MAGILL'S
LITERARY ANNUAL
2017

*Essay-Reviews of 150 Outstanding Books
Published in the United States During 2016*

_____

With an Annotated List of Titles

Volume II
L-Z

Edited by
Jennifer Sawtelle

SALEM PRESS
A Division of EBSCO Information Services, Inc.
Ipswich, Massachusetts

GREY HOUSE PUBLISHING

Magill's Literary Annual, 2017, published by Grey House Publishing, Inc., Amenia, NY, under exclusive license from EBSCO Information Services, Inc.

∞ The paper used in these volumes conforms to the American National Standard for Permanence of Paper for Printed Library Materials, Z39.48-1992 (R2009).

Publisher's Cataloging-In-Publication Data
(Prepared by The Donohue Group, Inc.)

Names: Magill, Frank N. (Frank Northen), 1907-1997, editor. | Wilson, John D., editor. | Kellman, Steven G., 1947- editor. | Goodhue, Emily, editor. | Poranski, Colin D., editor. | Akre, Matthew, editor. | Spires, Kendal, editor. | Toth, Gabriela, editor. | Sawtelle, Jennifer, editor.
Title: Magill's literary annual.
Description: <1977->: [Pasadena, Calif.] : Salem Press | <2015->: Ipswich, Massachusetts : Salem Press, a division of EBSCO Information Services, Inc. ; Amenia, NY : Grey House Publishing | Essay-reviews of ... outstanding books published in the United States during the previous year. | "With an annotated list of titles." | Editor: 1977- , F.N. Magill; <2010-2014>, John D. Wilson and Steven G. Kellman; <2015>, Emily Goodhue and Colin D. Poranski; <2016>, Matthew Akre, Kendal Spires, and Gabriela Toth; <2017->, Jennifer Sawtelle. | Includes bibliographical references and index.
Identifiers: ISBN 978-1-68217-276-6 (2017 edition : set) | ISBN 978-1-68217-280-3 (2017 edition : vol. 1) | ISBN 978-1-68217-281-0 (2017 edition : vol. 2) | ISSN: 0163-3058
Subjects: LCSH: Books--Reviews--Periodicals. | United States--Imprints--Book reviews--Periodicals. | Literature, Modern--21st century--History and criticism--Periodicals. | Literature, Modern--20th century--History and criticism--Periodicals.
Classification: LCC PN44 .M333 | DDC 028.1--dc23

FIRST PRINTING
PRINTED IN THE UNITED STATES OF AMERICA

CONTENTS

CONTENTS

COMPLETE ANNOTATED LIST OF CONTENTS

VOLUME I

13 Ways of Looking at a Fat Girl *is a collection of thirteen linked short stories that follow Elizabeth, a young woman who spends much of her life hating her body. Elizabeth goes from overweight to thin, but while her weight loss earns her the approval of others, she seems increasingly unhappy with herself.*

The philosopher A. C. Grayling presents a case that the seventeenth century was decisive in laying the foundations of the modern world view. It was in the seventeenth century that science and reason began to offer a new understanding of the universe and humanity's place in it. The scientific revolution led to a technological revolution that made Europe the engine of a global transformation.

David Szalay's All That Man Is *consists of nine thematically linked stories. The tales focus on a series of European men of various nationalities at key periods in life who attempt to resolve personal issues, often while traveling away from their homes.*

All the Birds in the Sky *blends the genres of science fiction and fantasy to explore the relationship between technology and nature. It is American writer Charlie Jane Anders's second novel.*

Rob Spillman, the founder of the literary magazine Tin House, *recalls his childhood and early adulthood in Berlin, both before and immediately after the fall of the Berlin Wall.*

American Heiress *is a nonfiction account of the high-profile, shocking abduction and trial of Patty Hearst, the granddaughter of wealthy publishing tycoon William Randolph Hearst, in the 1970s.*

In Helen Ellis's American Housewife, *twelve humorous, thought-provoking, and sometimes disturbing short stories expand upon, and even shatter, the common understanding of the titular archetype.*

    Another Brooklyn *is a powerful and lyric meditation on memory, friendship, and loss. Protagonist August, an adult when the story begins, reflects on her past and how a move to Brooklyn in the 1970s, while grieving the loss of her mother, led to strong but complicated bonds of friendship with three other girls of color in her neighborhood.*

    The Arab of the Future 2 *is the second installment in author and cartoonist Riad Sattouf's graphic memoir trilogy about his life growing up in France, Libya, and Syria.*

    In Are We Smart Enough to Know How Smart Animals Are? *Frans de Waal explores the complex subject of animal intelligence, presenting compelling evidence that many animals are far smarter than humans might think.*

    The fourth book by English author Sarah Bakewell, At the Existentialist Café *is an in-depth guide to the evolution of modern existentialism.*

    In Barkskins, *author Annie Proulx addresses the destruction of the world's forests over a three-hundred-year period, tracing the descendants of two men who arrive in New France (Canada) as indentured servants and choose opposite paths. One family becomes a powerful aggressor in the timber industry while the other struggles to live a more peaceful existence closer to nature and the trees.*

    An unusual blend of social satire and murder mystery, Before the Fall *presents an intriguing, suspenseful story. In the aftermath of a tragedy, the lives of victims and survivors alike are relentlessly scrutinized both by media outlets hungry for sensation and by the government agencies charged with investigating the event.*

    Imbolo Mbue's debut novel, Behold the Dreamers, *introduces a family of Cameroonian immigrants into the lives of a wealthy white American family and then observes their reactions as they become victims of a major national financial crisis: the recession of 2008.*

The Black Calhouns *is the story of a branch of the author's own family, traced
from emancipation through the 1960s. This multigenerational history of the family
situates Lena Horne, the author's mother, within a rich family context while also offering a valuable case study of African American history.*

*Journalist and author Joe Jackson has written an expansive biography of Black
Elk, one of the most revered Oglala Lakota holy men of the late nineteenth and early
twentieth centuries, whose life intersected with defining events in American history.*

The Black Widow *is the sixteenth installment of the best-selling series featuring
Gabriel Allon. In this entry, the wily Israeli agent is pitted against Saladin, a ruthless operative of the Islamic State of Iraq and Syria (ISIS), in a race against time to
prevent terrorist events that are intended to inflict maximum destruction in Europe
and the United States.*

Patrick Phillips's book Blood at the Root: A Racial Cleansing in America *explores the forced exodus of an African American community in Georgia in 1912.*

*Authors Randy Roberts and Johnny Smith draw on a wealth of previously un-
tapped evidence to provide an insightful portrait of the relationship between the fiery
Black Nationalist Malcolm X and Muhammad Ali, born Cassius Clay, a brilliant
boxer maneuvering his way through the boxing world toward a heavyweight champi-
onship bout. For a brief time, the two became like brothers, with Malcolm X helping
shape Ali's view of race in America. Then it all fell apart.*

Breaking Wild *presents a realistic, dramatic account of an attempt to search for
and rescue a female bow hunter lost in the vast Colorado wilderness as winter settles
in and a marauding cougar stalks the missing woman.*

In But What If We're Wrong? Thinking about the Present As If It Were the Past,
*Chuck Klosterman posits that much of what twenty-first-century society considers
objectively true and significant could one day be called into question.*

Science journalist Jo Marchant draws on the latest research, as well as personal interviews with experts and patients, to provide a cutting-edge look at the potential—and limitations—of the mind's ability to heal the body.

Bill Beverly's debut novel Dodgers *draws upon three genres—the travelogue, the coming-of-age story, and crime fiction—to tell the story of East, a fifteen-year-old caught in a large drug ring, who is sent on a dangerous mission.*

The Doll-Master and Other Tales of Terror *presents a half dozen short, disturbing stories by one of America's most notable authors of fiction. The stories are diverse in setting, plot, kinds of characters, and kinds of satisfaction offered.*

The rise and fall of a brilliant, but solipsistic and alcoholic, mathematician who abuses his family, demeans his colleagues, and exploits women, as told by his talented, drug-addicted son.

Brady Hartsfield is back in this final chapter of Stephen King's Bill Hodges trilogy. This time, Hartsfield uses mental manipulation to convince his victims to commit suicide. Bill, Holly, and Jerome fight to overcome the so-called Mercedes Killer before he can achieve an even higher kill rate.

Pulitzer Prize–winning novelist Richard Russo revisits the characters and setting of Nobody's Fool, *his beloved chronicle of the alternating day-to-day frustrations and triumphs of the citizens of fictional North Bath, New York. In this work, the focus has shifted to the town's hapless police chief, Douglas Raymer, sometime antagonist of the previous novel's main character, Donald "Sully" Sullivan.*

Evicted *is a heartrending study of inner-city poverty as it directly relates to housing affordability and to failures in the social safety net of the United States. Taking Milwaukee as its case study,* Evicted *follows the stories of tenants for whom the experience of eviction initiated a downward spiral.*

Helen Dunmore's novel Exposure *is a thriller set in London in the 1960s during the Cold War era.*

Set in the American South during the final year of the Civil War, this novel follows a young couple—Callum and Ava—as they flee a murderous band of bounty hunters who seek a prize on Callum's head. Moving through the devastated wasteland of the South, and integrating some brief encounters with Union forces, the book's principle focus is on the desperate plight of a young couple seeking to survive the ravages of war and rebuild a new life.

The Fire This Time: A New Generation Speaks about Race *is a collection of essays that explore the challenges facing African Americans today. The essays were compiled and edited by award-winning novelist Jesmyn Ward.*

Painstakingly researched and meticulously documented, The Firebrand and the First Lady *is an account of the sometimes contentious, always respectful, and ultimately warmly familiar relationship between two unlikely allies—African American activist Pauli Murray and aristocratic Eleanor Roosevelt, wife of the longest-serving US president—who bonded in common cause to fight for civil rights and women's rights in the United States.*

A novel of epic proportions from best-selling speculative fantasy-horror author Joe Hill, The Fireman *is an apocalyptic tale concerning the sudden appearance of a devastating worldwide plague that causes humans to spontaneously burst into flame, and the efforts of a handful of people fighting to escape being consumed in the conflagration.*

A suspenseful thriller, Fool Me Once *presents a strong-willed but deeply flawed US Army veteran investigating the murders of her husband and sister. It is a story about unsavory secrets from the past and the lengths to which ruthless people will go to keep them hidden.*

A study of the early years in the life of the sixteenth president of the United States, the historical novel A Friend of Mr. Lincoln *presents an intimate portrait of the complex, conflicted character of one of the most beloved figures of American history from the perspective of a fictional confidant.*

    The Gene: An Intimate History traces the history of attempts to understand and manipulate heredity, from the ancient Greeks down to the present day. Siddhartha Mukherjee explores such issues as gender, race, medical breakthroughs and medical malpractice as he leads up to the unlocking of the human genome and both the promises and perils this achievement may entail.

    Historian H. W. Brands recounts the story of the growing rift between US president Harry S. Truman and US Army general Douglas MacArthur during the Korean War, a dispute that led to Truman's decision to relieve MacArthur of command of United Nations forces against North Korea and Communist Chinese military units.

    Emma Cline's The Girls *is a fictional reimagining of the infamous Manson Family cult murders that shocked Southern California in 1969, symbolically marking the end of the sixties ideals of peace and love.*

    In The Glamour of Strangeness: Artists and the Last Age of the Exotic, *Jamie James chronicles the lives of six artists who found homes in countries far from their birthplaces.*

    In her sixth book, The Glass Universe, *Dava Sobel recounts the little-known story of the nineteenth- and twentieth-century women who were employed at the Harvard College Observatory to interpret hundreds of thousands of stellar photographs.*

    Naomi, born into slavery on an Alabama plantation, escapes on foot to Georgia after a horrific family confrontation with her master, and though her freedom is short-lived, she survives long enough to give birth to her daughter, Josey. Naomi narrates the story as a ghost, alternating between flashbacks of her own past with passages from her daughter's present life as she experiences the turmoil of the Civil War. In Grace, *Natashia Deón combines lyrical writing with expertly paced suspense to portray a mother's torment as she watches over her child, desperate, even in death, to help her survive.*

    The twelfth entry in the best-selling, award-winning mystery series featuring former homicide inspector Armand Gamache, A Great Reckoning *presents a pair of conundrums to be solved. One is the murder of a corrupt official at the Sûreté*

    Imagine Me Gone *is the history of a family and the ways in which each member is tortured differently but no less painfully by mental illness and addiction.*

    In a Different Key *is a sweeping chronicle of the seven decades that make up the history of autism, told through deeply reported biographical narratives and with uncommon empathy and even-handedness.*

    In Other Words *is a nonfiction account of the author's pursuit of the Italian language. The English-language edition features Italian and English on facing pages. Part linguistic exploration, part memoir, this book encompasses Lahiri's attempt to come to terms with her own transnational upbringing and multilingual heritage.*

    In the Darkroom *depicts author Susan Faludi's attempts to understand the personality of her domineering father, who left the family in Faludi's mid-teens. More specifically, the book examines her father's decision to undergo sex reassignment surgery at the age of seventy-six.*

    A carefully researched and meticulously executed history of the fight for freedom of the press in colonial America, Indelible Ink: The Trials of John Peter Zenger and the Birth of America's Free Press *tells the story of the impact of early publication practices for political gain. Led by a colorful cast of historical characters and concluding with modern analysis and examples of today's issues with freedom and the press, this comprehensive telling stresses why these rights mattered then and why they continue to matter now.*

    Irena's Children *describes the heroic efforts of a young Polish woman, Irena Sendler, to save Jewish children from death in Warsaw during World War II. Although Sendler and her colleagues were able to rescue roughly 2,500 children from the Holocaust, her story had not been widely publicized until fairly recently.*

    Jane Steele *is a dark satire inspired by Charlotte Brontë's Jane Eyre (1847) that reimagines the eponymous heroine as a serial killer. It is American author Lyndsay Faye's fifth novel.*

Claude Arnaud presents a brilliantly written and exhaustive biography of multi-faceted artist Jean Cocteau, a poet, playwright, set designer, and film director. From before World War I until his death, Cocteau pursued fame as a member of the artistic avant-garde. Arnaud situates this complex man at the heart of the rich artistic and intellectual world of twentieth-century Paris, a world without which he could not live.

This wide-ranging novel constructs a fictional world across a wide range of time, but closely connected to an impoverished neighborhood on the outskirts of Northampton in the United Kingdom. Tracing families across generations and orchestrating complex interconnections across time and place, Alan Moore weaves a fantasy world of religion and afterlife, which offers an alternative sense of place, space, and history.

Award-winning writer James McBride departs from the traditional chronological approach while telling the life story of one of America's greatest entertainers in Kill 'Em and Leave: Searching for James Brown and the American Soul. *Part biography, part autobiography, and part personal philosophy, the book concentrates on the multitude of ways Brown influenced the people who knew him.*

VOLUME II

In her memoir Lab Girl, *geobiologist Hope Jahren recounts the evolution of a life immersed in science—one inextricably interwoven with the lives of the plants to which she has devoted her career.*

When Landreaux Iron accidentally shoots and kills his neighbor's young son, he and his wife decide to share their own son in an effort to help the grieving family.

Dominic Smith's fourth novel, The Last Painting of Sara de Vos, *is a mystery and romance spanning over three continents and three hundred years.*

League of Dragons is the ninth and final installment of the Temeraire historical fantasy series by American writer Naomi Novik.

A look at the civil war raging in Syria, based on visits there in 2012. The author looks at the impact of the conflict on individuals and families through extensive interviews with people living through the war.

Distinguished historians Annette Gordon-Reed and Peter Onuf examine the mind and character of Thomas Jefferson, who worked diligently to create an image of himself as a member of the natural aristocracy and a modern-day patriarch, exhibiting behavior that could serve as a model for governance in the new nation.

Christine and Marcus Nilsson are preparing for the birth of their first child, a child for whom they struggled for years. However, their happiness is shattered when Christine sees a news program showing the arrest of a serial killer. Her belief that this serial killer is her sperm donor throws their lives into chaos, and her fight to find the truth could change everything in her life.

Graham Swift's novella is a fairy-tale romance about one magical day when a young British maidservant loses her lover, discovers her freedom, and decides to become a writer.

In her debut novel, The Mothers, *Brit Bennett tells the story of Nadia Turner after she makes the decision to end her pregnancy. As the novel progresses, Nadia and her friends struggle to confront both loss and acceptance of motherhood.*

Mr. Splitfoot *is a modern American gothic ghost story that examines the different ways the dead can haunt the living by focusing on the lives and both emotional and physical journeys of two women.*

My Name Is Lucy Barton *tells the story of its protagonist, Lucy Barton, through a series of flashbacks to her past, particularly a visit from her mother while Lucy was hospitalized with an extended and undiagnosed illness. With a sharp focus on the strained but loving relationship between the two women and the effect of Lucy's troubled childhood on her adult life, the novel explores themes of family, memory, and class.*

In his World War II thriller The One Man, *Andrew Gross imagines an elaborate plot to free one man—an important scientist whose knowledge and skills are necessary to construct the world's first nuclear bomb—from Auschwitz concentration camp.*

The Opposite of Everyone *is a novel by American author Joshilyn Jackson that examines the way storytelling can shape identity.*

Best-selling British novelist Jojo Moyes's collection Paris for One and Other Stories *contains one romantic novella and eight plot-based, female-focused short stories.*

An intriguing mystery-thriller, The Passenger *takes readers on a harrowing rollercoaster ride that follows the exploits of a chameleon-like female protagonist who takes countless risks while attempting to run from the events of her past and survive the many dangers she encounters.*

The Past *by Tessa Hadley takes place over a three-week vacation in the English countryside near the ocean. Four siblings are tasked with the decision to sell the family home and have come for one last gathering. While dealing with their present-day lives, the novel also reaches back to the past when three of the siblings lived at the summer home for a brief time during their parents' turbulent marriage. Comprised of strong characters and evocative landscapes,* The Past *creates a compelling, yet comforting reading experience.*

Luke Dittrich's book Patient H.M.: A Story of Memory, Madness, and Family Secrets *is a dual portrait of Patient H.M., the most famous test neurological subject in history, and the author's grandfather, a neurosurgeon who performed several lobotomies.*

The People and the Books *analyzes eighteen works of Jewish literature from over two thousand years of history. It is American poet and literary critic Adam Kirsch's ninth book.*

Daniel Borzutzky's poetry collection The Performance of Becoming Human *blends strong imagery with satirical prose to offer an indictment of the modern world. Exploring themes of privatization, overdevelopment, immigration, and neoliberalism, Borzutzky uses his own background as a poet of Chilean descent to blast the systems at play and create a wasteland of humanity in words and emotion.*

A memoir of John le Carré's writing career that describes the places he traveled while researching his novels and his encounters with many people who influenced his writing or were drawn to him because of his work. The focus is on his professional career, although le Carré's efforts to come to terms with his father and their strained relationship is an important part of the book.

An imaginative, satirical skewering of contemporary society's foibles, The Portable Veblen *offers a cast of wildly unorthodox but nevertheless believable characters, a convoluted but logically unfolding plot, a congenially off-center philosophical outlook, and an abundance of arboreal rodents.*

Pumpkinflowers *presents a brisk, tense account of an obscure and almost forgotten war that pitted Israeli forces against guerrillas in southern Lebanon—a conflict that mirrors the more widespread sectarian violence that has raged throughout the Middle East since the late twentieth century.*

Alexander Chee's The Queen of the Night *is a rich, complex, and sometimes melodramatic historical novel that tells the rags-to-riches story of an orphaned American farm girl turned international opera diva, set amidst the turmoil of Second Empire France.*

Redemption Road, *a crime thriller set in rural North Carolina, is American novelist John Hart's fifth book.*

The Road to Little Dribbling *is a humorous travel memoir by American author Bill Bryson that explores the municipalities, landscape, and culture of Great Britain.*

    In The Romanovs, *award-winning historian Simon Sebag Montefiore traces the nearly three-hundred-year history of the Romanov family, rulers of Russia from the seventeenth century until the abolishment of the monarchy during the Communist Revolution in 1917.*

    Secondhand Time: The Last of the Soviets *is a book of oral history that captures the last generation of those who lived under Soviet rule and the subsequent first generation to live under capitalism. Consisting of interviews with a wide range of individuals, the book is meant to create a symphony of voices that tell the story of how today's Russia came to be, politically, culturally, and emotionally.*

    In Seinfeldia: How a Show about Nothing Changed Everything, *Jennifer Keishin Armstrong chronicles the making of the sitcom Seinfeld and its enduring influence on popular culture.*

    A Series of Catastrophes and Miracles: A True Story of Love, Science, and Cancer *is Mary Elizabeth Williams's surprisingly witty account of her battle with a diagnosis of terminal cancer. Williams, now cancer free, benefited from cutting-edge immunotherapy treatment. Her book offers information about cancer and the history of its treatment.*

    Shirley Jackson: A Rather Haunted Life *recounts the life of the often misunderstood and historically undervalued American fiction writer and essayist Shirley Jackson. In providing a thorough discussion of Jackson's life and work, literary critic Ruth Franklin aims to reemphasize the author's significance.*

    In The Silence of the Sea, *attorney Thóra Gudmundsdóttir investigates the disappearance of the passengers and crew missing from a yacht that arrives on autopilot in Reykjavik harbor, piecing together details about their fate from sparse forensic evidence in the absence of eyewitnesses to the tragedy that occurred at sea.*

    The Silk Roads: A New History of the World *tells the history of the world through the perspective of the rise of the Persian Empire and the empire's subsequent effect on cultural evolution in the rest of the world.*

Ruth has been a beloved labor and delivery nurse for twenty years; however, after a racist couple ask for her to be removed from the care of their newborn baby, she is blamed for his death, and her life spins out of control.

Dan Vyleta's novel Smoke *imagines an alternate nineteenth-century England in which sinful thoughts and bad deeds manifest themselves as Smoke excreted from one's body.*

Soul at the White Heat is a collection of essays from writer Joyce Carol Oates that spans her career as critic and literature lover. Derived from previously published work—many pieces coming from the New York Review of Books and Kenyon Review—the pieces in the collection explore the writing life; offer lively discussion of literary figures, movements, and works; and afford brief glimpses into the author's own life. Beloved figures such as Virginia Woolf, Julian Barnes, and Margaret Atwood are all examined under Oates's careful eye, culminating in a respectful collection representative of contemporary literature.

The Sound of Gravel is a memoir that recounts American writer Ruth Wariner's experience growing up in a polygamist Mormon cult. It is her first book.

C. E. Morgan's sophomore novel, The Sport of Kings, *is a sprawling narrative about Kentucky, race, biology, and horse racing.*

Ibram X. Kendi's sweeping history illustrates how racist ideas have been constructed and perpetuated in America, focusing on their essential beginnings in fifteenth-century Europe and ending in the present day.

Sweetbitter is the debut novel from writer Stephanie Danler. Loosely based on her real life experiences working in the Union Square Café in New York, Sweetbitter tells the story of a twenty-two-year-old woman newly arrived to the city and is as involved with food obsession as it is with the social aspects of a young person's life. She takes a job as a backwaiter (busser) at an unnamed restaurant where a colorful cast of characters shows her the ins and outs of the restaurant business and life in the city. The story is told over the period of one year.

COMPLETE ANNOTATED LIST OF TITLES

Swing Time 573
In Swing Time, *acclaimed novelist Zadie Smith traces the divergent lives of two dance-obsessed childhood friends who grew up together in council estates in Northwest London. In doing so, she weaves a multifaceted narrative about coming of age, the false promises of philanthropy, and the strange turns that life can take.*

Their Promised Land: My Grandparents in Love and War 578
Based on a collection of family letters, Their Promised Land: My Grandparents in Love and War *recounts the story of the life and love of Bernard and Win Schlesinger. Spanning the eventful years between 1915 and 1945, this book uses the case study of this couple and their children to consider complex questions of identity and selfhood in a time of war and upheaval.*

Then Come Back: The Lost Neruda 583
In these manuscript poems, written on playbills, napkins, and odd scraps of paper, the Nobel Prize–winning poet Pablo Neruda writes about love, friendship, and the complicated joys of life. The discovery of these poems has prompted fresh assessment of Neruda's late poems.

This Must Be the Place 588
In This Must Be the Place, *author Maggie O'Farrell takes readers on a meandering trip through time to understand the complications of protagonist Daniel Sullivan's life. Conflicted relationships with the people he loves lead to choices that may change his life in ways he could never have imagined.*

To the Bright Edge of the World 592
Eowyn Ivey's second novel, To the Bright Edge of the World, *is an Alaskan adventure tale told through old letters, diary entries, photographs, and other ephemera.*

The Underground Railroad 596
Cora, born into slavery on a Georgia cotton plantation, was left behind as a child when her mother escaped. After the plantation's ownership changes hands to a much crueler master, a newly arrived slave named Caesar convinces Cora to escape north on the Underground Railroad. Cora's journey, with its gritty realism and elements of fantasy, is harrowing, and Ridgeway, a slave catcher hired to bring her back, is determined to find her.

The Unseen World 601
Liz Moore's third novel, The Unseen World, *is a science-fiction mystery about virtual reality, artificial intelligence, and one woman's quest to decode her father's past.*

Until We Are Free: My Fight for Human Rights in Iran 605
Writing in exile, Nobel laureate Shirin Ebadi chronicles her life and work in Iran under the brutal reign of former President Mahmoud Ahmadinejad.

Award-winning and best-selling author Reed Farrel Coleman introduces a new series character, Gus Murphy, in Where It Hurts. *A psychically damaged ex-police-man, Murphy embarks on an informal investigation into the murder of the son of a felon, encountering violent crime and deep-seated corruption in the process of criss-crossing his socially diverse home territory of Long Island, New York.*

A suspenseful examination of how past crimes, lies, and secrets can adversely affect present lives, Laura Lippman's Wilde Lake *continues the author's outstanding record of producing literary crime fiction featuring an intelligent, sympathetic, and strong-willed woman as the central protagonist.*

Elizabeth Wright is sent to Ireland for a nursing position. When she arrives, she discovers that her patient, eleven-year-old Anna O'Donnell, is an "extraordinary wonder" who has not eaten in four months. As she observes the child to determine whether this is a hoax, the nurse uncovers a dark twist behind the so-called miracle.

This generous collection of nonfiction by celebrated speculative fiction author Ur-sula K. Le Guin includes essays, addresses, reviews, and introductions to the works of others.

Sunjeev Sahota's critically acclaimed novel The Year of the Runaways *focuses on the vulnerabilities and hardships of Indian immigrants as they negotiate visas, jobs, and living conditions in England in their quest for a better life. Sahota narrates the story through four key characters, three men and one woman, whose struggles are compounded by issues of class, caste, spirituality, and moral obligation.*

Megan Abbott's novel You Will Know Me *is a psychological thriller and murder mystery that centers on the budding career of a teenage gymnast.*

Don DeLillo's new novel Zero K *imagines a world in which people opt to be cryogenically preserved in hopes of living again in a distant future.*

Lab Girl

Author: Hope Jahren (b. 1969)
Publisher: Alfred A. Knopf (New York). 304 pp.
Type of work: Memoir
Time: 1969–the present
Locales: Minnesota, California, Georgia, Maryland, Norway, Ireland, Hawaii

In her memoir Lab Girl, *geobiologist Hope Jahren recounts the evolution of a life immersed in science—one inextricably interwoven with the lives of the plants to which she has devoted her career.*

Principal personages:
HOPE JAHREN, the author, a professor of geobiology
BILL, her longtime friend and work partner
CLINT, her husband

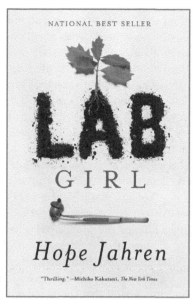

NATIONAL BEST SELLER

"Thrilling." —Michiko Kakutani, *The New York Times*

(Courtesy of Knopf)

"As a rule," geobiologist Hope Jahren writes in *Lab Girl*, "people live among plants but they don't really see them." Undoubtedly the exception to that rule, Jahren is a professor of geobiology at the University of Hawaii at Manoa who has dedicated her career to the study of plants, specifically with regard to how they interact with the broader environment. Over the course of her career, which has taken her from graduate studies in California through laboratories cobbled together from limited resources in Georgia and Maryland, Jahren has established herself as a persistent, devoted scientist whose research has taken on additional importance amid growing concerns about the fate of plants in a rapidly industrializing world. As a work that blends the scientific and the personal, *Lab Girl* interweaves the tale of Jahren's career trajectory with more personal stories, including powerful depictions of her childhood, struggles with mental illness, and later family life. Some parts of the book fall firmly into both categories, such as the many passages focusing on Jahren's decades-long friendship and scientific partnership with laboratory manager Bill Hagopian. Throughout it all, there are the plants, which serve as the scaffold for the memoir's structure.

Lab Girl consists of three parts, each broken up into chapters. The first part begins with Jahren's childhood in Minnesota, where she grew up immersed in science from infancy. Her father, a community college science professor, often brought her to his workplace, where she first played among the scientific equipment and later used the resources at her disposal to learn how to conduct experiments and fix broken equipment. Scientific inclinations were also passed down to Jahren through her mother, who had distinguished herself in science as a high school student but was unable to complete university studies in chemistry for financial reasons. Growing up, Jahren felt that her interest in science made her an anomaly, both in her town, where the majority of adults worked for the local factory, and in the wider world, where female scientists were not yet wholly accepted. After graduating from high school, however, her path was clear. "I knew that I was meant to be an extension of my indestructible mother," she writes, "a do-over to make real the life that she deserved and should have had."

Enrolling at the University of Minnesota, Jahren initially studied literature but soon switched her major to geology. While an undergraduate, she found her first job in a scientific field, working first as a medicine runner for the university hospital's pharmacy before transitioning into a role in the pharmacy's laboratory, where she prepared bags of intravenous medications. Jahren recounts her memorable experiences in the pharmacy, which not only gave her practical experience in precise lab work but also sparked in her the realization that she wanted to pursue work she truly cared about. Leaving her hospital job for a work-study position in one of the university's research laboratories, she prepared to "take a long, lonely journey toward adulthood with the dogged faith of the pioneer who has realized that there is no promised land but still holds out hope that the destination will be someplace better than here."

After graduating from the University of Minnesota, Jahren enrolled at the University of California, Berkeley, where she worked toward a doctorate in soil science. It was during this period that she made what would be perhaps the most significant connection of her professional life. While accompanying a class of undergraduates on a field trip to study the soil of California's Central Valley, she befriended a student named Bill, in whom she found a kindred spirit. Upon returning from the trip, she convinced her supervisor to hire Bill to work in their lab. This decision would prove to be a highly fortuitous one, as Jahren and Bill's friendship and scientific partnership would become one of the few constants in her life over the next decades, and their almost symbiotic relationship in many ways forms the heart of *Lab Girl*. Already inseparable by the time Jahren completed her PhD and Bill his bachelor's degree, they decided to begin their careers together, both traveling to Georgia when Jahren was offered an assistant professorship at the Georgia Institute of Technology (Georgia Tech).

Over the course of the remaining two parts of the memoir, Jahren recounts the development of both her career as a researcher and her personal life. Facing adversity in the form of severe budgetary limitations, the sexist attitudes of many of her colleagues, and her own struggles with mental illness, Jahren nevertheless built her own laboratory from scratch and succeeded in pursuing work that truly interested her. Accompanied by Bill, she relocated to Maryland's Johns Hopkins University in 1999, where her lab remained for nearly a decade. Jahren recounts her stint in Oslo, Norway, as well as research trips to locales such as Ireland before telling of her 2008 relocation to the University of Hawaii, where she continued to work as of the book's publication. Alongside this career trajectory, she chronicles personal milestones such as her first date with her husband, Clint, and the events leading up to the birth of their son.

Lab Girl concludes in a manner consistent with Jahren's long-standing dedication to plants and concern for the environment, which are evident throughout the book. In addition to an endnote that provides additional information about the scientific studies she cites throughout, she includes an epilogue in which she exhorts readers to consider the effects of deforestation and the eradication of plants in general from the natural landscape, encouraging readers to do their part in combating such potentially devastating phenomena.

As a whole, *Lab Girl* is a beautifully written memoir of a life in science. Jahren's devotion to her chosen field is palpable, and even readers minimally versed in biology may feel a newfound fondness for trees and other plants by the end of it. The author excels at explaining relevant scientific concepts—volatile organic compounds (VOCs), for instance—so that they are easily understood by lay readers, yet still written in the same evocative style as the remainder of the work. While much of Jahren's focus is on the development of her professional life and the associated scientific discoveries that have made her an important figure in her field, *Lab Girl* is also deeply personal. In vivid language, she describes her experiences with bipolar disorder and the effects of the periods of mania she experienced during her late twenties. One particularly memorable chapter in the memoir's second section takes the reader through one such period, illustrating her mental state at the time. As is perhaps appropriate, even her descriptions of these instances are rife with plant imagery: "Your raised arms are the fleshy petals of a magnificent lily bursting into flower. It deeply dawns on you that this new world about to bloom is *you*." Jahren's mania seems glorious at first, filled with infinite possibilities, but by the end of the chapter comes the crash: "And then it's too loud and it's too bright and there's too much too close to your head and you scream, scream, scream it away." The chapter provides a powerful depiction of the realities of mental illness, and although readers who have not personally experienced such incidents cannot hope to understand fully what Jahren was feeling at the time, her visceral description nevertheless gives the reader a very good idea. Further aspects of her personal life, including her relationship with her husband, Clint, and her shifting view of motherhood before and after the birth of her son, are likewise presented with remarkable honesty and power.

Hope Jahren is a professor of geobiology at the University of Hawaii at Manoa.

Perhaps the most striking element of *Lab Girl*, however, is the memoir's overarching emphasis on building what one needs—be it a laboratory or a family—from the ground up, overcoming the many roadblocks that stand in the way of professional and personal fulfillment. Persevering in the face of challenges such as budgetary restrictions and the sexism prevalent in the sciences—a topic that comes up on various occasions in *Lab Girl* and about which Jahren has written extensively outside of the book—Jahren succeeded in building and rebuilding a laboratory that would allow her to carry out her research in her way. With Bill, and later Clint and their son, she built a family that would weather every challenge that came its way. *Lab Girl* is an engrossing memoir and an enlightening peek into the careers of working scientists, but at its heart it is above all else a testament to persistence and the will to succeed, both Jahren's and that of the plants that fascinate her.

The critical response to *Lab Girl* was overwhelmingly positive, with reviewers for a broad range of publications praising her effective fusion of memoir and science writing. Writing for the *New York Times*, critic Michiko Kakutani called attention to the unusual yet fitting structure of the book, noting, "By crosscutting between chapters about the life cycle of trees and flowers and other green things, and chapters about her own coming-of-age as a scientist, Ms. Jahren underscores the similarities between humans and plants—tenacity, inventiveness, an ability to adapt." At the same time, Kakutani noted, Jahren calls attention to "the radical otherness of plants" as she describes the unique capabilities and limitations that render them a very different form of life than humankind. Critics likewise praised the beauty of Jahren's language, often likening it to poetry, and highlighted her discussions of topics such as sexism in science, the financial realities of scientific research, and mental health as being of particular interest.

Joy Crelin

Review Sources

Fabian, Ann. "Review: *Lab Girl* Is the Story of a Brilliant Scientist with Literary Flair." Review of *Lab Girl*, by Hope Jahren. *Huffington Post*, 26 Apr. 2016, www.huffingtonpost.com/the-national-book-review/review-lab-girl-is-the-st_b_9781566.html. Accessed 14 Oct. 2016.

Green, Lucie. "*Lab Girl*: A Story of Trees, Science and Love by Hope Jahren—Review." Review of *Lab Girl*, by Hope Jahren. *The Guardian*, 24 Apr. 2016, www.theguardian.com/books/2016/apr/24/lab-girl-hope-jahren-review-story-of-trees-science-and-love. Accessed 14 Oct. 2016.

Kakutani, Michiko. "Review: Lab Girl, Hope Jahren's Road Map to the Secret Life of Plants." Review of Lab Girl, by Hope Jahren. *The New York Times*, 28 Mar. 2016, www.nytimes.com/2016/03/29/books/review-lab-girl-hope-jahrens-road-map-to-the-secret-life-of-plants.html. Accessed 14 Oct. 2016.

Review of *Lab Girl*, by Hope Jahren. *Kirkus Reviews*, 15 Jan. 2016, p. 10.

LaRose

Author: Louise Erdrich (b. 1954)
Publisher: Harper (New York). 384 pp.
Type of work: Novel
Time: 1967–70, 1999–2003
Locale: Pluto, North Dakota, and adjacent Ojibwe reservation

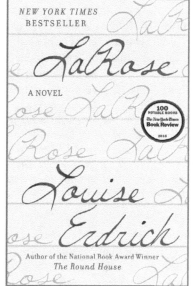

(Courtesy of HarperCollins Publishers)

When Landreaux Iron accidentally shoots and kills his neighbor's young son, he and his wife decide to share their own son in an effort to help the grieving family.

Principal characters:

LAROSE IRON, a five-year-old child who is shared with his friend's family
LANDREAUX IRON, his father, who accidentally shot his friend
NOLA RAVICH, his maternal aunt, the mother of the boy who died
MAGGIE RAVICH, the older sister of the boy who died
ROMEO PUYAT, his father's former friend
FATHER TRAVIS WOZNIAK, the local priest who counsels the families and tries to mentor Romeo

Novelist Louise Erdrich has been writing since childhood, but her first novel, *Love Medicine* (1984), firmly established her as an up-and-coming force in the literary world. The novel received the National Book Critics Circle Award for Fiction. In the years between that first novel and *LaRose*, which is her fifteenth, Erdrich has not gone unnoticed. She was given the Lifetime Achievement Award from the Native Writers Circle of the Americas in 2000, and her ninth novel, *The Plague of Doves* (2008), was a finalist for the 2009 Pulitzer Prize in Fiction. More recently, she was awarded the 2015 Library of Congress Lifetime Achievement Award for the Writing of Fiction. Readers of her fifteenth novel will find that she continues to follow the successful formatting that she used in many of her earlier works. *LaRose* is particularly reminiscent of her earlier writing in its strength of storytelling techniques, thematic content, and characterization.

The story of *LaRose* centers on the accidental shooting death of five-year-old Dusty Ravich by Landreaux Iron. Landreaux is a neighbor to and relative of the Ravich family, but he is also the father of another five-year-old child, LaRose. After Dusty's death, Landreaux and his wife, Emmaline, go into their sweat lodge to commune with their ancestors, and Landreaux feels that they ask him and Emmaline to give the Ravich family their own son in replacement of the dead child. This action sets off a series of events that guide the development of the rest of the novel as it traces the effects on both families as well as the surrounding community.

The novel skillfully uses multiple narrators, recalling earlier Erdrich books such as *Love Medicine* and *The Beet Queen* (1986), to follow a variety of characters as they deal with the repercussions of Dusty's death and work around the interpersonal relationships that tie them together. Among the point-of-view characters are Dusty's parents, Peter and Nola Ravich; LaRose's parents, Landreaux and Emmaline Iron; LaRose himself; several of LaRose's siblings, including Maggie, Dusty's sister; Father Travis, the local priest; Romeo, a former friend of Landreaux's; and several of LaRose's ancestors. Each point of view establishes a different perspective for the story, ultimately creating a broader picture of the tragedy and people involved.

Louise Erdrich is an award-winning full-time writer whose Ojibwe and German heritage are central to her work. Her body of work includes novels, short stories, poetry, children's literature, and nonfiction.

The sections focusing on Peter Ravich establish the depth of this father's grief and confusion. His sense of fairness leaves him struggling to know what to do as he learns to love the son of another man while he mourns his own child. It is his observation that LaRose is being harmed by the exchange. When he realizes the extent of that harm, he talks to Landreaux, telling him, "He's sad. Missing his family. Can't understand. You're right there down the road. I catch his face in the rearview when we pass. He's so quiet, just looking at his old house." Although Peter is willing to share that knowledge with Landreaux, he withholds information as well: "This was all Peter could stand to tell. About the muffled crying, nothing. About LaRose beating his head with his hands, nothing. About his secret questions whispered only to Peter, *Where is my real mom?*, he couldn't tell." Unfortunately, although Peter is aware of what is happening to LaRose, and although he observes a change in his daughter, Maggie, he remains somewhat blind to the depth of his wife's grief and seems unable to grasp the reality of Maggie's emotional trauma. In almost direct contrast to Peter's mostly calm reaction to Dusty's death and the events of the years that follow, when Nola becomes the focus of the narration, readers see a fragile woman who almost constantly fights against the reality of her son's death. Thoughts about and plans to commit suicide engulf her until Maggie catches her preparing to hang herself. It is only when her surviving child begs her to stop, to live, that Nola begins to slowly move forward.

The Iron family dynamic is only slightly different from that of the Ravich family. In Landreaux's chapters, readers learn about his difficult childhood, including abandonment, abuse at a residential government-run Indian boarding school, and an escape from that school that led to an accidental injury to his friend Romeo. His gentle spirit is challenged by addiction and tormented by Dusty's death and LaRose's life with the Raviches. Only a few snippets throughout describe Emmaline's experience, and these mostly concentrate on the emotional ordeal of giving up her youngest son to recompense for her husband's sin.

LaRose's chapters show a child who matures too early after Dusty is killed and he is sent to live with his friend's family. Despite his inability to truly comprehend why his world has been turned upside down and how he must carry Nola's sanity on his shoulders, he often has more insight than many of the adults in the novel. After Emmaline tells LaRose on a visit that she will not send him back to the Ravich family because his own family misses him too much, he concludes that he must return to the Raviches, saying, "Problem is, Nola, she's gonna be too sad. It might be death if she gets too sad, Maggie told me. . . . [Maggie and I] keep her mom going when she can't get out of bed and stuff." He then tries to console his mother: "It's okay, you're gonna make it. If you just get going you'll feel better. One step after another. One day at a time." LaRose's level of maturity and depth of personality often show him to be stronger than any of the other characters in the novel.

In addition to the chapters where the families are the focus, sections centering on Father Travis and Romeo Puyat are key to understanding the twisted web of relationships in the story. Their subplots create suspense and conflict beyond the problems the Irons and Raviches experience as a result of Dusty's death. There are four main plotlines in the novel: Dusty's death and the family reactions, an ancestral background story from LaRose's family, a subtle subplot involving Father Travis and the Irons, and an old revenge plot concentrated on Landreaux and Romeo. Each piece of the overall story has ties to a different time, and Erdrich skillfully intertwines those various times as she traces the main story line through the novel. The majority of the novel takes place at the turn of the twenty-first century, encompassing societal fears over Y2K, September 11, and the Iraq War. However, there are two major jumps back in time. One of those flashbacks is to LaRose's namesake. Readers meet the original LaRose and learn her story and legacy. More germane to the immediate plot, however, is an extended flashback to Landreaux's childhood with Romeo. In this section, readers learn of the boys' childhood friendship, their virtual incarceration in an Indian boarding school that attempts to kill anything native in them, and an attempted escape gone awry that destroys their relationship.

Erdrich intertwines assorted thematic issues throughout the varied narrative perspectives and multiple plotlines. As one would expect, grief and loss are primary to the two families' stories. Drug addiction and alcoholism create ties between a number of the characters as well. This creates tension for Landreaux and Romeo specifically, as both men struggle in different ways with the desire to escape from their painful pasts. Despite the sense of despair that drives much of the novel, Erdrich skillfully intersperses a sense of hope for several characters throughout the novel, with healing for the adults and strong, long-lasting relationships forming between the children. A number of characters even begin to find redemption.

Reviews of the book have been primarily positive. *Washington Post* reviewer Ron Charles argued that Erdrich's talent in this novel is in creating a piece where sensitivity reigns supreme, not sliding into sentimentality. Reba Leiding's *Library Journal* review focused on Erdrich's ability to intertwine families, plots, time periods, and the physical and spirit worlds. Overall, this novel will challenge readers to see characters, plotlines, and themes from various perspectives. Erdrich's talented description will draw even reluctant readers into the often difficult novel.

Theresa L. Stowell

Review Sources

Charles, Ron. "Louise Erdrich's *LaRose*: A Gun Accident Sets Off a Masterly Tale of Grief and Love." Review of *LaRose*, by Louise Erdrich. *The Washington Post*, 9 May 2016, www.washingtonpost.com/entertainment/books/louise-erdrichs-larose-a-gun-accident-sets-off-a-masterly-tale-of-grief-and-love/2016/05/09/e719aa04-1215-11e6-8967-7ac733c56f12_story.html. Accessed 11 Oct. 2016.

Hoffert, Barbara. Review of *LaRose*, by Louise Erdrich. *Library Journal*, 1 Dec. 2015, p. 73.

Leiding, Reba. Review of *LaRose*, by Louise Erdrich. *Library Journal*, 15 May 2016, p. 67.

The Last Painting of Sara de Vos

Author: Dominic Smith (b. 1971)
Publisher: Sarah Crichton Books (New York). 290 pp.
Type of work: Novel
Time: 1631, 1957, 2000
Locales: Amsterdam, Netherlands; New York, New York; Sydney, Australia

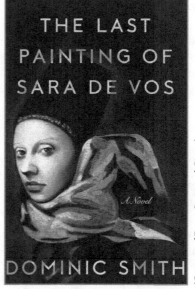

(Courtesy of Farrar, Straus and Giroux)

Dominic Smith's fourth novel, The Last Painting of Sara de Vos, *is a mystery and romance spanning over three continents and three hundred years.*

Principal characters:
SARA DE VOS, a painter in seventeenth-century Amsterdam
MARTY DE GROOT, a patent lawyer with vast inherited wealth
ELEANOR "ELLIE" SHIPLEY, an Australian art forger turned conservator and museum curator

Dominic Smith's novel *The Last Painting of Sara de Vos* centers on a seventeenth-century Dutch painting but begins in Manhattan in the autumn of 1957. Marty de Groot, a wealthy forty-year-old patent attorney, and his thirty-two-year-old wife, Rachel, are hosting an extravagant fundraiser in their Central Park penthouse. Rachel mingles awkwardly with society ladies rather than Marty's colleagues and their wives. Her mind is never far from her two miscarriages, and her new and grim reality, a life without children, has yet to settle in. Marty is too wrapped up in impressing his boss—he hopes to make partner soon—to shepherd his wife through the crowd of strangers, but Rachel feels some measure of uncharacteristic ease. She has a surprise: on a whim, she has invited a small coterie of bearded, barefoot beatniks to the party. Using a so-absurd-it-has-to-be-true service called Rent-a-Beat, she has paid them to drink wine and say provocative things to her guests. Of course, the beatniks turn out to be more of a handful than she bargained for, and after a deliciously awkward scuffle involving Marty's boss, the party ends. Only months later does Marty discover that a precious family heirloom, a seventeenth-century Dutch painting of a girl and a frozen lake, has been stolen.

In Marty's defense, the wall above his bed was not empty. Someone hung what he deems a "meticulous fake" in its place. If it were not for the rusting nails visible in the original frame, Marty might never have realized the theft at all. Swept up in a kind of midlife crisis—coming to terms with his boring job, his distant wife, his childless future—Marty becomes obsessed with pursuing justice for the crime, despite the fact that he secretly thinks that the painting might have been bad luck anyway. He hires a greasy private investigator, who turns up a strange lead that takes Marty to a dilapidated apartment in Brooklyn. Ellie Shipley, the young woman who lives there, painted the forgery for her own complicated reasons, but thanks to Marty's single-minded thirst for revenge (or perhaps something else), her fate becomes inextricably entwined with his. The consequences of Ellie's act—and, later, Marty's—reverberate through the years, reaching forward to the year 2000 and, thanks to Smith's lush and expansive palette, reaching backward as well, to one woman's tragedy in Amsterdam in the 1630s.

The Last Painting of Sara de Vos is not Smith's first historical fiction novel. Smith, a transplant from Australia, has written about turn-of-the-century Chicago, the South Pacific, and mid-nineteenth-century Paris, as inhabited by Louis Daguerre, pioneering photographer and inventor of the daguerreotype. In his 2011 novel *Bright and Distant Shores*, the lives of a poor, young Chicagoan and a teenage boy from Melanesia converge to tell an adventure story about cultural divides and the meaning of "civilization." In *The Mercury Visions of Louis Daguerre* (2006), Smith's first novel, he reimagines the life of the famous man and his contemporary, poet Charles Baudelaire, in a rich rendering of Paris in the 1840s. As a writer, Smith's greatest strength is his eye for period detail. Kathryn Harrison, in her review of *The Last Painting of Sara de Vos* for the *New York Times*, marveled at Smith's impressive moments of seamless time travel. "Smith's 1637 is as convincing a realization as his 1957 or 2000, Amsterdam in its Golden Age no less vivid than millennial Manhattan," she wrote. "The narrative has a supple omniscience that glides, Möbius-like, among the centuries without a snag."

The fictional painting referred to in Smith's title is called *At the Edge of the Wood*. As characters subsequently describe its contents, it appears vividly real in the reader's mind. The placard describes it as a "winter scene at twilight." In it, a dark-haired girl stands behind a silver birch, looking out at a small crowd of skaters on a frozen river. Despite the snow, her feet are bare and her dress torn. She holds a black ribbon in her hand and stares off at some distant point beyond the frame. The haunting scene was painted by a woman named Sara de Vos, a composite rendering of several real Dutch women painters of the era, and her story, too, is told in Smith's novel. In 1631, Sara lives with her painter husband, Barent, and their seven-year-old daughter, Kathrijn, in Amsterdam. Sara and her husband are both part of the prestigious Guild of St. Luke, whose members include Rembrandt van Rijn and Johannes Vermeer.

As a woman, Sara is constricted to painting only still lifes, though she often assists her husband in other projects. When the reader meets them, the family is on their way to see a beached whale that Barent hopes to paint. The scene is a happy one but also ominous. An enterprising local offers a glimpse into the dying animal's enormous eye for a small fee. After scant consideration, Kathrijn decides to take a look from atop the man's ladder. Sara, Smith writes, "imagines the eye backlit with bafflement, a dumbfounded predator looking out from the dark cave of his own skull and mind." Contrary to Sara's expectation that Kathrijn will be awed and find peace from months of nightmares, "Kathrijn's plodding ladder climb and the stilted way she leans over the eye socket suggests a girl carrying out a penance. She hoods her gaze and stares into the whale's eye for a long time, then climbs slowly down onto the beach, refusing to say a word about what she's encountered."

Weeks later, Kathrijn is dead, gone suddenly of the plague. Sara's grief is compounded by Barent, who drives the household to financial ruin and then leaves. But somewhere in between Kathrijn's death and Barent's departure, Sara is gripped by inspiration. Feverishly, obsessively, she completes *At the Edge of the Wood* and then hides it away. Centuries later, Ellie will feel an echo of the Sara's fervor when she looks at the same painting for the first time in a photograph and feels "her breath catch." Ellie decides to paint the copy, if only to imagine for a moment that she had made it herself.

(Courtesy of StacySodolak)

Dominic Smith is an Australian-born novelist and professor of creative writing. His past works include The Mercury Visions of Louis Daguerre *(2006),* The Beautiful Miscellaneous *(2007), and* Bright and Distant Shores *(2011).*

Young Ellie smothers her anger (at her emotionally absent father, at the men who discouraged her own painting) in her work as a conservator. In its description, her apartment mirrors Sara's studio. Bowls of cold-pressed linseed oil, raw sienna, and lead white, all components of the seventeenth-century painter's tool kit, litter her kitchenette. Even if she had friends, Ellie muses, she could never have anyone over, as the place always smells of the rabbit pelts that she boils down for glue. Smith's descriptions of conservation work, both technical and philosophical, are engrossing. In certain passages he teases out larger themes about how artworks and people change over time by describing the layer-by-layer "geology" (Ellie's word) of a painting.

In the structure of the book, this young and passionate Ellie lives alongside a much older Ellie, now an art professor, in 2000. The forgery has come back to haunt her and so, incidentally, has Marty de Groot. Ellie and Marty's relationship in the 1950s is a forgery of its own. Marty, pretending to have been referred by one of her professors and using an assumed name, enlists her as an art consultant, but a deeper relationship begins to blossom. In 2000, he travels to Sydney to offer its conclusion. In his early eighties, Marty is a humbler version of the dashing, patrician man Ellie once knew. He is certainly far too old to be traveling so far, but he is driven by a profound regret that has come to him with time and age.

Adult Ellie has made a name for herself as an expert on Sara de Vos, and in addition to her inevitable confrontation with Marty, she is grappling with the discovery of a new de Vos painting. (*At the Edge of the Wood* was believed to be her only surviving work.) This painting serves as an absorbing plot point in Sara's story but lacks shape in Ellie's. Her quest to uncover more paintings, or more accurately, to find closure in her understanding of Sara's life, is less compelling after the reader has already gleaned this information from its source. For Sara, the painting serves as a point of connection to another grieving parent; for Ellie, it is a plot point on the road to a conclusion that seems too pat. Smith's attempt to bring them together seems at odds with the novel's point about how people form personal relationships with art despite, and sometimes in contradiction to, their original meaning. Like the enigma of the whale's eye, a powerful piece of art has something singular to say to each person, though it cannot always be articulated.

Molly Hagan

Review Sources

Harrison, Kathryn. Review of The Last Painting of Sara de Vos, by Dominic Smith. *The New York Times*, 8 Apr. 2016, www.nytimes.com/2016/04/10/books/review/ the-last-painting-of-sara-de-vos-by-dominic-smith.html. Accessed 12 Dec. 2016.

Review of *The Last Painting of Sara de Vos*, by Dominic Smith. *Kirkus Reviews*, 15 Mar. 2016, p. 118.

Review of *The Last Painting of Sara de Vos*, by Dominic Smith. *Publishers Weekly*, 22 Feb. 2016, p. 62.

Shapira, Ian. "Review: *The Last Painting of Sara de Vos*, a Riveting Tale of Art Theft." Review of *The Last Painting of Sara de Vos*, by Dominic Smith. *The Washington Post*, 9 Apr. 2016, www.washingtonpost.com/entertainment/books/ review-the-last-painting-of-sara-de-vos-a-riveting-tale-of-art-theft/2016/04/05/46 5f55dc-f758-11e5-a3ce-f06b5ba21f33_story.html. Accessed 12 Dec. 2016.

Swinn, Louise. "*The Last Painting of Sara de Vos* Review: Dominic Smith's Brilliant Art Novel." Review of *The Last Painting of Sara de Vos*, by Dominic Smith. *The Sydney Morning Herald*, 2 June 2016, www.smh.com.au/entertainment/ books/the-last-painting-of-sara-de-vos-review-dominic-smiths-brilliant-art-novel- 20160526-gp4sq3.html. Accessed 14 Dec. 2016.

League of Dragons

Author: Naomi Novik (b. 1973)
Publisher: Random House (New York). 400 pp.
Type of work: Novel
Time: 1812–15
Locales: Russia, Europe

(Courtsy of Penguin Random House)

League of Dragons *is the ninth and final installment of the Temeraire historical fantasy series by American writer Naomi Novik.*

Principal characters:
CAPTAIN WILLIAM LAURENCE, former captain of HMS Reliant in the British Royal Navy before joining the Aerial Corps and becoming captain to Temeraire
TEMERAIRE, a heavyweight Chinese Celestial dragon in the British Aerial Corps
NAPOLEON BONAPARTE, the French military and political leader attempting to conquer the world
ADMIRAL JANE ROLAND, captain to the dragon Excidium and Laurence's love interest
ISKIERKA, a fire-breathing dragon in service to Britain with whom Temeraire mates

For Naomi Novik, the idea of a book series depicting the Napoleonic Wars with dragons came easily. In interviews, the author has stated that she started reading the books of historical fiction novelist Patrick O'Brien shortly before writing her own series. A longtime fan of the fantasy genre, Novik recognized fascinating similarities between dragons and the British Royal sailing ships in O'Brien's naval adventures. Dragons, she decided, could easily substitute for these ships in a swashbuckling Napoleonic War story by requiring entire military crews rather than single riders. With this image in mind, she began writing what would be known as the Temeraire series. Beginning with *His Majesty's Dragon* (2006), the Temeraire series consists of nine novels in total—many of which have been on the New York Times Best Sellers list. The books follow the adventures of Captain William Laurence, an Englishman who leaves the high society position of being an officer of the British Royal Navy to join the Aerial Corps after a young dragonet, whom he names Temeraire, chooses him to be his handler. Together, Laurence and Temeraire travel the world fighting the French army and seeking international alliances. *League of Dragons* (2016) is the ninth and final book to depict Laurence and Temeraire's adventures.

League of Dragons successfully combines an action-packed adventure story with a comedy of manners. In addition to concluding Britain's fight against Napoleon and depicting the numerous battles this effort involves, the novel also satirizes the British class system. Novik demonstrates how stiff and elitist the world that Laurence once belonged to is by presenting the Aerial Corps as a stark contrast. Where members of the Royal Navy are gentlemen of the upper class, the Aerial Corps officers are a diverse group, including men from various class backgrounds, women, and teenagers as well as the intelligent, sentient dragons. Although Laurence has shamed his well-to-do family by leaving the Royal Navy for the Aerial Corps, Novik ensures that his decision to do so always appears worthwhile to readers by illustrating how interesting the new world he has joined actually is.

The characters and their relationships are a large part of what makes *League of Dragons* so compelling. However, while the narrative is told from the perspective of Laurence, he is not the most interesting character. Temeraire, the enormous dragon to whom Laurence is captain, easily wins that designation. As a Celestial, which is a Chinese breed of dragon, Temeraire is extremely intelligent. Upon his hatching in 1805, he was able to speak English, French, and Mandarin. His curiosity about the world and thirst for knowledge gives him a playful, childlike quality. In the previous novels in the series, this endearing quality was furthered by his requests to have Laurence read to him on subjects such as science and mathematics. However, *League of Dragons* is in many ways the final chapter in Temeraire's bildungsroman, or coming-of-age story. Having traveled the world with Laurence while fighting for the British military, Temeraire has a better understanding of the injustices dragons face. In *League of Dragons*, he combines this knowledge with a growing feeling of confidence to become a leader in his community and spearhead the drafting of the Dragon Rights Act of 1813. Ultimately, what makes Temeraire and many of the other dragons of the series so interesting is that Novik presents them as a disenfranchised demographic of society. Their fight for political and economic autonomy from humans is powerful because it echoes actual civil rights struggles throughout history.

Naomi Novik is an American writer best known for the historical fantasy Temeraire series. Her first book, His Majesty's Dragon *(2006), won the 2007 Compton Crook Award for the year's best first novel in the categories of science fiction, fantasy, and horror.*

Just as Novik has rewritten history to include dragons, she has also given women a more prominent role. In the books' depiction of nineteenth-century Britain, women are welcomed as leaders and members of the military—although only in the more unconventional Aerial Corps. One of the best examples of Novik's efforts to showcase what history would have looked like had women had more power is Jane Roland, an aviator in the Aerial Corps who has led many successful dragon formations to win battles. She becomes an admiral in *League of Dragons*, the highest possible rank. Meanwhile her daughter, Emily Roland, is a wingman in Temeraire's crew. What is truly unique about Jane as a character is the fact that she is tough, older, and not especially beautiful, but still serves as Laurence's love interest. Jane exemplifies the multidimensional and nuanced nature of many of Novik's secondary characters. This is equally as true for the dragon characters as for the humans. Iskierka, for example, is a fire-breathing, bloodthirsty dragon in the Aerial Corps who convinces Temeraire to mate with her. While occasionally an obnoxious and dangerous character, she is also an excellent foil to Temeraire. Their offspring, Ning, also proves to be a complicated character.

When it comes to writing action, Novik is superb. There are several story lines within *League of Dragons*, all of which are continuations from previous novels in the series. The primary story line, however, focuses on the Aerial Corps's fight against Napoleon's army. When *League of Dragons* begins, Laurence and Temeraire are in Lithuania learning that Napoleon has retreated from Russia. Their plans to pursue him become more urgent when they learn that the French have stolen Temeraire and Iski-erka's egg. They make their way toward France, only to be held hostage in the Alps, where they learn that Napoleon has been both breeding thousands of dragons and has successfully developed a cure for the draconic plague. After escaping, they regroup in Britain before heading back to continental Europe to take care of Napoleon once and for all. From aerial battles between fleets of dragons to one-on-one pistol duels, Novik excels at raising the stakes and describing action sequences in an engaging way.

One of the most engaging aspects of *League of Dragons* is Novik's highly inventive world building. She takes great pains to describe each dragon's physicality, talents, and behavior. At this time in Novik's alternate history, every nation around the world has its own breeds of dragons, and each culture treats dragons differently. Where Britain views dragons predominantly as essential members of the military, China treats them as sacred beings. In Russia, however, dragons are kept in the gulags and abused. In addition to creating a detailed draconic world, *League of Dragons* also showcases Novik's skill for developing a unique military culture. In the Aerial Corps, dragons fly in fleets much like ship armadas. Each dragon has a crew that flies with it during battle. In addition to the captain, who gives them direction, a dragon also carries up to thirty or forty riflemen, bellmen, and lookouts. Although some dragons have fire-breathing capabilities and can attack during battle, the human officers they carry are largely responsible for attacking the enemy. The final layer that makes Novik's world come to life is her deft ability to weave history with fantasy. Many of the events that Laurence and Temeraire encounter are taken from real life; Britain is still dealing with the aftermath of losing the Revolutionary War against the United States, the East India Trading Company is smuggling opium to Europe, and Napoleon Bonaparte is attempting to conquer the world. The inclusion of these familiar historical elements makes it easy for readers to enter Novik's world. The addition of dragons not only makes the story more interesting but also changes the course of history in an exciting and suspenseful way.

League of Dragons has been met with mixed reviews. Many critics and fans have called the book's pacing slow, a problem that stems from Novik's decision to repeat several subplots from previous installments in the series. For example, much of the first part of *League of Dragons* focuses on Laurence's emotional tailspin after learning that his father has died. Laurence's father, a traditional nineteenth-century military man, never approved of his son being in the Aerial Corps. Where it once seemed that Laurence had finally made peace with his decision to join this ostracized branch of Britain's armed forces, in *League of Dragons* he again begins to agonize about his role in the wars. Novik's decision to spend a significant portion of the book on Laurence's complex feelings about his father does not move the plot forward and consequently gives certain chapters a frustrating, stagnant feeling. Fortunately, however, Novik resolves this conflict early in *League of Dragons* and the rest of the novel focuses on the exciting hunt for Napoleon.

Despite the fact that many critics felt *League of Dragons* was uneven, most agreed that it provided a rewarding conclusion to the series. In his review for National Public Radio's website, Jason Heller wrote, "*League of Dragons* masterfully wraps up so many plot threads and loose ends that had built up throughout the previous eight books." Similarly, *Kirkus Reviews* wrote that although *League of Dragons* was slow to gain momentum, it was "overall a satisfying conclusion to a remarkable series." In addition to providing readers with a fulfilling ending to Laurence and Temeraire's adventures, *League of Dragons* also succeeds at taking a thought-provoking look at injustice. By depicting the social and political plight of the dragons in a compelling manner, Novik makes poignant commentary on the devastating effects that systemic oppression has on disenfranchised groups. At the end of the day, however, what truly makes *League of Dragons* a superb read is its storytelling. As a writer, Novik is exceptionally talented at telling exciting stories driven by complicated, fleshed-out characters. Furthermore, she is brilliant at blending unlikely genres; fans of both fantasy and historical fiction novels are likely to enjoy *League of Dragons*.

Emily Turner

Review Sources

Heller, Jason. "Temeraire and Laurence, at Peace at Last in *League of Dragons*." Review of *League of Dragons*, by Naomi Novik. *National Public Radio*, 14 June 2016, www.npr.org/2016/06/14/481391755/temeraire-and-laurence-at-peace-at-last-in-league-of-dragons. Accessed 22 Jan. 2017.

Review of *League of Dragons*, by Naomi Novik. *Kirkus Reviews*, 14 June 2016, www.kirkusreviews.com/book-reviews/naomi-novik/league-dragons. Accessed 22 Jan. 2017.

Review of *League of Dragons*, by Naomi Novik. *Publishers Weekly*, 11 Apr. 2016, www.publishersweekly.com/978-0-345-52292-4. Accessed 22 Jan. 2017.

The Legends Club
Dean Smith, Mike Krzyzewski, Jim Valvano, and an Epic College Basketball Rivalry

Author: John Feinstein (b. 1956)
Publisher: Doubleday (New York). 416 pp.
Type of work: Nonfiction
Time: 1980–2016
Locale: North Carolina

(Courtesy of Doubleday)

Veteran sportswriter John Feinstein provides a multidecade portrait of the three major college basketball programs in North Carolina's Raleigh–Durham–Chapel Hill area, focusing on the legendary coaches who helmed each school's team—and the unlikely friendships that developed between these rivals.

Principal personages:

DEAN SMITH, head coach of the University of North Carolina men's basketball team, 1961–97

MIKE KRZYZEWSKI, head coach of Duke's men's basketball team, 1980–

JIM VALVANO, head coach of North Carolina State's men's basketball team, 1980–90

MICKIE KRZYZEWSKI, Mike Krzyzewski's wife

PAM VALVANO STRASSER, Jim Valvano's widow

LINNEA SMITH, Dean Smith's widow

TOM BUTTERS, athletic director at Duke who hired Mike Krzyzewski

MICHAEL JORDAN, star shooting guard for North Carolina, 1982–84

CHRISTIAN LAETTNER, star forward for Duke, 1988–92

In the world of college basketball, the players come and go, but the coaches remain. Unlike in the professional world of the National Basketball Association (NBA), where the best athletes enjoy careers of up to two decades, in the college ranks the stars stay for four years, at most. As a result it is the coaches who develop into legends, the best of them becoming synonymous with the schools they represent, as they assert control over every aspect of the basketball program.

In writing about college basketball, then, it makes sense for an author to take a top-down approach, and this is precisely the preferred methodology of John Feinstein. The prolific sportswriter made his name in 1986 with his now classic work *A Season on the Brink*, which provided an all-access look into the Indiana University basketball team's 1985–86 season, focusing particularly on the figure of their volatile head coach, Bobby Knight. The book became an instant sensation, leading the National Collegiate

Athletic Association (NCAA) to restrict reporter access to locker rooms and earning the years-long enmity of Knight, thanks to its warts-and-all portrayal of that coach.

Thirty years and several dozen books later, Feinstein decided to return to profiling NCAA coaches, albeit in a far less explosive manner, with his 2016 book *The Legends Club*. Unlike *A Season on the Brink*, this latest volume covers far more than just one basketball season and scrupulously avoids any explicitly negative commentary on its subjects. A graduate of Duke University and a man whose professional career has put him on an intimate footing with the college basketball powerhouses of North Carolina, Feinstein found his natural subject in the three legendary coaches who competed against each other in the 1980s (and in the case of two of them, throughout the 1990s and into the first decade of the twenty-first century).

"I wasn't born to write [this book], but I lived it," Feinstein writes, noting his long personal involvement with the three men who would come to define basketball in the Tar Heel state—Dean Smith, coach of the University of North Carolina (UNC) basketball team from 1961 to 1997; Mike Krzyzewski, top man at Duke from 1980 onward; and Jim Valvano, who headed up North Carolina State's program from 1980 to 1990. All three men worked in close proximity to each other in North Carolina's so-called Research Triangle and as a result developed a fierce rivalry. Drawing on his friendly acquaintance with Smith and Valvano and his ongoing friendship with Krzyzewski, Feinstein is able to provide unprecedented access to these archrivals. In writing the book, Feinstein interviewed Krzyzewski at length, drew on his previous interaction with the other coaches, both now deceased, and spoke with the spouses of all three men. While this access—along with the author's great admiration for the coaching trio—too often leads Feinstein to go easy on his subjects, ignoring any of their negative qualities, it also allows for the intimacy and the sense of behind-the-scenes observation that forms the book's greatest strength.

This privileged viewpoint is maintained throughout the book, endowing what is essentially a straightforward, chronological narrative with a rich stew of anecdote, personal reflection, and no shortage of on-the-court Xs and Os analysis. After a brief introduction, Feinstein begins his narrative proper in 1980, when both Krzyzewski and Valvano are hired to take over their respective schools' basketball programs. Although both Duke and NC State had had some success in the past, each school has had difficulty escaping from the shadow of UNC and their already legendary coach, Dean Smith. It was this inability to establish their own identities in the Research Triangle that led previous coaches Bill Foster (Duke) and Norm Sloan (NC State) to leave and be replaced by the two new recruits from the New York area. Years later, Krzyzewski would recall to Feinstein, "If Jimmy [Valvano] and I had landed in a spaceship from Mars instead of on airplanes from New York, we couldn't possibly have had less understanding of what an icon Dean was." Because of their ignorance, they launch into their new jobs undeterred, but they soon figure out the fraught lay of the land.

Although Valvano has some early success, improbably winning a national title in 1983, it takes Krzyzewski some time to establish his own identity on the court. Eventually he turns Duke into a destination for recruits—crucially winning a head-to-head battle with Smith to sign top high schooler Danny Ferry in 1985—and wins back-to-back national championships in 1991 and 1992. By then, Duke had become an undisputed rival to North Carolina, but NC State had long faded from elite status. Following a scandal involving the academic manipulation of student athletes, Valvano stepped down in 1990, and his replacement, Les Robinson, was unable to match his success.

Feinstein's account focuses primarily on the 1980s and 1990s, those years when the balance of power in the Research Triangle was at its most volatile, constantly shifting as the upstarts tried to take their place beside the legend. The process of Krzyzewski's development, in which he comes to not only rival Smith in coaching achievement but to resemble him in on-the-court approach, is the most dominant through line in the book, probably in part because Feinstein had the most access to the Duke coach, but also because Coach K's trajectory is the most narratively satisfying. From confident but unproven neophyte who barely survives getting fired in his early years to winningest

> *John Feinstein is a* New York Times *best-selling author of numerous sports books, including* A Season on the Brink *and* A Good Walk Spoiled. *He is a columnist for the* Washington Post, Golf World, *and* Golf Digest *and contributes to a number of radio programs, including the Golf Channel and Sirius XM Radio. He is also the author of a series of sports-themed children's mysteries.*

(and arguably most-hated) coach in NCAA history, with some setbacks along the road, Krzyzewski is an appropriate central figure and one who emerges vividly as a principled, obsessive, but fair-minded coach who genuinely cares about his players.

Valvano, although less central to the book than Krzyzewski, comes off as even more vivid, thanks to his large, gregarious personality and rollicking sense of humor. Everyone whom Feinstein interviews about him has a Jimmy V. story. Valvano also provides the emotional heart of the story as he becomes stricken with cancer and dies at the age of forty-seven. Detailing his final days, Feinstein describes the friendship between Valvano and Krzyzewski, which had developed after the former had left NC State, and takes readers inside Valvano's hospital room, where Coach K. is a frequent visitor. Here, Feinstein's level of access to his subjects allows for a greater form of intimacy than he had previously achieved by taking us into the locker room, and these scenes provide the emotional highlights of the book.

If Smith does not come off quite as vividly as the other two men, it is perhaps because, as *Wall Street Journal* reviewer Will Blythe suggests, he was an intensely private man who was averse to publicity, but he still registers as more than just the legendary figure that his Tobacco Road peers had to measure up to. In fact, one of the narrative coups in the later sections of the book is to chart the grudging respect and admiration that eventually developed between Smith and Krzyzewski.

This mutual esteem turns into a greater intimacy when Smith comes down with a terminal form of dementia and Krzyzewski visits him, registering the sadness that comes from someone with such a sharp mind now losing his memory. Later, Krzyzewski and his wife run into Smith's wife at the beach. Krzyzewski asks to visit Smith, now in the final throes of dementia. After sitting with the man, who is almost completely gone, he squeezes his hand and tells him he loves him. "At that moment,"

Feinstein writes, "Dean looked up at him and Mike saw something—he wasn't sure if it was recognition or not, but it was something—in his eyes." Without insisting on anything miraculous having occurred, Feinstein suggests a powerful connection between the two coaches, crafting a moving conclusion to his story.

As with many of Feinstein's previous books, *The Legends Club* was respectfully reviewed in the mainstream press, with several reviewers lauding the intimate nature of the author's portrayal of his subjects. Writing for the *Chicago Tribune*, Ed Sherman called the book a "fast-moving account of a memorable era in college basketball," concluding that *Legends* is among the author's best work. Blythe was especially taken with Feinstein's treatment of Krzyzewski, noting that the "portrayal of the Duke coach is the most revelatory in the book and goes a long way towards humanizing the man known by Tar Heels as the Rat, among the printable epithets." Because of the book's genre, it was not widely reviewed, but it did earn a respectable notice from Heather Havrilesky in *Bookforum* in which she considered the role that college basketball plays in the lives of its fanatical followers and discussed the ways in which Feinstein plays to his audience. The author, she wrote, "doesn't work around the inherent provincialism of his latest subject so much as lean in—way in," an approach that may render the book's appeal limited, but makes it of great interest to its target audience.

As many reviewers point out, Feinstein's primary achievement is to provide insight into the personal element of college basketball. By focusing on three coaches who worked in such close proximity to each other, Feinstein gives us not only a sense of the developing relationships between them, but of the long, twisting trajectories that a career in sports can take. We also see the personal toll the job takes on the three men, as well as the highs and lows they experience on the court. If Feinstein, on occasion, seems like more of a fan than an objective observer, it is a necessary gesture. That is because only by befriending his subjects and speaking with them in good faith is he able to achieve the level of access that makes *The Legends Club* such an engaging and dynamic read.

Andrew Schenker

Review Sources

Blythe, Will. "Full-Court Press in North Carolina." Review of *The Legends Club: Dean Smith, Mike Krzyzewski, Jim Valvano, and an Epic College Basketball Rivalry*, by John Feinstein. *The Wall Street Journal*, 16 Mar. 2016, www.wsj.com/articles/full-court-press-in-north-carolina-1458169205. Accessed 7 Dec. 2016.

Brady, Erik. "John Feinstein Relives Tobacco Road Coaching Rivalry in 'The Legends Club.'" Review of *The Legends Club: Dean Smith, Mike Krzyzewski, Jim Valvano, and an Epic College Basketball Rivalry*, by John Feinstein. *USA Today*, 14 Mar. 2016, www.usatoday.com/story/sports/ncaab/2016/03/14/john-feinstein-the-legends-club-book-dean-smith-mike-krzyzewski-jim-valvano/81795326. Accessed 7 Dec. 2016.

Havrilesky, Heather. "Hoop Dreams: How Obsessive Basketball Fandom Helps Us Find Our Bliss." Review of *The Legends Club: Dean Smith, Mike Krzyzewski, Jim Valvano, and an Epic College Basketball Rivalry*, by John Feinstein. *Bookforum*, Apr.–May 2016, p. 4.

Sherman, Ed. "'The Legends Club' by John Feinstein Showcases Smith-Krzyzewski-Valvano Dynamic." Review of *The Legends Club: Dean Smith, Mike Krzyzewski, Jim Valvano, and an Epic College Basketball Rivalry*, by John Feinstein. *Chicago Tribune*, 8 Mar. 2016, www.chicagotribune.com/lifestyles/books/ct-prj-legends-club-john-feinstein-smith-krzyzewski-valvano-20160308-column.html. Accessed 7 Dec. 2016.

The Lightkeepers

Author: Abby Geni (b. 1979)
Publisher: Counterpoint (Berkeley, CA).
361 pp.
Type of work: Novel
Time: Present day
Locale: Farallon Islands, California

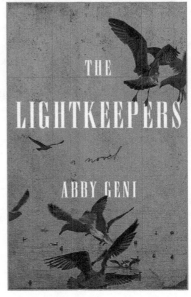

(Courtesy of Counterpoint Press)

A character study with an undercurrent of suspense, The Lightkeepers *concerns the soul-searching experiences of a young female photographer during a year spent in isolation among wild animals and the equally untamed scientists who study them, on the unforgiving archipelago known as the Farallon Islands.*

Principal characters:

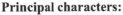

MIRANDA, a professional wildlife photographer
GALEN MCNAB, a biologist who specializes in sharks
MICK AUDINO, a young biologist who specializes in whales
FOREST COHEN, a young shark specialist
ANDREW METZGER, a bird specialist
LUCY CRAYLE, a young bird expert
CHARLENE WESTERMAN, an intern

Thirty miles off the coast of California, opposite San Francisco Bay, lie the Farallon Islands. Scattered, wave-splashed rocks in the Pacific Ocean, the Farallones were once known as "the Islands of the Dead" because mainland American Indians believed they were haunted by the spirits of the departed. Located in the rich California Current, the Farallones have long provided feeding and breeding stations for a variety of seabirds, fur seals, several species of whale, and unusually large great white sharks that prey on the other animals. The fur seals also attracted humans who decimated their population. The islands posed a hazard that claimed many ships before the erection of a lighthouse on the largest island in the nineteenth century. The Farallones became a protected reservation in 1909 and a National Wildlife Refuge in 1969. Now closed to the public, the islands are uninhabited by humans, except for the ninety-five-acre Southeast Farallon Island, where a handful of biological researchers are allowed to live while studying native fauna.

It is at this remote, rugged spot that Miranda, viewpoint character of *The Lightkeepers*, arrives after a five-hour ride by ferry. Miranda has spent her career fearlessly traveling the globe, from the tropics to the Arctic to the desert, shooting nature photographs. After seeing an image of the Farallon Islands, she applied for a grant to complete a personal project and was accepted for a year-long residence to capture images of the native wildlife.

Miranda narrates the rest of the novel, which is divided into the four seasons of research and study of specific animals (sharks, whales, seals, and birds). Each chapter prior to the epilogue is written as letter to her mother, who was killed in a freak traffic accident when Miranda was fourteen years old. This is a habit that Miranda, a loner with no permanent attachments, has maintained ever since her mother's death. Sometimes she mails the letters, addressing them simply to "Mom," knowing they will end up among dead, undeliverable letters at a post office. Other times, she sticks letters under rocks or in the cracks of trees, or allows the wind to carry them away. To her living father, meanwhile, she sends a single postcard with a few words.

In Miranda's first unsent letter on this excursion, she describes the hazardous transition from ferryboat to land, foreshadowing difficulties to come. Because the waters are too rough to permit the construction of a dock, Miranda and her luggage have to be lifted off the boat by a shore-mounted crane. On the island, she will bunk in a bedroom of an ancient, dilapidated cabin built a century earlier, alongside the few other humans living and working there, all individually odd and collectively more interested in and comfortable interacting with animals than with humans.

The senior member and leader of the biologists is Galen McNab, a cranky shark specialist and longtime island resident. He works with a fellow shark enthusiast, the much younger Forest Cohen. Andrew Metzger and Lucy Crayle are young ornithologists and lovers who enjoy intimidating and humiliating the newcomer, whom they misname "Melissa" and later disparagingly call "Mouse Girl," after Miranda's encounter with a horde of the mice that overrun the island. Burly whale watcher Mick Audino and eager young intern Charlene Westerman are the only human inhabitants who are friendly toward the photographer.

Miranda quickly learns the rules of the isolated retreat. The first lesson is to watch her step. The truth of this is painfully delivered when she stumbles on crumbling rock and gashes her side, a wound that Mick tenderly stiches. The second rule is to observe but not interfere, and to not impose human standards on the natural world. This is a rule Miranda will violate when nobody is watching, helping lead a lost seal pup to the water's edge. Third, she learns not to talk about her past. While Miranda follows this rule in communicating with others on the island, she nevertheless lives in the past, unable to disconnect from the memory of her late mother. While the island itself is isolated, these rules serve to keep its residents isolated from one another as well, allowing for the mysteries and misunderstandings to come.

As the days pass, Miranda adapts to the leisurely pace and brooding ambience of the island. She visits a nearby coast guard house, abandoned except for a colony of bats. She climbs Lighthouse Hill to appreciate the panoramic view. She learns local landmarks: Blowhole Peninsula, Sea Pigeon Gulch, Emperor's Bathtub. She is told animal lore and island history, including the tale of a female ghost who haunts the island. Using a variety of cameras, she snaps hundreds of shots of the various animals in their seasons.

(Courtesy of Dan Kelleghan)

Winner of a Friends of American Writers literary award for her story collection The Last Animal *(2013), Abby Geni also won first place in the 2008 Glimmer Train Fiction Open with her short story "Captivity." Geni was awarded a fellowship to the Iowa Writers' Workshop and became a writing instructor at the School of the Art Institute of Chicago in 2011.* The Lightkeepers *is her first full-length novel.*

While others engage in observing and researching their chosen fauna, Miranda also observes her cabinmates. She hears Lucy and Andrew noisily making love nightly in the room beneath hers. One night she spots Mick and Forest going off together and, using a telephoto lens, photographs their sexual encounter in the deserted coast guard house. She eavesdrops on conversations, surreptitiously fires off candid snapshots, and occasionally snoops in bedrooms while members of the group are absent.

The mood of the novel changes dramatically in November, during whale season, when the normal island routines are shattered. After a night of drinking wine—something she seldom indulges in—a tipsy Miranda awakens to find herself pinned to her bed by a man. By moonlight, she sees that her assailant is Andrew. As he rapes her, she sees the ghostly figure of a woman, who seems to wave at her. The assault leaves Miranda ill, feverish, and bed-bound. While Mick kindly nurses her, Andrew acts as though nothing happened. When she hears Andrew and Lucy having sex as usual, she can no longer stand being cooped up, and though she is still sick, dresses and leaves the house. She walks to the nearby coast guard house, and as bats, disturbed by her presence, flit about before leaving via a broken window, she passes out.

By dawn, Miranda, still feeling the effects of her illness, has returned to her own room. She is awakened and told that Galen has ordered everyone outside. She struggles to dress and meets the others at Sea Pigeon Gulch, where Andrew's battered body has been found floating face down in the water. Law enforcement is summoned by radiophone, the only link to the mainland, and a helicopter is dispatched to the island, bearing two plainclothes federal agents and a medical examiner. Andrew's body is retrieved to be flown to the city for an autopsy, which eventually concludes the cause of death was drowning, probably as the result of a fall. Meanwhile, the agents interview each living resident privately and individually, learning little of value. Miranda privately wonders if Andrew's death was indeed an accident.

The island, which holds dangers at every turn, becomes increasingly sinister as the book progresses. The situation becomes more complicated during seal season in January when a severely bruised, unconscious Charlene is found at the bottom of Lighthouse Hill.

The Lightkeepers is an intriguing novel with the elements of a locked-room mystery placed in a unique and evocative setting. There are a sudden death that could have been murder and a second potential assault, either or both of which could have been committed by one or more of a limited number of suspects, all with possible motives, in a geographically restricted environment. The story diverges considerably from the conventional mystery, however, in that no character takes up the role of detective to pursue scant clues potentially suggesting malfeasance. The characters' response is much more passive, as they are a group who have been trained to observe, to not take action, and to keep their thoughts to themselves. All of this creates an unreliable, but haunting and compelling narrative.

The major strength of *The Lightkeepers* is its sympathetic, complex protagonist. Though she manages to launch a successful career as a professional photographer, Miranda is emotionally crippled and connects more fully with animals than with her human counterparts. She is, in the end, an unreliable narrator whose thoughts are warped by her self-imposed isolation from normal interactions and whose impressions cannot always be believed. Until her arrival in the Farallones, she can relate only to her late mother via personal missives that are created for the moment, then left behind to make room for new temporary experiences. The dramatic experiences of this narrative finally spur Miranda to change.

Critical reception to this novel was overwhelming in its praise. Meredith Maran, in her review for the *Chicago Tribune*, compared *The Lightkeepers* to Alice Sebold's *The Lovely Bones* (2002) and wrote, "Like many literary classics and novels that are destined to be classics, *The Lightkeepers* raises questions about humanity that are anything but light. Unlike many classics, it's an accessible page-turner whose surprises, both fictional and stylistic, unfold so satisfyingly that the novel is also a pleasure to read." Critics praised Geni's masterful storytelling and the ways that she augments the traditional story structure by telling the story through Miranda's letters and playing with the conventions of mystery stories.

Jack Ewing

Review Sources

Leavitt, Caroline. Review of *The Lightkeepers*, by Abby Geni. *SFGate*, 31 Dec. 2015, www.sfgate.com/books/article/The-Lightkeepers-by-Abby-Geni-6730702. php. Accessed 23 Nov. 2016.

Review of *The Lightkeepers*, by Abby Geni. *Kirkus Reviews*, 1 Nov. 2015, p. 202.

Maran, Meredith. Review of *The Lightkeepers*, by Abby Geni. *Chicago Tribune*, 6 Jan. 2016, www.chicagotribune.com/lifestyles/books/ct-prj-lightkeepers-abby-geni-20160106-story.html. Accessed 23 Nov. 2016.

Prose, Francine. Review of The Lightkeepers, by Abby Geni. *The New York Times*, 29 Jan. 2016, www.nytimes.com/2016/01/31/books/review/the-lightkeepers-by-abby-geni.html. Accessed 23 Nov. 2016.

Look

Author: Solmaz Sharif (b. 1986)
Publisher: Graywolf Press (Minneapolis, MN). 112 pp.
Type of work: Poetry

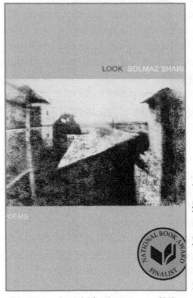

(Courtesy of Graywolf Press)

Look *is the first collection of poems by Solmaz Sharif, a prize-winning writer whose works in this volume often deal with the intersections of foreign wars and private lives. The often-political poems in* Look *are characterized by their stylistic inventiveness, particularly in their juxtapositions of different ways of using language.*

Anyone who values language as interesting in and of itself will find much to admire in *Look*, Solmaz Sharif's debut book of poems. Sharif is a variously inventive poet, especially in the way she shifts between different voices and techniques, often within the same poem. The primary conceit of the collection as a whole is the inclusion of phrases taken, as a note late in the text explains, "from the United States Department of Defense's *Dictionary of Military and Associated Terms* as amended through October 17, 2007." To begin with, the title of the collection, *Look*, plays with multiple meanings and subverts the *Dictionary of Military and Associated Terms* definition. The military definition of "look" is "a period during which a mine circuit is receptive of an influence"—an "influence" here being a person. Throughout the work, Sharif gives faces and feelings and crucial contexts to individuals being looked at in this way, while also issuing a call to arms for readers to really look at and observe events and dissect language.

The military terms are formatted in small caps when they appear in the text, giving more impact to terms that have been, by definition, intentionally sanitized of their full impact. The uses of these terms are many, but the poignancy of their juxtaposition with the phrases around them is one use Sharif commonly employs. For example, the first two poems in the collection, "Battlefield Illumination" and "Pinpoint Target," consist simply of the title in capital letters, followed by two short lines of text. These two brief works are typical of Sharif's writing in numerous ways. Their effectiveness depends very much on the use of juxtaposition: readers are led to expect one thing, and then the poem suddenly veers off in a different direction. Although Sharif often deploys this technique, she does so expertly and rarely allows it to become predictable. She also uses juxtaposition to put human meaning and feeling back into the military jargon: in a later poem, she uses the term "thermal shadow" to express the feeling of sexual desire; in another, "low dollar value items" is used to refer to human casualties.

Sharif is a minimalist: words are often simple and short, lines are often brief, and she relies on implications of stark brutality, rather than overt statements, to make her most effective points.

The two brief poems mentioned above also exemplify some of Sharif's other characteristic traits as a poet, including a rejection of predictable meters, a resistance to lyrical imagery, and a tendency toward prosaic phrasing. She employs many devices to lend interest to individual works, including prominent use of such techniques as anaphora, repetition, listings, and very brief lines (often just two or three words long). All of these methods work together to give her poems a strong sense of rhythm and propulsion. Here, for example, are the opening lines of a lyric titled "Lay"::

> LAY   down
>   to sleep then
>   to rest last night
>   to waste before
>   across a stretcher
>   across a shoulder
>   over a leg
>   beneath an arm
>   in a shroud

Poems such as these seem designed to be read aloud. They often have a chanting rhythm that is reminiscent more of oral traditions than of poetry designed primarily for the printed page. The ideas of Sharif's poems are arranged in terms of phrases rather than larger, more complex structures. She often eschews terminal punctuation, although this is not uniformly the case.

Look also contains various (usually short) prose poems that appear throughout the collection. In addition, although the collection is focused primarily on dark subjects, Sharif does employ humor on occasion. Thus one work, titled "SPECIAL EVENTS FOR HOMELAND SECURITY," begins as follows:

Leave your DOLLY at home—this is no INNOCENT PASSAGE. Ladies, bring your KILL BOX. Boys, your HUNG WEAPON. You will push WARHEAD MATING to the THRESHOLD of ACCEPTABILITY. Whether you're PASSIVE or on the HUNTER TRACK, there's a room for you.

The wit of the subtle sexual allusions in these sentences, and even more in the lines that follow, still works to subvert the military definitions of these terms and bring a stark humanity to them. For the most part, however, Sharif's tone is subdued and ironic. The voice that often speaks in this book is cool and intellectual, although moral urgency is also often implied by the text's frequent descriptions of, and implied protests against, the brutality of war. That brutality is often sanitized in its execution: soldiers can kill by pressing buttons thousands of miles away from the targets their weapons destroy. Modern war can seem more a technical exercise than a matter of personal risk and individual bravery. Euphemisms and technical language of the sort that appear throughout this book are often consciously metaphorical, as in the quoted reference to "WARHEAD MATING," functioning as a kind of Orwellian Newspeak. *Look* serves in part as a lesson in the ways language can be used to distort reality. Sharif uses her poems to expose and ridicule those distortions, or at least to call them more clearly to her readers' attention.

The imitation of military jargon is not the only kind of mimicry that Sharif employs. She is skilled at simulating a number of diverse voices and idioms in her poems, using language that variously calls to mind a public petition or legal brief, the voice of a sports announcer, and words shared in letters between intimates—sometimes all in a single poem. Her phrasing is often memorably dialogical as she switches from one tone or register to another within the same lyric. Reading this book is often like listening to a talented impersonator run through a whole series of varied voices.

The book's overarching theme is war. Sharif's parents are Iranians who left their country to escape war before she was born. Although she has not lived in the midst of actual war, she makes the argument in this work that by her own definition, she has been constantly at war, and asserts that she has as much right to discuss war as anyone else. Arguably the central poem of the work is one that looks at the ways in which war has directly affected her life: "Personal Effects," a thirty-one-page elegy for her uncle, Amoo, who died in the Iraq-Iran War. The poem itself encapsulates Sharif's variable style, including, as *New York Times* reviewer Natalie Diaz noted, passages of "prose, captions, sonnet, tercets, Wikipedia entries, bullet points, white space, and erasure."

It becomes clearer as the work progresses that Sharif is interested in wars of all kinds, not just the recent American wars in the Middle East. World War II and the Vietnam War are also mentioned or alluded to, as are the grim wars between Iran and Iraq. If the American military still seems mostly villainous, it is at least joined in villainy by the armies of Saddam Hussein and the Iranian mullahs. For example, "Personal Effects" includes the following prose excerpt:

> **Operation Ramadan** was an offensive in the Iran-Iraq War. It was launched by Iran in July 1982 near Basra and featured the use of human wave attacks in one of the largest land battles since World War II. **Aftermath:** The operation was the first of many disastrous offensives which cost thousands of lives on both sides. This one in general boosted the casualty limit up to 80,000 killed, 200,000 wounded, and 45,000 captured. [. . .][6]

Here, again, readers see examples of Sharif's formal inventiveness—in this case, an imitation of the tone and form of a Wikipedia entry, with the concluding reference to a "dead link" typifying the kind of ironic wit that often creeps into her poems. Sharif is often especially effective in the ways she concludes her works, frequently ending with phrasing that is memorable for presenting some striking image or implied bit of irony. Throughout *Look*, Sharif plays with meaning and the limits of language to great effect, ultimately creating a work that is varied and deeply thoughtful in its forms, as well as stark and powerful.

Robert C. Evans, PhD

Review Sources

Amico, Brandon. Review of *Look*, by Solmaz Sharif. *Rumpus*, 15 June 2016, therumpus.net/2016/06/look-by-solmaz-sharif/. Accessed 31 Jan. 2017.

Diaz, Natalie. "A Poet Subverts the Defense Department's Official Dictionary." Review of Look, by Solmaz Sharif. *The New York Times*, 21 Aug. 2016, www.nytimes.com/2016/08/21/books/review/look-poems-solmaz-sharif.html. Accessed 22 Feb. 2017.

Higgs, Lisa. "'Let Me LOOK at You': On *Look* by Solmaz Sharif." Review of *Look*, by Solmaz Sharif. *KR Online*, Nov. 2016, www.kenyonreview.org/kr-online-issue/kr-reviews/selections/look-by-solmaz-sharif-738439-2/. Accessed 22 Feb. 2017.

Johnson, Julie Swarstad. Review of *Look*, by Solmaz Sharif. *Harvard Review Online*, 5 July 2016, harvardreview.fas.harvard.edu/?q=features/book-review/look. Accessed 22 Feb. 2017.

Lund, Elizabeth. Review of *Look*, by Solmaz Sharif, et al. *The Washington Post*, 12 July 2016, www.washingtonpost.com/entertainment/books/look-by-solmaz-sharif-and-other-best-poetry-this-month/2016/07/12/a9b755de-4524-11e6-bc99-7d269f8719b1_story.html. Accessed 31 Jan. 2017.

Mad Enchantment
Claude Monet and the Painting of the Water Lilies

Author: Ross King (b. 1962)
Publisher: Bloomsbury Circus (New York).
  Illustrated. 403 pp.
Type of work: History
Time: 1914–29
Locales: Giverny, France; Paris, France

Ross King presents a fascinating study of Claude Monet's last masterpieces, the imposing paintings of water lilies, which reflected the artist's anguish at the loss of loved ones and the horrors of World War I.

(Courtesy of Bloomsbury USA)

Principal personages:
CLAUDE MONET, French Impressionist
  painter
GEORGES CLEMENCEAU, his friend and a
  French publisher, politician, and prime
  minister
BLANCHE HOSCHEDÉ-MONET, his stepdaughter, daughter-in-law, and assistant
SACHA GUITRY, his friend and an actor, playwright, and filmmaker
PAUL LEON, government official involved in the donation of Monet's Water Lilies to
  France

Ross King is a Canadian novelist turned award-winning historian who specializes in the history of art. In works such as *Brunelleschi's Dome: How a Renaissance Genius Reinvented Architecture* (2000), *Michelangelo and the Pope's Ceiling* (2002), and *Leonardo and the Last Supper* (2011), King has provided riveting stories about the creation of great masterpieces of Western art. In *The Judgement of Paris: The Revolutionary Decade That Gave the World Impressionism* (2006), King told the story of the origin of Impressionist painting in the late nineteenth century. His latest book, *Mad Enchantment: Claude Monet and the Painting of the Water Lilies*, is a companion piece to that work in which King describes the final magnificent flowering of Impressionism as the last of the Impressionist masters, Claude Monet, labored in his twilight years to create an imposing set of masterpieces that would soon point the way to the Abstract expressionism of the 1950s.

Monet helped give Impressionism its name with his 1874 painting *Impression, Sunrise*. He became one of the leaders of this artistic movement, which emphasized the transient effects of light and color. Impressionism challenged the realist approach to painting that dominated at the time by deemphasizing line and making use of bold, unmixed pigments. Monet became famous for his studies of light; in a famous series of thirty paintings, he captured the changing interplay of light and shadow on the face of the cathedral in Rouen. He would often set up several canvases at once before his subject and work on them one after the other as the light changed. In his early years, he suffered from critical disdain and struggled financially. This changed in the 1880s when the public finally embraced Impressionism, and Monet was seen as a French national treasure due in part to his brilliant depictions of the French countryside.

Monet's first wife Camille died of cancer in 1879. He then lived with Alice Hoschedé, who had been previously abandoned by her financier husband when he fled France in order to escape creditors. Monet brought his two children to the relationship and Alice her six.

Monet rented a large home in 1833 in the village of Giverny, forty miles northwest of Paris and not far from the suburban Parisian world that the Impressionists had made famous. He then purchased the house in 1890, and following the 1891 death of Alice's husband, he and Alice were married in 1892. He lived in Giverny for the rest of his life, expanding the property and building a studio. He was earning enough from the sale of his paintings to lay out lush gardens, which included a lily pond that was traversed by a graceful Japanese-style bridge. A team of six gardeners maintained his floral wonderland.

Monet spent freely on other interests, including the newly invented automobile. He soon had a small fleet of them garaged at his home in Giverny, and he terrified the neighbors with his speeding. He also enjoyed good food and kept a lavish table. Visitors to his home always hoped to be invited to lunch so they could partake in the excellently prepared fare. Dressing in conservative English tweed suits, he looked like a heavily bearded country gentleman.

Monet lived his life to the full, but there were shadows, even in his years of prosperity. Deeply disturbed by the governmental corruption revealed by the Dreyfus Affair in 1898, he abandoned his purportedly patriotic pictures of French scenery. He withdrew into his garden and focused on painting what he saw there. Aficionados of his work called him the "great anti-depressant" because of the beautiful play and intermingling of light and color in his paintings. Monet's own disposition was anything but sunny. He was a perfectionist and prone to depression. Over the course of his career, he destroyed hundreds of canvases while in a rage; the estimated value of these today would be many millions of dollars. He endured self-imposed agonies as he labored to achieve his pictorial effects.

In 1909, Monet exhibited forty-eight paintings of his water lilies. The exhibit was a great commercial success with more money flowing in to subsidize his world in Giverny, but while he was being lionized as one of the grand old men of French art, younger men were attracting attention with new and exciting approaches to painting. Pablo Picasso with Cubism and Henri Matisse with Fauvism were now the talk of Paris, and as the new century progressed, the painters of the Impressionist generation began to die off. An increasingly aged and artistically lonely Monet was in danger of becoming yesterday's news, a crusty relic of the Belle Époque, France's "Beautiful Age."

Profound personal crises also darkened Monet's mood. In 1911, Alice died of leukemia, and after this loss, Monet could not find the heart to paint. The next year, his eyesight began to dim. His painter's "eye" had become famous, awing his colleagues and delighting his public; now it was in danger of disappearing altogether because of a cataract. Even as he attempted to assimilate

Ross King is the author of seven books on history and art, including Brunelleschi's Dome *(2000) and* Michelangelo and the Pope's Ceiling *(2002). King won Canada's Governor General's Award for Non-Fiction for* The Judgement of Paris *(2006) and* Leonardo and The Last Supper *(2011).*

this unwelcome development, his eldest son Jean suffered a stroke. Jean lingered for two years and died in 1914. Reeling under these successive blows, Monet questioned whether he would ever pick up a brush again.

Monet's friends attempted to cheer him. The young playwright Sacha Guitry invited him to design a garden for his country estate. A much older friend, Georges Clemenceau, hoped to persuade Monet to resume painting when he paid him a visit in Giverny in April 1914. Clemenceau was seventy-three, a year younger than Monet, and the two men had known each other since the 1860s. While Monet was making his way as a painter, Clemenceau had pursued a career in journalism and politics. A ferocious controversialist, vehement anticlerical, and vociferous supporter of republican government in France, Clemenceau fought twenty-two duels against various rivals, earning the nickname the Tiger. Clemenceau served as France's prime minister from 1906 to 1909, and throughout his long and tumultuous life, he remained devoted to Monet, publically championing his art and privately offering unconditional emotional support.

It was artistic encouragement that Clemenceau offered during his April visit, and after lunch and a tour of the garden, he and Monet looked over some twenty-year old paintings that Monet had done of his water lilies. Privately, Clemenceau thought that these studies were not very interesting, but despite this, he praised the work and urged Monet to paint some larger, more ambitious canvases that could adorn the dining room of a wealthy patron. This challenge to undertake a grander scale project struck a spark with Monet. His paintings up to this point had rarely been larger than three feet wide by three feet high. By the spring and early summer, Monet was busy at work on canvases that were much larger than he typically painted. At first, these were six-and-a-half feet long and five feet high. Over time, they would get even bigger. In 1915, Monet built an enormous new studio to house these great stretches of canvas that then sat on specially designed easels that were built with casters to facilitate maneuvering them easily around the studio, which itself overshadowed Monet's house and was a measure of the artist's commitment to his task.

That commitment was tested by the outbreak of World War I in August 1914. Monet's remaining son Michel was called to serve, and when German armies threatened Paris, some feared that the enemy might appear in Giverny as well. Monet refused to contemplate evacuation, and the Germans were turned back at the Marne before he was forced to leave. The war cast a shadow over life at Giverny and cost France dearly. Around 1,400,000 French soldiers died, and nearly 2,000,000 French civilians became refugees. Great stretches of northern France were devastated by the fighting and scarred for years by the trenches. Monet worked steadily through these harsh years, and King makes a compelling argument that the war infuses these paintings, especially the enormous *The Two Willows*. Weeping willow trees had long been associated with mourning, and in Monet's stark representation, these trees evoke the profound suffering of the war years.

Moved by patriotism, Monet decided that the best way he could serve his country was to donate the growing collection of massive canvases that he called his Grandes Decorations to France. The gift was not unconditional; Monet expected his paintings to be properly displayed, and he had very precise notions of what that would entail. The result was prolonged negotiations with the French government, and it was Clemenceau, who had become prime minister at the climax of the war, who played a key role in overcoming the hurdles in the negotiations, making the donation possible. Much to Clemenceau's frustration, however, Monet, who was by then plagued by worsening problems with his eyes, kept finding reasons to delay the completion and delivery of his magnificent gift. It eventually became clear to Clemenceau that Monet was unable to part with his last creations while he was still alive. Monet died on December 5, 1926, and in May 1927, the Musée Claude-Monet à l'Orangerie des Tuileries opened in Paris. On permanent exhibition were Monet's vast paintings of waterlilies and willows, over three hundred feet of canvas in total. Over time, Monet's Grandes Decorations came to be seen as one of the masterworks of Western and world art.

Ross King's *Mad Enchantment* cannot recapture the full depths of Monet's creative process for the reader since the subtle interactive magic of inspiration and technical skill remains the mystery of great art. What King does magnificently accomplish is to place Monet's achievement into a vibrant historical context by allowing the reader to grasp the immense hurdles that Monet overcame to produce a work as monumental as his Grandes Decorations. In doing so, King's evocative narrative enables the reader to see Monet's paintings with fresh and more appreciative eyes.

Daniel P. Murphy

Review Sources

Carter, Maxwell. "Step Inside Monet's Garden." Review of *Mad Enchantment: Claude Monet and the Painting of the Water Lilies*, by Ross King. *The Wall Street Journal*, 18 Nov. 2016, www.wsj.com/articles/step-inside-monets-garden-1479494367. Accessed 22 Feb. 2017.

Hughes, Kathryn. "The Truth about Monet's Lily Pond." Review of *Mad Enchantment: Claude Monet and the Painting of the Water Lilies*, by Ross King. *The Guardian*, 3 Sept. 2016, www.theguardian.com/artanddesign/2016/sep/03/mad-enchantment-claude-monet-water-lilies-review. Accessed 22 Feb. 2017.

Simon, Linda. "Delightful Story of Claude Monet's Water Lilies." Review of *Mad Enchantment: Claude Monet and the Painting of the Water Lilies*, by Ross King. *Newsday*, 9 Sept. 2016, www.newsday.com/entertainment/books/mad-enchantment-review-delightful-story-of-claude-monet-s-water-lilies-1.12287900. Accessed 22 Feb. 2017.

Solomon, Deborah. "The Story of Claude Monet's Water-Lily Masterworks." Review of Mad Enchantment: Claude Monet and the Painting of the Water Lilies, by Ross King. *The New York Times*, 2 Dec. 2016, www.nytimes.com/2016/12/02/books/review/the-story-of-claude-monets-water-lily-masterworks.html. Accessed 22 Feb. 2017.

A Man Lies Dreaming

Author: Lavie Tidhar (b. 1976)
First published: 2014, in the United Kingdom
Publisher: Melville House (New York). 288 pp.
Type of work: Novel
Time: 1939
Locales: London, England; Auschwitz concentration camp in German-occupied Poland

Mind-bending and genre-blending, A Man Lies Dreaming *combines elements of such literary forms as factual and alternative history, tongue-in-cheek fantasy, classical noir, soft-core pornography, pulp detective fiction, Holocaust literature, and sly satire to create a wildly original romp of a novel.*

(Courtesy of Melville House Publishing)

Principal characters:
WOLF, a.k.a. The Drummer, a.k.a. Moshe Wolfson, a former German political leader and aspiring artist turned London private detective
ISABELLA RUBINSTEIN, his Jewish client
JUDITH RUBINSTEIN, Isabella's sister
JULIUS RUBINSTEIN, Isabella and Judith's father
SIR OSWALD MOSLEY, a member of Parliament and founder of the British Union of Fascists
LADY DIANA MOSLEY, a.k.a. Diana Freeman-Mitford, Oswald's wife, one of the famous and controversial Mitford sisters
RUDOLF HESS, leader of the Blackshirts
SHOMER, a Jewish novelist confined in Auschwitz
ILSE KOCH, the sadistic wife of a concentration camp commandant
KLAUS BARBIE, the operator of a bicycle shop used for nefarious activities
DETECTIVE INSPECTOR MORHAIM, a Jewish police officer
VIRGIL, an American employed by the Office of Strategic Services (OSS)

A Man Lies Dreaming begins much like a typical hard-boiled private-eye pulp novel. It is told partially through first-person diary extracts and partially through third-person narration. As the story opens on November 1, 1939, a shabby detective named Wolf sits brooding in his equally shabby office, which is located in a worn, prostitute-frequented section of London, England. A beautiful, well-dressed, dark-haired woman named Isabella Rubinstein soon enters Wolf's office, and the two characters engage in snappy banter. Isabella wishes to hire Wolf to find her sister, Judith, who has been missing for three weeks. Wolf is reluctant to work for someone of Jewish heritage, but he needs the money to pay rent on his office and his bleak, spartan apartment. Isabella mentions that Judith was to have been smuggled out of Germany in an arrangement made by her father. Wolf then realizes that Isabella's father is the German banker Julius Rubinstein, whom Wolf read about in a London newspaper and considers to be a ruthless gangster.

It soon becomes apparent to the reader that Wolf is, in fact, Adolf Hitler in disguise. Tidhar provides a series of explicit clues leading to this conclusion, such as Wolf's rampant anti-Semitism, his habits as a vegetarian and teetotaler, a reference to a book he published, the mention of his Austrian origin, his former distinctive mustache, and his sorrow over the suicide of his teenaged niece Geli, who used Wolf's own gun to kill herself. The fact that Hitler is a detective in London in November 1939 is an indication that *A Man Lies Dreaming* is set in an alternate, yet somewhat parallel universe. In the real world, Germany had already invaded Poland by 1939, initiating World War II. In the fictional world of this novel, Hitler and the National Socialists (Nazis) lost the power struggle within Germany to the Communists in the early 1930s in what is referred to as "the Fall." The would-be führer and most of his cohorts then fled Germany in order to avoid becoming victims of a purge, though a few stayed behind to join the Communists.

The Wolf's investigation is periodically interrupted by a seemingly unrelated story within the story. A man named Shomer, who, it is regularly stated, is in a different time and place, intrudes into the main story to relate his present life events. He is a novelist who is confined at Auschwitz concentration camp. During the day he digs graves for inmates who have died, and at night he dreams of a detective who is conducting an investigation. Later, after a stint in the infirmary, Shomer is put to work in a factory, making doors of all types that are actually portals to other times and places.

After Isabella leaves Wolf's office, Wolf begins the search for Judith. He leaves his office, plowing through throngs of prostitutes, whom he despises because he believes they are diseased. He visits a pub called the Hofgarten and solicits the help of a former colleague from Germany: Blackshirt leader Rudolf Hess, one of many characters in the novel who are real historical figures. Hess gives Wolf a card with the address of an East End club. When he leaves the pub, Wolf notices he is being followed, and he decides to return home to his apartment, where he finds an invitation from Sir Oswald Mosely to attend to a high-society event. Moseley, also a real historical figure, is a fascist and a candidate for prime minister.

Another subplot is then introduced when the reader learns of an unknown person with murderous tendencies who hides in the shadows opposite Wolf's building. This person preys on the prostitutes who congregate in the neighborhood, and the killer, who seems to know a great deal about the detective, subsequently taunts Wolf with typewritten letters.

Wolf continues the search for Judith, traveling to the club that Hess told him about. There, he is subdued with a hypodermic needle that knocks him unconscious, then drenched in the blood of an underling who is murdered in order to frame Wolf for the crime. The following day, Wolf is tortured sexually by the sadistic Ilse Koch—a process he secretly enjoys—before being released. He returns home to find policemen who are investigating the violent death of a prostitute. Wolf, who is covered in blood, is arrested as a suspect in the murder. He is questioned by Detective Inspector Morhaim and shown photographs of the dead prostitute, who has been mutilated with a swastika carved into her skin. A toy tin drummer—a reference to Wolf's German nickname, "the Drummer"—was found beside the body. Wolf denies any involvement in the crime and gives an expurgated version (minus the sexual torture) of what happened at the club.

Imprisoned overnight, Wolf is released the following day after the police visit the club and find it empty. Wolf cleans himself up and is transported via chauffeured Rolls-Royce to a party being held at the mansion of Sir Oswald and his wife, Lady Diana, whom Wolf knew previously in Germany. Oswald hires Wolf, paying him handsomely, to investigate several assassination attempts made on his life. Oswald suspects that Jews are trying to kill him. When he returns home later that evening, Wolf finds his office has been ransacked, and waiting in the office is Julius Rubinstein and two brutish minions. Julius warns Wolf to stay away from his daughters and then instructs the two men to tie up the detective and roughly circumcise him with a knife. Rubinstein urinates on the agonized Wolf in contempt, then leaves.

After taking several days to recover from his ordeal, Wolf continues his twin investigations. A second visit to Rudolf Hess produces the address of Klaus Barbie, in real life a Gestapo member who was known for torturing French prisoners. Wolf subdues Barbie, takes possession of a thick envelope, and finds dozens of women being held in the basement. They are all tattooed with numbers. As Wolf frees the captives, one woman gives him a possible lead to Judith's whereabouts. Wolf is subsequently confronted by an American named Virgil who shows the detective a warehouse full of military materiel and invites him to stage a coup against the Communists in Germany. Wolf contemplates the offer as he heads home, but he cannot think of any former associates who would be capable of assisting him. When he arrives at his apartment, Isabella is waiting. Wolf tells her what her father did to him, and Isabella beats and whips him in the course of sexually humiliating him, which Wolf likes. In the envelope he took from Barbie, he finds a passport for Moshe Wolfson and replaces the passport's photograph with his own, then forges the appropriate official stamps in order to assume Moshe Wolfson's identity.

Author of the popular Bookman Histories series of steampunk novels, Lavie Tidhar has also published two short-story collections, three graphic novels, four novellas, and six full-length novels. His novel Osama *(2011) won the World Fantasy Award for best novel, and* A Man Lies Dreaming *won the prestigious Jerwood Fiction Uncovered Prize.*

Eventually, most of the threads of the story converge, and the detective's two cases are essentially resolved. Wolf does not really care about the success or failure of the outcomes, since he has already been paid. As the conclusion approaches, the plot spirals faster, almost out of control. Wolf confronts and battles the prostitute killer and takes revenge on Julius Rubinstein. After Oswald Mosley announces at his victory rally that all foreigners will be deported, Wolf uses his forged passport to escape England and boards a ship to embark on a new journey.

A clever, twisted, and at times mind-bogglingly complicated story, *A Man Lies Dreaming* is populated with a multitude of genuine historical figures of the period that interact with the fictional characters. Notes at the end of the novel helpfully provide brief biographical sketches of people who actually existed. In addition to the Mosleys, Hess, Koch, and Barbie, the novel offers glimpses of such real historical personages as Roland Freisler, Leni Riefenstahl, Robert Bitker, Joseph Goebbels, Unity Valkyrie Mitford, Evelyn Waugh, C. S. Forester, Leslie Charteris, A. A. Milne, and Ian Fleming.

A Man Lies Dreaming presents an occasionally somber, but more often hilariously ironic, depiction of the people and attitudes that characterized a particularly stressful period of world history. In a technique that simultaneously honors and thumbs its nose at a variety of traditional genres, Tidhar—who has freely mixed and matched categories of literature elsewhere, especially in the graphic novel *Adolf Hitler's "I Dream of Ants!"* (2012) and the noir-flavored, Nazi-centric novella *The Vanishing Kind* (2016)—manages to create a new type of fiction in which the characters are really just figments of the imaginations of other characters, and vice versa.

Jack Ewing

Review Sources

Edwards, Maximillian. Review of *A Man Lies Dreaming*, by Lavie Tidhar. Strange Horizons, 12 Jan. 2015, strangehorizons.com/non-fiction/reviews/a-man-lies-dreaming-by-lavie-tidhar/. Accessed 30 Nov. 2016.

Heller, Jason. "Unnerving WWII Noir in A Man Lies Dreaming." Review of *A Man Lies Dreaming*, by Lavie Tidhar. NPR, 8 Mar. 2016, www.npr.org/2016/03/08/468941984/unnerving-wwii-noir-in-a-man-lies-dreaming. Accessed 29 Nov. 2016.

Merkin, Daphne. Review of *A Man Lies Dreaming*, by Lavie Tidhar. The New York Times, 18 Mar. 2016, www.nytimes.com/2016/03/20/books/review/a-man-lies-dreaming-by-lavie-tidhar.html. Accessed 30 Nov. 2016.

Roberts, Adam. "A Noir Novel about the Holocaust." Review of *A Man Lies Dreaming*, by Lavie Tidhar. *The Guardian*, 15 Oct. 2014, www.theguardian.com/books/2014/oct/15/a-man-lies-dreaming-lavie-tidhar-review-novel. Accessed 30 Nov. 2016.

Midnight in Broad Daylight
A Japanese American Family Caught Between Two Worlds

Author: Pamela Rotner Sakamoto (b. 1962)
Publisher: HarperCollins (New York). 464 pp.
Type of work: History, biography
Time: Early twentieth century through 2015, focusing on World War II (1939–45)
Locales: Auburn, Washington; Hiroshima, Japan; Los Angeles, California; Pacific theater of World War II; Japanese American internment camp in Gila, Arizona

Midnight in Broad Daylight *spins a masterful historical thread between the worlds of Japan and the United States, focusing on the years in which the nations faced one another in World War II. Through the true account of the experiences of the Fukuhara siblings, Sakamoto makes these international events personal and intimate.*

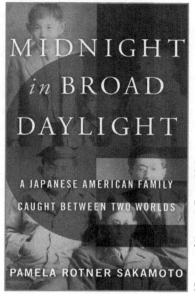

(Courtesy of HarperCollins Publishers)

Principal personages:

HARRY FUKUHARA, the middle son of the Fukuhara family, who serves with distinction in the US Army during World War II

FRANK, his youngest brother, also known as Katsutoshi, who is drafted into the Japanese Army during World War II

MARY, his sister, who also lives in the United States during World War II

VICTOR, his oldest brother, who is drafted into the Japanese Army

PIERCE, his brother, who is drafted into the Japanese Army

KATSUJI, his father, also known as Harry K. Fukuhara, who immigrated to the United States from Japan

KINU, his mother, who returns her family to Japan after being widowed

From the first pages of *Midnight in Broad Daylight: A Japanese American Family Caught Between Two Worlds*, the reader is aware of the harsh historical reality that awaits the Fukuhara family. In the prologue, historian Pamela Rotner Sakamoto describes how two brothers separately hear of the Japanese attack on Pearl Harbor on the island of Oahu, Hawaii, in December 1941: Harry Fukuhara is working as a gardener when he gets the news, while his younger brother Frank is in high school. The two brothers are Nisei, or first-generation American-born Japanese Americans, and they are emotionally close but geographically distant—Harry is in the United States, while Frank, also known as Katsutoshi, lives with his mother in Hiroshima, Japan. The two are the central protagonists of this true account of a uniquely transnational family strained by the devastation of World War II.

Improbably, both survive the war, and it is their detailed oral histories, along with extensive research, that allow Sakamoto to reveal the complex contours of lives caught between two national identities. *Midnight in Broad Daylight* is divided into six parts, which unfold sequentially, following the brothers from their childhood years through the aftermath of the bombing of Hiroshima. The book concludes with a brief consideration of the lives of Frank and Harry after the war. While Sakamoto offers an account of the entire Fukuhara family's war experience, Harry and Frank's stories bind together its diverse threads. The close bond between the two exceeds the ties between the other siblings. Furthermore, their diametrically different experiences of the war (Harry eventually serves in the US Army, while Frank, along with the other Fukuhara brothers, is drafted on the Japanese side), allows Sakamoto a convenient frame through which to present a very balanced view of the conflict between Japan and the United States. The focus on Harry and Frank, as well as the chronological structure, provides important grounding for the reader when the cultural and geographical scope of the subject matter is so broad.

Sakamoto leaves the inevitable atomic bombing of Hiroshima hanging and promptly rewinds to the happy early childhood of the Fukuhara brothers, born to their Issei (Japanese immigrant) parents in the small town of Auburn in Washington State. Harry, Frank, and their siblings offer the reader a privileged view into the prewar Japanese American experience, carefully weaving a sense of the complex duality of immigrant and first-generation life. Harry, in particular, grows up fully identifying as American, though connected to his Japanese heritage. However, the book reveals that self-identity is not enough to prevent a society from turning on those perceived as different.

Importantly, Harry and Frank's experiences as Nisei are contrasted to those of their Issei parents. Harry Katsuji Fukuhara and Kinu Fukuhara were proud immigrants to the United States, but did not want to abandon their heritage. They also wanted their children to remain connected to Japanese tradition, and sent their two eldest—Mary and Victor—back to Hiroshima, in hope they could attain a sufficient level of language mastery and cultural immersion. In making this decision, they followed the approach taken by many other Japanese immigrant parents in their day. Although they ultimately did not send their three younger sons away in this fashion, they did enroll them in Japanese language school. At home, the family enjoyed Japanese cooking and traditional family roles. Yet despite these careful cultural markers, Harry and Frank led a life that was closely integrated with the mainstream white community, privileged by their father's business success and the fact that their small town was less inclined toward the anti-Japanese xenophobia often evident in urban areas of the West Coast. However, their world was upturned by their father's death and their mother's decision to move the family to Hiroshima in 1933.

The immigrant experience and the sensation of cultural disconnect did not end with the family's return to Japan, however. Sakamoto skillfully traces the challenges of displacement that the Fukuhara children faced in Japan, perhaps even more acutely than in the United States. As Nisei, they were seen as not fully Japanese and therefore subject to bullying and isolation, particularly as nationalism and militarism took hold in Japan. Mary and Harry were particularly devastated by the family's return to Japan, and both would separately move back to the United States by 1938. Frank and the other siblings remaining in Hiroshima learned to conceal the fact that they spoke English and had spent years of their lives in the United

Pamela Rotner Sakamoto is a graduate of Amherst College and the Fletcher School of Law and Diplomacy at Tufts University. She has served as a professor at Punahou School in Honolulu, Hawaii, and as a consultant for the United States Holocaust Memorial Museum in Washington, DC.

States. As tension between the United States and Japan built, finally leading to Pearl Harbor and war, Frank, Victor, and their brother Pierce were drafted into the Japanese Army to face the country of their birth.

Across the Pacific, Harry and Mary experienced prejudice as well. American suspicion of anyone of Japanese heritage ran high after the attack on Pearl Harbor, and Harry faced discrimination in sharp contrast to his idyllic childhood. For example, he was fired on the spot by a woman whose lawn he was mowing when word of the attack was received. As the United States entered World War II, the situation rapidly deteriorated for the Japanese American community. Harry, Mary, and Mary's young child were eventually imprisoned in an internment camp in Arizona. In her account of the Fukuharas' interment experience, Sakamoto is able to integrate Harry's first-person reflections on the experience with detailed consideration of the larger historical and political context of the camps, shining new light onto a dark part of US history.

Perhaps the most remarkable part of this book, however, is its presentation of Harry's account of the next period in his life. Eager to escape from the internment camp, Harry responded to a military call for the enlistment of Japanese language experts. Though as a boy he had worked hard not to learn Japanese, he nevertheless had a high level of mastery of the language and easily passed the initial assessment exams. Shipped off to Minnesota, Harry began training in what would become one of the most secretive and elite units of the US military in the Pacific theater—an intelligence unit of specialists in the Japanese language. Harry and his peers received intensive language, intelligence, and cultural training, but no combat preparation. Their role on the front was to interrogate prisoners of war, to translate documents that had been obtained or intercepted, and, perhaps most importantly, to intervene with their military colleagues in order to create more opportunities for the collection of information. Harry quickly became one of the US Army's top translators, and his service brought him into very real wartime experience, even if most of the time he was carefully protected by other members of the military units to which he was assigned. Although he met with some terrifying incidents of racism, Harry's role as a highly prized intelligence asset ensured that systems were put into place to maximize his protection.

With Harry's enlistment in the US military, it was inevitable that the Fukuhara brothers would be divided across enemy lines. Harry never met his brothers in battle—indeed, the US Army went to some lengths to ensure that neither he nor his colleagues would be directed toward regions of Japan that were close to family—but he sought to be reunited with his family. None of the Fukuhara brothers in Japan served at such an elite level in the military. They were all, however, in the greater region of Hiroshima when the city was targeted by the US nuclear strike. Sakamoto provides a detailed and painful account of the experiences that they and their extended family endured both on the day of the bombing and in subsequent weeks and months. In the aftermath of the bombing, Harry finally reached Japan along with other US forces and made a remarkable journey home to Hiroshima in search of his family. This poignant climax is powerful even knowing in advance that Frank and Harry live to tell Sakamoto their tales.

Midnight in Broad Daylight was met with general critical enthusiasm. Many reviewers noted that the book exposes elements of the World War II experience that are little known to most American readers. The focus on the lives of Nisei in Japan during the war and the work of Nisei translators for US forces was particularly well-received, with critics praising Sakamoto's effective portrayal of the individual lives of Harry, Frank, and the rest of the Fukuhara family. David Takami, in his review for the *Seattle Times*, singled out Sakamoto's "sublime prose and prodigious research skills" as contributing to "as riveting and moving a book as has ever been written about World War II." Some reviewers, such as Gary Kamiya for the *New York Times Sunday Book Review*, noted that Sakamoto's straight historical style occasionally limits the characterization of the Fukuharas against the vast scope of the book's context, but recognized that in many ways this fits the unassuming nature of her protagonists and many other Nisei. Altogether, *Midnight in Broad Daylight* takes its place as a remarkable work both in the unique story it tells and in the way it adds to the historical understanding of World War II.

Julia Sienkewicz

Review Sources

Damsker, Matt. "*Midnight*, a Compelling History of a Japanese-American Family." Review of *Midnight in Broad Daylight: A Japanese American Family Caught Between Two Worlds*, by Pamela Rotner Sakamoto. *USA Today*, 18 Feb. 2016, www.usatoday.com/story/life/books/2016/02/18/midnight-in-broad-daylight-a-japanese-american-family-caught-between-two-worlds-book-review/80503404/. Accessed 1 Dec. 2016.

Kamiya, Gary. Review of Midnight in Broad Daylight: A Japanese American Family Caught Between Two Worlds, by Pamela Rotner Sakamoto. *The New York Times*, 15 Jan. 2016, www.nytimes.com/2016/01/17/books/review/midnight-in-broad-daylight-by-pamela-rotner-sakamoto.html. Accessed 1 Dec. 2016.

Quamme, Margaret. "*Midnight in Broad Daylight*: War Put Brothers on Opposite Sides of Conflict." Review of *Midnight in Broad Daylight: A Japanese American Family Caught Between Two Worlds*, by Pamela Rotner Sakamoto. *The Columbus Dispatch*, 31 Jan. 2016, www.dispatch.com/content/stories/life_and_ entertainment/2016/01/31/1-war-put-brothers-on-opposite-sides-of-conflict.html. Accessed 1 Dec. 2016.

Takami, David. "*Midnight in Broad Daylight*: World War II Sunders a Family."
Review of *Midnight in Broad Daylight: A Japanese American Family Caught Be-*
tween Two Worlds, by Pamela Rotner Sakamoto. *The Seattle Times*, 3 Jan. 2016,
old.seattletimes.com/html/books/2027823616_midnightbroaddaylightxml.html.
Accessed 1 Dec. 2016.

Modern Lovers

Author: Emma Straub
Publisher: Riverhead Books (New York).
 368 pp.
Type of work: Novel
Time: Present
Locale: Brooklyn, New York

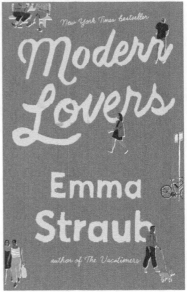

(Courtesy of Penguin Random House)

Modern Lovers is a novel about a close group of friends and former college bandmates all going through a midlife crisis. This novel explores the concepts of aging and adulthood—long after youth has gone away. It is New York Times best-selling novelist Emma Straub's third novel.

Principal characters:

ELIZABETH MARX, a real estate agent and
 the former singer for the punk band
 Kitty's Moustache
ANDREW MARX, her husband and the former bassist for Kitty's Moustache
HARRY MARX, Andrew and Elizabeth's teenage son
ZOE KAHN-BENNETT, Andrew and Elizabeth's friend, restaurateur, and a former
 member of Kitty's Moustache
JANE KAHN-BENNETT, Zoe's wife and the co-owner of the restaurant Hyacinth
RUBY KAHN-BENNETT, Zoe and Jane's teenage daughter

American novelist Emma Straub has built her literary reputation on works of fiction that explore the complexities of human relationships. Although she is not a plot-driven writer, Straub's narratives are still highly engaging. This is largely thanks to her talent for depicting the everyday tragedies and joys of contemporary life in an honest and humorous way. In her *New York Times* best-selling novel *The Vacationers* (2014), for example, Straub examines the dynamics of the Posts, a New York City family that goes on vacation to Mallorca, Spain, for two weeks. What makes this novel especially impressive is how entertaining it is despite the simplicity of its subject: the confines of a foreign paradise become an inescapable prison in which the characters' interpersonal conflicts begin to boil over. Similar to *The Vacationers*, Straub's latest novel *Modern Lovers* (2016) also focuses on the crumbling relationships of a tight-knit group of New Yorkers. In *Modern Lovers*, however, Straub explores the themes of adulthood and aging, something she has not done in the past.

 When *Modern Lovers* begins, most of the characters are in a state of prolonged personal stagnation. Set in the present, the novel follows the stories of the Marxes and the Kahn-Bennetts, two families that have known each other for nearly thirty years.

Early in the novel it is established that Elizabeth Marx, Andrew Marx, and Zoe Kahn-Bennett met while they were attending college at Oberlin in the late 1980s. Along with another Oberlin student named Lydia Greenbaum, the three began a punk band called Kitty's Moustache. The band enjoyed moderate success before the death of Lydia, who passed away at the age of twenty-seven from an overdose. After her death, Lydia's version of the band's song "Mistress of Myself" became a radio hit. Although Elizabeth, Andrew, and Zoe have not pursued music or fame since their Oberlin days, none of them can quite let go of their youth. Now in their late forties, Elizabeth and Andrew—now married—live half a block away from Zoe and her wife Jane in the Brooklyn neighborhood of Ditmas Park. Their lack of existential evolution is especially embodied by Andrew, who, despite being weeks away from turning fifty, has never had a career and cannot let go of his image as a member of a punk band. When a movie producer tries to buy the life rights to the band's story, Andrew refuses. His inaction ultimately becomes the catalyst that forces all of the characters to reckon with the current state of their lives.

Through her characters, Straub demonstrates how deceptive adulthood can be. In the throes of middle age, Elizabeth, Andrew, and Zoe have successfully achieved many of the milestones that constitute society's definition of maturity: they are all married, have children, and own real estate. Ostensibly they are adults, and yet their inability to acknowledge the passage of time and let go of their youth suggests otherwise. The fact that these protagonists still have a lot of growing up left to do is made clear by their children's storylines. When *Modern Lovers* begins, Zoe and Jane's daughter Ruby is graduating from high school and attempting to establish her autonomy as an adult. Similarly, Elizabeth and Andrew's son Harry is also developing his own independent identity. The characters of Ruby and Harry, however, serve two purposes. First, they provide an honest and external perspective on who their parents are as people. Second, Ruby and Harry's own coming-of-age adventures are compared to their parents' storylines. As Straub repeatedly illustrates, the parents and children of her novel are on a similar plane of emotional development.

Emma Straub is an American novelist known for her best-selling books Laura Lamont's Life in Pictures *(2012),* The Vacationers *(2014), and* Modern Lovers *(2016).*

In addition to exploring the terrain of contemporary adulthood, *Modern Lovers*, as its title suggests, is a novel about romantic relationships. Throughout the narrative, Straub follows the trajectory of three relationships over the course of one summer. With each one, she poses a different question about the nature of sexual and emotional intimacy. Zoe and Jane's relationship, for example, questions whether or not a marriage can be saved even if it has been completely destroyed. Where once their extreme personality differences allowed them to balance each other out, over time these differences made it impossible for them to see eye to eye. Consequently, they spend their days fighting about Hyacinth—the restaurant they co-own—and they spend their nights sleeping in separate beds. Meanwhile, the Marxes' ostensibly indestructible marriage is quickly thrown into disarray when Elizabeth learns that Andrew slept with their former bandmate Lydia twenty-five years earlier. Combined with Andrew's inability to let go of their Oberlin days, the Marxes' marriage is tested as both spouses try to reconcile who they thought they were with who they really are.

Where the relationships of the former band members of Kitty's Moustache examine the nature of long-term love and how it often contends with the past, Ruby and Harry's adolescent affair is demonstrative of the tension that exists between new love and the future. In personality, the teenagers are polar opposites. Ruby is moody and sarcastic while Harry is a sweet, earnest individual who enjoys fantasy novels. The two begin sleeping together after reconnecting in a class. Their relationship proves to be more than physical, however, as they bond over their parents' struggles. Despite the fact that they seem well suited for one another in many ways, they face the question of whether or not their relationship can survive the changes that will accompany their imminent adulthood.

One of the most engaging aspects of *Modern Lovers* is its setting. A native New Yorker, Straub infuses the novel's narrative with a detailed perspective on modern life in the city's outer borough of Brooklyn. Straub works hard to capture every aspect of her characters' reality: from the architecture of the Victorian houses in their neighborhood of Ditmas Park, to the food on the menus of trendy restaurants, to the book-club culture of its hip middle-aged residents. By depicting the novel's time and place with such accuracy, Straub successfully contextualizes the characters' conflicts for her readers. This is important because Elizabeth, Andrew, Zoe, and their families are members of a very specific, privileged New York demographic and subsequently their problems are not universally relatable. For example, a significant plot point in Andrew's storyline is the fact that he gets drawn into a cultlike yoga studio. In addition to bringing the unique and humorous details of this New York subculture to life, Straub also ensures all readers can get a grasp on the characters by focusing more on their emotions rather than their unique circumstances.

As a writer, Straub spends more time exploring her characters' internal dialogue and motivations than the novel's plot. Written in third-person past tense, each chapter of *Modern Lovers* assumes the perspective of a different character. Consequently, much of the narrative is about the characters' memories and how they are feeling about the state of their lives and relationships to one another. While this may not initially sound interesting to some readers, Straub's conversational tone and sharp sense of humor ensures the novel is always engaging. Although not all readers will be able to relate to the characters' lifestyles, they will be able to empathize with the pain of their shared midlife crisis.

Reviews of *Modern Lovers* have been largely positive. Many critics have praised Straub for her ability to depict some of the most flawed aspects of human nature in an authentic and funny way. Ultimately, Straub's ability to ensure that her characters remain empathetic and entertaining throughout the novel despite engaging in selfish behavior is a testament to her skills as a writer. She is equally talented at capturing burgeoning trends in contemporary American adulthood and the lives of Elizabeth, Andrew and Zoe in Brooklyn symbolize these trends. "*Modern Lovers* celebrates the updated look and feel of familial love and all of its complexities. Straub's clever and perceptive observations on growing up are gentle reminders that coming of age isn't just for kids," Carol Memmott wrote for the *Washington Post*.

While generally received as a light and fun read, *Modern Lovers* still has its flaws. For some readers, the characters' privileged lives are not fertile enough grounds for interesting conflict. Although it is understandable that many readers cannot empathize with the Kahn-Bennett and Marx families and see their problems as nothing more than ennui, this is a largely subjective issue. Many other critics recognized this shortcoming and still enjoyed the storytelling. *Kirkus Reviews* wrote, "Straub's characters are a quirky and interesting bunch, well aware of their own good fortune, and it's a pleasure spending time with them in leafy Ditmas Park." Others have argued that the novel is problematic in the number of sitcom tropes it hits. And while Emma Straub's novels are not groundbreaking, it is important to note that her storytelling feels fresh and entertaining rather than derivative. Attributing this to Straub's talent as a writer, Michiko Kakutani wrote for the *New York Times*, "In her capable hands, however, even the most hackneyed occasions are transformed into revealing or comic moments." Despite its shortcomings, *Modern Lovers* is an enjoyable, well-written novel that humorously showcases a very specific time, place, and type of people.

Emily Turner

Review Sources

Kakutani, Michiko. "Review: In Emma Straub's Modern Lovers, Passion and Regret in Brooklyn." Review of Modern Lovers, by Emma Straub. *The New York Times*, 30 May 2016, www.nytimes.com/2016/05/31/books/review-modern-lovers-by-emma-straub.html. Accessed 28 Jan. 2017.

Kuczynski, Alex. "Emma Straub's Modern Lovers." Review of Modern Lovers, by Emma Straub. *The New York Times*, 1 June 2016, www.nytimes.com/2016/06/05/books/review/emma-straubs-modern-lovers.html. Accessed 28 Jan. 2017.

Memmott, Carol. "Review: Emma Straub's Delightful New Novel, *Modern Lovers*." Review of *Modern Lovers*, by Emma Straub. *Washington Post*, 26 May 2016, www.washingtonpost.com/entertainment/books/review-emma-straubs-delightful-new-novel-modern-lovers/2016/05/16/adee4e0c-1b65-11e6-b6e0-c53b7ef63b45_story.html. Accessed 28 Jan. 2017.

Review of *Modern Lovers*, by Emma Straub. *Kirkus Reviews*, 31 May. 2016, www.kirkusreviews.com/book-reviews/emma-straub/modern-lovers/. Accessed 28 Jan. 2017.

Waldman, Katy. Review of *Modern Lovers*, by Emma Straub. *Slate*, 8 June 2016, www.slate.com/articles/arts/books/2016/06/emma_straub_s_modern_lovers_reviewed.html. Accessed 28 Jan. 2017.

The Morning They Came for Us
Dispatches from Syria

Author: Janine di Giovanni (b. 1961)
Publisher: Liveright (New York). 224 pp.
Type of work: Current affairs
Time: 2012
Locale: Syria

(Courtesy of Liveright Publishing Corporation)

A look at the civil war raging in Syria, based on visits there in 2012. The author looks at the impact of the conflict on individuals and families through extensive interviews with people living through the war.

Principal personages:

NADA, a Sunni Muslim and a supporter of the opposition who survived brutal torture and rape at the hands of supporters of the Assad regime

HUSSEIN, a supporter of the opposition in Homs who is not involved in fighting he survived horrific torture by government troops

UMM HAMID, a Muslim woman in Aleppo trying to keep her family fed and safe as the war engulfs their city

KHALED, a doctor running a makeshift hospital in Aleppo, striving to deal with lack of medicines and other supplies

MARYAM, a Sunni Muslim resident of Darayya, where it is believed government forces massacred up to five hundred supporters of the opposition

SHAZA, a "minder" sent by the Syrian government to accompany di Giovanni as she visited Homs; a strong supporter of Assad's government

RIFAF, a soldier in the Syrian Army fighting in Homs

The Morning They Came for Us: Dispatches from Syria is a difficult book. Though well written and researched, this account of the civil war in Syria is difficult to read because of the tragedies and atrocities described. Janine di Giovanni, an experienced war correspondent, writes in an engaging style and her prose flows effortlessly; however, as she observes, when you see the kinds of things she saw in Syria, and know that you can insulate yourself from them simply because you have the ability to leave, it makes you "feel ashamed to be a human." Di Giovanni says she wrote the book so that people will never forget what is happening in Syria, and the powerful descriptions of suffering and brutality she provides work successfully toward this end. Di Giovanni puts a face to the atrocities of the Syrian Civil War, both through her own reactions and through the stories she relates, that conveys reality far more effectively than statistics do. Because of how vividly and compassionately di Giovanni illuminates the stories of the civilian victims of war, many reviewers have declared *The Morning They Came for Us* required reading.

Di Giovanni recounts her experiences traveling in Syria in 2012, when the civil war there had been going on for about a year. For the period that she was there (from June to December) she witnessed a tipping of the scales and the country descending into all-out war. She describes the surrealism of the sense of denial she witnessed in the early days of war, and the ability of the Syrian people to deceive themselves about what was going on around them. She was staying in a relatively safe hotel in Damascus, where United Nations (UN) monitors were also staying. These monitors were no longer allowed to go out and patrol or investigate, however, because they had been attacked too many times and the situation had become too dangerous. But in those early days, there were extravagant pool parties on the hotel rooftop on Thursday afternoons—the beginning of the weekend in many Muslim countries. Wealthy Syrians and their foreign guests swam and danced and enjoyed good music as they could see smoke rising from fighting on the outskirts of Damascus. For several weeks, di Giovanni witnessed this "fevered hedonism," although as the weeks went by, people tended to leave the parties earlier, because it was becoming too dangerous to be out after dark.

The book is largely made up of sketches of different people di Giovanni met as she traveled in Syria, although she often makes comparisons to what she was seeing there to her experiences in covering other wars, which were the subjects of her several earlier books. There is also an epilogue written in March 2015 that provides some updates on what has happened in Syria since 2012.

Most of the people di Giovanni interviews and describes were part of the opposition—those fighting against the regime of Syrian president Bashar al-Assad, and she is clearly sympathetic to their cause. But she also interviewed supporters of Assad's government, and she is judicious in describing their views and experiences. Many of the Syrian people, on either side of the conflict, expressed pride in how Syria was previously a place of tolerance, where different sects of Islam coexisted peacefully, and Syrian Christians mixed freely with Muslims in daily life and commerce. To the rest of the world, the conflict in Syria brings to mind the flood of refugees who have fled the country and moved to other Islamic nations in the region, or to Europe. But di Giovanni deals for the most part with people still living in Syria. In some cases, some of her interviewees initially fled their homes but eventually came back, because they had no other place to go.

In the book, di Giovanni gives readers a picture of what was going on at the particular time she was in Syria. Confusion was such on the ground that the Syrian people did not fully understand what was happening to their country, and how it came about. Like the uprisings of the Arab Spring, the civil war began with peaceful demonstrations against the oppressive actions of the Assad regime. Peaceful protest soon devolved into violence, and eventually became something more than an internal civil war. What the Syrian people she talked to understood and agreed upon was that life there would never be the same. As di Giovanni asks, "How can Syria ever be what it once was? It has been burnt alive by hatred."

(]Courtesy of Peter Nicholls)

Janine di Giovanni has been covering civil wars and international conflicts for more than twenty-five years. Considered one of the leading foreign correspondents working today, she is the Middle East editor for Newsweek *and a contributing editor for* Vanity Fair.

She tells the story of Mohammad, a baker who was threatened by Assad forces with being kidnapped and killed if he continued to provide bread to a neighborhood held by the opposition. Di Giovanni relates the heartbreaking story of Nada, who was a student activist for the opposition—she brought sandwiches and medicines to rebel soldiers and spread their messages on social media. She was arrested and held for eight months, during which she was tortured and raped. Her parents were told she was dead. Di Giovanni also details the kinds of torture that doctors are recruited to perform, such as pulling out intestines and puncturing lungs. One interviewee, Hussein (a pseudonym), was a victim of this form of torture. He was not a member of the opposition but was arrested anyway; he only survived because a doctor took pity on him and declared him dead. He was able to escape after a night spent in a cell sleeping on corpses. She also spoke with pro-regime nuns in a convent in Ma'Loula and actor Fadwa Suleiman, who fronted protests in Homs. Di Giovanni presents these stories unsparingly, but does not ask any of her interviewees to explain their actions.

In the midst of the fighting, di Giovanni also relates the resilience of people trapped in their home towns, or in hideouts, who tried to go on with their lives with whatever normality was possible. She paints a stark reality of the landscape, describing, for example, cities covered in rubble and heaps of trash because city services had ceased to function and there was no trash removal. Children still went to school in some places thought "safe," but what is safe one day may not be the next. Just getting food and fuel became virtually impossible, and people sometimes spent hours standing in line for the few commodities that might be available. Men on the street sold fuel in old soda bottles. Di Giovanni was taken to a dinner at the home of one of her Syrian associates and was fed a sumptuous meal. She was embarrassed to partake, however, because she knew how hard it was for the people to get enough to feed themselves daily. Her friend told her to eat what was set before her and say nothing about it, because she would embarrass her hosts if she did not eat. Small glimmers of humanity such as this show through the grim realities of a nation self-destructing.

As di Giovanni notes, even in war, there is camaraderie and intimacy among those caught up in the struggle. But wars in urban areas have their own brand of terrors. By the nature of the battlefield, they are not just wars between fighting armies—civilians are quite literally caught in the crossfire. Buildings that once were beautiful architectural masterpieces become piles of rubble that provide cover for snipers, and paths between the rubble became the only way to move about without being exposed to fire. At a lunch in another home, everyone tried to avoid talking about the war—people were often afraid to talk to anyone, because informers seemed to be everywhere. But when a large bomb hit somewhere nearby, one of her hosts remarked, "This is the background music of our lives."

The parts of the book that are most distressing to read deal with the widespread use of torture and the systematic use of rape as an instrument of terror. While both sides are guilty of these types of brutality, it does seem it is a more common tactic of Assad's forces, especially the Shabiha, a kind of paramilitary force known as "the ghosts." Sexual violence against both women and men is used to terrorize and demoralize the enemy, and threats of rape or torture are used to elicit confessions or other information about opposition forces.

Di Giovanni has earned a reputation as a hard-hitting investigator in her other books on some of the regional wars of the past three decades. Like those earlier works, this book has been highly praised by reviewers, both in the United States and Great Britain. Michiko Kakutani, writing for the *New York Times*, called *The Morning They Came for Us* a "searing and necessary book." The reviewer for *Publishers Weekly* praised her ability to capture complicated violent conflict from multiple sides and to make war's "reality fully tangible and tragic." Reviewers across the board commended di Giovanni for the book's beautiful writing and for not holding the reader's hand by allowing any distance between the reader and the gruesome realities she describes.

Given the 2016 Courage in Journalism Award by the International Women's Media Foundation, di Giovanni also received the Hay Medal for Prose at the literary festival in Hay-on-Wye in Wales. A major strength of di Giovanni's book is its coverage of ordinary people trying to go about everyday life in whatever ways they can manage while their homeland is engulfed in brutal fighting.

Mark S. Joy, PhD

Review Sources

Kakutani, Michiko. "Review: *The Morning They Came for Us* Reports on the Hell of Syria." Review of *The Morning They Came for Us: Dispatches from Syria*, by Janine di Giovanni.
The New York Times, 23 May 2016, www.nytimes.com/2016/05/24/books/review-the-morning-they-came-for-us-reports-on-the-hell-of-syria.html. Accessed 18 Nov. 2016.
Kiley, Sam. Review of *The Morning They Came for Us: Dispatches from Syria*, by Janine di Giovanni. *Evening Standard*, 18 Feb. 2016, www.standard.co.uk/lifestyle/books/the-morning-they-came-for-us-dispatches-from-syria-by-janine-di-giovanni-review-a3183861.html. Accessed 18 Nov. 2016.
Review of *The Morning They Came for Us: Dispatches from Syria*, by Janine di Giovanni. *Publishers Weekly*, 18 Jan. 2016, www.publishersweekly.com/978-0-87140-713-9. Accessed 18 Nov. 2016.

Yassin-Kassab, Robin. "*The Morning They Came for Us* by Janine di Giovanni—Heroic Dispatches from Syria." Review of *The Morning They Came for Us: Dispatches from Syria*, by Janine di Giovanni. *The Guardian*, 26 May 2016, www.theguardian.com/books/2016/may/26/the-morning-they-came-for-us-janine-digiovanni-syria. Accessed 18 Nov. 2016.

"Most Blessed of the Patriarchs"
Thomas Jefferson and the Empire of the Imagination

Authors: Annette Gordon-Reed (b. 1958)
and Peter S. Onuf (b. 1946)
Publisher: Liveright (New York). 400 pp.
Type of work: History
Time: 1760–1826
Locales: Virginia; Washington, DC; and
Paris, France

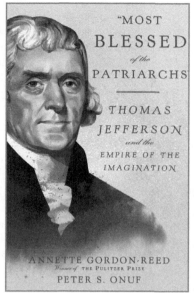

(Courtesy of Liveright Publishing Corporation)

Distinguished historians Annette Gordon-Reed and Peter Onuf examine the mind and character of Thomas Jefferson, who worked diligently to create an image of himself as a member of the natural aristocracy and a modern-day patriarch, exhibiting behavior that could serve as a model for governance in the new nation.

Principal personages:
THOMAS JEFFERSON, third president of the
United States (1801–9)
MARTHA JEFFERSON, his wife
MARTHA JEFFERSON RANDOLPH, his older daughter
MARIA JEFFERSON EPPES, his younger daughter
SALLY HEMINGS, one of his slaves and mother to several of his children

There is a prodigious amount of scholarship on Thomas Jefferson; books published or reprinted just since 2000 dealing exclusively or in large part with Jefferson number in the hundreds. Biographies, collections of Jefferson's sayings, scholarly editions of his papers, and even advice books based on his writings are available to twenty-first-century readers looking to learn more about the author of the United States' Declaration of Independence and the country's third president. The sheer volume of recently published work suggests that Jefferson remains a topic of interest to millions of readers and a subject for continuing study by academics, whose methodologies and ideologies have undergone significant transformation in the preceding four decades.

Sorting through the piles of books (not to mention scholarly and popular articles) can be a daunting task. Nevertheless, it is certain that some work will stand apart, either because of the reputation of the authors or the controversial approach they employ to study Jefferson's life and character. *"Most Blessed of the Patriarchs": Thomas Jefferson and the Empire of the Imagination* is distinguished on both counts. Any book by Annette Gordon-Reed published after her groundbreaking 1997 study *Thomas Jefferson and Sally Hemings: An American Controversy* and her Pulitzer–Prize winning book *The Hemingses: An American Family* (2008), is virtually guaranteed to garner significant attention. Her partnership with distinguished University of Virginia historian Peter Onuf made *"Most Blessed of the Patriarchs"* a highly anticipated release, and reviews were plentiful and generally laudatory. Among major publications, only the *Wall Street Journal* offered a skeptical assessment, the focus of which is telegraphed in the title: "It's Always about Slavery." Jefferson's complex, contradictory, and often confused attitudes toward this most controversial subject is certainly at the heart of *"Most Blessed of the Patriarchs"*; why it is so and how Gordon-Reed and Onuf deal with the problem provide a good indication of what they are aiming to do in this unusual revisionist study.

Gordon-Reed and Onuf's approach is hinted at by two words in their book's title: "patriarch" (with its direct tie to "patriarchy") and "empire" are terms of opprobrium in contemporary scholarship. Hence, one might expect that this book will not continue in the tradition of Dumas Malone's Pulitzer Prize–winning six-volume biography of Jefferson (1948–81), which treats Jefferson reverentially. By contrast, *"Most Blessed of the Patriarchs"* is part of a larger, decades-long project to revise earlier assessments that elevated the Founding Fathers to near-sainthood. For many historians of the nineteenth and early twentieth centuries, Jefferson shared first place with George Washington (or stood only slightly behind him) in that pantheon, whose collective wisdom set the United States on its path to becoming the world's foremost democracy. Before World War II, few historians (and few in the general public) sought to challenge the myths that had grown up around these men—and the women associated with the Founders were often either ignored or politely honored as supporters keeping the home fires burning while their men did the real work of revolution and governance. As putative author of the Declaration of Independence, Jefferson has been especially admired for the ideas in this document that many ascribe to him alone, since Americans are familiar with the Enlightenment philosophers on whom Jefferson drew for his ideas. Many elide Jefferson's declaration with the Constitution, a document written when he was serving his country in France and which he influenced only through correspondence with those actively engaged in its writing. Nevertheless, many outside the scholarly community consider Jefferson the guiding hand in these foundational writings that shaped the nation. The myth of Jefferson that has emerged presents him as a selfless, morally incorruptible, far-sighted visionary and patriot who was committed unquestionably to the notion that "all men are created equal" and have certain inalienable rights. It is a portrait of the saint as patriot.

Scholarship in the past four or five decades has exploded that myth, recasting Jefferson and his fellow Founders as men with personal flaws. Alexander Hamilton, always a bit suspect, has come to be seen as a man of overwhelming ambition. John Adams is now confirmed to have been officious, opinionated, and jealous of the Virginians who dominated the early government. Benjamin Franklin has been recognized as something of a libertine. Even Washington has been exposed as somewhat imperious, with a sense of self-aggrandizement that made him either oblivious to—or averse to confronting—political wrangling that almost destroyed the new country before it could hold its third election for president.

Both Gordon-Reed and Onuf have written books that contribute to a refashioning of Jefferson's image, and their collaborative effort in *"Most Blessed of the Patriarchs"* further explodes some of the traditional hagiography to reveal Jefferson as a more complex figure than received opinion suggests. The authors take deconstruction to an extreme, choosing to interrogate Jefferson's ideas topically rather than chronologically to explain how Jefferson embarked on a systematic effort at self-fashioning, creating the image of himself he wished to project to the world, and how he sought to control events and rationalize ideological inconsistencies to make sure his contemporaries and posterity would view him as he wished.

Early in their narrative, Gordon-Reed and Onuf make an important statement about their aims, saying that they "seek to understand what Thomas Jefferson thought he was

(Courtesy of Tony Rinaldo)

Annette Gordon-Reed, professor of law and history at Harvard University, is author of The Hemingses of Monticello: An American Family, *which won the 2009 Pulitzer Prize for history.*

doing in the world," and that they "take Jefferson at his word about his beliefs, goals, and motivations." However, they continue, "this does not mean that we always endorse Jefferson's formulations of why he did things or what he thought about matters." This claim of disinterestedness holds up in many portions of their book, breaking down at only one point—but a key one—that links their study with the deflationary efforts of contemporary scholars described above.

The sections of *"Most Blessed of the Patriarchs"* in which Gordon-Reed and Onuf are able to offer balanced assessments focus on Jefferson's efforts to create an image of himself as an Enlightenment gentleman and natural aristocrat who would stand first among equals in the new republic he and his fellow Americans were creating. Citing a letter Jefferson wrote in which he describes himself as "most blessed of the patriarchs," the authors claim that the statement "provides a window into his thinking about his place in the world and his sense of self." Gordon-Reed and Onuf rely on that epithet, and the term "master," to describe Jefferson in both public and private life. Jefferson's vision of his ideal self as a patriarch meant he was master of his domain and all within it, head of an extended family (both free and enslaved) that looked to him for guidance and direction, submitted to his will (and whim) as if it were law, and served his every need. Of course, as the narrative explains, this worked best for Jefferson when he was at home at Monticello.

Exercising meticulous control over the development of the architecture, layout, and daily life at Monticello allowed Jefferson to create a place where he truly was the center of his world. As the authors point out, Jefferson was often less successful away from his mountaintop domain in maintaining his sense of mastery. In France,

(Courtesy of Kristin K. Onuf)

Peter S. Onuf, retired professor of history at the University of Virginia, has published numerous books on Jefferson, colonial America, and the early years of the United States.

he found that while the culture and sophistication he had admired from afar met (and sometimes exceeded) his expectations, he was not always comfortable—because he was not always the smartest or most sophisticated person in the room. Similarly, when he stepped forward to act in the political arena, he found much of the work distasteful, because others did not engage in what he considered civilized discourse over the principles and aims of the new United States. As the authors note, however, while Jefferson expected that the new national government would "rise above partisanship," his own behavior while vice president and even later as president shows that he was often blind to the self-serving nature of his own efforts to denounce the "self-interested partisan intentions" of political opponents.

Where the authors' contemporary values are most in evidence are in discussions of slavery. Admittedly, Jefferson's writings on the evils of slavery seem starkly at odds with his reliance on slave labor at Monticello. After quoting a passage from *Notes on the State of Virginia*, in which Jefferson rails against the institution, Gordon-Reed and Onuf ask, how could Jefferson "exempt himself, and his plantation, from this devastating indictment?" Their answer, developed in several sections of *"Most Blessed of the Patriarchs"*, is that through a deft bit of intellectual sleight of hand, Jefferson opted to believe that Southern slave owners would eventually become more enlightened and abandon the practice, and in the meantime those who owned slaves could ameliorate conditions by behaving benevolently toward them. Of course, this self-serving evasion does not stand up to Gordon-Reed and Onuf's unflinching critique, and the portrait of Jefferson as slave owner is none too flattering. Ultimately, they argue that he let himself be convinced of the righteousness of his behavior because he needed his slaves—his property—to maintain the kind of lifestyle he envisioned for himself as a modern-day patriarch. The judgmental nature of the authors' analysis comes through in observations such as the following: "For their part, the enslaved could make a show of devotion to Jefferson with a clear understanding of the precariousness of their position. . . . They could not possibly have loved him in any meaningful sense." They are quick to point out the irony of Jefferson's innate bias: "The philosophical Jefferson claimed that blacks could not employ reason, and he spoke patronizingly of his hopes for their intelligence. . . . Yet the plantation owner Jefferson gave black people tasks that he knew required reason and that he fully expected them to complete—which they did." One can see behind the idealized community of Monticello, they claim, "the legally enforced labor of the enslaved and the culturally imposed domestic labor of white female family members that made it all possible." Such judgments may not be wrong, but they display a bias born of twentieth- and twenty-first-century attitudes toward social issues.

Despite the exceptional scholarship and keen insight that Gordon-Reed and Onuf bring to this book, it is unlikely that *"Most Blessed of the Patriarchs"* will be the last word on Jefferson. As they observe, "There is evidence that, as close as Jefferson was to them, members of his own family were unable, at times, to read his emotions effectively." How are succeeding generations to reach an understanding when contemporaries could not penetrate the mask Jefferson wore when dealing with even his most intimate acquaintances? Joseph Ellis may have captured Jefferson's character best in the title of his 1996 book *American Sphinx*. Like the mythological creature, Jefferson seems unlikely to yield up all of the mysteries that combine to make up his complex, enigmatic, and sometimes maddening character. He continues to remain, like the Grecian urn in Keats's famous 1820 ode, a figure that "dost tease us out of thought, as does Eternity."

Laurence W. Mazzeno, PhD

Review Sources

Baker, Peter. Review of "Most Blessed of the Patriarchs": Thomas Jefferson and the Empire of the Imagination, by Annette Gordon-Reed and Peter S. Onuf. *The New York Times* Book Review, 10 Apr. 2016, www.nytimes.com/2016/04/10/books/review/most-blessed-of-the-patriarchs-by-annette-gordon-reed-and-peter-s-onuf.html. Accessed 30 Jan. 2017.

Kendall, Joshua. "Jefferson: Brilliant but Self-Absorbed, Troubled." Review of *"Most Blessed of the Patriarchs": Thomas Jefferson and the Empire of the Imagination*, by Annette Gordon-Reed and Peter S. Onuf. *Boston Globe*, 19 Apr. 2016, www.bostonglobe.com/arts/2016/04/18/portrait-jefferson-brilliant-but-self-absorbed-troubled/p18g3HAVWnQttMrTuYoqsK/story.html. Accessed 30 Jan. 2017.

Muyumba, Walton. "*Most Blessed of the Patriarchs'* Sketches Profoundly Human Portrait of Thomas Jefferson." Review of *"Most Blessed of the Patriarchs": Thomas Jefferson and the Empire of the Imagination*, by Annette Gordon-Reed and Peter S. Onuf. *Chicago Tribune*, 8 Apr. 2016, www.chicagotribune.com/lifestyles/books/ct-prj-thomas-jefferson-most-blessed-of-the-patriarchs-20160408-story.html. Accessed 30 Jan. 2017.

Simpson, Matthew C. "Thomas Jefferson's Double Life." Review of *"Most Blessed of the Patriarchs": Thomas Jefferson and the Empire of the Imagination*, by Annette Gordon-Reed and Peter S. Onuf. *New Republic*, 10 May 2016, newrepublic.com/article/133386/thomas-jeffersons-double-life. Accessed 30 Jan. 2017.

Stewart, David O. "Thomas Jefferson: Master of All and of Everything." Review of *"Most Blessed of the Patriarchs": Thomas Jefferson and the Empire of the Imagination*, by Annette Gordon-Reed and Peter S. Onuf. *Washington Post*, 29

Apr. 2016, www.washingtonpost.com/opinions/thomas-jefferson-master-of-all-
and-of-everything/2016/04/27/c40eb5ae-d4d0-11e5-9823-02b905009f99_story.
html. Accessed 30 Jan. 2017.

Swaim, Barton. "It's Always about Slavery." Review of *"Most Blessed of the
Patriarchs": Thomas Jefferson and the Empire of the Imagination,* by Annette
Gordon-Reed and Peter S. Onuf. *The Wall Street Journal,* 8 Apr. 2016, www.wsj.
com/articles/its-always-about-slavery-1460148148. Accessed 30 Jan. 2017.

Most Wanted

Author: Lisa Scottoline (b. 1955)
Publisher: St. Martin's Press (New York). 448 pp.
Type of work: Novel
Time: Present day
Locales: Glastonbury, Connecticut; West Chester, Pennsylvania

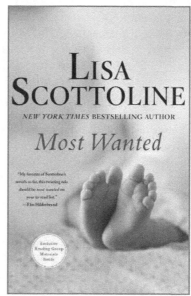

Christine and Marcus Nilsson are preparing for the birth of their first child, a child for whom they struggled for years. However, their happiness is shattered when Christine sees a news program showing the arrest of a serial killer. Her belief that this serial killer is her sperm donor throws their lives into chaos, and her fight to find the truth could change everything in her life.

Principal characters:

CHRISTINE NILSSON, an elementary school teacher who is pregnant with her first child
MARCUS NILSSON, her husband, an architectural engineer
LAUREN WEINGARTEN, her best friend, a fellow teacher
ZACHARY JEFFCOAT, accused serial killer and potential sperm donor for the Nilssons
FRANCES XAVIER "GRIFF" GRIFFITH, Jeffcoat's lawyer
GAIL ROBINBRECHT, the last victim of the Nurse Murderer

Christine and Marcus Nilsson have been trying to conceive for quite some time when they decide to use a sperm donor. Now, two months pregnant, Christine is leaving her teaching job and preparing to be a stay-at-home mom. Just as she is getting ready to leave her farewell party at the school, however, one of the other teachers tunes the television into a news alert about the arrest of an alleged serial killer, a man named Zachary Jeffcoat. As the camera pans in to focus on the accused man's face, Christine freezes: "She recognized those eyes. She would know that face anywhere. The serial killer was their donor, Donor 3319." This revelation sets Christine and Marcus up for the fight of their lives.

The multiple meanings behind the title of the book set up the double plot of the novel, which explores a variety of ethical and emotional issues. The first potential meaning refers to the baby; for Christine, the baby is what she wants most, but for Marcus, this may not be the case. Marcus's main concern when choosing a donor is the man's health, followed by the physical attributes that would identify the child as a full part of their family; Christine, meanwhile, is simply happy for the chance to have a baby. The insemination is the starting point of one of the main conflicts of the novel. As the story progresses, the suspicion that Jeffcoat is their donor begins a downward spiral that threatens their marriage.

Christine's excitement about her baby is threatened as she worries about potential genetic repercussions of having a serial killer for a biological father. This brings up the controversy of nature versus nurture while she struggles with fears over her baby's future. She comes to the conclusion, however, that she wants this baby despite any fears: "She made a silent vow to love the baby, to take care of it, and to shield it from any and all harm. Because it wasn't Rosemary's baby, it was her baby, and she was its mother."

The issue of family further resonates throughout the novel as Christine and Marcus learn what it really means to be parents. Marcus, particularly, struggles with not being the baby's biological father, feeling jealous of their donor. Marcus's relationship with his own parents also complicates his feelings about parenthood: Marcus's mother is deceased and his father treats Marcus as a competitor more than a child. Christine, who is the baby's biological mother and has a good relationship with her father despite his advancing dementia, struggles less with such issues.

Because all Christine and Marcus have to identify their donor is a brief family history, along with a couple of pictures of the man, they can only go on Christine's gut feeling that Jeffcoat is the donor. Marcus does not want to believe it. Marcus's emotional conflict leads the couple to challenge their fertility clinic to release Donor 3319's identity, but when the sperm bank refuses, they become entangled in a legal battle. Marcus hires a lawyer, and though Christine is hesitant to sue for information because she has become emotionally attached to her physician, she finally agrees to pursue a suit that will reveal whether Donor 3319 is Jeffcoat.

This identification becomes an obsession for both Marcus and Christine, but it is for slightly different reasons, and their reasons set the two on a bumpy marital ride. As the novel progresses, it is revealed that the infertility is a result of Marcus's inability to father a child, and he struggles with the idea that he is not a complete man. This issue comes to the fore when he and Christine find out that Marcus's father and his second wife, Stephanie, are expecting a baby. Stephanie's admission that "Marcus shared with us why you had problems conceiving, that you didn't produce enough eggs, and that's why it took you so long to get pregnant" throws Christine into further confusion as she realizes that Marcus has lied to his family, and she feels betrayed by the lie. Ironically, her anger over Marcus's lie comes after her secret trip to visit Jeffcoat in prison, so the double standard introduces a moral dilemma about honesty. Marcus's anger over the situation raises the question of abortion when he hints that he is not sure he can raise the child of a serial killer. As the biological mother of the baby, Christine is shocked and saddened by her husband's attitude. Ultimately, the two must decide whether their marriage can withstand the double storm of infertility and doubt.

In the second portion of the double plot, Jeffcoat has been arrested for the brutal slayings of three nurses. Christine's obsession over the images of Jeffcoat that she has seen on screen lead her to decide to go visit him in jail, so she lies to Marcus about her plans while he is on a business trip, and she takes a trip to Graterford prison in West Chester, Pennsylvania, where Jeffcoat is being held. Posing as reporters, she and her best friend Lauren meet with the young man. His charismatic personality wins her over, and she sets out to prove his innocence.

The first step Christine takes in helping Jeffcoat, which is also an attempt to help herself, is to find him an attorney who will take his case seriously. She stumbles across Frances Xavier "Griff" Griffith, a grumpy semiretired defense attorney who agrees to take on the case if someone pays his retainer. Christine knows that covering Jeffcoat's legal expenses is going too far, but a mysterious woman covers the cost, and the case takes off.

Christine cannot let it go, and she hires on as Griff's assistant. In this role, she investigates the murder of Gail Robinbrecht, the last Nurse Murderer victim. While trying to convince not only herself, but Griff as well, of Jeffcoat's innocence, Christine is embroiled in a dangerous game as an untrained and naïve detective. Her questions cause problems for a number of innocent people, but Christine is nevertheless determined to uncover the truth.

Characterization, plot conflict, and layered meanings are all strengths of Scottoline's writing in this novel. *Kirkus Reviews* called the exposition of the novel "irresistible." Carol Memmott for the *Washington Post* wrote that *Most Wanted* is an example of the kind of domestic realism that has made Scottoline popular. Christine Tran for *Booklist* also lauded the "humor and soul-bearing characterization" in the novel.

The reviews also mentioned a few weaker points. The story wraps up neatly, which could be considered a problem, but is more likely a reflection of Scottoline's audience's expectations. *Kirkus Reviews* commented, "The fairy-tale ending calls for some convenient coincidences and changes of heart, but Scottoline's legion of fans will be too relieved to object." Tran commented that the book was "a gripping, although often incredible, suburban crime tale." *Publishers Weekly* also questioned the emotionalism in the novel, saying it "often sinks to the melodramatic." Despite these issues, however, *Most Wanted* remains an entertaining read.

Lisa Scottoline is an award-winning and best-selling author of twenty-seven novels. In addition, Scottoline has written a number of popular nonfiction books, most in collaboration with her daughter Francesca Serritella.

There are also a number of extras available for this novel. The "Reading Group Gold Selection" section at the end of the book includes an essay by Scottoline about her inspiration for not just this novel but most of her works about motherhood, a note on book clubs, and ten reading group questions. Each question is prefaced with a short exposition about an issue that the novel covers. These exposition-question combinations are meant to provoke deeper discussion regarding the issues in the novel. Sample topics include fertility issues in the family, fertility issues in the courts, and familial tensions between spouses and parental relationships.

Theresa L. Stowell, PhD

Review Sources

Cooper, Jackie K. "*Most Wanted* Has Scottoline's Most Inventive Plot to Date." Review of *Most Wanted*, by Lisa Scottoline. *The Huffington Post*, 21 Apr. 2016, www.huffingtonpost.com/jackie-k-cooper/most-wanted-has-scottolin_b_9749874. html. Accessed 12 Jan. 2017.

Dahlman, Madeline. "Fiction from Coben and Scottoline, Plus a Nonstop Debut." Review of *Most Wanted*, by Lisa Scottoline. *Library Journal*, 3 Mar. 2016, reviews.libraryjournal.com/2016/03/books/fiction/fiction-from-coben-and-scot-toline-plus-a-nonstop-debut-xpress-reviews/. Accessed 12 Jan. 2017.

Memmott, Carol. "Lisa Scottoline's *Most Wanted*: A Nail-Biting Story that Asks 'What Would You Do?'" Review of *Most Wanted*, by Lisa Scottoline. *The Washington Post*, 6 Apr. 2016, www.washingtonpost.com/entertainment/books/lisa-scottolines-most-wanted-a-nail-biting-story-that-asks-what-would-you-do/2016/04/06/fdfb291e-e56a-11e5-a6f3-21ccdbc5f74e_story.html. Accessed 12 Jan. 2017.

Review of *Most Wanted*, by Lisa Scottoline. *Kirkus Reviews*, 12 Apr. 2016, www. kirkusreviews.com/book-reviews/lisa-scottoline/most-wanted-scottoline. Accessed 12 Jan. 2017.

Review of *Most Wanted*, by Lisa Scottoline. *Publishers Weekly*, 8 Feb. 2016, www. publishersweekly.com/978-1-250-01013-1. Accessed 12 Jan. 2017.

Tran, Christine. Review of *Most Wanted*, by Lisa Scottoline. *Booklist*, 15 Mar. 2016, p. 28.

Mothering Sunday
A Romance

Author: Graham Swift (b. 1949)
Publisher: Knopf (New York). 177 pp.
Type of work: Novella
Time: March 30, 1924
Locale: Berkshire, England

Graham Swift's novella is a fairy-tale romance about one magical day when a young British maidservant loses her lover, discovers her freedom, and decides to become a writer.

Principal characters:
JANE FAIRCHILD, a twenty-two-year-old maidservant to the Niven household at Beechwood
PAUL SHERINGHAM, the twenty-three-year-old heir to Upleigh
MILLY, the cook at Beechwood
ETHEL, the maid at Upleigh
MR. NIVEN, the owner of Beechwood

(Courtesy of Knopf)

Bearing an epigraph from "Cinderella" ("You *shall* go to the ball") and beginning "Once upon a time," Graham Swift's short novel immediately announces its fairy-tale intentions. However, this "once upon a time" is a very specific time: a single day in March 1924, which is also celebrated as Mothering Sunday, a day when domestic servants are given time off to visit their mothers.

Reviewers have emphasized that *Mothering Sunday* is a novella and not a novel and that it is a fairy tale and not realism. As is typical of that form, what makes *Mothering Sunday* distinctive is not a complex plot (it only lightly narrates the events of one day) nor its intricate character interactions (there are only two important characters, and all they do together is have sex), but rather its literary formality, its precise language, and its self-reflexive focus as a story of the adventure of life. Consequently, reviewers have heaped praise on the tight, poetic structure of the story, with Michiko Kakutani, writing for the *New York Times*, calling it a "carefully chiseled story."

Although several reviewers have called attention to the similarities of the book to the popular PBS television program *Downton Abbey* (2010–15) during its coverage of the Edwardian decline of the manor and its need for servants, the focus is less on the social implications of the split between classes and more on a day that marks the beginning of a writer's life; the young Jane Fairchild, readers learn in several flash-forward references, will become a famous novelist who will live until the age of ninety-eight.

Jane, who has been having an affair with Paul, the only remaining son of the Sheringham family (two sons having been killed in World War I), for almost eight years and since she was fifteen, takes advantage of her Mothering Sunday holiday and of Paul's parents being out of the house for a luncheon to spend the day in bed with him rather than meeting in the woods or the other places they have secretly met over the years. This is a special day for several reasons, not the least of which is that it will be Jane's last day with Master Paul because he is scheduled to marry Miss Emma Hobday in two weeks. It is also special because Paul has invited her to his bedroom for the first time, making her heart "soar" like a stranded heroine in a story, which the narrator calls "a phrase you read in books"—one of the first of several references to the world of books in this small literary novella. Swift's narrator announces: "Feast your eyes. A story was beginning."

The novella begins by yoking British history to the world of fairy tale by following the "once upon a time" phrase with a reference to a time when there were more horses than cars and before the male servants disappeared. The social and the literary are also linked in the introduction by a metaphor of the Sheringham's race horse, in which they placed their hopes for fame and glory, whose head and body the parents said belonged to them, while the three sons had a leg each. Unlike most fairy tales, the relationship between Paul and Jane is not built on a perfect, pure, and predestined love. Instead, their connection to each other is purely physical, and Jane does not seem distraught or even sad to lose Paul to marriage and another woman. She seems to know that she never exactly had him, except in their physical relationship.

The fairy-tale context of the story is sustained throughout the first half of the book, with numerous references to the conventions of that genre. For example, when Jane brings her bike to a halt at the front door of Upleigh, it opens "as if by a miraculous power of its own." Since their previous meetings have been in various make-do, outdoor venues, this is the first time Paul has ever undressed Jane, and he goes about it, "religiously," with a kind of "reverence" as an "unveiling." As they lie in the bed, Jane feels the "magic" of nakedness that removes them from the role of maid and master. She thinks, "There never was a day like this, nor ever would or could be again." When Paul mentions that he has to meet his fiancé at the Swan Hotel at Bollingford, it is like the "breaking of a spell," and there is a passing of a "magic dispensation."

Graham Swift's novel Wonderland *(1983) was short-listed for the Booker Prize and won the Guardian Fiction Award. His novel* Last Orders *(1996) won the Booker Prize.*

A central image that dominates the background of the scene as Paul begins to dress is the sexual stain that is left on the bed. Paul might have noticed it, but it is part of his "fine disdain" not to notice it, for it is one of those things that the "magic army" of servants take care of to make the secret life of the upper class possible. Jane knows that the housemaid Ethel will make the stain vanish, "like the good fairy she was." Thinking like the novelist she is yet to become, Jane imagines that in a more common, comic story she might already be scurrying downstairs, still adjusting her clothing, while another man in a different kind of story might be madly tugging at and tucking in his clothes, saying, "I have to damn well scoot." Seeing him standing in the room with only his shirt on might have, "in another story," made her giggle.

After Paul leaves, Jane wanders about the house, still completely naked, feeling that no one would know she had ever been here, as if her nakedness conferred on her not just invisibility but an "exemption from fact," that is, as if she were a character in a tale. She looks into a tall mirror in the hall, and having never had the chance to see her whole body naked, she says, "This is Jane Fairchild! This is me!" Like Alice in Lewis Carroll's *Through the Looking-Glass* (1872), she wonders if one can step through a mirror and be someone else. At this point, about halfway through the novel, there is a single, abrupt statement when the grandfather clock chimes two: "She had not known he was already dead."

The most important room Jane enters naked is the library, which is significant for Jane because she has learned to read and with permission spends much of whatever spare time she can manage reading adventure books by H. Rider Haggard, Robert Louis Stevenson, and Rudyard Kipling. When she asked the head of the household, Mr. Niven, if she could read some of his books and he acquiesced, she describes his response as "magic, door-opening words."

In one of the several flash-forward references to Jane's later life as a novelist, the narrator notes that Jane would say in interviews that she read boys' adventure books, not "sloppy girls' stuff," as they were like reading across "a great divide." She sees adventure stories as having a "subtext," as scholars might call them now, that life itself was an adventure—the adventure of "constant mental hazarding"—the writer's life of the imagination.

The most important moment in the story occurs when Jane gets on her bicycle and rides away, when "a sudden unexpected freedom flooded her," and she feels her life is beginning. She has a sense that life is both cruel and bounteous at the same time; she feels completely untethered. When she is asked later in life how she became a writer, she tells interviewers that she came into the world a foundling, with "an innate license to invent" and "an intimate concern for how words attach to things." She would never tell anyone that the seed of becoming a writer was planted in her on a warm day in March when she was twenty-two and had wandered around a house naked, feeling more like Jane Fairchild than she had ever felt before.

Through the voice of the narrator, Jane ponders the "inconstancy of words"—what if orphans were called orchids and a tree were called a daffodil? Would it make any difference to the actual nature of things? Or their mystery? She thinks, "Words were like an invisible skin, enwrapping the world and giving it reality." She tells one inter-viewer, her eyes twinkling, "Words are only words, just bits of air."

Readers do not learn much about Jane's life after she leaves the world of service, other than that she went to Oxford, that she was married for twelve years to a phi-losopher, that her husband died in 1945,and that she began publishing novels, the most famous being *In the Mind's Eye*, which shocked British society for its sexual suggestiveness.

In the last section of the book, Jane thinks about her earlier plans to read Joseph Conrad's collection *Youth, a Narrative; and Two Other Stories* (1902), which leads to a somewhat literary consideration of the various words for "story." Jane likes the word "narrative," as well as the word "tale," and she thinks about the question hovering in the background to these words—the relationship between the story and the truth—although she thinks the word "fiction" seems totally dismissive of truth. She knows that Conrad's short story "Youth" is not just an adventure story. Rather, it is about men telling stories, including one named Marlow, who, of course, also tells the famous story in *Heart of Darkness* (1902). She begins to read more Conrad and thinks "that Conrad himself must be a sort of secret agent. . . . And much later she'd think and sometimes say that all writers are secret agents."

The novella ends with Jane thinking that although she tells stories of her life, there was one story she would never tell: the story of that one day in March 1924. The last paragraph considers the implications of telling stories, trading in lies, but somehow getting at the heart of it all. Truth-telling, which Jane concludes is "the very stuff of life," was about "trying to capture, though you never could, the very feel of being alive," accepting that many things in life can never be explained at all. Readers looking for a multilayered world fraught with the busy lives of ladies, masters, and their servants will not find it here. What they will find instead is the finely wrought literary world of fairy tale.

Charles E. May

Review Sources

Charles, Ron. "*Mothering Sunday*, by Graham Swift, Reveals One Writer's Beginnings." Review of *Mothering Sunday*, by Graham Swift. *Washington Post*, 12 Apr. 2016, www.washingtonpost.com/entertainment/books/review-mother-sunday-by-graham-swift-reveals-one-writers-beginnings/2016/04/12/e11379d2-ff82-11e5-9203-7b8670959b88_story.html?utm_term=.9f0bf3017c0c. Accessed 22 Feb. 2017.

Kakutani, Michiko. "Graham Swift's Mothering Sunday, a Haunting Day Forever Relived." Review of Mothering Sunday, by Graham Swift. *The New York Times*, 28 Apr. 2016, www.nytimes.com/2016/04/29/books/review-graham-swifts-mothering-sunday-a-haunting-dayforever-relived.html. Accessed 22 Feb. 2017.

Kent, Christobel. Review of *Mothering Sunday*, by Graham Swift. *The Guardian*, 20 Feb. 2016, www.theguardian.com/books/2016/feb/20/mothering-sunday-a-romance-by-graham-swift-review. Accessed 22 Feb. 2017.

McAlpin, Heller. "One Life Changes Forever on 'Mothering Sunday.'" Review of *Mothering Sunday*, by Graham Swift. *NPR*, 19 Apr. 2016, www.npr.org/2016/04/19/474225803/one-life-changes-forever-on-mothering-sunday. Accessed 22 Feb. 2017.

Review of *Mothering Sunday*, by Graham Swift. *Financial Times*, 19 Feb. 2016, www.ft.com/content/5976c500-d3ff-11e5-829b-8564e7528e54. Accessed 22 Feb. 2017.

Review of *Mothering Sunday*, by Graham Swift. *Kirkus*, 31 Jan. 2016, www.kirkus-
reviews.com/book-reviews/graham-swift/mothering-sunday/. Accessed 22 Feb.
2017.

The Mothers

Author: Brit Bennett (b. 1990)
Publisher: Riverhead Books (New York).
  288 pp.
Type of work: Novel
Time: Present day
Locale: Southern California

(Courtesy of Penguin Random House)

In her debut novel, The Mothers, *Brit Bennett tells the story of Nadia Turner after she makes the decision to end her pregnancy. As the novel progresses, Nadia and her friends struggle to confront both loss and acceptance of motherhood.*

Principal characters:
NADIA TURNER, a seventeen-year-old girl
  who becomes pregnant
ROBERT TURNER, her father
ELISE TURNER, her mother
LUKE SHEPPARD, the father of her unborn child
PASTOR SHEPPARD, Luke's father, the minister of Upper Room Chapel
LATRICE SHEPPARD, his wife and Luke's mother
AUBREY EVANS, Nadia's friend, a congregant of Upper Room Chapel

Brit Bennett's debut novel, *The Mothers*, is a compelling story that, as the title suggests, explores the theme of motherhood, starting with a mother's suicide and a teenager's decision to end her pregnancy. The narrative is unique partly because it is related in the first-person plural by the titular mothers, a group of church women. In this story, which takes place in a small African American church community in Southern California, Bennett closely examines the fundamental role of a mother and its impact on the lives of her characters.

The main character of *The Mothers* is Nadia Turner, a seventeen-year-old girl who becomes pregnant about six months after her own mother, Elise Turner, commits suicide. She feels that her mother's death is her fault to some extent, because Nadia herself was an unwanted child. Nadia comes to the realization, or perhaps knew all along, that her birth prevented her mother from having an accomplished life. This understanding leads Nadia, who has been given a scholarship to attend the University of Michigan, to terminate her pregnancy to avoid repeating her mother's history. The baby's father, Luke Sheppard, offers no objection to Nadia's decision. Luke's father is Pastor Sheppard, and he, along with his congregation, once led a protest against a local abortion clinic. Nevertheless, Pastor Sheppard and his wife, Latrice Sheppard, offer to pay for the abortion procedure. They do this without telling Robert Turner,

Nadia's father and a faithful congregant. Nadia's decision stays with her throughout the rest of the novel.

Immediately after the abortion, Luke ends his relationship with Nadia. In the aftermath of her mother's death and Luke's abandonment, Nadia eventually befriends Aubrey Evans, another girl at her high school. Aubrey has escaped from her mother's abusive partner, which, in a way, has also left her motherless. Both girls must come to terms with what it means to live without a mother. They know, however, their losses are not the same, and Nadia's stays with her in the following years; for example, she refuses to walk at her college commencement ceremony because it seems pointless to do so without her mother there as a witness. Nadia often wonders what her mother's life might have been if she had not had a child so early. She also compares the loss of her mother with Aubrey's suffering: "[Nadia's] mother was dead, but what could be worse than knowing that your mother was alive somewhere but she wanted a man who hit her more than she wanted you?"

The complex depiction of motherhood in *The Mothers* curtails condemnation of Nadia's choice to terminate her pregnancy, and Bennett's subtle treatment of her protagonist's psychology makes it difficult to trivialize this choice. After her mother's death and her subsequent abortion, Nadia's imagination is drawn relentlessly to images of motherhood. When she wakes up from the abortion procedure, Nadia fleetingly mistakes the nurse for her own mother. Especially haunting is Nadia's imagining of her mother's death: she pictures Elise driving along a curving road, "the morning light as pink as a baby girl's nightgown." This light of life, however idealized and sentimental, leads to death. For years after her abortion, Nadia continually imagines her unborn child at different stages of life. She pictures a gurgling baby, a running toddler, and a six-year-old tearing around the living room. These mental images may come as a surprise to the reader, given Nadia's immediate, unwavering decision to end her pregnancy, but they illustrate the fact that grief is not a linear process. As she struggles to forget Luke and their unborn child, Nadia realizes that "grief [i]s not a line, carrying you infinitely further from loss. You never knew when you would be sling-shot backward into its grip."

Nadia is not the only character in *The Mothers* affected by her decision. Luke, too, suffers throughout the novel, which may come as another surprise to the reader, and perhaps to Luke himself. Having abandoned Nadia at the clinic after the abortion procedure, he at first gives every indication of not caring about the girl who once carried his child. Only later does he come to terms with his love for Nadia, and when she is about to leave for college, he confesses to her that he wanted to keep the baby. For years while Nadia is away, he struggles to contain his grief, stuck in his reckless patterns, until he eventually becomes engaged to Aubrey. When Nadia returns home years later to care for her sick father, a complicated triangle ensues, as the three characters struggle with love and grief.

The Mothers confronts and subverts stereotypes of African American mothers and fathers, in particular the stereotypical depictions of absent fathers and unfit mothers. Bennett humanizes Luke through her depiction of his experience of losing an unborn child; he cannot seem to move on from this negative experience, even though he has never met the child. In addition, Nadia's father, Robert, is always present, and though he is reserved and disciplined to a fault, he clearly supports and loves his daughter. Meanwhile, Nadia decides to end her pregnancy partly because she does not yet feel qualified to become a mother, and Latrice, while judgmental and cruel to Nadia, becomes a mother figure to Aubrey.

Then there are the mothers of the community, a group of elderly church-women who serve as a chorus-like narrator throughout the novel. They lack individuality, and their function as a narrative voice does not always work, in part because they are presented as both individual characters and as a group. The reader eventually learns their names—which include Mother Betty, Mother Agnes, and Mother Flora—but other than such superficial details, Bennett does not reveal much about them, and sometimes it is difficult to tell them apart. This creates a puzzling contrast with the intense specificity of the other characters. The mothers' generic nature seems to work against the carefully crafted individuality of Nadia, Aubrey, and Luke, which means it also, perhaps, undermines the notion of motherhood as multifarious. Although the mothers are the bedrock of the church, they rarely mention their faith, as Joy Lanzendorfer pointed out in her review of *The Mothers* for the KQED Arts website: "The mothers rarely mention Jesus, for example. Prayer to them isn't communion with God but an act of empathy, where you 'slip inside' the person you're praying for. That's an interesting idea, but unlikely to be the thoughts of women so religious they practically live at church." Lanzendorfer attributed this decision to Bennett's attempt to avoid disrupting the carefully crafted moral nuances of her characters with too many religious allusions.

Another flaw in this novel is the way the narrative ultimately punishes Pastor Sheppard for his handling of Nadia's pregnancy. By agreeing to help pay for Nadia's abortion, Pastor Sheppard and his wife act with blatant hypocrisy, given the pastor's strong public condemnation of the same procedure. Latrice even boasts arrogantly of having paid for Nadia's abortion—"I did what any mother would've done. . . . That girl should be thanking me. I gave her life"—and for years afterward goes out of her way to be cruel to Nadia, blaming her alone for the pregnancy. There is no question that, in this context, the Sheppards deserve to be humbled, which they eventually are. Their comeuppance, however, seems like a concession to relieve the reader of the story's sadness, and it works against what the novel otherwise shows to be true. The Sheppards' punishment suggests an artificial world where hypocrisy is punished, but in fact the world often tolerates and even rewards hypocrisy, and part of what makes *The Mothers* so credible is its portrayal of the world as an unfair place—a place where mothers commit suicide, choose abusive partners over their own children, and blame other women for their sons' mistakes.

Brit Bennett graduated from Stanford University and earned an MFA from the University of Michigan. The winner of the 2014 Hurston/Wright Award for College Writers for fiction, she has had her work published in the Paris Review, *the* New Yorker, *and the* New York Times Magazine, *among other publications. The Mothers is her first novel.*

These are choices that can never be undone or made right, only negotiated. How Nadia chooses to do so, and how her choices change her forever, is what makes *The Mothers* a compelling story. "[Bennett's] decision to put abortion front and centre in the story is in itself extraordinary, given how absent it is in cultural narratives about young women, but she doesn't linger on it, nor does she judge her characters," Marta Bausells wrote in her review for the *Guardian*. Although abortion is an important part of the novel, the book, as the title suggests, is fundamentally about motherhood. Throughout the novel the reader witnesses how the role of mothers deeply influences the characters. Reviewing the novel for the *Washington Post*, Bethanne Patrick wrote, "If you read *The Mothers*, you will learn a lot. You will learn what it's like to experience a mother-shaped absence at the center of your life, as well as what it's like to feel your mother's hot, judgmental breath on your shoulder every second." The relatable themes and impeccable writing of *The Mothers* make Bennett's debut novel a great achievement.

Ashleigh Imus, PhD

Review Sources

Bausells, Marta. "A Bold New Voice in American Fiction." Review of *The Mothers*, by Brit Bennett. *The Guardian*, 27 Nov. 2016, www.theguardian.com/books/2016/nov/27/the-mothers-brit-bennett-review-bold-new-voice-american-fiction. Accessed 26 Feb. 2017.

Eddo-Lodge, Reni. "An Impressive Coming-of-Age Debut." Review of *The Mothers*, by Brit Bennett. *The Guardian*, 15 Oct. 2016, www.theguardian.com/books/2016/oct/15/mothers-brit-bennett-review-debut-novel. Accessed 26 Feb. 2017.

Lanzendorfer, Joy. "Church, Abortion and Family Converge in Debut Novel *The Mothers*." Review of *The Mothers*, by Brit Bennett. *KQED Arts*, KQED, 6 Oct. 2016, ww2.kqcd.org/arts/2016/10/06/church-abortion-and-family-converge-in-debut-novel-the-mothers/. Accessed 26 Feb. 2017.

Review of *The Mothers*, by Brit Bennett. *Publishers Weekly*, 11 July 2016, www.publishersweekly.com/978-0-399-18451-2. Accessed 20 Feb. 2017.

Patrick, Bethanne. "*The Mothers*: A Fantastic Debut Novel by Brit Bennett." Review of *The Mothers*, by Brit Bennett. *The Washington Post*, 18 Oct. 2016, www.washingtonpost.com/entertainment/books/the-mothers-a-fantastic-debut-novel-by-brit-bennett/2016/10/13/ee701c72-9148-11e6-9c85-ac42097b8cc0_story.html. Accessed 20 Feb. 2017.

Mr. Splitfoot

Author: Samantha Hunt (b. 1971)
Publisher: Houghton Mifflin Harcourt (Boston). 336 pp.
Type of work: Novel
Time: 1990s–the present day
Locale: Upstate New York

(Courtesy of Houghton Mifflin Harcourt)

Mr. Splitfoot is a modern American gothic ghost story that examines the different ways the dead can haunt the living by focusing on the lives and both emotional and physical journeys of two women.

Principal characters:
RUTH, a young woman with a scar across her face
NAT, her closest friend, who claims he can speak to the dead
CORA, her niece, with whom she embarks on a journey across upstate New York
FATHER ARTHUR, the founder of the Love of Christ! foster home
MR. BELL, a young con man who helps emancipate Ruth and Nat

Central to the story of *Mr. Splitfoot* (2016) is the supposition that the living need the dead. It is a narrative line that first becomes evident during an early scene sequence when teenaged orphans Ruth and Nat conduct séances for the other children at the Love of Christ! foster home. In exchange for five dollars, Nat allegedly speaks to the dead through an unseen spiritual entity named Mr. Splitfoot. Despite the fact that these foster kids differ in backgrounds and personalities, the events that transpire once Mr. Splitfoot has been summoned are always the same. Inevitably, the children want to speak to their mothers who, through the corporeal conduit of Nat, say that they love them and wish that they could be there. In response, some children cry, while others get angry. Regardless of what emotions they react with, however, it is clear that each one of them needs to believe that they are speaking to those they lost.

In interviews, author Samantha Hunt has argued that because everyone eventually dies, all stories are ghost stories. In *Mr. Splitfoot*, her third novel, she posits that this is not necessarily a bad thing. Labeled an American gothic ghost story, *Mr. Splitfoot* explores the different ways that the dead can haunt the living. For Hunt, the phenomenon of haunting is defined as when someone or something has been left behind like a residue. While many of *Mr. Splitfoot*'s characters are haunted in some capacity, no one symbolizes the idea as effectively as the primary protagonist, Ruth. Like many of the other children at the Love of Christ! foster home, Ruth is haunted by the memories of her mother. However, Ruth is unique in that her haunting has a physical manifestation;

the "wormy mess" of scars that cover a large part of her face is from the time that her mother deliberately poured bleach on her as a baby. It is arguably because Ruth is reminded every day of her painful past that she believes that talking to the dead is not only possible but also necessary.

The narrative of *Mr. Splitfoot* alternates chapter by chapter between two story lines. The primary story line takes place in the late 1990s, when Ruth is seventeen years old and subsequently in her last year at the foster home. Quiet and unassuming, Ruth is inseparable from her best friend, a handsome seventeen-year-old boy named Nat. The relationship between Ruth and Nat is meticulously crafted by Hunt to drive the plot of *Mr. Splitfoot*. She depicts the two characters as intertwined beings willing to go to extreme measures to avoid being separated from one another. Ruth and Nat's spiritual bond is also often illustrated by their physical interactions. They hold hands, sit on one another's laps, and even share a bed. Hunt clarifies that their feelings and actions are strictly platonic, however, by giving their relationship a familial designation. Throughout the narrative, Ruth refers to Nat as her "sister," a nickname from their first encounter when they were five years old and Ruth was missing her biological sister, El, who had aged out of the foster-care system.

Set years later in the mid-2010s, *Mr. Splitfoot*'s second story line follows Ruth's niece, Cora. Twenty-five and unhappy with her life, Cora works at an insurance company, where she wastes most of her days ruminating about her boyfriend, Lord, a former marine who is married to another woman. When Cora tells him that she is pregnant with his child, Lord tries to give her an abortion against her will. In addition to being highly disturbing, the scene also functions as the inciting incident of Cora's narrative. The threat that Lord poses to her unborn child is ultimately what makes Cora willing to follow her Aunt Ruth, who shows up unexpectedly one night, on a trip across upstate New York. Hunt utilizes Ruth's sudden arrival in Cora's life to infuse the narrative with mystery. Despite being the same woman from the primary story line, Ruth has changed dramatically. In addition to having become inexplicably mute, Ruth's motives for the trip are unclear. Furthermore, she does not indicate to her niece where they are going and insists that they travel by foot. By ensuring that the circumstances surrounding Ruth and Cora's journey inspire more questions than answers, Hunt amplifies the plot's suspense.

More than anything, *Mr. Splitfoot* is about two women fighting for their agency. When Hunt introduces the characters of Ruth and Cora, it is clear that both lack any real power in their lives. This impotence is especially evident with Ruth, who is a ward of the state and subsequently unable to leave Love of Christ! until she becomes a legal adult. Her imminent eighteenth birthday, however, does not represent freedom but an introduction to a new set of problems; most of the children who age out of Love of Christ! become homeless and unable to support themselves. To make matters worse, Nat is several months younger than Ruth, meaning that he will have to stay behind at the foster home and the two will be separated. The fear of being without Nat is Ruth's call to action. Rather than allow Father Arthur, the abusive man who runs the foster home, to control her fate, Ruth begins devising her own plan. First, she allows a young con man named Mr. Bell to help her and Nat find more clients for their séance act.

Once they start making money, Ruth asks Mr. Bell to marry her so that she can adopt Nat. Hunt's depiction of Ruth's transformation is gradual but inspiring; the more action she takes, the stronger she becomes.

Despite being well into adulthood, Cora is also largely powerless in the beginning. First she is paralyzed by her romantic feelings for Lord, later by her fear of him. However, she stops being a victim of her circumstances the moment she decides to trek through the woods of New York with her aunt. Although Ruth is leading the way, it is truly Cora's journey. Hunt employs several stylistic cues to signify this fact. For one, Ruth is presented as a silent, peripheral figure at the edges of all of Cora's scenes. Furthermore, Cora's first-person narration reveals the evolution of her thoughts and fears in the form of internal dialogue. As the weeks pass, she grows stronger both physically and emotionally, transitioning slowly from having the mindset of a daughter to the mindset of a mother. It is a powerful use of symbolism; as Cora's baby grows inside her, so does her sense of self.

Samantha Hunt is an American novelist and the author of The Seas *(2004) and* The Invention of Everything Else *(2008).*

Ultimately, *Mr. Splitfoot* is an enjoyable addition to the annals of American gothic literature. Although it explores several contemporary social issues, the novel's themes and imagery align neatly to classic works of the genre such as *The House of the Seven Gables* (1851), by Nathaniel Hawthorne, and H. P. Lovecraft's short story "Beyond the Wall of Sleep" (1919). Historically, American gothic writers such as Hawthorne and Lovecraft used monsters and spirits in their stories to symbolize their characters' sins and fears. Similarly, Hunt implements ghosts throughout the novel as a device to represent both the characters' twisted emotions and unsettled issues. *Mr. Splitfoot* is also rife with the dark imagery that has come to define American gothic literature. Like Edgar Allan Poe's description of the old man's blue, filmy eye in "The Tell-Tale Heart" (1843), Hunt leverages the face of one of the antagonists of Ruth's story line, a man named Zeke, for the purpose of horror. After months of snorting powdered bleach, Zeke has burned the nose off his face and refuses to cover the subsequent open nasal cavity. It is a disturbing image that intensifies the novel's eerie tone and demonstrates the evil that Ruth and Nat are up against.

Arguably, *Mr. Splitfoot*'s most significant American gothic quality, however, is the irrationality that many of its characters are incapable of overcoming with logic. In *Mr. Splitfoot*, irrationality often takes the form of religion. Hunt demonstrates the horror and destructiveness that accompanies irrationality through the character of Father Arthur, who justifies severely neglecting his foster children with the misguided belief that he is saving their souls. She furthers this point with the Etherists. A cult that believes a meteor is destined to crash into Earth and transform them all into particles of light, the Etherists are willing to take violent measures in the name of their beliefs.

The critical reception of *Mr. Splitfoot* has been mixed. Ubiquitous among the novel's positive reviews has been praise for the inventiveness of Hunt's storytelling and setting. Writing for the *Chicago Tribune*, Ron Charles extolled Hunt's ability to capture the "dark spirit" of upstate New York forests. It can be argued that the novel's setting has been a universal point of acclaim because it establishes the narrative's dark and twisted tone effectively. In addition to creating a landscape befitting of a ghost story, Hunt is also successful at using the unsettling quietude and shadows of upstate New York to elevate her characters' feelings of pain and uncertainty.

Among the less favorable evaluations of *Mr. Splitfoot* is critic Sarah Ditum's review for the *Guardian*, in which she argued that "suspense runs short and horror is too often undercut by an infuriating structure that serves symbolism over story." For some, Hunt's choice to alternate between the two story lines may derail the tense momentum of the plot, since many of the short chapters end in action or suspense and then are followed by a chapter dedicated to the other story line. However, while this structure can have a jerky, frustrating quality, it does not necessarily dilute the narrative's suspense. Instead, it requires readers to wait, which creates anticipation. The prose of *Mr. Splitfoot* has also been a divisive point among critics. Although she initially praised Hunt's writing for its "hallucinatory detail," *Chicago Tribune* critic Amy Gentry concluded her review by arguing that the level of description becomes tedious and distracts from the storytelling. In contrast, Gregory Maguire of the *New York Times* claimed that he was so enamored with Hunt's vivid prose that the corners of his copy were "fattened" by the number of passages he felt compelled to dog-ear. Despite the fact that some readers may not enjoy Hunt's literary style, the originality of the novel is undeniable. With compelling characters and innumerable plot twists, *Mr. Splitfoot* is a highly enjoyable read.

Emily Turner

Review Sources

Charles, Ron. "*Mr. Splitfoot* Review: A Gothic Tale in the Woods of New York." Review of *Mr. Splitfoot*, by Samantha Hunt. *Washington Post*, 4 Jan. 2016, www. washingtonpost.com/entertainment/books/mr-splitfoot-review-a-gothic-tale-in-the-woods-of-new-york/2016/01/04/efd0b168-afca-11e5-b711-1998289ffcea_story.html. Accessed 11 Oct. 2016.

Ditum, Sarah. "*Mr Splitfoot* by Samantha Hunt Review—American Gothic with Lashings of Symbolism." Review of *Mr. Splitfoot*, by Samantha Hunt. *The Guardian*, 30 Dec. 2015, www.theguardian.com/books/2015/dec/30/mr-splitfoot-samantha-hunt-review. Accessed 11 Oct. 2016.

Gentry, Amy. Review of *Mr. Splitfoot*, by Samantha Hunt. *Chicago Tribune*, 27 Jan. 2016, www.chicagotribune.com/lifestyles/books/ct-prj-mr-splitfoot-samantha-hunt-20160127-story.html. Accessed 11 Oct. 2016.

Maguire, Gregory. Review of Mr. Splitfoot, by Samantha Hunt. *The New York Times*, 5 Jan. 2016, www.nytimes.com/2016/01/10/books/review/samantha-hunts-mr-splitfoot.html. Accessed 11 Oct. 2016.

My Name Is Lucy Barton

Author: Elizabeth Strout (b. 1956)
Publisher: Random House (New York). 208 pp.
Type of work: Novel
Time: 1960s–2000s
Locales: New York City; Amgash, Illinois

My Name Is Lucy Barton tells the story of its protagonist, Lucy Barton, through a series of flashbacks to her past, particularly a visit from her mother while Lucy was hospitalized with an extended and undiagnosed illness. With a sharp focus on the strained but loving relationship between the two women and the effect of Lucy's troubled childhood on her adult life, the novel explores themes of family, memory, and class.

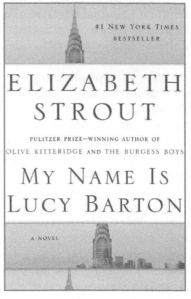

(Courtesy of Penguin Random House)

Principal characters:

LUCY BARTON, the novel's protagonist, who was raised in poverty and worked her way to a successful life in New York City

LUCY'S MOTHER, her estranged mother, whom she has not seen in years and still lives in the town and house where Lucy grew up

BECKA AND CHRISSIE, her daughters, who age from small children to college-aged young adults through flashbacks to the present

WILLIAM, her husband, who comes from a middle-class New England family of German descent

As Elizabeth Strout's short novel *My Name Is Lucy Barton* (2016) comes to a close, the eponymous protagonist, Lucy Barton, meditates on the landscape of her childhood home in rural Illinois: "A view of the horizon, the whole entire circle of it, if you turned, the sun setting behind you, the sky in front becoming pink and soft, then slightly blue again, as though it could not stop going on in its beauty, then the land closest to the setting sun would get dark, almost black." She continues to meditate on the trees and crops that are still visible in the near dark, with everything finally fading to black. "All life amazes me," she concludes. So much of *My Name Is Lucy Barton* deals with the lingering effects of the past—from one's upbringing as a child to its effect on one's ability to cope and adapt as an adult. With this final passage, Lucy seems like she is finally able to mend the two parts of herself and come to terms with her early years while standing firm in her adult self.

The novel opens sometime in the early 2000s with Lucy narrating a story about a hospital stay in the mid-1980s when she was suffering from a mysterious illness. She was in the hospital to have her appendix removed, a simple procedure, only to find herself too ill to be released for nine weeks. Her husband and two young daughters are at home. Her husband rarely visits and a family friend brings her daughters to see her in the hospital. Then one afternoon, Lucy's mother is sitting at the food of her bed. "Hi, Wizzle," she says, as her daughter stares shocked after not having seen her in years. It is this complicated mother-daughter relationship that forms the heart of the story.

Lucy is from poverty-stricken Amgash, Illinois, where she was raised with two siblings by her parents: her mother, a seamstress who worked from the house, and her father, a day laborer and veteran of World War II. Lucy, however, pulled herself out of the cycle of poverty after being offered a full scholarship to a college in Chicago and has since worked to distance herself from her past as she pursues a successful career as a writer in New York City. The past, or her childhood memories perhaps, is the root of all pain in this tale. Her father carried demons from his time in the war and cannot accept Lucy's husband, who is blond and of German descent, thus alienating his daughter. The reader soon learns that Lucy's thirty-six-year-old brother is still living at home; he reads children's books and sleeps in the barn with farm animals the night before their slaughter, and her thirty-four-year-old sister lives nearby their parents with her own small children and a bitterness that encircles her rural life. When Lucy expresses surprise at her brother's adult life, her mother shrugs her shoulders. Much like during Lucy's rough and sometimes violent childhood, there is no room for sentimentality in her mother's twilight years.

In her review of the book for the *New York Times*, novelist Claire Messud pondered, "One of this nation's most abiding myths is that social origins don't matter. Each of us is Gatsby, or can be, with the potential to be reinvented and obliterate the past. This is nowhere more true than in New York City, where, surrounded by millions, each person supposedly stands upon his or her own merits." Messud elaborated, "Lucy Barton's story is, in meaningful ways, about loneliness, about an individual's isolation when her past—all that has formed her—is invisible and incommunicable to those around her." It is this intense pressure that has guided Lucy's adult life. Therefore, it comes as no surprise that she feels a great relief and joy at seeing her mother at her bedside after so many years of estrangement. Lucy notes that she has slept fitfully every night of her stay, but with her mother there she finally is able to sleep through the night. Lucy recalls one professor whom she had been in love with, only to be ridiculed for her poverty at one point in their relationship, which ultimately makes her realize that their relationship will end, that the two will never see the world in quite the same way. "I have since been friends with many men and women and they say the same thing: Always that telling detail. What I mean is, this is not just a woman's story. It's what happens to a lot of us, if we are lucky enough to hear that detail and pay attention to it." Her husband, who the reader later learns will eventually divorce her, is kinder but still aware of her social class, frequently making excuses for her ignorance of certain topics in public situations.

Strout's characters are simple in their demeanors; the story is fueled by stark language and muted actions that allow the intense emotions at play to truly come through. The feelings between mother and daughter are so intense and the topics they grapple with are so unspeakable that the two often simply wiggle their fingers at each other as a way to check in. If her mother is finished with a conversation, she closes her eyes and seems to disappear inside her head. In flashbacks from her earlier college and post-college years, Lucy is struck mute in situations when she's forced to reckon with her past. Her mother is never seen sleeping through a night; she takes brief naps, telling her daughter that she learned to do this as a child because she never felt safe. These small details in quiet moments are the ones that end up defining the story and to a degree the characters. Sometimes it is easier to accept a situation for what it is, while at other times it is easier to create a new reality.

Elizabeth Strout is the author of five novels, including the Pulitzer Prize–winning Olive Kitteridge *(2008).* My Name Is Lucy Barton *was named to the long list for the Man Booker Prize.*

Strout is ultimately asking what each person has given up in these cases and how a person can become or remain whole while wrestling with pain, hardship, and inequality.

The book's structure allows Strout to examine the adult life of Lucy with a tenderness that a linear narrative would likely not provide. Moments with her mother in the hospital are juxtaposed with moments Lucy spends with her two young daughters, watching them grow in an urban setting that is foreign to her but has become home. The reader sees Lucy as a young child amid the violence of her home life and then is transported back to New York and the hospital room. Each night the two women watch as the Chrysler Building becomes a shining beacon against the dark sky; Lucy notes that it looks like any other building during the day, but the darkness transforms it into something unforgettable.

Memory is fallible, and Strout uses this to her advantage. Each of her characters is haunted by memories, but many are not even sure if these memories are accurate or if they have been created or enhanced by their imaginations. At one point, Lucy speaks about a former teacher she had been close to in the sixth grade, Mr. Haley, and how he left at the end of that school year. "In my memory he was going into the service, and this could only have been Vietnam, since it was during that time." However, she later tried to look up his name on the Veterans Memorial in Washington, DC, and his name was not listed. At other moments she is not even sure of something that may have happened with her mother during her hospital stay. The effect creates a dreamlike state. As Lucy is infantilized by her hospital stay, feeling reassured by her mother's presence, she has also fallen into a state that seems to break down the wall between her past and present. Of course, it must be remembered that Lucy herself is narrating this story from many years beyond her hospital stay, and in that intervening time both her parents have died, she has divorced and remarried, and her children have grown. What is the half-life of a memory, the story seems to ask.

Strout, who was born in 1956 in Portland, Maine, and raised in small towns in Maine and New Hampshire, is the Pulitzer Prize–winning author of *Olive Kitteridge* (2008), a novel set on the coast of Maine and the subject of a 2014 HBO miniseries. Her most popular work deals with rural life and, in the case of *My Name Is Lucy Barton*, the juxtaposition between rural and urban life.

Included on the long list for the Man Booker Prize in 2016, *My Name Is Lucy Barton* received accolades from critics and the literary community. In a review for the *Washington Post*, author Lily King wrote, "Strout is playing with form here, with ways to get at a story, yet nothing is tentative or haphazard. She is in supreme and magnificent command of this novel at all times." Hannah Beckerman said in a review for the *Guardian*, "*My Name Is Lucy Barton* confirms Strout as a powerful storyteller immersed in the nuances of human relationships, weaving family tapestries with compassion, wisdom, and insight."

Strout has created a relatable and unforgettable character in Lucy Barton, someone who struggles to find and maintain her identity while constantly questioning what she has lost in the process. Through the vagueness of memory, the sharpness of environment, and the pain of her upbringing, Strout brings to the surface the many facets of cycling through life and the hardships and rewards that come with them.

Melynda Fuller

Review Sources

Beckerman, Hannah. Review of *My Name Is Lucy Barton*, by Elizabeth Strout. *The Guardian*, 2 Feb. 2016, www.theguardian.com/books/2016/feb/02/my-name-is-lucy-barton-review-elizabeth-strout. Accessed 1 Nov. 2016.

Hampson, Sarah. "Review: Elizabeth Strout's *My Name Is Lucy Barton* Is an Exploration of Memory." Review of *My Name Is Lucy Barton*, by Elizabeth Strout. *Globe and Mail*, 22 Jan. 2016, www.theglobeandmail.com/arts/books-and-media/book-reviews/review-elizabeth-strouts-my-name-is-lucy-barton-is-an-exploration-of-memory/article28338507. Accessed 1 Nov. 2016.

King, Lily. Review of *My Name Is Lucy Barton*, by Elizabeth Strout. *Washington Post*, 4 Jan. 2016, www.washingtonpost.com/entertainment/books/elizabeth-strouts-my-name-is-lucy-barton-review/2016/01/04/8df36b98-afca-11e5-b711-1998289ffcea_story.html. Accessed 1 Nov. 2016.

Messud, Claire. Review of My Name Is Lucy Barton, by Elizabeth Strout. *The New York Times*, 4 Jan. 2016, www.nytimes.com/2016/01/10/books/review/elizabeth-strouts-my-name-is-lucy-barton.html. Accessed 1 Nov. 2016.

Vanderhoof, Erin. "Her Name Is Lucy Barton." Review of *My Name Is Lucy Barton*, by Elizabeth Strout. *Nation*, 22 Mar. 2016, www.thenation.com/article/my-name-is-lucy-barton-elizabeth-strout-review/. Accessed 1 Nov. 2016.

My Struggle
Book 5

Author: Karl Ove Knausgaard (b. 1968)
First published: *Min kamp 5*, 2010, in Norway
Translated from the Norwegian by Dan Bartlett
Publisher: Archipelago Books (Brooklyn, NY). 624 pp.
Type of work: Autobiography; memoir; novel
Time: 1988–2004
Locale: Norway

My Struggle Book 5 *is the fifth volume of Norwegian author Karl Ove Knausgaard's six-volume autobiographical novel series, originally published in Norway as* Min Kamp *(2009–11).*

(Courtesy of Archipelago)

Principal personages:
KARL OVE KNAUSGAARD, the narrator, a struggling Norwegian novelist
YNGVE, his older brother
INGVILD, a young woman with whom he falls madly in love
TONJE, his first wife
TORE RENBERG, his friend, a less experienced but more successful writer

In interviews, Norwegian novelist Karl Ove Knausgaard has stated that his goal with *Min Kamp*, translated into English as *My Struggle* starting in 2012, was initially to create something as majestic and grand as *Moby Dick* (1851). However, he found that the smallness of his life lacked the inspiration necessary for a literary epic. As a result, he began writing about the mundane events that made up his days and how they made him feel. He discovered that although he did not necessarily like the prose that he was generating, it was something rather than nothing. Eventually writing "plainly" about his life became the point of his work; by documenting everything from the most shameful humiliations of his adolescence to the banalities of middle age, Knausgaard was capturing the human experience in an unprecedentedly honest way.

 My Struggle is a six-volume series about Knausgaard's personal and professional life. Each of these six volumes focuses, mostly, on a specific period in Knausgaard's life. In *My Struggle: Book 1* (2012), Knausgaard reflects on his early childhood and the role that his judgmental, alcoholic father played in shaping his identity. In *My Struggle: Book 2* (2013), Knausgaard jumps forward in time to write about his marriage to his second wife, Linda, and his experience as the primary caregiver of their four young children. *My Struggle: Book 3* (2014) returns to the dark depths of his childhood, and *My Struggle: Book 4* (2015), which is lighter and more comical in tone, recalls his adolescence. The two overarching themes that connect all of the *My Struggle* books are Knausgaard's feelings of inadequacy and his desire to fulfill his creative ambitions as a writer.

These themes are not only continued in *My Struggle: Book 5* (2016) but are finally brought to the forefront of the narrative. This fifth installment in the series begins when Knausgaard is nineteen years old and has been admitted to a prestigious writing academy in Bergen, Norway, taught by the country's best-known authors. The youngest and most inexperienced member of his class, Knausgaard is arrogant and self-assured about his talent. Consequently, when the other students begin criticizing his work as immature and clichéd, he lashes out at them. This behavior proves to be formative, ulti-mately shaping the way he approaches writ-

(Courtesy of Andre Løvning)

Karl Ove Knausgaard is a writer from Oslo, Norway. His debut novel, Out of the World *(1998), won the Norwegian Critics Prize for Literature. His six-volume autobiographical novel series* My Struggle *has earned him international acclaim. He resides in Österlen, Sweden, with his wife and four children.*

ing throughout the rest of his career. Knausgaard becomes saddled with feelings of inadequacy about his own accomplishments and pettiness about the success of others. Arguably one of the most significant outcomes of his time at the Bergen writing academy is that Knausgaard starts to believe that his shortcomings as a writer stem from the fact that he is, as he says, too much of a "goody-goody." He concludes that in order to become a true artist he must stop being so normal. It is a decision that has enormously self-destructive effects.

The primary focus of *My Struggle: Book 5* is the first fourteen years of Knausgaard's writing career, which he depicts as dark and chaotic. After leaving the academy, he continues to write with little success besides getting one short story printed in a literary magazine. He grows increasingly frustrated as his colleagues, like his younger, less experienced friend Tore Renberg, start getting their novels published. Meanwhile, his quest to transform himself from a "goody-goody" to a true artist causes him to engage in dangerous behavior. When Ingvild, a girl he becomes infatuated with, breaks his heart by kissing his older brother, Yngve, for example, he gets revenge by throwing a pint glass at his brother's face. Although the two brothers make amends, Yngve's betrayal causes irreparable damage to Knausgaard's already fragile self-esteem.

Knausgaard's self-loathing emerges repeatedly throughout the story, often driving him to episodes of drunken blackouts, theft, vandalism, infidelity, and violence. In an especially dramatic scene, Knausgaard's demons come to a head when he slices his

own face repeatedly with a broken beer bottle after witnessing Yngve and his girlfriend Tonje getting along. It is in this moment of unhinged jealousy that it becomes
clear that he has truly succeeded in his goal of becoming a disturbed artist. Despite the
fact that he finally achieves his goal, soon afterward when his first novel, *Out of the
World* (1998), is published to positive reviews, Knausgaard's feelings of inadequacy
and unworthiness continue. More than anything, *My Struggle: Book 5* seems to argue
that Knausgaard's skills as a writer were the result of years of pain and setbacks.

Despite the fact that publishers have designated *My Struggle* a novel, readers often
interpret it as an autobiography. It is difficult to determine how to categorize the work,
because it includes true events and actual people from Knausgaard's life; nothing is
fabricated. Furthermore, Knausgaard writes with such detail and attention to triviali-
ties that it is easy to believe that it is nothing more than a well-written journal. This,
however, is an illusion. *My Struggle: Book 5* is a work of literature in the way that
Knausgaard masterfully shapes the material through his choices of which stories to
include and which to discard. Furthermore, his prose is crafted to draw readers in
through its distinct literary style, pacing, and focus. It is this distinct literary style that
somehow makes pages of observations about a mundane interaction that he had with
a stranger fascinating. With such merits, it seems appropriate that many critics have
come to the conclusion that *My Struggle* can be labeled an autobiographical novel.

In addition to the high quality of the writing, *My Struggle* has earned international fame because of the numerous controversies that surround it. Initially, the public
was shocked when it was learned that the book would be published with the name
Min Kamp, which was the title of the Norwegian translation of Adolf Hitler's 1925
autobiography, *Mein Kampf*. Additionally, Knausgaard's work has been considered
controversial for his decision to write about the personal lives of his friends, family,
and colleagues without their permission. Knausgaard's depictions of the people in his
life, including several of his ex-girlfriends, are often deeply critical and humiliating
and thus inherently invasive. Although Knausgaard changed some people's names in
the books, Norway is a small country, and the media was able to identify most of
them. One response to Knausgaard's treatment of others in his books is that he utilizes
the same level of unwavering scrutiny when writing about himself. Throughout *My
Struggle*, Knausgaard continuously reveals and examines every one of his own humiliating, morally reprehensible actions and thoughts. While it is this level of honesty
and willingness to share his flaws that makes Knausgaard relatable to readers, it is also
what makes him the book's primary antagonist.

Like previous volumes in the series, the critical reception of *My Struggle: Book
5* has been overwhelmingly positive. In his *Washington Post* review, critic Rodney
Welch writes, "This fifth volume feels more insular than the others, but that's where
Knausgaard has always been at his best. The inner life inspires him. It's what gives
the sentences their urgency." It is true that where previous volumes of the series have
been more circuitous and allowed Knausgaard to jump back and forth in time, *My
Struggle: Book 5* is more narrowly focused on Knausgaard's career as a writer. As
most of Knausgaard's "struggle" has been both directly and indirectly about him trying to become a writer capable of producing great art, *My Struggle: Book 5* provides

readers with some satisfaction. After years of pain, self-doubt, and obstacles, Knausgaard finally lands a book deal. And although his existential misery does not cease with this achievement, for readers it comes across as a tremendously rewarding payoff; his aspirations no longer appear to be as futile as he claims.

My Struggle: Book 5 has also received enormous praise from critics for the quality of its writing. In his review for the *New Yorker*, Joshua Rothman argues, "Knausgaard writes beautifully about landscapes, and he describes his inner life the way he describes a landscape, simply noting, with tender exactness, what is there. Using the same flat tone, he will describe the green mountainside, the tea in a cup, the feeling of fear." A large part of what makes *My Struggle: Book 5* a worthwhile read is the way that Knausgaard presents common ideas, images, and experiences in a new light. He does this by describing everything in great detail. While his meticulously detailed, lengthy passages are arguably the most distinct stylistic aspect of his work, they are also the most divisive. Where many find his decision to spend pages depicting banal events a sign of his literary genius, others may find it to be tedious. Regardless of whether readers enjoy the detailed realism of Knausgaard's prose, however, it is undeniably unique and evocative. Therefore, *My Struggle: Book 5* can be considered a successful continuation of his critically acclaimed solipsistic epic. Like Vladimir Nabokov's *Lolita* (1955), *My Struggle: Book 5* is an important piece of literature because it embraces the fact that its confessional perspective is contradictory, uncomfortable, and therefore thought-provoking.

Emily Turner

Review Sources

Kunzru, Hari. Review of My Struggle: Book 5, by Karl Ove Knausgaard. *The New York Times*, 27 Apr. 2016, www.nytimes.com/2016/05/01/books/review/my-struggle-book-5-by-karl-ove-knausgaard.html. Accessed 30 Jan. 2017.

Morrison, Blake. "Some Rain Must Fall: My Struggle Volume 5 by Karl Ove Knausgaard Review—Merciless Self-Exposure." Review of *My Struggle: Book 5*, by Karl Ove Knausgaard. *The Guardian*, 9 Mar. 2016, www.theguardian.com/books/2016/mar/09/some-rain-must-fall-my-struggle-volume-5-by-karl-ove-knausgaard-review. Accessed 30 Jan. 2017.

Rothman, Joshua. "Knausgaard's Selflessness." Review of *My Struggle: Book 5*, by Karl Ove Knausgaard. *The New Yorker*, 20 Apr. 2016, http://www.newyorker.com/books/page-turner/knausgaards-selflessness. Accessed 30 Jan. 2017.

Smee, Sebastian. "Portrait of a Writer as a Young Man." Review of *My Struggle: Book 5*, by Karl Ove Knausgaard. *The Boston Globe*, 22 Apr. 2016, www.bostonglobe.com/arts/2016/04/22/knausgard/mWS1c5YKtAbmfimJcHFUzH/story.html. Accessed 30 Jan. 2017.

Welch, Rodney. Review of *My Struggle Book 5*, by Karl Ove Knausgaard. *The Washington Post*, 11 Apr. 2016, www.washingtonpost.com/entertainment/books/review-book-five-of-karl-ove-knausgaards-monumental-memoir/2016/04/11/82818150-f5b1-11e5-8b23-538270a1ca31_story.html. Accessed 30 Jan. 2017.

Necessity

Author: Jo Walton (b. 1964)
Publisher: Tor (New York). 336 pp.
Type of work: Novel
Time: Twenty-sixth century
Locale: A planet called Plato

Courtesy of Tor Books

Necessity, the conclusion to Jo Walton's Thessaly trilogy, takes place on the planet Plato. There, the civilization—a mix of aliens, robots, and humans—grapples with the meaning of time and fate.

Principal characters:
APOLLO, a Greek god, known as Pytheas in
  his human form
JASON, a human fisherman
CROCUS, the first Worker (robot) to achieve
  consciousness
MARSILIA, Pytheas's granddaughter and a member of the ruling council
THETIS, her sister

Jo Walton's 2016 novel *Necessity* is the conclusion to her Thessaly trilogy, an elaborate and thought-provoking series about philosophy and time travel. The trilogy is inspired by Plato's most renowned work, *The Republic*. To comprehend this third part, however, it is important to understand the context of Walton's world.

In the first book of the trilogy, *The Just City* (2015), the Greek god Apollo attempts to seduce a nymph, but she rejects his advances, choosing instead to be turned into a tree. Apollo goes to his sister, Athene, the god of reason, to ask her why someone would go to such lengths to avoid his love. Athene's response is really a proposition: she invites Apollo to join a city she has built and populated with children from throughout the ages. She has done this as a way to recreate the "just city" of Plato's *Republic*. Accepting the proposition, Apollo assumes the form of a human child named Pytheas and goes to live there.

The second book of the trilogy, *The Philosopher Kings* (2015), takes place thirty years later. The original city, fraught with unresolved philosophical questions, has fractured into five different cities. These cities have competing points of views, and because of this, each has founded its own version of *The Republic*. In pursuit of a villain named Kebes, who has stolen a ship and escaped with his accomplices, the characters wrestle with the meaning of justice. The book ends with a surprising twist: Zeus, the father of all gods, moves the cities to a distant planet called Plato sometime in the twenty-sixth century.

The third book of the trilogy, *Necessity*, takes place mostly on Plato, which orbits a distant sun. Apollo, who has lived as the human Pytheas and has married and spawned two generations, dies in the first part of the book. After his death, he quickly resumes his mantle as a god. The next generations have adapted to the unforgiving and arid climate of Plato as well as they can, and they have welcomed a species of humanoid aliens called the Saeli. There are also sentient robots called Workers, originally supplied by Athene when she first established the original city, who perform chores and interact with humans and Saeli as equals. One of the main characters in *Necessity* is Crocus, the first Worker to achieve consciousness; since his introduction in *The Just City*, Crocus has become a philosopher and a poet.

Two problems are presented early on in the book: a human spaceship from Earth has made contact with Plato and asked for permission to land, and Athene has disappeared outside the bounds of space and time. In this universe, the gods can move through space and time at will and can locate one another within that continuum, but Athene's disappearance is different; she appears to have traveled outside of the continuum, to a place known as the Chaos. To find her, Apollo and a host of other characters, including his granddaughter Marsilia, must find and solve a complicated string of riddles that Athene has planted throughout history.

Walton, as is evident from her fusion of Greek philosophy with futuristic adventure, is a singular voice in the science fiction and fantasy genres. Although her first novel, *The King's Peace* (2000), and its two sequels were set in a more traditional fantasy world of kings, magic, and war, her fourth book established her as a writer with an unusual and exciting perspective. *Tooth and Claw* (2003) is a gripping tale of political intrigue and romance inspired by the Chronicles of Barsetshire, a six-novel series by Victorian writer Anthony Trollope, with one major departure: all of the characters in Walton's novel are dragons. Her next novel, *Farthing* (2006), and its sequels, *Ha'penny* (2007) and *Half a Crown* (2008), present an alternative history in which Great Britain made peace with Adolf Hitler and withdrew from World War II; *Farthing* begins the story in 1949, and the next two books follow Britain's subsequent transformation into a fascist dictatorship. *Among Others* (2011), one of Walton's most celebrated novels, is a tale of magic and fairies that draws on Walton's own history growing up in Wales.

Walton wrote the Thessaly series because she wanted to continue the conversation Plato had started in *The Republic*. In his celebrated work, Plato, speaking through his mentor Socrates, aims to determine the nature of a just person and the nature of a just city. *The Republic*, however, is rife with contradictory arguments. In an essay for the Tor.com eBook Club, published on the website on August 22, 2016, Walton wrote, "[Plato]'s so great on some things, and so wrong on others, so crazy, and simultaneously so thoughtful, that I can get a lot of power out of these kinds of contradictions." Plato and Socrates learned about the world by asking questions. Walton is adamant that the city in *Necessity* is neither a utopia nor a dystopia, but a physical Socratic dialogue; in her essay, she continued, "[Plato] wanted people to examine the societies they lived in, and consider if the way they lived really was the best way, the good life, the thing that made people the best people they could be." The civilization living on the planet Plato continues doing this, although, as third-generation inhabitants, they take a lot of things for granted—the equality between women and men, for instance. Although remnants of sexism remain, as evidenced by the way many men treat the beautiful Thetis, men and women are represented equally in the city's government. Marsilia, for example, is a member of the ruling council. She is also part of the group responsible for deciding what to do when a ship arrives from Earth.

The spaceship, while not the book's focus, also raises important questions. The narrative suggests that humans from Earth are looking to exploit Plato's resources, or at least profit from them. The team in charge of communicating with the ship is perplexed by the Earth humans' use of the word "profit," and Crocus, the leader of the team, struggles to explain its meaning. Although people from Earth also have robots, they treat them as non-sentient beings. The team is appalled by the way they treat their

Jo Walton is an award-winning science fiction and fantasy writer. Her previous novels include Tooth and Claw *(2003),* Among Others *(2011), and* My Real Children *(2014).* Necessity *is her thirteenth novel.*

Workers and makes clear to the Earth natives that Workers are treated equally on Plato and that slavery is outlawed on their planet.

As the book progresses, more abstract questions present themselves. In the novel, the gods are bound by Necessity—a physical force that compels them to take particular actions to influence the universe's timeline. As Socrates (here spelled Sokrates) observes to Apollo at one point, "You said once that Fate is the line drawn around what we can do, and Necessity prevents us overstepping that line, but within the lines we are free to do what we want." For the gods, the pull of Necessity is powerful and often painful. A Saeli trickster god who plays an important role in the plot explains that Necessity is like walking with a pebble in one's shoe, only the pebble gets bigger and more painful if it is not addressed. Discussions about the concept of Necessity touch on freedom, choice, morality, need, and fate. These, however, are complicated and subjective ideas, and readers are likely to question not only the characters' definitions of them but their own views as well—which very well may have been Walton's intention.

The principal characters in *Necessity* include Apollo, Marsilia, and a fisherman named Jason. Jason has no real agency in solving the central problem of the book—Athene's disappearance—but he serves as a good surrogate for the reader, being just as awed and baffled by the gods as readers would be in the same situation and having no working knowledge of godly time travel. His arc, however, is far less exciting than the arcs of the other characters, because he spends the duration of the book sitting at a table in the Original City, watching gods flit in and out of the room. Herein lies one of the novel's biggest weaknesses: in an effort to tie up story lines begun in *The Just City* and *The Philosopher Kings*, the characters spend a lot of time sitting and talking. Their philosophical conversations are interesting, especially after Sokrates shows up, but the reminiscences slow the story down. Furthermore, many pages are devoted to the various paradoxes implicit in the gods' method of time travel. In Walton's defense, she does a good job trying to explain them, but the resulting passages feel odd and uncharacteristically awkward next to the author's fleeter and more familiar prose.

In the end, it is difficult to say if readers of *The Just City* and *The Philosopher Kings* will find *Necessity* to be a satisfying conclusion to the Thessaly trilogy. It is clear, however, that the wild and seemingly random deviations of plot and genre throughout the series are calculated parts of Walton's vision. In a review for Tor.com, classical historian Liz Bourke noted that *Necessity* is clearly influenced by Plato's *Timaeus*, a dense Socratic dialogue about the origin of the universe, which she described as "Plato's least accessible work, and one of his most theoretical." Bourke concluded her review with a warning and a qualified recommendation: "*Necessity*, like its predecessors, won't be for everyone. Its structure is less tightly focussed . . . though its characters and voice are equally charming. But if you enjoyed *The Just City* and *The Philosopher Kings*, then you'll almost certainly enjoy *Necessity* too." *Necessity* is an adventure story, and it is fun to read, but some elements seem out of place, part of a larger dialogue with a source material that might not be known to many readers.

Molly Hagan

Review Sources

Bourke, Liz. "'No, Sokrates, We Have Certainly Been Paying Attention': Jo Walton's *Necessity*." Review of *Necessity*, by Jo Walton. *Tor.com*, 12 July 2016, www.tor.com/2016/07/12/book-reviews-jo-walton-necessity/. Accessed 9 Feb. 2017.

Boyce, Joel. "Walton's Platonic Sci-Fi Trilogy Terrific." Review of *Necessity*, by Jo Walton. *Winnipeg Free Press*, 29 Oct. 2016, www.winnipegfreepress.com/arts-and-life/entertainment/books/waltons-platonic-sci-fi-trilogy-terrific-399131931.html. Accessed 9 Feb. 2017.

Review of *Necessity*, by Jo Walton. *Kirkus Reviews*, 1 June 2016, p. 52.

Review of *Necessity*, by Jo Walton. *Publishers Weekly*, 6 June 2016, p. 67.

The Nest

Author: Cynthia D'Aprix Sweeney
Publisher: Ecco (New York). 368 pp.
Type of work: Novel
Time: Present
Locale: New York City

(Courtesy of HarperCollins Publishers)

Cynthia D'Aprix Sweeney's first novel The Nest *is a dark comedy about a privileged, dysfunctional New York family fighting for their inheritance.*

Principal characters:

LEO PLUMB, the eldest Plumb sibling, a charming addict who is going through a messy divorce

BEATRICE PLUMB, a formerly successful fiction writer

JACK PLUMB, an antiques dealer in the midst of a financial crisis

MELODY PLUMB, the youngest sibling whose fortieth birthday marks the date that the Plumb children are entitled to receive their inheritance

STEPHANIE, Beatrice's literary agent and Leo's ex-girlfriend

MATILDA RODRIGUEZ, a young waitress and aspiring singer whose life is destroyed by Leo

Most reviews of Cynthia D'Aprix Sweeney's debut novel *The Nest* (2016) are quick to acknowledge the timeliness of its story. Published in an era when baby boomers are retiring and passing their legacies onto their children, the novel focuses on the complex issue of inheritance. Experts anticipate that over the next few decades, trillions of dollars will be passed from one generation to the next. *The Nest* examines this phenomenon and the many challenges it brings to families through the story of the Plumbs. Four middle-aged siblings based in New York City, the Plumbs have been estranged for years. However, when they learn that their oldest brother's scandalous behavior has drained what was intended to be a shared inheritance or trust fund, nicknamed "the nest," they are forced back into one another's lives.

The Nest is a story about the multifaceted nature of family, a theme that is especially evident in Sweeney's depiction of the Plumbs as individuals. In addition to providing each of the four siblings with a story line of equal importance, Sweeney also ensures that every family member brings a completely different perspective to the family conflict at hand, the state of their inheritance, through strong character development. Leo, the oldest Plumb sibling, initially provides an apathetic perspective on the matter, which is partially a result of the fact that his recklessness is what has destroyed "the nest." A handsome lothario, Leo's problems with substance abuse and womanizing cause a young waitress named Matilda Rodriguez to lose an appendage in a car accident. Leo is then forced to ask his mother to use the shared inheritance to pay Matilda off. Meanwhile, his sister Beatrice, a formerly successful fiction writer, is the optimist of the family who believes that Leo has the ability to make things right.

Contrary to Leo and Beatrice, the youngest Plumb siblings view the loss of "the nest" as a travesty. Sweeney presents the youngest brother, Jack, a gay man who owns a failing antiques store, as the living embodiment of the Plumbs' resentment toward one another. Early in the novel, it is revealed that Jack's ill will toward his family runs so deep that he did not invite any of them to his wedding. Leo's accident has exacerbated the duress of Jack's precarious finances and familial umbrage. Similarly, Melody, the youngest Plumb sibling whose imminent fortieth birthday once marked the date all four siblings were supposed to receive their share of "the nest," has had her life plans ruined by Leo. Unlike her siblings,

Cynthia D'Aprix Sweeney is a former copywriter. The Nest (2016) is her debut novel.

Melody is a more timid soul whose main concern is taking care of her teenage twin daughters and husband. Without her share of the inheritance, Melody is unable to pay her mortgage and daughters' college tuition.

The adage of not counting one's chickens before they hatch provides the narrative of *The Nest* with a thematic spine. Ultimately, Leo's desperate misuse of "the nest" becomes the inciting incident for the rest of the characters' story lines simply because they have built their entire lives around the anticipation of a significant influx of cash. Once they learn that they will not be receiving the money that they long believed would be the solution to all of their problems, the Plumbs are forced to readdress the current state of their lives from a new lens. For most of them, this is a challenging process that requires the admission of mistakes and personal shortcomings. With great skill and humor, Sweeney successfully captures how difficult and even painful introspection can be.

In addition to forcing the Plumbs to acknowledge their life choices head on, the loss of "the nest" ultimately galvanizes each of the characters to take action. For the first time in years, Leo is forced to start working again. Once a successful businessman, he pledges to his siblings that he will develop a plan to return their inheritance to them within three months. Similarly, the conflict inspires Beatrice to start writing fiction again. Not all of the Plumbs' actions are positive, however. Now under serious financial pressure, Melody has no choice but to sell her family's house. Jack, who is also in serious need of money, starts engaging in desperate and deceptive behavior. When he meets a firefighter who kept a priceless Auguste Rodin sculpture that he found in the rubble of the World Trade Center, Jack tries to manipulate the man into selling it to him for significantly less than it is worth. As Jack and Leo's selfishness often demonstrates, Sweeney is more concerned with her characters' humanness than their likeability. By focusing on the Plumbs' flaws and interpersonal struggles, she succeeds in this effort.

Although *The Nest* is about a privileged group of people, it effectively maintains an undercurrent of universality. Ostensibly, the novel is a story about upper-middle-class white siblings who are confronted with the elitist problem of a trust fund. However, underpinning this conflict is a multitude of arguably ubiquitous family issues. For example, the contention among the Plumbs surrounding their lost inheritance is exacerbated by the fact that they have become estranged over the years and subsequently are resentful toward one another. Like the Plumbs, many siblings grow apart during adulthood as a result of geography or the people they marry. While the problem of a lost inheritance is one that only the wealthy might have, the underlying issue of familial money trouble is highly relatable. As the plot of *The Nest* demonstrates, Sweeney has a deep understanding of how quick many people are to fight with their families over the issue of money.

Sweeney is a character-driven writer. Although the novel's numerous story lines are well paced and include a number of effective twists and turns, ultimately Sweeney prioritizes character development over plot. This observation is evident in what is arguably one of the most unique stylistic features of *The Nest*: Sweeney's decision to explore the feelings and motivations of all of the novel's secondary and tertiary characters. Despite the fact that she writes from a third-person, omniscient point of view, she often delves into her characters' inner thoughts in a manner that feels as intimate as a first-person narration. For example, in an early scene when Francie, the Plumbs' mother, explains to her children what has happened to "the nest," Sweeney engages in a multipage detour of how Francie actually feels about her children. In comical prose written in a stream-of-consciousness style, Francie reflects on how Jack has always tried to sell her overvalued antiques, causing her to wonder if he is senseless or just thinks that she is. Sweeney examines the perspective of all of her characters in a similar fashion—from Melody's twin daughters, to the firefighter who Jack is trying to rip off, to the Plumbs' dead father, Leonard Plumb Senior. By providing readers with the inner thoughts of all of the novel's wide cast of characters, Sweeney not only prevents its narrative from becoming too myopic but also demonstrates how the loss of "the nest" has direct and indirect consequences on people outside of the Plumb siblings.

Critical reception of *The Nest* has been mixed. Writing for the *New York Times*, Janet Maslin argued that the primary flaw of the novel was that it was unable to break out of the tropes of dysfunctional family literature. Additionally, Maslin's review claimed that the novel had too many "sugary" plot twists and not enough compelling stakes for the characters. She concluded by writing, "In the idiom of the genre, nothing's gotta give." It is true that, in many ways, *The Nest* comes across as a familiar rather than groundbreaking story. Sweeney's literary style, while effective, does not take any risks. Furthermore, the narrative's central conflict of estranged siblings being forced back together over a family issue feels derivative of Jonathan Tropper's *This Is Where I Leave You* (2009) and Jonathan Franzen's *The Corrections* (2001). Despite its predictable elements, however, what arguably makes *The Nest* a unique story is the lens through which Sweeney examines it. Unlike Tropper, Sweeney is unafraid to use acerbic humor to skewer her characters' outrageous, unchecked privilege.

The satire present throughout *The Nest* has been a common point of praise among critics. In her review of the novel, book critic Leah Greenblatt reported for *Entertainment Weekly* that Sweeney's writing "is like really good dark chocolate: sharper and more bittersweet than the cheap stuff, but also too delicious not to finish in one sitting." Similar to Greenblatt's argument, it can be concluded that although *The Nest* is not a revolutionary piece of literature, it is immensely entertaining. Sweeney is a sharply proficient storyteller with a particular talent for developing fascinating, nuanced characters. As Amy Weiss-Meyer wrote in her review for the *Atlantic*, "The Plumbs are ridiculous, and it's fun to pass judgment and worry on their behalf." It is the novel's sizeable and often despicable cast, which comprises roles ideal for an ensemble comedy blockbuster, that originally earned *The Nest* significant prepublication buzz and a bidding war that ended in Sweeney receiving a seven-figure advance from Ecco. While the novel may not live up to the publishing industry's initial expectations, ultimately it succeeds as an engaging examination of families, money, and the humorous tensions that can arise when the two are mixed.

Emily Turner

Review Sources

Charles, Ron. "*The Nest* Review: What Happens When That Nest Egg Cracks?" Review of *The Nest*, by Cynthia D'Aprix Sweeney. *Washington Post*, 14 Mar. 2016, www.washingtonpost.com/entertainment/books/the-nest-review-what-happens-when-that-nest-egg-cracks/2016/03/14/30cf270e-e571-11e5-a6f3-21ccdbc5f74e_story.html. Accessed 10 Nov. 2016.

Greenblatt, Leah. Review of *The Nest*, by Cynthia D'Aprix Sweeney. *Entertainment Weekly*, 17 Mar. 2016, www.ew.com/article/2016/03/17/the-nest-cynthia-daprix-sweeney-review. Accessed 10 Nov. 2016.

Maslin, Janet. "In The Nest, a Family Pot to Split Sets Sibling Relations to a Slow Boil." Review of The Nest, by Cynthia D'Aprix Sweeney. *The New York Times*, 27 Mar. 2016, www.nytimes.com/2016/03/28/books/review-in-the-nest-a-family-pot-to-split-sets-sibling-relations-to-a-slow-boil.html. Accessed 10 Nov. 2016.

Weiss-Meyer, Amy. "*The Nest*: A Tale of Family, Fortune, and Dysfunction." Review of *The Nest*, by Cynthia D'Aprix Sweeney. *The Atlantic*, 31 Mar. 2016, www.theatlantic.com/entertainment/archive/2016/03/the-nest-cynthia-daprix-sweeney-review/476115/. Accessed 10 Nov. 2016.

Night of the Animals

Author: Bill Broun (b. ca. 1966)
Publisher: Ecco (New York). 560 pp.
Type of work: Novel
Time: 2052
Locale: London, England

Night of the Animals *imagines a near-future dystopia where technology is used to control people and the natural world is on the verge of extinction. It is American author Bill Broun's first novel.*

Principal characters:
CUTHBERT "CUDDY" HANDLEY, a ninety-year-old homeless man with mental illness who is on a mission to protect the last remaining animals on Earth
SARBJINDER SINGH BAJWA, his physician and the only person who genuinely cares about his well-being
DRYSTAN HANDLEY, his older brother who allegedly died when they were children
MUEZZA, an Islamic sand cat living in the London Zoo
HENRY IX, a.k.a. Harry9, the monarch who rules the United Kingdom with an iron fist

(Courtesy of HarperCollins Publishers)

In reviews, American author Bill Broun's debut novel *Night of the Animals* (2016) is often described as a reimagining of the story of Noah's ark. As there are many similarities between the two stories, the comparison is warranted. Both stories have protagonists facing apocalyptic scenarios in which they must save the world's animals from extinction. Where Noah has to save the animals from a great flood, Cuthbert Handley, the protagonist of *Night of the Animals*, must protect what few creatures still exist on Earth from a violent cult. Noah is compelled to act by the voice of God; Cuthbert is motivated by the voice of animals that he believes can speak to him. The most important parallel shared by the two stories, however, is the underlying message about the relationship between people and animals. The story of Noah's ark and *Night of the Animals* both demonstrate that humans are the stewards of the natural world and that the fate of Earth depends on them taking this responsibility seriously.

One of the most prominent themes of *Night of the Animals* is that technology has the potential to destroy nature. The science-fiction novel imagines a near-future dystopian England in which King Henry IX, known as Harry9, wields oppressive power through "WikiNous," an Internet that is transmitted across human flesh. With their corneas serving as "screens," British citizens are subjected to a constant barrage of alerts, government propaganda presented as news, and spam, which only the wealthy can pay to remove from their WikiNous feed. In addition to the nation devolving into a tyrannical surveillance state, England's class divide has also become extreme. Broun's depiction of London in the near future is comparable to Charles Dickens's Victorian England. Under Harry9's reign, the lower class is so poor that they are willing to trade their right to vote for jobs on government-run soybean farms because they provide food, housing, and access to "Nexar hoods," personality-killing devices that tranquilize users. There are a number of technologies and innovations such as Nexar hoods throughout the novel, and while they demonstrate Broun's vivid imagination, they also provide commentary on contemporary society. Technology, Broun seems to suggest, is stripping people of their agency.

The feeling of a looming "judgment day," or the end of the world, is omnipresent throughout *Night of the Animals*. In addition to the oppressed, impoverished life that most British citizens endure in the year 2052, Earth has been bulldozed, deforested, and "poisoned." A comet called Urga-Rampos hangs ominously in the sky and the few animals that still exist are being systematically killed off by Heaven's Gate, an American suicide cult on a mission to extinguish all living creatures before ending their own lives. Consequently, *Night of the Animals* often has a dark, twisted feeling. This sense of darkness is furthered by its strange imagery, which consists of a blend of majestic living creatures with cold, synthetic hardware. In many ways, the London Zoo, where the world's last remaining animals are kept, is symbolic of the state of Broun's futuristic world: what little hope is left for Earth is trapped behind manmade steel bars.

What saves *Night of the Animals* from becoming overwhelmingly dire is its protagonist, Cuthbert. In the context of mainstream literature, Cuthbert is an unlikely leading man. In addition to being ninety years old, homeless, obese, and addicted to a hallucinatory drug called Flōt, Cuthbert also believes that he has "the Wonderments," the magical ability to speak to and understand animals. His mission to free the inhabitants of the London Zoo is motivated both by his desire to protect them from Heaven's Gate and because they have promised to reunite him with his brother Drystan, who drowned back in 1968. Despite his seeming inability to grasp reality, Cuthbert provides the narrative with a feeling of childlike hope. While there are countless obstacles, including his mental health, that stand between him and his goal of freeing the animals from the zoo, Cuthbert never stops trying. Ultimately, Broun portrays Cuthbert as the kind of human hero that the natural world needs in order to survive. He is brave, devoted, and willing to stand up against evil forces. His heroism is even suggested in his name: Saint Cuthbert was the seventh-century Anglo-Saxon holy man known for being a protector of animals.

Bill Broun is a former journalist and copy editor originally from Los Angeles, California. A professor at East Stroudsburg University in Pennsylvania, Broun has a master's degree in creative writing from the University of Houston. Night of the Animals *is his first novel.*

What arguably makes *Night of the Animals* so enjoyable is how richly detailed and original it is. These qualities are especially evident in the characters' dialogue. In Broun's dystopia, people speak a dialect of English that blends old slang from industrial cities across Britain and Guyana with speculative, futuristic words and phrases.

The subsequent language is colorful and engaging. Broun's depiction of politics in 2052 is similarly nuanced. In his imagining of the country's future, England leaves the European Union and is ruled by Harry9, who breaks the electoral system to give the monarchy more power. The country becomes a police state in which the rich are kept away from the "indigents," a name given to the poor. Meanwhile, England's welfare system and the middle class are disappearing due to legislation such as the Positive Disenfranchisement Act of 2028. Broun's attention to detail provides insight into how important he believes these parts of the story are. In interviews, Broun, who was raised by a British father, has stated that *Night of the Animals* is demonstrative of his painful love affair with England. Furthermore, it is intended to make a case for the abolishment of vestigial monarchy as kings and queens will always be threats to democracy.

Despite the high stakes of its plot, *Night of the Animals* is largely character driven. As a writer, Broun excels at developing unique, compelling characters. For example, Cuthbert's general practitioner, Dr. Bajwa, provides a sliver of humanity to a narrative that operates in a seemingly hopeless world. While their appointments start out as state mandated, they begin meeting more frequently once Dr. Bajwa grows to care about Cuthbert. In these meetings, he tries to protect Cuthbert from the neuralpike-wielding police by deterring him from breaking into the London Zoo. However, his efforts are in vain. The majority of the novel takes place when Cuthbert is inside the zoo, and it is here that he, believing that he has the ability to talk to animals, encounters some of the most intriguing characters. As he frees each animal one by one using a pair of bolt cutters, they bestow their wisdom upon him. A gorilla named Kibali informs him that while humans are not their foes, their cruelty proves that they are less decent than animals. Later, Muezza, a Muslim sand cat, provides Cuthbert with spiritual guidance, telling him that anyone who is kind to the creatures of God is also kind to God. It is a simple yet powerful sentiment that proves to be the cautionary message of *Night of the Animals*.

Critical reception of *Night of the Animals* has been mixed. A common gripe among less favorable reviews has been the novel's length. As *Night of the Animals* comprises more than five hundred dense pages of story and Broun's meticulous prose unfurls at a slow pace, it is easy to understand how many readers' engagement could wane over time. However, while Broun's unhurried, specific style of storytelling may not be universally appealing, it is still undeniably skillful and provides a worthwhile payoff in the final act. The ambiguity surrounding the narrative of *Night of the Animals* is another element that has been criticized. The novel shifts back and forth in style and tone from what can be described as a dystopian satire to a psychological thriller. Additionally, it is often unclear whether the extreme events are actually happening or are Cuthbert's hallucinations. Despite this potentially frustrating quality, many critics have praised the novel's nebulousness. In her review for *Vox*, Constance Grady wrote that much of the *Night of the Animals* is "not clear, but the richness of the ambiguity just adds to the book's sense of sweeping melancholy."

Even with its shortcomings, *Night of the Animals* is an exceptional work of speculative fiction. Broun's fantasy-world building and the manner in which he blends different international cultures, religions, and historical events with fantasy have been extolled repeatedly by many critics. *Kirkus Reviews* called *Night of the Animals* "richly imagined," while praising its ability to fuse ancient lore with contemporary technology. The *Publishers Weekly* review called Broun's debut novel "witty" and "engrossing," claiming that "through precise and eloquent prose and a hint of political satire, Broun creates a near future filled with bioelectric technology and characters with patois as diverse as their desires." Ultimately, the imagination and creativity of Broun's characters, setting, plot, and language are comparable to J. K. Rowling's Harry Potter series. Fans of the science-fiction and fantasy literary genres are likely to enjoy *Night of the Animals*.

The novel's timeliness has also been a common highlight among critics. By coincidence, *Night of the Animals* was published within weeks of Brexit, the 2016 referendum during which a small majority of Britons voted for the United Kingdom to leave the European Union. As a result, many people, including Broun, have called the novel eerily prescient. *Night of the Animals*'s seemingly prophetic insight into the rocky state of the United Kingdom provides its narrative with urgency and codifies Cuthbert as a true hero. While many works of fiction attempt to explicate contemporary cultural trends and politics, few succeed. *Night of the Animals* is different. In interviews, Broun has said that the novel took him fourteen years to write. For many readers, the thoroughness of his political, technological, and social analyses will satisfyingly demonstrate this fact. With well-crafted characters, a strong message, and an imagining of a wholly original, near-future dystopia that seamlessly blends ancient lore and technology with fantasy, *Night of the Animals* is an important new addition to the speculative fiction genre.

Emily Turner

Review Sources

Grady, Constance. "*Night of the Animals* Is a Stunning Postmodern Rendition of Noah's Ark." Review of *Night of the Animals*, by Bill Broun. *Vox*, 19 Aug. 2016, www.vox.com/2016/8/19/12457894/night-of-the-animals-bill-broun-review. Accessed 3 Jan. 2017.

Hightower, Nancy. "*Night of the Animals* and Other Best Science Fiction Books This Month." Review of *Night of the Animals*, by Bill Broun, et al. *Washington Post*, 19 July 2016, www.washingtonpost.com/entertainment/books/night-of-the-animals-and-other-best-science-fiction-books-this-month/2016/07/19/52648dec-4 9f2-11e6-bdb9-701687974517_story.html. Accessed 3 Jan. 2017.

Memmott, Carol. "*Night of the Animals*: A Novel to Stoke Post-Brexit Anxiety." Review of *Night of the Animals*, by Bill Broun. *Chicago Tribune*, 13 July 2016, www.chicagotribune.com/lifestyles/books/ct-prj-night-of-the-animals-bill-broun-20160713-story.html. Accessed 3 Jan. 2017.

Review of *Night of the Animals*, by Bill Broun. *Kirkus*, 13 Apr. 2016, www.kirkusreviews.com/book-reviews/bill-broun/night-of-the-animals/. Accessed 3 Jan. 2017.

Review of *Night of the Animals*, by Bill Broun. *Publishers Weekly*, 23 May 2016, www.publishersweekly.com/978-0-06-240079-6. Accessed 3 Jan. 2017.

Russell, Anna. "In Bill Broun's *Night of the Animals*, a Post-Brexit Dystopia." Review of *Night of the Animals*, by Bill Broun. *Wall Street Journal*, 7 July 2016, www.wsj.com/articles/in-bill-brouns-night-of-the-animals-a-post-brexit-dystopia-1467905323. Accessed 3 Jan. 2017.

Ninety-Nine Stories of God

Author: Joy Williams (b. 1944)
First published: *99 Stories of God*, 2013, in the United States
Publisher: Tin House Books (Portland, OR). 168 pp.
Type of work: Short stories

Joy Williams's Ninety-Nine Stories of God is a compendium of brief stories, annotations, observations, and anecdotes, many of which feature God as a central character interacting with animals and humans.

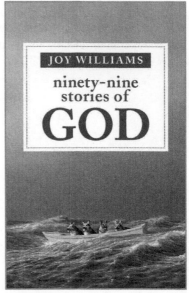

(Courtesy of Tin House Books)

Since her first collection, *Taking Care*, was published in 1982, Joy Williams's short stories have always taken some getting used to. Without a clear plot, likeable characters, or an easily graspable themes, her stories have been described as "quirky." In an essay on her most recent collections for the August 22, 2016, issue of the *New Yorker*, James Wood wrote, "Her fiction is easy to follow and hard to fathom; easy to enjoy and harder to absorb." This seems especially true for this new collection of "pithy" mysteries, called "micro fiction," "flash fiction," aphorisms, and conundrums by reviewers trying to make sense of them.

Ninety-Nine Stories of God was originally published, with very little attention, as an e-book in 2013. Now that Tin House Books has published it, reviewers have taken a new look. In a review for the *New York Times*, Justin Taylor wrote that "all Williams's work is informed by a learned yet half-feral Christianity" that aligns her with "desert mystics" and described the pieces in the collection as "wry and playful, except for when densely allusive and willfully obtuse." Although Joy Williams is not widely known, she has been called a "writer's writer" enough times in the past to have this work praised as a collection of conundrums worthy of Franz Kafka. However, the ninety-nine pieces in this book vary in their level of complexity. Although some are indeed like Zen koans that evoke a complex response, many are merely bits and pieces of data that at some point caught Williams's attention. The pieces are headed simply by their number, but are followed by an "after-title." Sometimes, it is the after-title that makes the story, as in story 84, when a poet says, "We all have one foot in the grave," to which a pretty girl says she should probably get a pedicure every week then. People wonder later who first noticed the swelling on her instep. Although this takes place in summer, when "the grass [i]s green as jade and freshly cut," the ominous after-title of the piece is "Winter."

Although in some way, depending on one's theology, all stories could be called stories of God, in Joy Williams's book, the stories' relationships to God begin somewhat tangentially and then gather momentum until, as the book moves toward its end, God plays a more predominant role, often becoming the central character. There are interconnections between some pieces, as when one story segues into another on the same or similar subject. For example, story 6, "See That You Remember"—a three-line piece about Leo Tolstoy's dream of being suspended between an abyss below and an abyss above, which the Lord says he gave to him—is followed by a story 7, "Not His Best," about Kafka's dream of jumping out a window at fifteen-minute intervals and being run over by a train. The Lord says he did not give this dream to him.

The opening story, "Postcard," introduces the reader to the mysteries of longing, loneliness, and death. A woman who deeply misses her dead mother comes across some postcards in an old antique store. When she sends a card to her mother, she gets a reply letter in her mother's handwriting. She does not open the letter but puts it in a drawer. As Joy Williams would say, some mysteries are better left as mysteries.

The second story, "Noche," is a segue to another spooky mystery, making a little joke at Williams's own expense. Known for always wearing prescription sunglasses, Williams writes about a woman who always wears sunglasses, so her dog has never seen her eyes. Whenever she invites people over, she sets out a bowl of sunglasses, for, she says, it is easier to do this than to lock the dog in the bedroom. She muses that the dog being from a kennel in Jerome, Arizona, an old ghost town, has something to do with this.

The book's central thematic statement lies in the very middle piece—number 49—which asserts: "We must push our minds to the limits of what we could know, descending ever deeper into the darkness of unknowing." This has always been Williams's mantra. She once wrote in "Why I Write," an essay in her collection *Ill Nature* (2001), "A writer loves the dark, loves it, but is always fumbling around in the light."

Some pieces reflect Williams's well-known reverence for animals. In story 5, "Nevertheless," a four-line piece, she notes that after Kafka became a vegetarian, he could go into an aquarium and look at the fish in peace because he did not eat them anymore. In story 29, "Ignorance," the narrator tells of being taken to a slaughterhouse as a child and of a newspaper article about a pig who saved a man from drowning. When the reporter asks the pig's owner if the animal would have rescued the man had she had known he and his companions had just enjoyed a picnic of ham sandwiches, the owner replies that although pigs are more intelligent than dogs, they are not omniscient. Perhaps the most thought-provoking animal story is story 93, entitled "Fathers and Sons," which has the Lord in a den with a pack of wolves, asking them why they are hounded so, for they are so intelligent. The wolves say that sentiment is very much against them, but they thank the Lord for inviting them to participate in his plan anyway.

Some pieces are simple human anecdotes. In story 9, "Clean," a child is killed in a drive-by shooting, and the family has a car wash to pay for funeral expenses; people come in their nice clean waxed cars that do not need washing. Then, in story 11, "Arrangement," there is the poignancy of an immigrant from El Salvador killing her three-year-old daughter; court records indicate that the woman may have used a rose

(Courtesy of Anne Dalton)

Joy Williams is best known for her frequently anthologized short stories but has also written several novels and nonfiction works. Her essay collection Ill Nature *(2001) was a finalist for the 2001 National Book Critics Circle Award for criticism, and her novel* The Quick and the Dead *(2000) was a finalist for the 2001 Pulitzer Prize for Fiction. She has won a Guggenheim fellowship, the Harold and Mildred Strauss Living Award from the American Academy of Arts & Letters, and the 1999 Rea Award for the Short Story.*

to suffocate the child—a horror that elicits complex emotions about mercy and motivation.

Some of the pieces focus on the Lord challenging human indifference to the world. In story 10, "Wet," when God drinks water from a glass and complains of its terrible taste, he asks the people what they have done to his "living water." The human reply is, "We thought that was just a metaphor." In Williams's world, metaphors are real, and the "as if" is as important as the thing itself.

Some of the pieces are narrative conundrums. In story 32, "Shaken," a female student of literature who loves the life of the mind is so shocked at a "long, glistening coil of blond excrement" she produced in the woods, she gives up intellectual life and lives the rest of her life in seclusion. The next story, "Irreducible," features another person who suddenly deserts the intellectual life, a prize-winning author who, while giving a lecture on the irrelevancy of the representative element in works of art, is suddenly seized by such "stupefying boredom" that he leaves the stage.

Some are reactions to well-known public events. A piece on the O. J. Simpson trial notes that the blood found near the victims could have come only from one person in 170 million—O. J. Simpson—and that the blood found on a sock in Simpson's bedroom was consistent with only one person out of 6.8 billion—that of Nicole Brown Simpson. This straightforward reporting of facts is followed by this postscript: "Courtroom analysts conclude that most jurors find DNA analysis 'boring.'"

Some are parables. In story 19, a great-grandfather tells a boy about a traveler meeting three men pushing wheelbarrows. When asked what work they are doing, one man says he toils from sunrise to sunset for a few francs, another says he is happy for he has not had work for months and has a family to feed. The third says he is building Chartres Cathedral. But the boy hearing the story has no idea what a "chartres cathedral" is. The amused after-title is: "Perhaps a Kind of Cake?"

Some are shocking extremes that communicate a sense of justice. In story 16, when two women are talking about the death by drowning of a young girl, one of the women, a vicious gossiper, says the child's father's brother also drowned, but he was sort of a "bad apple." When she stoops to pick some flowers called pearly everlastings, the other woman grabs a stone and hits her in the head with it, making "a sharp, even satisfying crack." The story ends with the line, "There were two funerals but only one trial." The after-title is "If Picked or Uprooted These Beautiful Flowers Will Disappear."

When the Lord appears as a character, it is usually to record his puzzlement or disappointment at the behavior of humans. In story 55, "Neglect," when the Lord is asked if he believes in reincarnation, he says he does, for it explains so much, adding he once saw a hot-dog-eating contest, which he calls the stupidest thing he has ever witnessed. In story 60, "Party," when the Lord is invited to a gala party in which caviar, which has cost the lives of thousands of female wild salmon, is served, he does not show up.

In one piece, a nun who has visions during epileptic seizures has surgery that cures her. But she discovers that life without epilepsy is dull, as though she had tumbled from a sacred mountain into a ruined village. A piece on the physical nature of dew and its metaphysical effects ends simply with the observation that dew has long been a subject of interest.

Story 79, "Example," arguably the most poignant in the book, seems to be about Williams's own experience after the death of her husband, *Esquire* fiction editor and author Rust Hills. It is an anecdote about a famous writer inviting another writer, whose husband died unexpectedly only two days earlier, to be a house guest. When the widowed writer wants her dog to stay in the guest house with her, the owner reluctantly agrees. The widow lies in the guest house with her dog and wishes she requested her husband's belt before he was cremated, for he had worn it every day for years and often put some leather preservative on it. The last line is simply: "Oh God, she thought."

At the end of an interview with Paul Winner for the *Paris Review*, published in the magazine's summer 2014 issue, Williams said, "I'm going to do one more story about God. He's really going to confide in me. Then I'm done."

Charles E. May, PhD

Review Sources

Matthews, Ramsey. "What If the Lord Came to Dinner Uninvited?" Review of
    Ninety-Nine Stories of God, by Joy Williams. *Los Angeles Review of Books*, 28
    July 2016, lareviewofbooks.org/article/what-if-the-lord-came-to-dinner-uninvited/. Accessed 17 Jan. 2017.
Review of *Ninety-Nine Stories of God*, by Joy Williams. *Kirkus Reviews*, 1 May
    2016, p. 39.
Review of *Ninety-Nine Stories of God*, by Joy Williams. *Publishers Weekly*, 8 Feb.
    2016, www.publishersweekly.com/978-1-941040-35-5. Accessed 17 Jan. 2017.
Taylor, Justin. "Joy Williams's Micro-Fictions Are a Trove of God's Bafflements."
    Review of Ninety-Nine Stories of God, by Joy Williams. *The New York Times*,
    5 Aug. 2016, www.nytimes.com/2016/08/07/books/review/joy-williams-ninety-nine-stories-of-god.html. Accessed 17 Jan. 2017.

The Nix

Author: Nathan Hill (b. 1976)
Publisher: Alfred A. Knopf (New York).
640 pp.
Type of work: Novel
Time: 1968–2011
Locale: Chicago

The Nix *is a tragicomedy about the relationship between a mother and son. It is the debut novel of American author Nathan Hill.*

Principal characters:
SAMUEL ANDRESEN-ANDERSON, an English
professor who decides to write a tell-all
book about his mother, Faye
FAYE ANDRESEN-ANDERSON, his mother who
abandoned him as a child; a political
activist known as the "Packer Attacker"
BETHANY, the love of his life; a violinist prodigy
BISHOP, Bethany's twin brother
LAURA POTTSDAM, Samuel's nemesis, a student (whom he catches cheating) in the
English literature class he teaches
PWNAGE, a gamer obsessed with the online game World of Elfscape

"Hugely entertaining."—*The New York Times Book Review*

THE NIX

Nathan Hill A novel

NEW YORK TIMES BEST SELLER

(Courtesy of Knopf)

According to Norwegian mythology, a nix is an evil spirit that likes to take the form
of beautiful and enticing creatures. Children are easily fooled by the nix, which often
appears to them as a horse. As the myth goes, once children climb onto its back, the
nix will start galloping and then jump off of a cliff to kill them both. This idea of being
haunted by something ostensibly beautiful is a fitting motif for *The Nix* (2016), the debut novel from American writer Nathan Hill. In many ways, Faye Andresen-Anderson,
one of the novel's protagonists, is like the horse in the Norwegian myth—after providing her son Samuel with a false sense of maternal security throughout his early life,
she disappears without warning when he is eleven years old. A tragicomedy, *The Nix*
explores the emotional and psychological impetus, and the aftermath, of Faye's decision, and it questions whether or not the things people love the most are in fact the ones
that eventually hurt them the worst.

The Nix is a novel about reckoning with one's past. When the novel begins, Samuel, the primary protagonist, is a thirty-something English professor who has become
utterly disenchanted with his life. Years earlier, he had been called one of the country's
twenty-five best writers under the age of twenty-five and was awarded a generous
book deal. His Great American Novel never came into fruition, however, thanks to
a combination of writer's block and emotional demons. Instead of writing, Samuel

wastes all of his free time playing an online game called *World of Elfscape*. When he learns that he is going to be sued by his publisher to force him to return the book deal's cash advance, Samuel panics and offers to write a book on his mother instead. Although Samuel has not spoken to his mother since she walked out on their family more than twenty years earlier, he has recently learned of her whereabouts after she made national headlines for throwing gravel at the conservative Wyoming governor, Sheldon Packer. His mother agrees to be interviewed by Samuel because he has promised her lawyer that he will write a letter on her behalf to be presented to the judge during her trial. Ultimately, the narrative's setup of forcing an alienated mother and son back together proves to be powerful. This is because Hill uses the literary tool of irony in a bittersweet way. Faye needs the son she abandoned to write a letter saying she is a good person; Samuel was tortured by the fact that he had no idea why his mother left, and now he must write a book on how she spent those years without him.

The Nix is Nathan Hill's first novel and was a finalist for the 2016 Leonard Award from the National Book Critics Circle for best debut novel. Hill, a former English professor, has also written short stories, many of which have been published in literary journals.

The literary structure of *The Nix* is not only highly unique, but it also demonstrates Hill's prowess as a writer. Hill breaks the novel down into ten parts, each of which comprises a different time period, location, literary style, and character perspective. As the novel's parts weave in and out of different decades, Hill provides readers with snippets from the past and the present lives of Samuel and Faye. Samuel's story line is split mostly between 2011, when he is writing the book on Faye, and in the late 1980s just before his mother left. A composite of diverse events and experiences, his narrative includes everything from young love, video games, and the Occupy Wall Street movement. Meanwhile, Faye's story line ends up being even more complex. Throughout the novel, readers follow Faye from her restrictive 1950s childhood in a Norwegian immigrant family to her participation in the 1968 Democratic Convention riots in Chicago to her unhappy life as a housewife and mother to a trip to Norway where she uncovers long-kept family secrets. Although there are many dark, depressing aspects of both Samuel and Faye's pasts, Hill uses humor and experimental prose to prevent the novel from becoming too heavy or depressing. For example, Hill transforms one heartbreaking chapter between Samuel and the love of his life, Bethany, into a Choose Your Own Adventure story.

As a writer, Hill excels at creating unique, compelling characters. In addition to ensuring that his protagonists and antagonists reflect universal hopes, anxieties, and egocentricities, Hill also provides each with an original, entertaining voice and set of idiosyncrasies. For example, one of Samuel's English class students, a young woman named Laura Pottsdam, is self-interested enough to outrightly refuse being punished for plagiarizing her essay on *Hamlet*. When Samuel informs her that she will fail the class because of her actions, Laura quickly employs a number of humorous retaliatory strategies. In a span of a twenty-minute meeting with Samuel, she tries everything from denying that she copied the essay to claiming that she did not know plagiarizing was forbidden to crying and saying that she will lose her scholarship to claiming that

Samuel is sexually interested in her and is trying to blackmail her into sleeping with him. Hill presents their conflict as a comedic, ridiculous matter; constantly escaping the consequences of her actions, Laura becomes a Bugs Bunny-like antagonist to Samuel's Elmer Fudd.

Hill's talent for crafting colorful characters is further exemplified by Samuel's childhood friends, twins Bishop and Bethany, who represent an antithesis of forces. A bully who likes to pick on other bullies, Bishop embodies the machismo and physical power that Samuel lacks. When Bishop first meets the sensitive Samuel in sixth grade, he tells him that he is going to toughen him up before smearing symbolic frog blood on his cheeks. Meanwhile, Bethany is a gentle, ethereal musical prodigy who provides Samuel with feelings of kindness, intellectuality, and love. Arguably the most interesting character, however, is Faye. By delivering the details of Faye's life slowly, piece-by-piece throughout *The Nix*'s chapters, Hill ensures that she remains a mystery to both readers and to Samuel. When Samuel first begins to write the book on his mother in 2011, he is convinced that she had always been a good Iowan farm girl rather than the "Packer Attacker" hippie radical that the media paints her. The truth, he eventually finds out, is not only much more complicated than anyone initially believed, but it also makes her motivations for leaving him when he was a child, in some ways, more sympathetic.

The Nix is comparable to the works of David Foster Wallace, Thomas Pynchon, and Charles Dickens. In addition to its expansive narrative, the novel follows many different characters and story lines in a way that effectively blends fiction with historical realism. While some elements of the novel are fantastical, Hill's depiction of the 1968 Chicago riots, complete with characters like Allen Ginsberg, are crafted with impressive accuracy. Hill uses these historical events often to make poignant social and political commentary on things like the significance of protests. Through Faye's time in 1960s Chicago and Samuel's later experiences living in New York City during the 2011 Occupy Wall Street movement, Hill demonstrates that the act of political protest is simultaneously necessary and destructive in times of social unrest. Hill also uses the novel to comment on the role that technology plays in modern life. This is primarily evident through Samuel and another character named Pwnage, both of whom choose to waste hours and days of their lives playing *World of Elfscape* rather than face reality. Similarly, the iFee app allows characters in *The Nix* to express all of their emotions to others while their followers can choose whether or not to "Autocare." Ultimately, Hill aims to point out how absurd human dependence on technology can be.

Reviews of *The Nix* have been overwhelmingly positive. For many critics, the novel has been an exciting introduction into Hill's talent as a novelist. In his *New York Times* review, book critic Teddy Wayne wrote, "*The Nix* is hugely entertaining and unfailingly smart, and the author seems incapable of writing a pedestrian sentence or spinning a boring story." Critics have also been quick to praise Hill's humor and dexterous storytelling. Writing for the *Guardian*, Anthony Quinn stated, "Hill, hopscotching back and forth through a 50-year span, swaps the masks of comedy and tragedy so deftly you can't always be sure which is which." Where lesser writers would not have been able to pull off such a complex first novel, Hill's sprawling narrative and humorous prose consistently come across as effortless. Although its specific humor and emotionally challenging narrative are unlikely to please all readers, it is safe to assume that most will appreciate *The Nix* as, in the very least, an ambitious work of fiction. Hill's talent for balancing multiple story lines while switching perspective, tone, and literary style is undeniably impressive. Furthermore, he succeeds in sustaining this complex storytelling style for more than six hundred pages.

It is important to note, however, that some critics found the novel's expansiveness to be superfluous. In his *Washington Post* review, Ron Charles wrote that while it is not unusual for authors or publishers of large, highly marketed novels to claim that the excessive length is necessary, "hundreds more pages could have been sliced away from *The Nix*." It is true that several parts of the novel could have been trimmed or cut out completely, based simply on the fact that they are tangential and do not move the plot forward. Still, Hill proves to be a talented enough writer to keep even these lengthy tangents entertaining. In her *Entertainment Weekly* review, Leah Greenblatt wrote, "At 600-plus pages, some of those threads inevitably snag or run on too long, but Hill weaves it all into the wild tragicomic tangle of his imagination." Despite these shortcomings, *The Nix* is still a worthwhile read thanks to its fascinating characters, impressive storytelling, and humor.

Emily Turner

Review Sources

Charles, Ron. "With *The Nix*, Nathan Hill Announces Himself as a Major New Comic Novelist." Review of *The Nix*, by Nathan Hill. *Washington Post*, 30 Aug. 2016, www.washingtonpost.com/entertainment/books/with-the-nix-nathan-hill-announces-himself-as-a-major-new-comic-novelist/2016/08/30/760da1f2-6bd0-11e6-ba32-5a4bf5aad4fa_story.html?utm_term=.0127151c314f. Accessed 28 Jan. 2017.

Greenblatt, Leah. Review of *The Nix*, by Nathan Hill. *Entertainment Weekly*, 31 Aug. 2016, ew.com/article/2016/08/31/nix-nathan-hill-ew-review/. Accessed 28 Jan. 2017.

Quinn, Anthony. "*The Nix* by Nathan Hill Review—A Novel of Extravagant Appetite." Review of *The Nix*, by Nathan Hill. *The Guardian*, 17 Jan. 2017, www.theguardian.com/books/2017/jan/17/the-nix-nathan-hill-review. Accessed 28 Jan. 2017.

Sheehan, Jason. "*The Nix* is a Vicious, Sprawling Satire with a Very Human Heart." Review of *The Nix*, by Nathan Hill. *NPR*, 31 Aug. 2016, www.npr.org/2016/08/31/490101821/the-nix-is-a-vicious-sprawling-satire-with-a-very-human-heart. Accessed 28 Jan. 2017.

Wayne, Teddy. "The Nix Is the Love Child of Thomas Pynchon and David Foster Wallace." Review of The Nix, by Nathan Hill. *The New York Times*, 2 Sept. 2016, www.nytimes.com/2016/09/04/books/review/the-nix-nathan-hill.html. Accessed 28 Jan. 2017.

The Obelisk Gate

Author: N. K Jemisin (b. 1972)
Publisher: Orbit Books (New York). 433 pp.
Type of work: Novel
Locale: The Stillness

The Obelisk Gate, *the second in N. K. Jemisin's Broken Earth trilogy, begins immediately where the first book,* The Fifth Season *(2015), left off.*

Principal characters:
ESSUN, a powerful orogene in her forties
NASSUN, her young daughter and a blossoming orogene prodigy
ALABASTER, her former lover and the most powerful orogene in the Stillness
YKKA, the headwoman of Castrima; a feral, or untrained, orogene
HOA, a stone eater who assumes the shape of a young human boy to help Essun

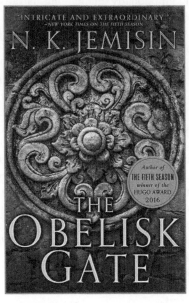

(Courtesy of Orbit)

The season has begun in earnest and Essun—along with her traveling companions, the feisty lorist Tonkee and a stone eater that looks like a human child named Hoa—has found a welcoming comm (a community) deep underground called Castrima. When the trilogy's first book, *The Fifth Season*, ended, Essun had just come across Alabaster, the formidable orogene who had once been her closest friend, mentor, and lover and whom Essun had assumed was dead. Alabaster has also sought refuge in Castrima, but he is dying after using his powers to literally tear the world apart. He is now slowly turning to stone and soon he will be nothing but rock. Most people aim merely to survive a season—a period of earthly turmoil and destruction that can last for thousands, sometimes millions, of years. But Essun does not have that relative luxury. After spending the Fifth Season in search of her daughter, Nassun, Essun is given a second and much more difficult task that, with Alabaster's tutoring, she only completely understands at the book's end. *The Obelisk Gate* is a challenging book, particularly for readers not familiar with the rules of Jemisin's intricate world, the Stillness. Jemisin's choice not to rehash the events from the *The Fifth Season* allows her to jump more quickly into the heart of her complex story and expand and elevate her allegory about oppression and race.

In 2016, Jemisin's *The Fifth Season* won the Hugo Award for best novel, the most prestigious literary prize specifically devoted to the science-fiction and fantasy genre. But as Jemisin, a prolific writer, revealed in a 2016 interview with Alexandra Alter for the *New York Times*, she almost did not finish the book because she questioned her ability to adequately tell the story "in a way that brings justice to it" and wondered whether she was "trivializing the things that are happening in the real world by treating them in this allegorical fashion in a world that doesn't exist." She has proven, however, that the Broken Earth series joins other classic works that use science-fiction and fantasy tropes to describe racial injustice.

The orogenes in *The Fifth Season* and *The Obelisk Gate* are humans who are born with the power to interact with and shift the plates of the earth, and they face the kind of oppression that mirrors the experience of many African Americans in the United States. Stills, or non-orogene people, are taught to hate and fear orogenes, who are in turn taught to hate and fear themselves. Some orogenes are enslaved, and those who are not face constant persecution and violence.

Other works that share this theme are more literal. For example, the 1979 novel *Kindred*, by award-winning novelist Octavia Butler, portrays an African American woman named Dana who lives in California during the late 1970s. On her twenty-sixth birthday, she suffers a dizzy spell, only to wake up over one hundred years earlier in the antebellum South. Dana, who cannot control when she travels through time, is tossed back and forth between eras, living as both a free, contemporary woman and a slave. Butler's exquisitely wrought narrative forces Dana to reckon with her ancestral past in a very literal way. She discovers that she has been sent back in time to save the life of a cruel slave master who is one of her distant relatives. Such complexity is also inherent in Jemisin's *The Obelisk Gate*. The book's protagonist, Essun, goes to great and sometimes violent lengths to protect the identity of her children, both of whom are orogenes. In *The Fifth Season*, a young Essun must kill one of her children, a young child she had with Alabaster, to protect the child from an invasion of Guardians, who have the power to control orogenes. The act is an homage to Toni Morrison's Pulitzer Prize–winning 1987 novel *Beloved*, as well as to every enslaved mother who was forced to make the same unthinkable choice. Butler once said, as quoted in her *New York Times* obituary, that she was inspired to write *Kindred* by her mother, who worked as a maid and endured the humiliations of segregation and racism to raise her. Both Dana in *Kindred* and Essun must make moral sacrifices to survive, but also to guarantee the survival of those that come after them.

In *The Fifth Season*, Essun desperately searches for her ten-year-old daughter Nassun, who has been kidnapped by her father, Essun's husband, Jija. In *The Obelisk Gate*, the reader meets Nassun for the first time, and the book shifts perspective between mother and daughter. Nassun is forced to grow up quickly. Thanks to her mother's genes and guidance, she is already a powerful orogene, but she must bear the burden of Jija's unpredictable and deadly rage. Jija, who killed Nassun's infant brother after discovering that he was an orogene, walks a terrifying line with his young daughter. He loves her, but he hates orogenes. In order to stay alive, Nassun must carefully perform for her father by manipulating his emotions to remind him of her humanity. Jija takes Nassun to a faraway comm called Found Moon rumored to house a school that "cures" orogeny. In a remarkably successful twist, the leader of this school is Schaffa, Essun's terrifying Guardian who was introduced in *The Fifth Season*. Schaffa has literally been given a new lease on life; he is no longer universally cruel but has become kind, and

(Courtesy of Laura Hanifin)

N. K. Jemisin is an award-winning novelist. Her work includes the Inheritance trilogy, the Dreamblood duology, and The Fifth Season *(2015), the Hugo Award–winning first book of her Broken Earth trilogy.*

he develops a deep bond with Nassun and resolves to help her develop her powers rather than "cure" them.

Nassun's plotline is a coming-of-age story, but it reveals something important about orogeny. Nassun's gifts are different from her mother's in that she is able to see and manipulate the energies that give orogenes their power. She calls these glowing strands that are found in humans and the earth magic, and for Nassun, sensing magic is innate. Meanwhile, far away in Castrima, Alabaster struggles to teach Essun what Nassun never needed to learn. Magic is key to utilizing the obelisks, he tells her. Obelisks were first introduced in *The Fifth Season* and are enormous stones from a past civilization that float in the sky. Like ancient ruins, people in the Stillness are aware of the obelisks but have little curiosity about what they were actually used for. The obelisks are for orogeny, it turns out, and Alabaster wants Essun to harness their power. Metaphorically, the obelisks bring Jemisin's entire breathtaking allegory into view. Alabaster used the obelisks to generate enough power to tear the continent apart, engendering the current, deadly season in hopes of initiating a revolution that will destroy the hierarchical social order rooted in a long-forgotten war between humans and the earth. In other words, he hopes to end the world so that it can be reborn.

As she did in *The Fifth Season*, Jemisin writes Essun's tale in the second person. The result is surprisingly effective, lending the novel a particular charge and immediacy, as if Jemisin were nearby, whispering the story to the reader. In *The Obelisk Gate*, the identity of the narrator is revealed, but the information is less important to the novel (at least at this point in the trilogy) than the style itself. The novel's conversational asides help the reader better understand the complexities of the Stillness and its history. For readers still struggling, there is a glossary at the back of the book.

The Fifth Season was included on the *New York Times* list of the 100 Notable Books of 2015. *The Obelisk Gate*, published in 2016, was well received, and both *Kirkus* and *Publishers Weekly* gave the novel a starred review, though *Tor.com* was more reserved in its praise. *Tor.com* reviewer Niall Alexander made a compelling argument about Essun's story line; in comparison to her daughter's arc, Essun's story seems static and pointed to too much quibbling over the mundanities of running a comm—is the water system running smoothly? Is everyone doing their chores?—and not enough action. However, Essun's odd turn as a bureaucrat allows Jemisin the opportunity to illustrate the growing animosity between the Stills and the orogenes in Castrima. The two groups do not usually live openly and harmoniously together like they do in this comm, and predictably, given the treatment of orogenes in the Stillness, tensions boil over when the comm is threatened by outsiders. This is arguably one of Jemisin's greatest achievements in *The Obelisk Gate*: showcasing how the lives of orogenes are threatened—and crucially, what that means for each individual character—on both a large and small scale.

Writer Amal El-Mohtar, who reviewed the book for *National Public Radio* (NPR) was effusive in her praise and wrote that the work surpassed *The Fifth Season* in depth and scope. "Every insight is deeper, every observation sharper," she wrote. "Beyond the meticulous pacing, the thorough character work, and the staggering ambition and revelations of the narration, Jemisin is telling a story of our present, our failures, our actions in the face of repeated trauma, our responses to the heat and pressure of our times." El-Mohtar evoked Jemisin's own words in the book's dedication, in which Jemisin, like Morrison and Butler before her, makes clear the real-world tradition in which she is writing. *The Obelisk Gate*, she writes, is for "those who have no choice but to prepare their children for the battlefield."

Molly Hagan

Review Sources

Alexander, Niall. "New Moon." Review of *The Obelisk Gate*, by N. K. Jemisin. *Tor. com*, 17 Aug. 2016, www.tor.com/2016/08/17/book-reviews-the-obelisk-gate-by-n-k-jemisin/. Accessed 19 Jan. 2017.

El-Mohtar, Amal. "Riveting *Obelisk Gate* Shatters the Stillness." Review of *The Obelisk Gate*, by N. K. Jemisin. *NPR*, 18 Aug. 2016, www.npr. org/2016/08/18/489497592/riveting-obelisk-gate-shatters-the-stillness. Accessed 19 Jan. 2017.

Review of *The Obelisk Gate*, by N. K. Jemisin. *Kirkus*, 27 June 2016, www.kirkusreviews.com/book-reviews/nk-jemisin/the-obelisk-gate-the-broken-earth/. Accessed 19 Jan. 2017.

Review of *The Obelisk Gate*, by N. K. Jemisin. *Publishers Weekly*, 1 Aug. 2016, www.publishersweekly.com/978-0-316-22926-5. Accessed 19 Jan. 2017.

Of Arms and Artists
The American Revolution through Painters' Eyes

Author: Paul Staiti (b. 1948)
Publisher: Bloomsbury Press (New York).
  Illustrated. 400 pp.
Type of work: History, fine arts
Time: Late eighteenth and early nineteenth
  centuries
Locales: Colonial America, later the United
  States; London, England

(Courtesy of Bloomsbury USA)

In Of Arms and Artists: The American Revolution through Painters' Eyes, *the distinguished art historian Paul Staiti presents a lively account of the careers of five American artists who lived through the American Revolution and memorably portrayed its leaders and turning points in their art. Staiti makes a compelling case that these artists helped the inhabitants of the young American republic develop a common identity by providing inspiring images that helped form the basis of a new nationalism.*

Principal personages:
CHARLES WILLSON PEALE, American soldier, politician, and painter
JOHN SINGLETON COPLEY, American painter who moved to London
BENJAMIN WEST, American painter who became a favorite of King George III
JOHN TRUMBULL, American soldier, diplomat, and painter
GILBERT STUART, American painter who became famous for his portraits

Paul Staiti, professor of fine arts at Mount Holyoke College, tackles a highly ambitious theme in *Of Arms and Artists: The American Revolution through Painters' Eyes*, exploring the impact of art on national identity. He argues that the men who painted the founding fathers of the United States themselves helped establish the republic by creating enduring images that would become integral to the evolving intellectual and emotional fabric of the American nation. Just as the men who waged war against the British army and framed the Constitution had to abandon the established path of the past and build a "new order of ages," so did a small band of painters have to pioneer an artistic vocabulary to capture the values of a revolution. In doing so, they created a powerful iconography for the embryonic United States, one that contributed to a unifying mythology that would bind Americans together over the ensuing generations.

When Americans in the twenty-first century think about George Washington, Thomas Jefferson, and Benjamin Franklin, it is the imperishable images created by these artists that come to mind. Most unforgettable of all is Gilbert Stuart's portrait of

George Washington, originally painted in the 1790s and gracing the dollar bill since 1869. Americans and countless others around the world know the father of his country through Stuart's evocation of an aging but dignified and determined statesman. Stuart's Washington looks the part that he played for Americans, brilliantly personifying paternal and patriotic authority. In 1939, Grant Wood satirized the vision of George Washington that Stuart's painting enshrined in the American consciousness in his own work *Parson Weems' Fable*. This picture portrays the legendary fiction devised by Mason Locke Weems, better known as Parson Weems, that as a boy, George Washington fatally sliced up his father's prized cherry tree with a hatchet; when questioned by his irate father, Washington allegedly said, "I can't tell a lie, Pa," and confessed. In Wood's painting, the youthful Washington has the face of Gilbert Stuart's portrait of the president at sixty-four. Wood's mordant commentary would have made no sense if, for most Americans, Stuart's Washington had not early on indelibly idealized the real man. Long before Mount Rushmore, the painters of the revolutionary era had made George Washington an icon.

The first artist Staiti discusses is Charles Willson Peale. Born in Maryland in humble circumstances—his father was a convicted felon who died when he was nine— Peale was the quintessential self-made man. Apprenticed to a saddlemaker at the age of thirteen, Peale eventually opened his own saddlery. A growing family that eventually included ten children convinced Peale that he needed to increase his income, and a gift for drawing led him to take painting lessons from a neighboring artist. Soon he was painting portraits of local luminaries. In late 1766, he set sail for London, where he studied the successful American painter Benjamin West for three years. Upon his return to America, Peale became an ardent patriot, and during the early stages of the Revolutionary War he saw action as a captain in the Pennsylvania militia.

In 1779, the Supreme Executive Council of Pennsylvania commissioned Peale to paint a life-sized, full-length portrait of General George Washington. Intended for the Council Chamber of the Pennsylvania State House, the building now known as Independence Hall, this would be the first officially sanctioned public art to be displayed in the United States. Peale took his charge very seriously, as did his subject, George Washington; the busy commander in chief of the Continental Army gave the artist several sittings between January 20 and February 2, 1779. Peale had to decide how to portray Washington. In the end he chose to depict him at the moment of victory at the 1777 Battle of Princeton. Peale's Washington is calm and confident, a leader who eloquently displays the righteousness of his cause. Enemies of American independence soon provided evidence of the power of this artistic expression of nascent American nationalism: in 1781, a band of Loyalists broke into the State House and slashed the painting. Peale quickly repaired the portrait, but the knives of its attackers had demonstrated the political significance of public art in the revolutionary years. Peale went on to a brief career as a politician and a much longer one as an artist. He eventually produced some sixty portraits of George Washington, valued for the accuracy of their representation as well as their patriotic message.

Benjamin West and John Singleton Copley stand out among Staiti's group of subjects because these men, though Americans by birth and by sentiment, never lived in the new United States. West was born in Pennsylvania and launched his career as a painter in his home colony, but in 1763 he moved to London to test his skills in the heart of the British art world. There he flourished, benefiting from both his artistic abilities and a good head for business. West mixed with the leading lights of the British art world, such as Joshua Reynolds, and soon attracted lucrative commissions from influential patrons. West won the attention of King George III, an avid connoisseur of fine painting. The king eventually appointed West historical painter to the royal court, with a generous yearly salary. In 1771 West exhibited his ambitious masterpiece *The Death of General Wolfe* (1770) at the Royal Academy in London. In his composition of the painting, which depicts the death of General James Wolfe at the climax of his victory over the French at the Battle of Quebec in 1759, West sacrificed historical verisimilitude for dramatic effect and a symbolic evocation of the glory of the British Empire. The painting caused a sensation, confirming West's status as an artistic master, and George III commissioned him to produce a replica for the Royal Collection.

Over the years, West proved to be an unselfish benefactor to American painters studying in London, including Peale, Stuart, and John Trumbull. His self-consciously emotive and didactic approach to historical painting would prove to be a potent inspiration to the American painters of the revolution. While West was sympathetic to his countrymen during the Revolutionary War, his position as the king's painter and his sensitivity to his British market kept him from producing any pro-American paintings. At the end of the war, he did begin an impressive painting of the American and British diplomats who negotiated the peace treaty, but the reluctance of the British delegation to pose for him kept the painting from being finished.

John Singleton Copley established himself as one of the ablest and most popular portrait painters in Boston during the 1760s. He painted portraits for whoever paid him, including Samuel Adams and other Patriot leaders who led the resistance against British tax legislation. Copley was largely silent on the topic of his own political sympathies; unfortunately for him, his wife's family consisted entirely of Loyalists, and in fact her father, Richard Clarke, was the importer of the tea thrown in Boston Harbor during the Boston Tea Party of 1773. Copley was uneasy with the increasingly violent tenor of politics in Boston, and he was also increasingly frustrated by the limited artistic horizons in America. Encouraged by West and other friends, he decided to relocate to London in 1774. In the cosmopolitan hub of the British Empire, Copley honed his skills and thrived economically. He continued to avoid commenting on the American Revolution or appearing to endorse it in his work while the fighting still raged, but once peace was in sight, he began to paint notable depictions of American leaders, including a massive portrait of John Adams. Copley never returned home, but the end of the Revolutionary War enabled him to re-embrace his American identity.

Staiti describes Gilbert Stuart as "the master artist of the early republic." Enormously gifted and a portraitist without peer, Stuart was also an alcoholic who ran up enormous debts and often had to move his family to escape his creditors. In 1775, he traveled to London to study under Benjamin West, and he eventually attained fame in Britain as a portrait painter. Success, however, only brought the spendthrift artist increasing debts. In 1793 Stuart fled back to the new United States, were his abilities placed him in demand. In 1795 George Washington agreed to sit for him. By this point much used to having his portrait painted, Washington was intrigued by this new talent, and Stuart did not disappoint the image-conscious president. His portrait forever preserved the popular conception of Washington as the wise and benevolent father of his country. In the short run, Stuart's compelling depiction of Washington aided the president as he attempted to rally his administration's battered authority in the wake of intense controversy surrounding the ratification of the Jay Treaty, which ensured peaceful trade between the United States and Great Britain during the French Revolutionary Wars—much to the dismay of members of Thomas Jefferson's Democratic-Republican Party, who advocated for closer ties to France instead. Contemporaries noted that Stuart's portrait of Washington was not the most accurate representation of an aging Washington, but that did not matter. Stuart had given the new nation the Washington that it wanted and needed.

John Trumbull was born into a distinguished family in Connecticut. His father was a long-serving governor of first the colony and then the state. Showing a gift for drawing early in life, Trumbull worried his father by dreaming of becoming a painter. Politics distracted the young artist for a time, and he became caught up in the unrest that led to revolution. Trumbull joined the Continental Army during the early stages of the war, and for a time he acted as an aide to George Washington. However, Trumbull left the army in 1777. Anxious to launch a career as a painter, he followed the path blazed by other American artists before him, traveling to the metropolis of London in 1780. This was a reckless action for a man known to have been an officer of the Continental Army, and indeed Trumbull was arrested and imprisoned for months before being released and forced out of the country.

Paul Staiti is a professor of fine arts at Mount Holyoke College. He has been the recipient of three fellowships from the National Endowment for the Humanities. He is the author of Samuel F. B. Morse *(1990).*

Trumbull returned to London following the end of hostilities, and he, too, studied with Benjamin West. He yearned to emulate West's success with dramatic historical compositions, but he wanted to do so using the American Revolution as his source material. His breakthrough success came with his painting *The Death of General Warren at the Battle of Bunker's Hill, June 17, 1775*, which he began in fall 1785 and completed in 1786. This picture does not attempt documentary realism, but instead stunningly evokes action and movement. What it lacks in accuracy it more than makes up for in emotional impact. From this point on, Trumbull's course was set. He began painting large representations of pivotal moments of the American Revolution, most notably a depiction of the Declaration of Independence being presented to the Second Continental Congress. Eventually four large paintings by Trumbull would be placed in the Capitol Rotunda. Here, in the very heart of representative government in the United States, Trumbull's idealized rendering of the American Revolution would be seen by countless visitors. Along with Stuart's portrait of George Washington on the dollar bill, this would be the apotheosis of artistic influence on the American civic imagination.

Staiti ends his story in the Rotunda. By this point he has made his case. The artists of the revolutionary generation shaped not only Americans' understanding of the founding of the nation but also how it continues to be seen.

Daniel P. Murphy

Review Sources

Anderson, Virginia DeJohn. "Examining the Artists of the Revolutionary Era." Review of Of Arms and Artists: The American Revolution through Painters' Eyes, by Paul Staiti, and A Revolution in Color: The World of John Singleton Copley, by Jane Kamensky. *The New York Times*, 2 Dec. 2016, www.nytimes. com/2016/12/02/books/review/of-arms-and-artists-paul-staiti-revolution-in-color-jane-kamensky.html. Accessed 1 Feb. 2017.

Review of *Of Arms and Artists: The American Revolution through Painters' Eyes*, by Paul Staiti. *Kirkus Reviews*, 1 July 2016, p. 88.

Review of *Of Arms and Artists: The American Revolution through Painters' Eyes*, by Paul Staiti. *Publishers Weekly*, 18 July 2016, p. 199.

Seaman, Donna. "Painting and the American Revolution." Review of *Of Arms and Artists: The American Revolution through Painters' Eyes*, by Paul Staiti, and *A Revolution in Color: The World of John Singleton Copley*, by Jane Kamensky. *Booklist*, 1 Sept. 2016, p. 4.

Sherman, Jacob. Review of *Of Arms and Artists: The American Revolution through Painters' Eyes*, by Paul Staiti. *Library Journal*, 15 June 2016, p. 89.

The One Man

Author: Andrew Gross
Publisher: Minotaur Books (New York).
432 pp.
Type of work: Novel
Time: 1944
Locales: Washington, DC, and Oswiecim,
Poland

In his World War II thriller The One Man, *Andrew Gross imagines an elaborate plot to free one man—an important scientist whose knowledge and skills are necessary to construct the world's first nuclear bomb—from Auschwitz concentration camp.*

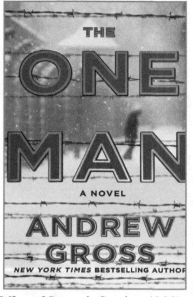

(Courtesy of St. Martin's Press)

Principal characters:
NATHAN BLUM, a Polish Jew who escaped to the United States from the Krakow ghetto early in the war; he works for the US Office of Strategic Services (OSS) as a translator
ALFRED MENDL, a world famous electromagnetic physicist
LEO WOLCIEK, a sixteen-year-old chess prodigy with a photographic memory
GRETA ACKERMANN, the wife of the terrifying Lagerkommandant at the Auschwitz concentration camp
CAPTAIN PETER STRAUSS, a Jewish operations officer with the OSS and the mastermind behind Operation Catfish

The One Man, Andrew Gross's historical thriller set during the height of World War II, follows the story of a young man named Nathan Blum. Blum was born in Poland to a milliner and a music-loving mother. His sister, Leisa, is an extraordinary pianist. But Blum's life changes forever after the Nazi invasion in 1939. He and his family are Jewish, and forced to move to the decrepit and overflowing Jewish ghetto in Krakow. Blum establishes himself as a wily thief, stealing and sneaking to help his family survive. His skills offer him a ticket out of the ghetto after he is asked to smuggle a priceless tract of the Talmud to Sweden. Blum is anguished about his mission—if he leaves, what will happen to his family? On his father's orders, Blum escapes, completes his mission, and immigrates to the United States, where he finds out that his entire family has been shot and killed in retribution for the shooting of a German officer. Blum enlists to fight in the war, but his language skills land him at a desk at the Office of Strategic Services (OSS) in Washington, DC, translating cable messages. He wants to do something more to avenge his family, or, at the very least, sacrifice for them in the same way they sacrificed their lives for him. Blum has made his desire known, and one

(Courtesy of Lynn Gross)

Andrew Gross is a best-selling suspense writer who began his career collaborating with James Patterson on titles in the Women's Murder Club series and other thrillers. His most recent novels include No Way Back *(2013) and* Everything to Lose *(2014). He is also the author of a series of books about a detective named Ty Hauck.*

day in the spring of 1944—shortly before the invasion of Normandy, or D-Day, June 6— he is given a chance to fulfill it in the form of a mission far more deadly than his first.

Blum is summoned by his superiors and directed to a man named Captain Peter Strauss, a chief operations officer with the OSS. Strauss, who is also Jewish, has spent over a year plugging away at a pie-in-the-sky mission code-named Operation Catfish. True to real-life events, the United States was made aware of Nazi concentration camps and the Reich's methods of mass extermination as early as 1942. (In July of that year, the *New York Times* ran a story about the "liquidation" of the Warsaw ghetto, in which inhabitants were sent to concentration camps throughout Poland.) After the escape of two Auschwitz prisoners in 1944—another true story and one that is told in *The One Man*— President Franklin D. Roosevelt reportedly explored ways that the United States might stop the killing. The president and his advisors ultimately decided that the Normandy invasion was more strategically advantageous, and that the prisoners of Auschwitz and other camps would have to wait for Allied soldiers to reach them on foot. Gross imagines that Strauss, a fictional character, was present at this meeting. Strauss is charged with tracking down Alfred Mendl, an electromagnetic physicist who holds the key piece of information necessary to the construction of the world's first nuclear bomb. Based on information from the two Auschwitz escapees, Strauss knows that Mendl was sent to Auschwitz, though he has no way of knowing if the aging scientist is still alive. Strauss enlists Blum to track him down. Blum, with the help of a network of Polish partisans, has only three days to sneak into Auschwitz as a prisoner and sneak back out again with Mendl in tow.

Gross is a suspense novelist best known for his collaboration with famous writer James Patterson on the second and third installments of the best-selling Women's Murder Club series, as well as three other titles. Gross's subsequent books, including a series of books about a detective named Ty Hauck, have fared just as well. *The One Man* is also a suspense novel, but its historical setting is a stark departure for Gross. The novel was inspired by the author's family history. His Jewish father-in-law, Nathan Zorman, was raised in prewar Warsaw, but fortuitously immigrated to the United States before the Nazi invasion in 1939. Zorman, who never heard from his family in Poland again, served as a translator in the OSS during the war. In his acknowledgements, Gross laments his father-in-law's resistance to speaking about his past or ever taking steps to find out what happened to his family. In *The One Man*, Gross writes, he sought to capture Zorman's incalculable and unspoken "anguish" in a book.

The novel's frame speaks to Zorman's experience as well as the experience of many other World War II survivors. An old man, unnamed, sits in a hospital bed. His adult daughter comes to visit him, showing him a cigar box of strange items, including a prestigious military medal that she found in his house. She begs him to tell her what they mean. "We've wanted to know for so long," she says. After some prodding, the man, who Gross suggests is nearing the end of his life, launches into a tale that forms the bulk of the book's story.

The One Man is well-wrought; its suspenseful turns are plotted with skill, and its various threads come together at the end in a way that is both satisfying and surprising. Philosophically, Gross fruitfully explores the well-known Talmudic principle about the importance of one life. (Readers unfamiliar with the Talmud might also recognize the quote "He who saves a single life, saves the entire world," from the 1993 Holocaust film *Schindler's List*.) Blum cites the passage when he agrees to Strauss's mission, but he struggles with its meaning after embedding himself in the camp. Gross's depiction of daily life at Auschwitz is notable for its banality—prisoners bicker among themselves and look for ways to bribe guards for extra food and cigarettes, or a chance to visit the woman's camp next door. But even these unremarkable interactions carry a frightening weight. Each prisoner knows his or her time could come at any moment. Some prisoners are beaten to death, while others are shot. Others still are marched to the gas chambers; Blum encounters them all, and each time he is forced to ask himself if the life of one man, Mendl, is worth more than all of the others.

Blum's dilemma however, is only one piece of Gross's larger plot. The reader also follows Mendl's heartbreaking separation from his wife and daughter, and the coming-of-age of a teenage chess prodigy named Leo. Mendl is fully aware of his value to the Allies—though as one reviewer pointed out, just how he knows this is unclear—and befriends Leo, who also has a photographic memory, in the hope that he might teach the young man what he knows. As Leo tries to glean what he can from the old man, he also develops an unusual friendship with a woman named Greta Ackermann, the Lagerkommandant's wife. (Ackermann is a fictional character who—in Gross's rendering—has stepped in to run the camp while Rudolf Höss, the real commander of Auschwitz, is in Berlin. Höss was hanged for war crimes in 1947.) Greta discovers Leo's talent and invites him to play chess with her at her house outside of the camp. Greta hates her husband and finds Nazis despicable; in her mind, her friendship protects Leo and that protection becomes a way for Greta to exorcise her guilt. Gross writes lovingly of their relationship, though it's more troubling than tender. The story line is one of several story elements in *The One Man* that strain credulity.

Greta performs an important sacrificial act near the end of the book. It makes for an exciting tale, but readers interested in the Holocaust or even the Manhattan Project (the secret project to develop a nuclear bomb) might be disappointed by how far afield it strays from actual history. In this regard, *The One Man* should be viewed as a historical thriller. For better or worse depending on the reader's expectations, Gross does not engage with the larger body of Holocaust literature, a genre that is anxiously concerned with representation and historical accuracy. This anxiety is best described in the words of Elie Wiesel, a Holocaust survivor and the author of *La Nuit* (1958; *Night*, 1960), when he wrote for the *New York Times* in 1989: "Just as no one could imagine Auschwitz before Auschwitz, no one can now retell Auschwitz after Auschwitz. The truth of Auschwitz remains hidden in its ashes. Only those who lived it in their flesh and in their minds can possibly transform their experience into knowledge. Others, despite their best intentions, can never do so." With all due respect to the late Wiesel, this hardly seems fair. Those in subsequent generations still grapple with the Holocaust—in fact, Gross is a perfect example. He wrote *The One Man* in attempt to understand the stories he was never told.

Molly Hagan

Review Sources

Ayers, Jeff. "Review: 'The One Man' (Minotaur) Is Heartfelt and Compelling." Review of *The One Man: A Novel*, by Andrew Gross. *The Washington Post*, 24 Aug. 2016, www.washingtonpost.com/entertainment/books/review-the-one-man-is-heartfelt-and-compelling/2016/08/24/dd51a0dc-6a2e-11e6-91cb-ecb5418830e9_story.html. Accessed 3 Oct. 2016.

Land, Jon. "Thriller Roundup: 4 Nail-Biters from the Long-Buried Past to Modern-Day Florida." Review of *The One Man: A Novel*, by Andrew Gross. *Providence Journal*, 15 Sept. 2016, www.providencejournal.com/entertainmentlife/20160915/thriller-roundup-4-nail-biters-from-long-buried-past-to-modern-day-florida. Accessed 3 Oct. 2016.

Review of *The One Man: A Novel*, by Andrew Gross. *Kirkus*, 30 May 2016, p. 109. *Literary Reference Center*, search.ebscohost.com/login.aspx?direct=true&db=lfh&AN=117663614&site=eds-live. Accessed 3 Oct. 2016.

Review of *The One Man: A Novel*, by Andrew Gross. *Publishers Weekly*, 30 May 2016, p. 38. *Business Source Complete*, search.ebscohost.com/login.aspx?direct=true&db=bth&AN=115859328&site=eds-live. Accessed 3 Oct. 2016.

The Opposite of Everyone

Author: Joshilyn Jackson (b. 1968)
Publisher: William Morrow (New York). 304 pp.
Type of work: Novel
Time: 1980s–Present
Locale: Atlanta, Georgia

The Opposite of Everyone *is a novel by American author Joshilyn Jackson that examines the way storytelling can shape identity.*

Principal characters:
PAULA VAUSS, a cutthroat divorce lawyer who lives in Atlanta
ZACH BIRDWINE, a private eye and her love interest
KAI, her estranged mother
JULIAN, her half brother
HANA, her half sister
CANDACE, a girl whom she knew while in foster care who ultimately betrays her

(Courtesy of HarperCollins Publishers)

Joshilyn Jackson's seventh novel *The Opposite of Everyone* (2016) begins with her protagonist Paula Vauss recounting the story of her birth. Paula describes in poetic prose how, as a result of the umbilical cord wrapped around her neck, she was born blue. Her mother then named her Kali after the azure, multiarmed Hindu goddess. However, because her mother was a sixteen-year-old serving time in juvenile detention, Paula was immediately given to her grandmother, who refused to write the foreign-sounding name on the birth certificate. While brief, this anecdote of Paula's birth establishes several important things about the narrative that subsequently unfolds. For one, it provides insight into Paula's background and the way she perceives herself. More important, however, it brings to life what Jackson has stated is the central idea of the novel: that the stories people tell can define them, destroy them, or connect them to others.

Throughout *The Opposite of Everyone*, Jackson utilizes the device of storytelling in several different capacities. In addition to being a vessel for delivering essential exposition to readers, it is also the way that the characters relate to one another. The two primary storytellers in the novel are Paula and her mother, Kai. When Paula shares stories from her tumultuous childhood it is with a kind of style and imagery that is reminiscent of folklore. Meanwhile, Kai's colorful and expertly crafted stories are revealed in flashbacks to Paula's childhood. Early on in the novel, it becomes clear that Paula grew up in a largely itinerate lifestyle, with her mother moving the two of them between different boyfriends' houses. Kai's storytelling, a collection of Hindu myths told with a southern twist, was the one constant in Paula's childhood. As a result, tales of Kali, Hanuman, and the elephant god Ganesha became the pillars that upheld Paula's understanding of the world.

As a protagonist, Paula is atypical. A mixed race, thirty-something woman who spent her formative years in and out of the foster care system, Paula is the kind of narrator who is rarely given a platform in mainstream literature. Furthering Paula's uniqueness as a female character is her unapologetic aggressiveness in both her personal and professional life. She is not just tough but willing to take down others, a quality that has enabled her to become a successful divorce attorney in Atlanta. Still, Jackson never presents Paula's cutthroat nature as a negative attribute. Unlike other mainstream narratives, where female characters embrace docility after learning the hard way that being aggressive makes them unlovable to men, Paula's ferocity is a characteristic that Jackson depicts with enthusiasm. Ultimately, Paula embodies her namesake Kali, the goddess of destruction who tears down old things to make way for the good and new.

The Opposite of Everyone revolves tightly around the themes of karma and family. The idea of karmic retribution first emerges in one of the novel's early scenes when Paula sends Kai, with whom she has been estranged for fifteen years, a check in the mail. Paula does not mind the ritual but sees it as a way to pay off her karmic debt. She is seeking forgiveness for a mistake that she made as a teenager that ultimately sent Kai to prison. Despite the fact that she refuses to speak to her, Kai always cashes Paula's checks. However, this all changes one day when a check is sent back to Paula with the word "void" emblazoned on it. On the back, Kai has written that she has enough money to last her the rest of her life, which has been cut short by cancer. Soon afterward, a young man named Julian shows up at Paula's law office claiming to be her half brother who Kai gave up while in prison. When she learns that she and Julian have a ten-year-old half sister who may be lost in the foster care system, Paula is given one last opportunity to clear the bad karma of her and her mother's past.

Joshilyn Jackson is an award-winning, New York Times best-selling author of seven novels including Gods in Alabama *(2003),* Backseat Saints *(2011), and* Someone Else's Love Story *(2013), as well as an e-original short story,* My Own Miraculous *(2013).*

Once Paula and Julian begin to track down Hana, their half sister, *The Opposite of Everyone* engages in a tonal shift that is comparable to a crime thriller. Although Jackson's imagery is colorful rather than dark and she sparingly employs narrative twists and incidents of violence, the plot comprises a number of standard detective procedural beats driven by the character of Birdwine. Birdwine has a personality that is arguably from the hardboiled mystery genre: he is private eye with a drinking problem and a former police officer. Despite the fact that he is also Paula's former boyfriend, Jackson does not spend much time leveraging the tension of whether or not the two will reunite. Instead, she establishes their mutual attraction early in the narrative and then depicts their subsequent interactions as steps toward an inevitable romantic relationship. It is a refreshing angle for a female-driven narrative, especially because both characters are equal to one another in strength, intelligence, and emotional complexity.

The narrative of *The Opposite of Everyone* is driven by two mysteries. The first involves Paula, Julian, and Birdwine as they try to determine what happened to Kai and Hana. To elevate the feeling of suspense around this plotline, Jackson utilizes the invisible ticking clock set by Kai's last note, which stated that she only had a few weeks to live. Determined to prevent Hana from also spending her childhood in foster care, Paula works as fast as she can to track her down. The novel's second mystery is one that Jackson poses exclusively to the readers—the reason behind Paula and Kai's estrangement. Although she introduces the fact that the two no longer speak to one another in the first chapter, Jackson reveals the details of the actual event slowly through a series of interconnected flashbacks. These flashbacks ultimately provide *The Opposite of Everyone* with a secondary story line from which Paula's narration weaves in and out.

In many ways, Jackson presents the story line of Paula's childhood in a manner similar to a superhero's origin story. Where Paula was once a shy, scared girl who was picked on in middle school, she transformed into a hardened fighter during her years in foster care. Paula undergoes this process of becoming self-reliant and emotionally withdrawn as a result of spending time with two other foster kids, Joya and Candace. From Joya, Paula learns street smarts. Although she never gets along with Candace, it is from her that Paula learns the painful lesson of how to be both deceptive and ruthless. Candace is ultimately presented as the antagonist in Paula's childhood story line. She represents an opposing point of view; a motherless being willing to deceive others to get what she wants. After being seriously hurt by Candace, Paula ultimately becomes more like her. In the other story line, Julian replaces Candace as Paula's foil. Where Paula has become cynical and fiercely self-reliant, Julian represents youthful optimism and the need to belong to a family. Just like Candace, his beliefs slowly begin to influence Paula's perception of both the world and herself.

The novel's tone is reflective of Paula's voice and character. Consequently, the prose is sharp, poetic, and darkly funny. To prevent the narrative from becoming too heavy, Jackson mines the divorce cases that Paula is working on as sources of comedy. Paula's clients are often rich, white, and privileged, and so she likes to mock how clueless they are to how the rest of the world lives. This is not the only place where Jackson strategically injects levity, however. As a writer, Jackson excels at exploring emotionally trying events, like Paula's time in foster care, in an evenhanded way. Throughout *The Opposite of Everyone*, Jackson deftly abstains from the kind of heavy-handed melodrama that is commonly associated with dysfunctional childhoods and death. Although Paula knows she may never see her mother again, she approaches the issue in a way that feels true to life. Paula's feelings upon learning of her mother's impending death are mixed; a reflection of how complex and deeply flawed their relationship is. In this way Jackson demonstrates that as a writer she prioritizes exploring the truth of human emotion, no matter how messy it may be, over tidy resolutions.

Ultimately, *The Opposite of Everyone* is an original, entertaining read. Reviews of the novel reflect this opinion. A common point of praise among critics has been for Jackson's diverse cast of characters. Writing for the *New York Times*, Bobbi Dumas states that the "unconventional characters in Jackson's books often provide thought-provoking studies of love and loyalty." Dumas's commendation is not unfounded; while Jackson demonstrates her adroit writing skills in a number of different ways, *The Opposite of Everyone* showcases her ability to craft compelling characters. Arguably one of the qualities that makes the novel's characters interesting is the fact that many of them represent the kinds of people who are typically depicted as existing on the fringes of society. Instead of dismissing them into supporting roles, however, Jackson makes them her protagonists. This provides the well-worn narrative of a dysfunctional family with a new perspective.

The Opposite of Everyone has also been extolled by critics for its success in repurposing literary devices typically found in murder mysteries. *Publisher's Weekly* deems the novel "an excellent read with a fresh take on the detective genre." Although the character of Birdwine ostensibly appears to wink at the trope of the hardened detective who plays his own rules, he is neither suave nor a womanizer but a man with predominantly good intentions who struggles with substance abuse issues. The only character that truly can be compared to iconic detectives like Dashiell Hammett's Sam Spade is Paula. In addition to having a complicated woman at the helm, the novel's mystery is also unique in that it is personal rather than criminal in nature.

At times, the narrative of *The Opposite of Everyone* can feel stagnant and claustrophobic. Despite the fact that she is trying to identify where in the country the ten-year-old Hana could be, Paula never leaves Atlanta. Combined with the fact that Paula's scenes take place in a limited set of locations, the world in which Jackson has created for her characters often comes across as small and uninspired. Furthermore, by keeping Paula in Atlanta throughout the entirety of her adult story line, Jackson inadvertently dilutes the urgency of finding Hana. Although suspense is arguably one of the novel's weakest points, Jackson still manages to tell a highly engaging story. This is largely the result of her hypnotic prose as well as her ability to capture the dynamics of human relationships with unwavering honesty. Despite its flaws, ultimately *The Opposite of Everyone* is a compelling, entertaining novel.

Review Sources

Dumas, Bobbi. "Romance." Review of The Opposite of Everyone, by Joshilyn Jackson. *The New York Times*, 12 Feb. 2016, www.nytimes.com/2016/02/14/books/review/romance.html. Accessed 6 Oct. 2016.

Review of *The Opposite of Everyone*, by Joshilyn Jackson. *Kirkus Reviews*, 10 Dec. 2015, www.kirkusreviews.com/book-reviews/joshilyn-jackson/the-opposite-of-everyone/. Accessed 6 Oct. 2016.

Review of *The Opposite of Everyone*, by Joshilyn Jackson. *Publishers Weekly*, 1 Feb. 2016, www.publishersweekly.com/978-0-06-210568-4. Accessed 6 Oct. 2016.

Paris for One and Other Stories

Author: Jojo Moyes (b. 1969)
Publisher: Pamela Dorman Books (New York). 288 pp.
Type of work: Short fiction

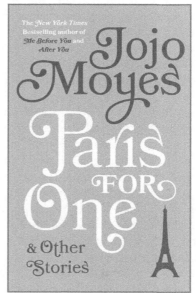

(Courtesy of Penguin Random House)

Best-selling British novelist Jojo Moyes's collection Paris for One and Other Stories *contains one romantic novella and eight plot-based, female-focused short stories.*

The stories in *Paris for One and Other Stories* are tales of romantic comedy with a central focus on themes of female empowerment. The collection has been recommended for "genre readers" looking for something "short and sweet." Five of these stories originally appeared in the British women's magazine *Woman & Home*, which publishes beauty and fashion tips, recipes, entertainment news, and sometimes short stories. The other three stories were originally read on BBC Radio 4.

Jojo Moyes worked for the British newspaper the *Independent* for ten years before publishing her first novel, *Sheltering Rain*, in 2002. Of her thirteen novels, many of them best sellers, her best-known, *Me before You* (2012), was called "swoonworthy" by reviewers.

Paris for One and Other Stories, her first collection of short stories, opens with the title novella, which takes up more than half the book and which has been the favorite piece of reviewers. The novella's appeal is dependent on that of the central character, named Nell after a well-known Dickens character. Nell, a twenty-six-year-old risk-assessment specialist, is not the kind of woman who can rely on her looks, and she is not adventurous. She has never been away for a weekend with her boyfriend. However, overhearing his colleagues talk about her timidity, she has decided to arrange it—booking the best budget hotel, getting the best tickets on a special deal, laying all her plans out on a spreadsheet as she would at work—determined to make herself into the kind of girl who goes to Paris with her boyfriend. The boyfriend, Pete, whom Nell's friends dislike, is not enthusiastic about the idea.

When Pete fails to show at the Eurostar station, saying he is held up at work, Nell must reluctantly go to Paris alone and wait for him at the hotel. Things get worse when she gets a text message from Pete saying he cannot make it at all and telling her to have a great trip. At this point, the story shifts to the point of view of Fabien, an aspiring writer in Paris who, while revising his manuscript on the rooftop of his flat, sees all 332 carefully edited pages of his only copy blown away. When Nell shows up at the restaurant where Fabien works and spills wine on him, it is fated (or rather plotted) that Fabien is heartbroken over a recent breakup with his girlfriend. When Nell runs into Fabien again and he shows some interest in her, she begins to try to turn herself into a more sophisticated person, buying a Parisian dress.

In the meantime, back in England, Nell's friends have hijacked Pete and forced him into going to Paris to meet with Nell, who now feels "something magical" has happened. The premise of the story, of course, is that Nell falls under the spell of Paris and its romantic attitude toward life, summed up by the phrase, "Sometimes you just have to do what feels good." Pete's arrival leaves Nell definitely underwhelmed, and so she sneaks away from him and meets Fabien, who takes her to his flat, which she also thinks is "magical," like being in a story. He takes her out on his rooftop and, at her urging, reads to her

(Courtesy of Stine Heilmann)

Before becoming a best-selling novelist, Jojo Moyes was a journalist for the Independent *for ten years. She is among the few writers to have won the Romantic Novelists' Association's Romantic Novel of the Year Award twice.*

from the few pages he has rescued of his work in progress. Nell says, "I feel like I fell in love with an entire city"—the defining sentence of the story.

Although the novella might well have ended here, a final chapter entitled "Six Months Later" brings Nell and Fabien's story to a satisfying conclusion while demonstrating Nell's growth into a confident, vibrant young woman willing to take charge of her own life.

The eight shorter stories can be summed up more briefly, though, despite their brevity, most employ multiple plot twists. The protagonists of these stories are mainly women who are underappreciated by those around them, and the events of the stories often conspire to deliver poetic justice for their heroes.

In "Between the Tweets," Declan Travis, a presenter on a morning television show, seeks professional help because a woman has posted messages on Twitter saying that Travis has had an affair with her for two years. The narrator, an investigator named Bella, soon finds out that the accuser is none other than Travis's wife, who has created this ruse to boost his failing profile, but the story still has some surprises remaining.

"Love in the Afternoon" is a story about a husband and wife who have been married for fourteen years and whose relationship has turned stale; they have not made love for five weeks and two days when the story begins. Then, uncharacteristically, the husband reserves a hotel room for them. Encouraged by this, the wife seductively suggests they could stay in; the husband agrees that this is a great idea and goes down to the lobby to get the movie *Snakes on a Plane*. The wife's embarrassed seduction attempts and his unromantic responses make up the rest of the story.

"A Bird in the Hand" focuses on a couple going to a party at which the wife is seated next to a man with whom she once had an adulterous affair. There is a whispered give-and-take between them as she accuses him of dumping her. When he tells her that no one has ever made him feel the way she did, "the world stall[s] around her" and she feels her blood rising and her heart racing. The woman's choice between the stability of her relationship with her husband and the passion she shared—and might again share—with her former lover is the crux of the story.

In "Crocodile Shoes," perhaps the lightest piece in the collection, a drab, middle-aged woman named Samantha finds that she has switched bags with another woman by accident; she finds in the stranger's bag a pair of red crocodile-skin Christian Louboutin sling pumps instead of her own comfortable pumps. Putting on the other woman's shoes, Samantha finds new confidence in both her work and her love life.

The appeal of "Holdups" is the brave, smart-talking protagonist, a clerk who outsmarts and befriends a baseball-bat-wielding thief who has taken part in a jewelry store holdup with two other men. Her conversation with the erstwhile thief while the other two men are robbing the store becomes a kind of flirtation—a rapport that complicates the clerk's decision to turn the robbers over to the police.

"Last Year's Coat" is about a woman, Evie, who needs a new coat, but because she and her husband have been caught in the economic downturn, she cannot afford it. To make matters worse, she knows the other women she works with have nicer clothes than she does, especially Felicity, who has a new handbag that would cost Evie a month's salary. A surprising revelation, however, leads Evie to greater contentment with what she has.

"Thirteen Days with John C" is another story of a woman who is taken for granted by her husband. When Miranda finds a mobile phone while on a walk, she sees a recent text message received from a man named "John C" reading, "Where U darling? It's been 2 days!!!" The message makes Miranda feel unbalanced by raw emotion, as if someone has broken into her safe haven. She continues to read new messages from John C, some of which make her blush with their explicitness, all of which make her more excited and intrigued. When the messages become even more insistent, she finally responds as if she is the woman he is writing to and makes arrangements to meet him, but the encounter is not what she was expecting.

Finally, "The Christmas List" is about a woman who is not just unappreciated by her husband but also taken advantage of by him. Dispatched to buy some hard-to-find perfume for his mother for Christmas, she is befriended by a taxi driver who helps her locate it. The story follows the dialogue in the cab as the woman gets phone messages from her husband scolding her for not performing the errands he has given her and the driver increasingly sympathizes with her, at last trying to convince her not to put up with her husband's treatment of her. It is a feel-good Christmas story—the final gift in this little collection of confections from a master of the rom-com genre.

Charles E. May

Review Sources

Maguire, Susan. Review of *Paris for One and Other Stories*, by Jojo Moyes. *Booklist*, 15 Sept. 2016, p. 24.

McClurg, Jocelyn. "You'll Fall for Jojo Moyes' Romantic *Paris for One*." Review of *Paris for One and Other Stories*, by Jojo Moyes. *USA Today*, 19 Oct. 2016, www.usatoday.com/story/life/books/2016/10/17/paris-for-one-and-other-stories-jojo-moyes/91959938. Accessed 16 Dec. 2016.

Ogle, Connie. "*Me before You* Author Is Back with Her Favorite Subjects: Romance, Laughter, Escape." Review of *Paris for One and Other Stories*, by Jojo Moyes. *Miami Herald*, 29 Oct. 2016, www.miamiherald.com/entertainment/books/article108938832.html. Accessed 16 Dec. 2016.

Review of *Paris for One and Other Stories*, by Jojo Moyes. *Kirkus Reviews*, 27 July 2016, www.kirkusreviews.com/book-reviews/jojo-moyes/paris-for-one-and-other-stories. Accessed 16 Dec. 2016.

Review of *Paris for One and Other Stories*, by Jojo Moyes. *Publishers Weekly*, 12 Sept. 2016, pp. 31–32.

The Passenger

Author: Lisa Lutz (b. 1970)
Publisher: Simon & Schuster (New York). 320 pp.
Type of work: Novel
Time: 2005–15
Locales: Waterloo, Wisconsin; Lincoln, Nebraska; Norman, Oklahoma; Austin, Texas; Casper and Recluse, Wyoming; Denver; Chicago; Albany, Saratoga Springs and Saranac Lake, New York; Burlington, Vermont; Philadelphia; Everett and Bilman, Washington

An intriguing mystery-thriller, The Passenger *takes readers on a harrowing rollercoaster ride that follows the exploits of a chameleon-like female protagonist who takes countless risks while attempting to run from the events of her past and survive the many dangers she encounters.*

Principal characters:

TANYA PITTS, a.k.a. Tanya Dubois, Jane Green, Amelia Keen, Debra Maze, Emma Lark, Sonia Lubovich, Paige, Moira Daniels, and Nora Jo Glass, a thirty-year-old woman on the run from the law

BLUE, a.k.a. Debra Maze, Debra Reed, Carla Wright, Amelia Keen, Amelia Lightfoot, Laura Cartwright, and Laura Bainbridge, a sympathetic, devious, and ruthless female Texas bartender who befriends Tanya/Amelia

ROLAND OLIVER, the wealthy owner of a Washington State construction company

RYAN OLIVER, his younger son, former classmate of Tanya/Amelia

LOGAN OLIVER, his elder son

EDIE PARSONS OLIVER, a former classmate and friend of Tanya/Amelia

KING DOMENIC LOWELL, a Wyoming sheriff

JACK REED, Blue's abusive ex-husband

MELINDA LYONS, a former classmate of Tanya/Amelia's

NAOMI GLASS, a.k.a. Mrs. Webber, Tanya/Amelia's mother

The motif, or recurring theme, of a character trying to evade capture is a common feature in fiction, and many scholars believe that its first use was employed by ancient Greek storyteller Homer in his epic poem *The Odyssey.* Homer's hero Odysseus traveled across real and fictional terrain in order to escape threats and injury from the gods while simultaneously rushing toward his own fate and the resolution of his quest. Since then, myriad authors have created characters who share common traits:

they are both innocent and guilty, usually male, and they demonstrate resourcefulness in escaping the law or in running from shadowy nemeses. The problems encountered by an individual who eludes justice were particularly well-drawn in the 1960s television drama, *The Fugitive* (1963–67). In each episode, Dr. Richard Kimble, who was accused of murdering his wife, assumed new names and identities while traveling and working at a variety of jobs in order to avoid arrest and pursue his own quest of identifying his wife's true killer.

Running and hiding were easier before the Internet, cell phones, facial recognition software, global positioning satellites, closed-circuit television, and other advanced technology. In the twenty-first century, it is hard to travel indefinitely without proper documentation like a driver's license, passport, or birth certificate and almost impossible to find steady work without a Social Security card. These are some issues author Lisa Lutz explores from the first-person perspective of a wanted woman, in her fun, fast thriller *The Passenger*.

As the novel opens, readers meet protagonist Tanya Dubois at a moment of intense crisis: she finds her slovenly husband of seven years, Frank, dead in their home after falling down the stairs. The first clue that Tanya is not an ordinary new widow is the fact she avoids calling emergency services for help and instead hastily packs, collects all the cash she can find, loads her belongings into the family truck, and speeds west, away from Waterloo, Wisconsin. Along the way, she uses automated teller machines (ATMs) and credit cards to withdraw extra cash before throwing the cards away. In Lincoln, Nebraska, she trades in her truck for an older car, buys supplies and a disposable phone, and hides out at a motel. Tanya then calls a man named Roland Oliver and demands he supply her with a documents for a fresh identity and $5,000. Tanya calls Roland back in two days and learns that a Social Security card and a passport have been created for Amelia Keen, who had died a year prior and whose identity Tanya would assume. Tanya tells Roland to overnight the documents to Jane Green at an address in Norman, Oklahoma, and to wire the cash to Amelia Keen in the same city. To fit the new person she has to become, Tanya/Amelia cuts and dyes her hair and dresses more casually than she formerly did.

This is the first of many transformations the heroine will undergo in the process of slipping from one identity into another as circumstances demand. Over time and as she zigzags across the country avoiding discovery, she changes internally as well as externally, moving from relative innocence toward increasingly criminal behavior. She becomes an expert at lying and brazenly steals wallets from women's purses to obtain fresh identification. She breaks into places in order to hide, and she even kills someone in self-defense. During a harrowing decade on the run as Jo, she maintains sporadic e-mail contact with a person from her past named Ryan. It is clear that Ryan cares about her, and he also provides information about people she once knew. The details provide the reader with tantalizing glimpses of who Tanya/Amelia used to be and why she fled.

At several of her temporary stops, the heroine's life becomes more permanently entangled with the lives of others. Arriving in Austin, Texas, Amelia drops into a bar and meets a sympathetic female bartender named Blue. When Blue asks for ID and is given Amelia's passport, she immediately recognizes it as an excellent forgery and wants to know where Amelia obtained it. As the two women go off to trade life stories, they are abducted by two men with guns—Amelia figures they have been sent by Roland Oliver to kill her—and are forced into a car. While the foursome is driving, Amelia causes the car to crash. Blue grabs a dropped pistol and shoots both of the men to death.

Afterward, Amelia moves in with Blue and learns that Blue was originally named Debra Maze then later Debra Reed and is a former third-grade teacher with a checkered past. Neither woman is confident with her current form of identification, so they search the obituaries looking for potential new identities to assume. They begin going to funerals to glean additional details about their targets. Before they can find an appropriate subject, however, Blue involves Amelia in the cover-up of a crime: to protect herself, Blue shot her abusive ex-husband Jack Reed and needs help burying the body. The two women then exchange identities, and with hair dyed blonde and blue contact lenses, Amelia becomes Debra Maze, a grade-school teacher with Ohio credentials, while Blue becomes brunette, brown-eyed Amelia Keen.

(© David Middleton)

Lisa Lutz's first novel, The Spellman Files *(2007), which won the Alexa Award and was nominated for several other mystery honors, spawned a series featuring the Spellman family. Lutz, an occasional screenwriter, has also written several standalone novels, including* How to Start a Fire *(2015).*

The new Debra Maze drives north in Blue's old Cadillac to search for a job at a small private school in Wyoming where authorities are said to be lax in checking identification. In Jackson, she meets and has romantic relations with King Domenic Lowell, who she later learns is the local sheriff. She quickly leaves him, continues her journey, and settles into a teaching position in tiny Recluse, Wyoming, where she lives in an apartment in the basement of the schoolhouse. During her tenure, she heroically rescues a small boy from drowning during a fishing party.

Amelia/Debra's low-key existence begins to unravel after a few months. A stranger shows up in town and seems to be watching her. Domenic then tracks her down and tells her he knows she is not really Debra Maze. Later, the stranger shows up at her door to announce he is Jack Reed, Blue's former husband, who is looking for his ex-wife. When Jack threatens her with violence, she is forced to kill him, and she sinks his body in a nearby lake. Afterward, she flees again, and has to knock-out a persistent Domenic in order to get away.

She travels by bus, train, and car and changes identities frequently and as opportunities present themselves, moving through Denver and Chicago to rural New York where she squats at a succession of cabins and vacation homes that are unoccupied during the fall and winter. She eventually realizes that no matter how far she travels or how many identities she assumes, she will never find peace until she accepts responsibility for her own fate by returning to the scene where her troubles began and make restitution in order to solve the problems that haunt her.

The Passenger (the title perhaps refers to the fact the protagonist is not really in control of her own destiny but is merely along for the wild ride) incorporates many interesting twists to the theme of the hunted person. As a woman, the main character has a unique set of strengths and weaknesses that both help and hinder her flight. She can look completely different and in effect become invisible simply by changing her hairstyle and color, adding or subtracting weight, or dressing up or down. On the other hand, beyond the mysterious and untrustworthy Roland Oliver and her occasional (and inconsistent) e-mail contact Ryan, she knows no one at any of the places she settles and must survive by her own wits, which sometimes fail her. The heroine lacks experience in deceiving others, which causes her to make errors of judgment that present fresh problems to be overcome. Lutz is adept at providing insight into the mind of the frequently frightened, often uncertain, but always self-aware protagonist, which allows readers to decide for themselves whether they would make the same choices she does or look for alternative solutions to her dilemmas.

The novel is equal parts thriller and mystery to be solved from clues inserted into the e-mails to and from Ryan, from brief flashbacks, and from information updates gleaned by the protagonist's regular library-computer searches. *The Passenger* mixes lyrical, noir-flavored passages about what constitutes a person's identity, the nature of guilt and innocence, and instinctual behavior with moments of dark humor, a technique also seen in Lutz's comedic Spellman mystery series. The scenes in which Tanya/Amelia and Blue/Debra are at funerals in order to learn about newly dead young women and then attempt to deflect questions from the deceased's relatives are especially memorable. Other scenes, such as when the protagonist encounters a survivalist preparing for a major terrorist event, are less believable. Though occasionally uneven in pace and sometimes repetitious, *The Passenger* nonetheless presents a spunky, all-too-human viewpoint from a character who is easy to root for. It is a suspenseful, well-told story with multiple philosophical points to ponder and a reasonable mystery to unravel.

Jack Ewing

Review Sources

Anderson, Patrick. "'The Passenger' Review: First a Dead Husband, Then a Wife on the Run." Review of *The Passenger*, by Lisa Lutz. *The Washington Post*, 28 Feb. 2016, www.washingtonpost.com/entertainment/books/the-passenger-review-first-a-dead-husband-then-a-wife-on-the-run/2016/02/28/8bd70acc-d978-11e5-891a-4ed04f4213e8_story.html?utm_term=.bef5c48307f8. Accessed 29 Sept. 2016.

Frazier, G. Robert. "'The Passenger': Run, Run, as Fast as You Can." Review of *The Passenger*, by Lisa Lutz. *BookPage*, ProMotion, 1 Mar. 2016, bookpage.com/reviews/19542-lisa-lutz-passenger#.WEc7TbIrJhF. Accessed 29 Sept. 2016.

Review of *The Passenger*, by Lisa Lutz. *Kirkus*, 22 Dec. 2015, www.kirkusreviews. com/book-reviews/lisa-lutz/the-passenger-lutz/. Accessed 29 Sept. 2016.

Strafford, Jay. Review of *The Passenger*, by Lisa Lutz. *Richmond Times-Dispatch*, 26 Mar. 2016, www.richmond.com/entertainment/books/article_10ce7bf9-1768-5fb8-91db-6b48c8bf1af2.html. Accessed 29 Sept. 2016.

The Past

Author: Tessa Hadley (b. 1956)
First published: 2015, Great Britain
Publisher: Harper (New York). 320 pp.
Type of work: Novel
Time: 1968; present day
Locale: A small English coastal town

(Courtesy of HarperCollins Publishers)

The Past by Tessa Hadley takes place over a three-week vacation in the English countryside near the ocean. Four siblings are tasked with the decision to sell the family home and have come for one last gathering. While dealing with their present-day lives, the novel also reaches back to the past when three of the siblings lived at the summer home for a brief time during their parents' turbulent marriage. Comprised of strong characters and evocative landscapes, The Past *creates a compelling, yet comforting reading experience.*

Principal characters:

FRAN, the youngest of the four Crane siblings, a schoolteacher with two children.
ALICE, the middle Crane sister, a passionate artist who struggles to find stability in her life.
HARRIET, the oldest sibling, a former revolutionary who works with asylum seekers.
ROLAND, brother to the three women, a professor and writer at the height of his career.
PILAR, Roland's beautiful Argentine wife (his third), who is meeting his sisters for the first time.
MOLLY, Roland's quiet teenage daughter from a former marriage.
KASIM, the son of Alice's ex-boyfriend, who accompanies Alice to the family cottage.
IVY, Fran's nine-year-old daughter, somewhat spoiled but overall a curious child.
ARTHUR, Fran's six-year-old son, quick to follow his older sister's lead.
JILL, the deceased matriarch of the Crane family.

Tessa Hadley's sixth novel, *The Past*, opens with the four Crane siblings—sisters Fran, Alice, and Harriet and their brother Roland—arriving at the family's long-time rural homestead for a three-week summer vacation. Subtle in structure and storyline, the novel gives Hadley space to develop full characters and a plot that builds to a crashing climax. It is a story rooted in the pastoral setting, particularly the crumbling country house itself, which has deep layers of meaning for each character. The former home of the siblings' grandparents, the cottage has become a financial burden for the family.

The decision to sell it or spend money to restore the roof is the major overarching tension of the novel; however, as happens with many quiet family dramas, *The Past* deals with much more: how much of the characters' lives are still lingering in the past, how regret has shaped their adult selves, and what the structure means to them, to the past, and familial legacy.

"The house was a white cube two storeys high, wrapped around on all four sides by garden, with French windows and a veranda at the back and a lawn sloping to a stream; the walls inside were mottled with brown damp, there was no central heating and the roof leaked," Hadley writes, creating the setting skillfully. When Alice arrives at the house with her ex-boyfriend's son Kasim, in his twenties, she notices that her sister Harriet is already there, but off on a hike in the acreage surrounding the home, and Alice has forgotten her keys. She and Kasim approach the French windows and look in on the cottage, further describing the setting within, including glimmering wallpaper, rooms furnished with her grandparents' wares, an upright piano, and paintings. Alice has dreamt about this house for years, it is noted, as it holds a life that she's never found in other surroundings.

With the setting solidly in place at the start, *The Past* introduces each sibling as they arrive, carefully describing their relationships to each other. Alice, the middle sister, is an artist, a failed actor in fact, who is middle-aged and considered scattered by her siblings. Harriet is the eldest, a stable presence, if not a bit too matronly for her age. Fran is the youngest, married to a musician named Jeff but coming only with her two children, Ivy and Arthur. Roland arrives the next day with a new wife, Pilar, an Argentine lawyer who the sisters have not previously met, and his teenage daughter Molly. Hadley's way of introducing the characters within the established setting of their ancestral home is masterful, and allows the reader to experience each one through a crisp, unbiased lens. Unlike many family-centric stories, there is no festering sibling rivalry or jealousy here, just normal tension, forcing Hadley to find other, subtler sources of dramatic force.

The house holds a mythical quality as events unfold within and outside. A romance develops between Molly and Kasim, the sisters bond over dinner after dinner, and Ivy and Arthur explore the boundaries between reality and the supernatural. Most notably, the house acts as a way for the siblings to recall their mother, Jill, who died at a young age from cancer (it was Harriet, in fact, who raised Fran), their absentee father, and the lives of their grandparents, a homemaker and a religious man who was also a great poet. Nearby, the children regularly explore an abandoned cottage, which becomes an alternate realm for them, where they slowly and steadily find independent footing away from the watchful eyes of the adults.

The novel is separated into three parts, with action set in the present bookending a flashback to when Jill brought Harriet, Roland, and Alice to live with their grandparents at the cottage. Hadley uses the first portion to construct the inner and outer lives of her main characters, alluding to their dead mother in details and establishing the homestead as a place of great importance to the family. When the novel transitions to the past, Hadley introduces us to the siblings' mother as a young woman who has just left her husband, Tom, and fled to the house in the country. Hadley brings Jill and Tom to life at a critical juncture, and discloses some family secrets at the same time. The layering of the past and present members of the family is particularly effective in that the reader is allowed to see the direct results of choices of the past, while also creating a grander landscape by incorporating the members of four generations, from Jill's own parents to Jill to the four siblings to their offspring.

Central relationships of the book include the love affair between Molly and Kasim and a budding friendship between Pilar and Harriet. However, much of the novel revolves around those relationships and expectations of one's life that never quite found their footing. Harriet regrets never having found love, while Alice wonders if she has been too frivolous. The otherwise successful Roland is on his third marriage, and Fran is worried about her marriage to the absent Jeff. The central conflicts of the novel are those inside of the characters. Hadley uses this to deftly explore the nuances of ambiguity, uncertainty, and quiet tension and introduce important character development. Despite the fact that novel ends with an explosive climax, *The Past* celebrates the smaller moments of its characters' lives.

Hadley, a native of England herself, has written five previous novels, as well as several collections of short stories and a work of nonfiction. *The Past* continues her trademark style of writing largely realistic fiction that focuses on the details of contemporary British life—Hadley's other novels are all also set in Great Britain and occur between 1950 and the present day. A focus on women is another hallmark of her work, exploring their worlds as they transition through stages of life like marriage, raising children, divorce, and meeting and maintaining relationships with friends and lovers, all the while examining the delicate balances and imbalances created by life. Hadley's women characters are typically smart and resourceful, and this standard is carried on in the complex Crane sisters. Similarly, The Past picks up subtle themes regarding sexuality, class issues, and modern society that have also permeated Hadley's other works.

Critical reception of *The Past* has been largely positive. This novel has been called the most commercial of Hadley's works, but most reviewers appreciated her continued exploration of the interior life of characters, life outside the city center, the relationships between women, particularly as they age, and family dynamics. Anthony Quinn said of the book in his review for the *Guardian*, "In her patient, unobtrusive, almost self-effacing way, Tessa Hadley has become one of this country's great contemporary novelists. She is equipped with an armoury of techniques and skills that may yet secure her a position as the greatest of them." Margot Livesey reviewed the novel for the *Boston Globe* and had a similar stance, saying, "I finished "The Past". . . with a sense that I had understood something profound about both Hadley's characters, and my own life.

Tessa Hadley is the author of several acclaimed novels and short story collections. She received a Windham-Campbell Literature Prize in 2016, and her books have been listed for many other awards and prizes. She is a Fellow of the Royal Society of Literature and the Welsh Academy.

Many readers will, I suspect, in the presence of this exhilarating novel feel the same." Livesey also noted similarities between the book and Kazuo Ishiguro's "Remains of the Day" and Ian McEwan's "Atonement." Writing for the *New York Times Sunday Book Review*, Fernanda Eberstadt found that Hadley occasionally explains her characters' emotions too much in *The Past*, but stated that even if the book was not quite as sharp as her previous works, it was an enjoyable entry in her growing catalog.

Upon the novel's shocking climax and slow resolve, *The Past* seems to tell readers that the events of the story won't unimaginably alter the lives of its characters. Though it would be easy to label such an understated story inconsequential, or even boring, Hadley's skill with language means that nothing is farther from the truth. In fact, the smaller details that have forged the strong bonds evident between the family members and others are what allow them to survive the more dramatic moments of life. The final message of the novel steers the reader back to the deep past, reassuring readers that life is cyclical, and people are rarely destroyed by it.

Melynda Fuller

Review Sources

Charles, Ron. "Family Tensions Simmer in Tessa Hadley's Exquisite Novel 'The Past.'" Review of *The Past*, by Tessa Hadley. *The Washington Post*, 22 Dec. 2015, www.washingtonpost.com/entertainment/books/family-tensions-simmer-in-tessa-hadleys-exquisite-novel-the-past/2015/12/22/9798cb12-a597-11e5-ad3f-991ce3374e23_story.html. Accessed 1 Dec. 2016.

Eberstadt, Fernanda. Review of The Past, by Tessa Hadley. *The New York Times*, 22 Jan. 2016, www.nytimes.com/2016/01/24/books/review/the-past-by-tessa-hadley.html. Accessed 1 Dec. 2016.

Livesey, Margot. Review of *The Past*, by Tessa Hadley. *The Boston Globe*, 2 Jan. 2016, www.bostonglobe.com/arts/books/2016/01/02/book-review-the-past-tessa-hadley/Ju0prpRxjoceEKkHxMqnfN/story.html. Accessed 1 Dec. 2016.

Quinn, Anthony. "The Past by Tessa Hadley Review—a Brilliant Excavation of Family and Inheritance." Review of *The Past*, by Tessa Hadley. *The Guardian*, 28 Aug. 2015, www.theguardian.com/books/2015/aug/28/the-past-by-tessa-hadley-review. Accessed 1 Dec. 2016.

Patient H.M.
A Story of Memory, Madness, and Family Secrets

Author: Luke Dittrich
Publisher: Random House (New York). 464
pp.
Type of work: Literary history, biography
Time: 1944–2008
Locale: Primarily Connecticut

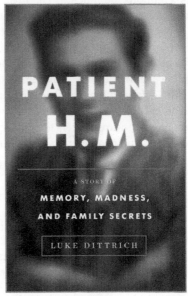

(Courtesy of Penguin Random House)

Luke Dittrich's book Patient H.M.: A Story
of Memory, Madness, and Family Secrets
*is a dual portrait of Patient H.M., the most
famous test neurological subject in history,
and the author's grandfather, a neurosurgeon who performed several lobotomies.*

Principal personages:
HENRY MOLAISON, the world's most famous
   lobotomy patient, known as Patient H.M.
WILLIAM BEECHER SCOVILLE, a famous
   neurosurgeon and champion of lobotomy, the author's grandfather
SUZANNE CORKIN, a researcher at the Massachusetts Institute of Technology (MIT)
   who conducted experiments on Molaison over several decades

Luke Dittrich had just won an award for his work at *Atlanta* magazine when he received a call from an editor at *Esquire*, requesting a pitch. Dittrich's idea, about a
death row inmate, was rejected. The editor turned him down touting a common writing adage, asking him: what story are you "uniquely" qualified to tell? For Dittrich,
that story began with his grandfather, a famous neurosurgeon, and one of his grandfather's patients, a man known to generations of psychology students as Patient H.M.
Research on Patient H.M., an amnesiac named Henry Molaison, who died in 2008,
provides a solid basis for our understanding of memory and the brain, but like the
brain itself, Dittrich's story is not so simple as it may appear. Dittrich set out to write a
profile of Patient H.M. but ended up with a story much, much larger than he bargained
for, uncovering startling facts about the scientists that studied Patient H.M. and about
members of his own family. *Patient H.M.: A Story of Memory, Madness, and Family
Secrets* is a sometimes discursive but ultimately absorbing exploration of ethics and
empathy, scientific hubris, and the quixotic quest to understand the human brain.
   Dittrich describes his grandfather, William Beecher "Bill" Scoville, as a dashing
and ambitious young neurosurgeon who began his career in the 1940s, operating on
returning World War II veterans. By the 1950s, Scoville, a meticulous dresser who
slicked his hair back with olive oil, was a rising star in his field, who became a Yale
professor. But Scoville was also quite reckless, a daredevil in his personal life—he

ultimately died in a car crash precipitated by his decision to throw his car into reverse on the New Jersey Turnpike—and, Dittrich suggests, dangerously experimental in his work. Scoville was a pioneer of psychosurgery, a discipline that sought to treat mental illness with brain surgery. Psychosurgery principally referred to a defunct procedure that will be familiar to most readers, even today: the lobotomy. Popularized by a man named Walter Freeman, the lobotomy seemed progressive and convenient in midcentury America. State asylums, as they were then called, were overcrowded, and doctors and patients alike were happy to grasp on to the lobotomy—billed as a simple cure-all—as a solution. In a glowing portrait of Freeman from the late 1930s, Dittrich writes, the *New York Times* praised this "new surgical technique . . . which, it is claimed, cuts away the sick parts of the human personality." Why should one suffer through the available, and frankly, tortuous, therapies of the day, when one could simply treat one's ailment—depression or anxiety, for instance—with an outpatient procedure? Lobotomies didn't even require patients to be fully unconscious.

Scoville streamlined Freeman's crude lobotomy technique—later in his career, Freeman used an ice pick to dig behind his patient's eye sockets, mutilating parts of their brain by feel. Here's how Scoville went about it: first, he made an incision at the patient's scalp and rolled down their skin like a "carpet," Dittrich writes. Using a custom-made drill, he drilled two inch-and-a-half-sized holes in the patient's skull, just above their eyes. Scoville reached through those holes with a scalpel, slicing through the brain's protective matter, and then used a brain spatula that looked like a shoehorn to lever up the patient's frontal lobes. Reaching behind those lobes, Scoville did one of several things. For the purposes of this story, as it relates to Patient H.M., he used a tiny vacuum to suction out the patient's medial temporal lobes.

Scoville had performed this operation countless times before he operated on Molaison, Patient H.M., in 1953. He had an agreement with an asylum called the Institute of Living in Connecticut, where he lobotomized many patients—sometimes as many as five in one day. One of the more remarkable aspects of Dittrich's story though, is that Scoville's wife, Emily, was also a patient at the Institute of Living. (Scoville's interaction with her there is one of the book's lingering questions.) This detail allows Dittrich to explore the genuinely horrifying "treatments" available to the mentally ill at the time. Dittrich also—significantly—touches on the Nuremberg Code, a code of medical ethics established after World War II. During the Holocaust, Nazi doctors tortured prisoners to test the bounds of human endurance. The Nuremberg Code dictates, among other things, that patients must provide consent to participate in experiments and that the risks to the human subject must be proportionate to the "expected humanitarian benefits." For example, Dittrich tells the story of the eighteenth-century British physician Edward Jenner, who intentionally infected his gardener's eight-year-old son with a disease. Jenner made the right gamble, though; his unethical test yielded not only a vaccine for smallpox, but the concept of a vaccine as a treatment and the birth of modern immunology. Also, the boy survived. In other words, the Nuremberg Code dictates that the ends must justify the means. Dittrich returns to this idea again and again in what is the most successful aspect of the book. Patient H.M. was invaluable to science, but at what cost to Molaison?

Henry Molaison was born in 1926. After a childhood accident, he became severely epileptic. Dittrich writes that Molaison's constant seizing cost him three years of school. He was not even allowed to walk onstage to receive his high school diploma for fear that he would disrupt the ceremony. Molaison was a smart man, but his condition made it difficult for him to hold a job or live on his own—so the Molaisons contacted Scoville in hopes that something could be done to fix their son's problem. If Scoville could locate the part of the brain responsible for the seizures, could he remove it? Like the desperate doctors at the Institute of Living, Molaison was willing to explore this unorthodox solution. As Dittrich writes, this is where things get tricky. Unlike Scoville's other lobotomy patients, Molaison was not mentally ill. If Scoville was unable, through the means available, to discover the source of Molaison's epilepsy when he saw Molaison's brain, he was obligated—according to medicine's oldest dictate, "First, do no harm"—to patch Molaison back up and send him on his way. But the desire to study the effects of a lobotomy on a "normal" brain, Dittrich argues, was too great. Instead of doing nothing, Scoville removed both of Molaison's medial temporal lobes.

After the surgery, it became clear that Molaison was suffering from something called "anterograde amnesia," meaning that he was unable to form new memories. Even the long-term memories he did possess, Dittrich explains, were complicated in their structure, but for Molaison, as he later said himself, "every day is alone in itself." Each day, he met his doctors anew, and if they left his presence, sometimes only for a few minutes, he would meet them again. Molaison's unusual condition, exhaustively studied over the course of more than fifty years, led scientists to understand, among other things, that the hippocampi, structures inside the medial lobes, are necessary for making new memories.

Remarkably, Dittrich's connection to Molaison's story does not end with Scoville. A woman named Suzanne Corkin, a psychologist who devoted her career to studying Molaison, happens to have been his mother's closest childhood friend. Dittrich's depiction of Corkin, who died after the book was completed but before it was published in 2016, raised the hackles of MIT, where Corkin worked, and prompted over two hundred scientists to sign a letter in support of her. Dittrich responded to their letter on his blog. One of their chief complaints has to do with Dittrich's suggestion that Corkin did not procure proper consent for later experiments with Molaison; Dittrich found that, for a significant portion of Molaison's adult life, Molaison signed his own consent forms. Dittrich raises a question that the reader, now familiar with the Nuremberg Code, might be wondering as well—is such consent meaningful?

Luke Dittrich is journalist and contributing editor to Esquire. *He won the 2012 National Magazine Award for reporting on the aftermath of the Joplin, Missouri, tornado.* Patient H.M. *is his first book.*

Corkin's story gets even more complex, and Dittrich does an admirable job of dramatizing the nuances of scientific infighting over Molaison's person, and later, his brain, while maintaining Molaison's humanity as a test subject. In fact, Dittrich is particularly good at balancing complicated information and heart. His biggest downfall, as nearly all of his reviewers have pointed out, is his lack of references outside the text. Unlike most nonfiction books—particularly ones that contain new and potentially explosive information—*Patient H.M.* contains no source notes or bibliography. This frustrating omission diminishes Dittrich's achievement. Dittrich committed himself to his subject far beyond the bounds of the story as he originally conceived it; he wrestles a serious amount of information—ranging from memories of his own life, to complicated science, to the contents of the Nuremberg Code—into a vast but ultimately cohesive whole. (Steven Rose, a reviewer for the *Guardian*, might disagree with this assessment.) In an August 12, 2016, interview with *Atlantic* magazine, Dittrich suggested that the structure of *Patient H.M.* mimics the "fragmented" way in which the human mind stores memories and creates narratives. Throughout the book, Dittrich makes imagistic leaps, the way a smell or a song might trigger a memory in the brain. Some reviewers found these bits of "time travel," as he calls them, off-putting, but gathered together, none seem totally out of place. In fact, they serve to underscore the philosophical implications of using one's brain to understand the brain. Like the enduring mystery of Patient H.M. (what was it really like to be him?), one must be satisfied with incomplete answers.

Molly Hagan

Review Sources

Mnookin, Seth. "A Book Examines the Curious Case of a Man Whose Memory Was Removed." Review of Patient H.M.: A Story of Memory, Madness, and Family Secrets, by Luke Dittrich. *The New York Times*, 29 Aug. 2016, www.nytimes.com/2016/09/04/books/review/patient-h-m-luke-dittrich.html. Accessed 6 Dec. 2016.

Review of *Patient H.M.: A Story of Memory, Madness, and Family Secrets*, by Luke Dittrich. *Neuroskeptic*, Discover, 2 July 2016, blogs.discovermagazine.com/neuroskeptic/2016/07/02/book-review-patient-h-m. Accessed 6 Dec. 2016.

Rose, Steven. "*Patient H.M.* Review—A Botched Lobotomy That Changed Science." Review of *Patient H.M.: A Story of Memory, Madness, and Family Secrets*, by Luke Dittrich. *The Guardian*, 25 Aug. 2016, www.theguardian.com/books/2016/aug/25/patient-hm-by-luke-dittrich-review. Accessed 6 Dec. 2016.

Senior, Jennifer. "Patient H.M. Recalls the Story of a Surgery That Took a Man's Memories." Review of Patient H.M.: A Story of Memory, Madness, and Family Secrets, by Luke Dittrich. *The New York Times*, 24 Aug. 2016, www.nytimes.com/2016/08/25/books/patient-hm-recalls-the-story-of-a-surgery-that-took-a-mans-memories.html. Accessed 6 Dec. 2016.

The People and the Books
18 Classics of Jewish Literature

Author: Adam Kirsch (b. 1976)
Publisher: W. W. Norton (New York). 432 pp.
Type of work: Religion
Time: Fourth century BCE to twentieth century CE

The People and the Books *analyzes eighteen works of Jewish literature from over two thousand years of history. It is American poet and literary critic Adam Kirsch's ninth book.*

THE
PEOPLE
——AND THE——
BOOKS

—— *18 Classics of Jewish Literature* ——

ADAM KIRSCH

(Courtesy of Norton, W.W. & Company, Inc.)

One of the most powerful facets of literature as an artistic medium is its ability to capture and preserve cultural moments in history. By providing firsthand insight into the past, ancient texts can give readers the context necessary to better understand their present. This was the primary intention of American literary critic Adam Kirsch when writing *The People and the Books* (2016)—to create a fuller, better understanding of Jewish identity today. What makes *The People and the Books* especially compelling is its close examination of the rich Jewish literary tradition. As Kirsch points out early on, Jews have been called the People of the Book and yet most members of the faith are unfamiliar with Jewish literature outside of the Hebrew Bible.

In its scope, *The People and the Books* is highly ambitious. With the exception of Simon Schama's *The Story of the Jews* (2013), few books have ever tried to analyze more than two thousand years' worth of Jewish history and literature. Not only does Kirsch welcome this challenge, but he also uses his experience as a literary critic to bring a fresh perspective to classic works. Consequently, every one of the eighteen Jewish texts summarized and analyzed in *The People and the Books* come across as expertly chosen. Kirsch also ensures the collection feels cohesive, rather than disjointed, when read back to back by highlighting how each text represents both a continuation and shift in traditional Jewish thought. For example, in his analysis of the biblical book of Esther, Kirsch first pinpoints the hallmark Jewish themes present in the story. Like many Jewish texts, the book of Esther, which recounts the story of a Jewish girl named Esther who becomes queen of Persia before thwarting the genocide of her people, depicts the Jews as living in exile under a foreign ruler while having their ancestral customs challenged. Still, Kirsch argues, the book of Esther is highly unique. For one, *God* does not save the Jewish people—they save themselves by slaughtering seventy-five thousand of their enemies. Furthermore, Kirsch notes, the story depicts

Jews as living a more secular lifestyle in a pluralist society. This is a stark difference from the more pious biblical book of Deuteronomy that Kirsch examines in the previous chapter.

Kirsch does not assume his readers have any previous knowledge of the Jewish faith, which contributes significantly to the accessibility of *The People and the Books*. When examining *The Exposition of the Laws* by the Greco-Roman writer Philo of Alexandria (15 BCE–45 CE), for example, Kirsch takes the time to explain the significance of Hanukkah. Although Hanukkah is arguably the most well-known Jewish holiday, Kirsch writes about it in a simple, explanatory way. Consequently, *The People and the Books* often feels as though it is for readers of all backgrounds. This feeling is reinforced by Kirsch's language. Rather than employ the vocabulary of a religious scholar, Kirsch writes in a casual, everyday style. His prose includes a number of colloquialisms. For example, he describes Purim as the holiday where Jews remember their "skin-of-the-teeth rescue" from their would-be assailants and Esther's transformation in the book of Esther as a "year-long makeover."

If there is a central idea to *The People and the Books*, it is that historically there has never been a singular, enduring Jewish mindset. Each of the eighteen texts that Kirsch analyzes in the book presents a completely different perspective on the faith and purpose of the Jewish people. For example, Philo of Alexandria wrote in the *Exposition of the Laws* that he believed both Greek philosophy and the Bible should act as guides to Jewish life. Centuries later, the Enlightenment philosopher Baruch Spinoza made a case for secularism in his *Theological-Political Treatise* (1670). The Bible, Spinoza argued, could provide logic and reason but the idea that the Jewish people were "the chosen" by God should be regarded as fiction. Representing a contrary point of view was Moses Mendelssohn, who argued in *Jerusalem* (1783) that Jewish people were not only chosen but should strictly obey Jewish religious law. Rabbi Nachman of Bratslav introduces a new layer to Jewish thought with his posthumous *Tales* (1816). By combining Jewish mysticism with elements of European folktales, Nachman makes a case for Jews to value the qualities of "spontaneity and sincerity" over traditional piety. Ultimately, what makes *The People and the Books* so fascinating is how it challenges many people's perception of the faith as always having been the same by illustrating the diversity of Jewish thought over time.

Ultimately, the diversity in texts of *The People and the Books* demonstrates the alternation of Jewish cosmopolitanism and conservatism through the centuries. Many early works, like the book of Esther, which was written around the fourth century BCE, come across as more modern than texts published thousands of years later. This is largely because the Jews depicted in the book of Esther were intermarrying with outsiders, eating non-kosher food, and viewing their background as an ethnicity rather than a faith to practice. In these ways, they are comparable to secular Jews in contemporary America. While there was a call for stricter observation of Jewish law in later texts collected in *The People and the Books*, Kirsch notes small indications of modernity emerging at random. This is especially evident in Kirsch's analysis of the *Memoirs of Glückel of Hameln*, the recollections of a seventeenth-century Jewish businesswoman. Glückel of Hameln's accounts mark a progressive chapter of the religion's history for both Jewish men and women. As her memoirs prove, Western European Jews at this time were slowly becoming less devoted to religious authorities and the Torah. As Glückel reflects on her life, she writes about what Jewish women like her cared about most at this time: family and business. In this way, her experience is not unlike many modern Jewish American women.

One recurring theme found throughout these classics of Jewish literature is the idea that the Jewish relationship with God is a tumultuous one. As such, many of their writers find different ways to explain why God is often silent during times of hardship and struggle. The authors of the book of Deuteronomy, for example, argue that the divine presence of God is always there for the Jewish people but often too overwhelming and miraculous for them to bear. Later, Moses Maimonides explains in his twelfth-century *Guide of the Perplexed* that God often ap-

(Courtesy of Remy Kirsch)

An American poet and literary critic, Adam Kirsch teaches Jewish studies at Columbia University's Center for American Studies. His works include The Thousand Wells: Poems *(2002),* Invasions: New Poems *(2008), and* Why Trilling Matters *(2011).*

pears absent because God is, contrary to previous belief, an impersonal force. In contrast to this perceived distance, the *Zohar* (ca. 1290), a book of Jewish mysticism, states that with careful study and practice, God can be found in everyday actions such as prayer and sex.

Another point of continuity that Kirsch finds among the different historical texts is that all of the writers ruminate about the past and present while worrying about the fate of the Jewish people. In Theodor Herzl's *Old New Land* (1902) and numerous other texts, the idea of a homeland with Jewish sovereignty is presented as a means to solve the ongoing issue of Jewish exile and foreign oppression. Strangely, Kirsch does not include texts written after 1948, when the Jewish people declared the State of Israel an independent nation. *The People and the Books* would arguably feel more complete had he decided to do so.

Reviews of *The People and the Books* have been largely positive. Much praise has been given to Kirsch's ability to explain complex ancient manuscripts in a clear and comprehensive way. The critic for *Kirkus Reviews* called *The People and the Books* "a fascinating, impeccably written, personal tour of the great books of Judaism." Simply put, a lesser writer would not have been able to make dense religious works such as the book of Deuteronomy interesting to a broad audience. However, all eighteen of Kirsch's analyses are succinct and engaging—a testament to his talent. Thanks to the conversational tone and relatively open perspective that Kirsch maintains throughout these analyses, *The People and the Books* has also been extolled for being universally accessible. As Robert Alter wrote in his review for the *New York Times*, "the summaries of the books are lucid, vivid and likely to provide helpful instruction even to those who will never read the books." Similarly, *Publishers Weekly* called *The People and the Books* "eloquent and articulate," before praising Kirsch's ability to "pull together the social, intellectual, religious, and political threads of every era" in an engaging way.

It is important to note that some people will be frustrated by Kirsch's decision to accommodate nonreligious readers. By maintaining simple, straightforward summaries and analyses, Kirsch also avoids the nuances of the texts as well as the complicated circumstances that surrounded their authors' lives. For instance, he does not spend much time exploring whether or not these Jewish writers' works were crafted to appease the non-Jewish societies in which they lived. For readers looking for a truly in-depth understanding of these works of literature, *The People and the Books* may disappoint. On the other hand, *The People and the Books* may come across as too dry for other readers. Kirsch's primary purpose with the book is to analyze ancient texts; consequently, it has an academic undertone that may not appeal to everyone. Nonetheless, Kirsch's ability to connect these ancient texts to the present day is likely to capture the attention even of readers who did not previously believe they were interested in history or theology. Many others will enjoy how Kirsch's fresh perspective on classic works succeeds in creating a more complete understanding of the Jewish identity. Ambitious, insightful, and thorough, *The People and the Books* expands today's often-narrow perception of Judaism in a warm and empowering way.

Emily Turner

Review Sources

Alter, Robert. "Seeing the Diversity of Jewish Thought in 18 Classic Texts." Review of The People and the Books: 18 Classics of Jewish Literature, by Adam Kirsch. *The New York Times*, 16 Nov. 2016, www.nytimes.com/2016/11/20/books/review/people-and-the-books-jewish-literature-adam-kirsch.html. Accessed 22 Jan. 2017.

Horn, Dara. "Adam Kirsch's Anthology of Jewish Civilization's Greatest Hits." Review of *The People and the Books: 18 Classics of Jewish Literature*, by Adam Kirsch. *The Wall Street Journal*, 10 Oct. 2016, www.wsj.com/articles/adam-kirschs-anthology-of-jewish-civilizations-greatest-hits-1475871472. Accessed 22 Jan. 2017.

Review of *The People and the Books: 18 Classics of Jewish Literature*, by Adam Kirsch. *Kirkus*, 19 July 2016, www.kirkusreviews.com/book-reviews/adam-kirsch/the-people-and-the-books. Accessed 22 Jan. 2017.

Review of *The People and the Books: 18 Classics of Jewish Literature*, by Adam Kirsch. *Publishers Weekly*, 8 Aug. 2016, www.publishersweekly.com/978-0-393-24176-1. Accessed 22 Jan. 2017.

The Performance of Becoming Human

Author: Daniel Borzutzky (b. 1974)
Publisher: Brooklyn Arts Press (New York).
   96 pp.
Type of work: Poetry

Daniel Borzutzky's poetry collection The Performance of Becoming Human *blends strong imagery with satirical prose to offer an indictment of the modern world. Exploring themes of privatization, overdevelopment, immigration, and neoliberalism, Borzutzky uses his own background as a poet of Chilean descent to blast the systems at play and create a wasteland of humanity in words and emotion.*

(Courtesy of Brooklyn Arts Press)

In his collection *The Performance of Becoming Human*, which won the 2016 National Book Award for poetry, Daniel Borzutzky has constructed a monolith made from fragments of society's darkest moments and most violent tendencies. The title itself is a bucket for the many ways in which people's humanity has been stripped from them through deregulation and privatization. As the narrators of Borzutzky's poems come to terms with the new nightmares surrounding them—public officials and policemen watching their every move; brutal torture, beatings, and killings happening in the United States and abroad for political ends; the disembodied sense of self that many of these voices are left with after they have been initiated into the new system—the images become more disturbing and vivid, and the culture that emerges cannot be considered entirely what one might call human.

Clearly one of Borzutzky's preoccupations is the body and how it performs within the parameters that are allowed it. One of the poems in this volume, "The Broken Testimony," begins with the lines,

> There is a beat behind this writing
> A nervous tap
> Against a plastic-coated table
> A body is trying to move forward
> It is blocked by its insistence on movement
> The performance of stasis played backwards
> It disappears or its absence appears

giving a claustrophobic tone to an already uncomfortable setting.
With his poems, Borzutzky taps into the viral mood of modern culture, whether

that means a never-ending supply of new "personality" quizzes, a single violent image spreading across the ether, or a listicle packaging the seemingly complex into something superficial and digestible for a distracted audience. In fact, many of these pieces read like lists of the horrid and the mundane. Damaged and destroyed bodies inhabiting uninhabitable landscapes, a narrator's quick inward observations, and analyses of a doom-inducing government power are delivered as one-liners, one after another, with the tragic punch line being the irresistible demise of a recognizable civilization. Other selections read like a fragile madman's response to the evening news, as if the speaker has seen one image too many and was pushed to insanity. In something like a brilliant corporate marketing campaign, Borzutzky has come to sell readers the end of times, lumping himself and his audience in with the maligned and sick who inhabit his poems.

In addition to his examination of the body and of physical infirmity, Borzutzky uses his work to explore and undermine a modern neoliberal agenda by aligning its rhetoric with many of the forms of violence he presents and urging readers to do the same. In this relatively slim volume, Borzutzky relentlessly makes his case while never straying from his point or purpose. His speakers

(Courtesy of Angel Dean Lopez)

Daniel Borzutzky has published several poetry collections and chapbooks, including The Ecstasy of Capitulation *(2006) and* The Book of Interfering Bodies *(2011), as well as* Arbitrary Tales *(2005), a book of short fiction. He is also an avid translator, having brought the works of Chilean poets Raúl Zurita and Jaime Luis Huenún to English-speaking audiences. He has taught at Wilbur Wright College in the City Colleges of Chicago system, at the School of the Art Institute of Chicago, and at Koç University in Istanbul.* The Performance of Becoming Human *won the 2016 National Book Award for poetry.*

obsessively examine the violence done to the bodies around them while also cataloging their own levels of dis-ease. This is urgent writing, at times desperate, always learned and necessary. The opening poem, "Let Light Shine out of Darkness," begins, "I live in a body that does not have enough light in it / For years, I did not know that I needed to have more light / Once, I walked around my city on a dying morning and a decomposing body approached me and asked me why I had no light," setting the tone for the rest of the collection. If the reader is asking why this narrator has no light, Borzutzky is about to answer that question with the sixteen poems that follow; or perhaps he is about to offer a light to such bodies, highlighting their experiences and forcing the reader to face their realities. The decomposing body—the first of many that will appear throughout this collection—is sometimes the government, sometimes those who have been destroyed by harmful government policies, and at times even a direct mirror of the narrator. By the poem's end, the reader has been bombarded by images carefully described by the narrator. Images of electrocutions, a boy's ear bitten off, and the disappeared being tossed from airplanes litter this sparse prose poem. Using a modified list format, Borzutzky creates a cacophony of voices and images that mirrors the modern shock-value news cycle, designed for ratings glory rather than truth telling. He is saying, yes, the truth is in these details, but not in the way people think.

In another poem, "The Privatized Waters of Dawn," a disembodied police force has taken over the narrator's life. They are in his bathroom, lobbing questions at him and putting out cigarettes on his body; they are on the street, harassing a long-haired, starving driver while the narrator hides behind his window blinds; they represent a chorus of bureaucrats making demands upon the bodies of citizens. By the poem's end, the narrator concedes that he can no longer afford to own himself, or his freedom. "I cost much less than my historical value," he tells the reader, yet the bank has denied the loan that would allow him to buy back himself.

Though Borzutzky's narrators are clearly victims of the system, the poet himself once worked for the city of Chicago, and he alludes to this detail several times in the collection. In the poem "In the Blazing Cities of Your Rotting Carcass Mouth," for instance, the speaker says, "Once I made $60,057 a year working for the city. This was before it blazed," admitting that even he has been on the side he seeks to implicate. In this same poem, the speaker seeks to commodify the art he is performing for his audience with two "imagination challenges" for the reader, one in the middle of the piece and one to end it. In the first, after posing an absurd hypothetical situation that strings together an incongruous series of images and cultural touchstones—matzo balls mixed with jalapeños and Fritos and then set on fire, a Manchester United game featuring the team's former player Javier "Chicharito" Hernández, and a Skype session conducted with one's mother while simultaneously "sexting with your boyfriend who works for the secret police"—the speaker implores the reader, "Write a sonnet or a villanelle about this experience and do not use any adjectives." The second challenge details a more gruesome scene, in which the reader is "decomposing in a cage or a cell" while the reader's father tells the story of a man who was forced to watch his children being burned to death by the military; the speaker then instructs the reader, "Write a free-verse poem about the experience. Write it in the second person. / Publish it some place good." In the world Borzutzky envisions, even poetry is doing the work of capitalism, and the by-products of inhumane treatment are nothing more than fodder for the next piece of art to be sold. A story is simply material to be harvested and exploited for one's own gain.

The consistently exciting language and variety of form in *The Performance of Becoming Human* makes for a captivating collection. Borzutzky's mastery of voice perfectly presents the stories and images, offering an evocative and affecting experience that leaves a lasting impression. His effective use of satire and parody forces the difficult subject matter to be translated into sympathy, even empathy. In an interview with Matthew Reed Corey and Joel Craig for the online journal *Matter*, published in January 2015, Borzutzky said of his writing process and subject matter, "I'm sympathetic to the idea that it's utopian to write about the horribleness of the world in beautiful ways. That to write through violence, to reimagine and recontextualize it and try to show just how awful the world actually is—that there's something beautiful about doing this. It's old fashioned, right?" Adding to this, Borzutzky carefully and brilliantly evokes place in his work, whether writing about what seems a postapocalyptic version of Chicago, Mexico, Chile, or Brazil. Often his examples and images are what reflect these locations. Borzutzky was born in Pittsburgh, Pennsylvania, to Chilean parents, and his unique view of Rust Belt cities, aligned with an international, outward-looking sensibility, is part of what allows this work to resonate so deeply.

In a review for the online magazine *decomP*, Spencer Dew wrote vividly about Borzutzky's use of place, politics, and violence, making the claim that "politics is theater" and asking, "What of literature attempting to address and engage with such theatrics?" Tyrone Williams, reviewing the collection for the *Lana Turner* journal, provided a thoughtful analysis of Borzutzky's performance as a poet, noting his studied "self-flagellation" in one of the book's prose poems and the ways in which he "inhabit[s] the forms of comedy," setting up "'jokes' that are only performing the form of the joke," to further his vision. The collection was reviewed in many smaller journals and positively received.

Ultimately the collection asks, What is to be done? Borzutzky's speakers are at times complacent and even complicit, while they seem to bemoan the state of the world at others. Do the images presented rattle readers to action, or has the poet created another commodity out of the pain and grief found on the nightly news? And if readers are rattled, what can they do? What are the options for action, or is it already too late? The collection's final piece, "The Mountain at the End of This Book," does not offer easy answers to any of these questions. Near the end of this last poem, Borzutzky writes, "On the mountain, the free-market poems absorb themselves and regenerate into billions of the blankest verses there ever were," calling into question the purpose of the poet in the first place and suggesting that artists are as susceptible to capitalism as anyone else. The poem closes with an image of abandoned children behind windows, writing "Come find us" on the glass "as they disappear into the bubbling mud." With this one final image, Borzutzky further complicates the image of creator versus commodifier, and the ambiguity is a terrifying delight.

Melynda Fuller

Review Sources

Dew, Spencer. Review of *The Performance of Becoming Human*, by Daniel Borzutzky. *decomP*, May 2016, www.decompmagazine.com/theperformanceofbecoming-human.htm. Accessed 1 Feb. 2017.

McClure, J. G. Review of *The Performance of Becoming Human*, by Daniel Borzutzky. *Center for Literary Publishing*, Colorado State U, coloradoreview.colostate.edu/reviews/the-performance-of-becoming-human/. Accessed 1 Feb. 2017.

Review of *The Performance of Becoming Human*, by Daniel Borzutzky. *Publishers Weekly*, 5 Dec. 2016, www.publishersweekly.com/978-1-936767-46-5. Accessed 1 Feb. 2017.

William, Tyrone. Review of *The Performance of Becoming Human*, by Daniel
Borzutzky. *Lana Turner*, no. 9, 2016, www.lanaturnerjournal.com/contents/the-
performance-of-becoming-human-by-daniel-borzutzky-brooklyn-arts-press-2016.
Accessed 1 Feb. 2017.

The Pigeon Tunnel
Stories from My Life

Author: John le Carré (pseudonym of David
  Cornwell; b. 1931)
Publisher: Viking (New York). 320 pp.
Type of work: Memoir
Time: 1960s to the present
Locale: Various places around the world;
  usually locales associated with the settings
  of le Carré's novels or where he has lived

*A memoir of John le Carré's writing career
that describes the places he traveled while
researching his novels and his encounters
with many people who influenced his writing
or were drawn to him because of his work.
The focus is on his professional career, although le Carré's efforts to come to terms
with his father and their strained relationship is an important part of the book.*

(Courtesy of Penguin Random House)

Principal personages:
JOHN LE CARRÉ, the author, whose given name is David Cornwell
RONNIE CORNWELL, the author's father
NICHOLAS ELLIOTT, an agent of the British Secret Service, friend of the double agent
  Kim Philby
SIR MAURICE OLDFIELD, one-time head of the British Secret Service
SIR ALEC GUINNESS, British actor who played George Smiley in a 1979 television
  adaptation of le Carré's 1963 novel Tinker, Tailor, Soldier, Spy
SIR RICHARD BURTON, Welsh actor who portrayed Alex Leamas in the 1965 film ver-
  sion of le Carré's 1963 novel The Spy Who Came in from the Cold
YASSIR ARAFAT, leader of the Palestine Liberation Organization until his death in 2004
MARGARET THATCHER, prime minister of the United Kingdom from 1979 to 1990

The Pigeon Tunnel deals primarily with two aspects of the life of writer John le Carré
(which is the pen name of David Cornwell). The major focus is on his writing career,
beginning with the publication of his first novel, *A Call for the Dead*, in 1961, but really taking off with his first spy novel, *The Spy Who Came in from the Cold*, in 1963. A
secondary focus is on the people he has encountered throughout his long career. Some
of these are people he worked with in his brief time in the British intelligence service
or has encountered over the years because of his reputation, both real and perceived.
Others are people that le Carré based characters on in his novels—some of whom have
no connection to the fields of intelligence or spying. For example, le Carré notes that

Vivian Green, his mentor at Oxford, "gave me by example the inner life of George Smiley." There are also brief glimpses of editors who have worked with le Carré, actors who have played some of his major characters in films and television adaptation of his books, and some of the producers with whom le Carré worked on these endeavors.

Like many memoirs, this work is not strictly an autobiography. It is instead a series of stories from le Carré's long and successful career, with little attempt to provide an overall theme or framework for these stories. For readers unfamiliar with le Carré's work or life, this can be frustrating. More intimate details of his life, such as his marriages and his children, receive very little coverage. He writes lovingly about his home in Cornwall, England, and about the cabin he had built in a village near Bern, Switzerland, in the 1960s. There is relatively little attention to the years he spent as an intelligence officer, mostly in Bonn, in what was then the Federal Republic of Germany. Le Carré gives some brief attention to his education but notes that the best training he ever received in writing

(Courtesy of Anton Corbijn)

Writing under the pen name John le Carré, David Cornwell has written more than twenty novels dealing with espionage and intelligence services generally, several of which have been adapted as feature films or television productions. He served briefly in the British intelligence service in the early days of the Cold War. In 2008, the Times of London listed him among the fifty greatest British writers since World War II.

techniques was not from any school or editor, but from his supervisors in the intelligence service, all of whom were classically educated at major British universities—these were the people who taught him to write clearly, succinctly, and to say precisely what he meant to say. Le Carré, however, gives only brief comments about how he writes. He notes that he likes the privacy of writing and thus has avoided, as much as possible, interviews and presentations at writing conferences. However, he has also made it a point to travel to the locales that he plans to use as a setting for a novel—a commitment he made after narrowly avoiding making an embarrassing mistake about a place he had not visited. From the people he encountered in these travels, le Carré collected bits and pieces of potential characters like a geologist collects rock samples.

Throughout his career, le Carré has said little about his work in British intelligence, in part because he feels a debt of loyalty to the people he worked with, and also because British law prohibits it. Here he notes another reason: he wanted his novels about spies to be seen not simply as exposés of what he learned as an insider, but as "works of imagination that owed only a nod to the reality that spawned them." But because he has written so much about the world of espionage and undercover operations, he is often approached by those who consider him an expert on such matters. His novels are generally seen as realistic and accurate in their portrayal of the "tradecraft" of spies and others in the world of espionage. Therefore, he has often been sought out by people working for various intelligence agencies and even by heads of governments, who want his advice and input on their own operations. He frankly admits his embarrassment at the fact that these people assume he knows much more than he does, and sometimes he can respond with only the most broad and generic observations. He tells of one person who mistakenly believed that he had been the chief of secret services for the British intelligence system. When le Carré tried to make it clear he had never held such an exalted position, the response was along the lines of "of course that is what you would say." Sometimes, as when British prime minister Margaret Thatcher asked him to have lunch with her and the prime minister of the Netherlands in 1982, le Carré admits coming away from the meeting not knowing why he had been summoned.

One of the longest chapters in the book is titled "Son of the Author's Father" and deals with the unhappy, complicated relationship between le Carré and his father, Ronnie Cornwell. Ronnie was a grafter and con man, and while he had failed on several occasions on a massive scale and spent several stretches in prison in various nations, he always projected the con man's eternal optimism that the next grand scheme would produce the big break. While this chapter is near the end of the book, there are bits of foreshadowing earlier on that alert the reader to the significance of Ronnie and the rocky father-son relationship le Carré had with him. Le Carré's mother, Olive, Ronnie's first wife, walked out on the family when he was five years old. However, while she was merely absent, Ronnie's stream of frequent departures and reentries were a constant source of trouble and embarrassment to his son. Le Carré admits to knowing little about his father's early life or the precise details of many of his scams.

While they never became close or even fully reconciled, le Carré does note the impact his father had on his writing career, as well as his work in espionage. Because of his family background, deception and the fabrication of stories came to him naturally, and when he was invited to join the British intelligence service, he felt in a way that he was coming home. The men and women associated with Ronnie's life provided le Carré with "a cast of characters to make the most blasé writer's mouth water." He quotes Graham Greene's saying that "childhood is the credit balance of the writer" and concludes, "By that measure, at least, I was born a millionaire." Realizing that his own father was a character too good to let go to waste, le Carré modelled the character of Rick Pym in *A Perfect Spy* (1986) after his father. In that novel, Rick Pym appears primarily in the recollections of the main character, Magnus Pym, about his father.

Le Carré had made a previous attempt at a memoir. However, proving as skilled a liar as his father, he found that he could not always separate fact from fiction in his memories. He hired two private detectives and charged them with fact-checking his life. Eventually, they had to prepare a report about his father's life—but they soon gave up in frustration. It was already too late, they reported, to separate the truth from the fiction about Ronnie's life. He gave up, too, and abandoned the memoir. *The Pigeon Tunnel* has had generally good reviews from critics, although some have noted the rather haphazard arrangement of some fairly significant encounters mixed in with brief stories of lesser importance. Several reviewers have noted the fact that this memoir came out only a year after Adam Sisman's massive biography *John le Carré: The*

Biography (2015), for which le Carré had given over fifty hours of interviews and had allowed Sisman access to his own papers—raising the question of why le Carré should write a memoir at all so close to the biography's release. Le Carré was reportedly less than satisfied with certain aspects of the biography and began this memoir immediately after its release. Those wanting details, or even a straightforward chronology of le Carré's life, however, will want to consult Sisman's work. In *The Pigeon Tunnel*, readers get le Carré's own take on his feelings and impressions about what was significant in the events he does choose to describe.

Early on in this book, le Carré claims that he has not fabricated any of these stories, although certain names may appear as aliases and certain details are deliberately omitted. He states that he has never kept a diary, so his reflections are based on memory and on a few scattered notes saved over the years. But these notes, he admits, were often written down through the eyes or the mind of a character he was inventing—thus they were not simply records of what le Carré saw or experienced, but what George Smiley or Alec Leamas might have taken away from these events. Some reviewers have raised the obvious question—since espionage and fiction writing both deal with creating deceptions and selling them to an audience, how can the reader be sure that what is presented here is factual? Certain parts, such as the material about his relationship with his father, reveal a pain and a depth of feeling that certainly ring true. For the rest, perhaps it is best to leave the matter just as le Carré does in the subtitle—these are stories from the author's life, and they are told with the humor and art of a masterful storyteller.

Mark S. Joy, PhD

Review Sources

Boyd, William. "*The Pigeon Tunnel* by John le Carré Review—What Made Him Write a Memoir?" Review of *The Pigeon Tunnel: Stories from My Life*, by John le Carré. *The Guardian*, 8 Sept. 2015, www.theguardian.com/books/2016/sep/08/ the-pigeon-tunnel-john-le-carre-review-memoir-autobiography. Accessed 17 Dec. 2016.

Isaacson, Walter. "John le Carré's Memoir about His Journey from Spy to Novelist." Review of The Pigeon Tunnel: Stories from My Life, by John le Carré. *The New York Times*, 18 Sept. 2016, www.nytimes.com/2016/09/18/books/review/john-le-carre-pigeon-tunnel.html. Accessed 12 Jan. 2017.

Morton, Brian. "His Greatest Story Yet: The Memoirs of John le Carré." Review of *The Pigeon Tunnel: Stories from My Life*, by John le Carré. *BBC*, 5 Sept. 2016, www.bbc.co.uk/programmes/articles/1kkNBxzxcFwxqkXvLWN0xQ6/his-greatest-story-yet-the-memoirs-of-john-le-carre. Accessed 17 Dec 2016.

Woog, Adam. "John le Carré's *The Pigeon Tunnel*: Some Spellbinding True Tales of a Master Spy Novelist." Review of *The Pigeon Tunnel: Stories from My Life*, by John le Carré. *Seattle Times*, 18 Sept. 2016, www.seattletimes.com/entertainment/ books/john-le-carrs-the-pigeon-tunnel-some-spellbinding-true-tales-of-a-master-spy-novelist/. Accessed 17 Dec. 2016.

The Portable Veblen

Author: Elizabeth McKenzie (b. 1958)
Publisher: Penguin Press (New York). Illustrated, with appendices. 430 pp.
Type of work: Novel
Time: Present day
Locales: California; Washington, DC; Arlington, Virginia

(Courtesy of Penguin Random House)

An imaginative, satirical skewering of contemporary society's foibles, The Portable Veblen *offers a cast of wildly unorthodox but nevertheless believable characters, a convoluted but logically unfolding plot, a congenially off-center philosophical outlook, and an abundance of arboreal rodents.*

Principal characters:

VEBLEN "VEB" AMUNDSON-HOVDA, an eccentric young woman who lives a directionless life and talks to squirrels
DR. PAUL VREELAND, her fiancé, a medical researcher
MELANIE DUFFY, her hypochondriac, controlling mother
RUDGEAR "RUDGE," her erratic biological father, confined to a mental health facility
BILL VREELAND, Paul's father, a former hippie
JUSTIN VREELAND, Paul's mentally disabled older brother
CLORIS HUTMACHER, a fabulously wealthy recruiter for Hutmacher Pharmaceuticals, for whom Paul works
MUU MUU, a gray squirrel to whom Veblen talks

In *A Midsummer Night's Dream*, William Shakespeare notes that the course of true love never runs smooth. That sentiment serves as an underlying theme of Elizabeth McKenzie's *The Portable Veblen*, an entertaining and original novel bursting with ideas presented in the course of detailing the difficult romance between two protagonists whose flaws are more the result of external forces than internal ones.

One half of the couple is Veblen Amundsen-Hovda, a young woman who toils as a semipermanent temporary worker at Stanford University School of Medicine and translates documents into Norwegian in her spare time. A normally cheerful free spirit, Veblen's lack of ambition is mainly due to her domineering mother, Melanie, a larger-than-life figure whose overbearing influence causes Veblen to take antidepressants, visit psychiatrists, and bite her own arm in times of stress. An extra complicating factor is her biological father, Rudgear, known as Rudge, an angry, mercurial individual confined to a mental health institution. Veblen, named for economist Thorstein Veblen, was an only child, and was terribly lonely during her youth because of her attention-seeking mother's frequent hypochondriac emergencies. Veblen enjoys talking to squirrels, because she can say anything to them without being criticized, ridiculed, or made to feel inferior.

Her intended mate is Dr. Paul Vreeland, a neurological researcher at the same facility where Veblen is employed. Paul has his own familial cross to bear: he was raised by drug-addled parents in a commune-like environment in Humboldt County, alongside a mentally disabled older brother who demanded all his parents' care and who seemed always to purposely sabotage Paul's life. Just before meeting Veblen, Paul, who conducted experiments on small mammals while working towards a treatment for brain injuries of wounded military personnel, developed a device to perform field craniotomies. The device is a gun-like machine that uses compressed air to punch a three-inch-diameter hole in a patient's skull to relieve pressure. Paul was subsequently recruited by beautiful, predatory Cloris Hutmacher, a scout for the massive, powerful family conglomerate Hutmacher Pharmaceuticals. Envisioning fame and fortune after being stifled in his youth, Paul signs a contract with the company for a cash bonus and stock options. After meeting in Washington, DC, with representatives from health and military institutions his device is approved for trial at a Veterans Affairs (VA) facility, first on cadavers and later on live volunteer subjects who were brain-injured in battle.

Veblen and Paul become constant companions, and within months of their meeting he moves into her bungalow in Palo Alto. He gives her a large, gaudy engagement ring and they begin to discuss wedding plans. A bone of contention in their relationship is the presence of an aggressive squirrel that takes up residence in the attic. Nature-loving Veblen is happy to have the rodent there, but Paul is annoyed and tries to capture it with a baited humane trap. Though each of the lovebirds, like any couple, has peculiarities—she prefers meatballs made of turkey, he hates corn on the cob—they manage to overcome minor differences and draw closer together.

An editor at Chicago Quarterly Review *and* Catamaran Literary Review, *Elizabeth McKenzie previously published a story collection,* Stop That Girl *(2005), and a novel,* MacGregor Tells the World *(2007). Her fiction has appeared in such periodicals as the* New Yorker *and the* Atlantic Monthly.

The strength of Paul and Veblen's union is tested, however, by their meetings with each other's families. When Melanie meets Paul, she gives him her complete medical history, discusses her most intimate physical symptoms, and pries a diagnosis out of him, with which she angrily disagrees. Further exacerbating the situation, Melanie cajoles Paul into accompanying her husband, kindly, mild-mannered Linus, in an onerous chore: retrieving the roof of a chicken coop that blew off during a storm to land into a deep, brush-choked ravine.

Veblen's meeting with Paul's family is similarly trying. During a meal at a fancy restaurant, Paul's brother, Justin, begins choking, and his father, Bill, has to perform the Heimlich maneuver, which is disgustingly successful. When Paul talks about his new job, Bill launches into a long diatribe about Hutmacher Pharmaceuticals as a corporate profiteer. Later, after the group assembles at Veblen's bungalow for dessert, it is discovered that Justin masturbated into a pair of Veblen's panties.

Meanwhile, tests of Paul's device are conducted on corpses at the VA facility, during which time a slight flaw in the mechanism is detected. Paul makes notes for improving the device, but before changes in the instrument can be carried out and appropriate tests can be made on living subjects, Paul is required to travel to San Jose to attend a Hutmacher-sponsored medical and pharmaceutical trade show. Upon arrival, he is outraged to learn that his still-unproven device has been packaged and is being prematurely marketed as the Pneumatic Turbo Skull Punch. When he voices his objections, first to Carter Locke, Hutmacher vice president of sales, and afterward to Cloris Hutmacher herself, he is thrown out of the trade show.

While Paul is away, Veblen rescues the squirrel trapped in the cage in her attic, and drives away with the animal to release it, but is reluctant to let it go. She checks into a motel with the cage, gets tipsy on beer, and talks intimately with the squirrel. Paul, distraught because of what happened, tries to call Veblen. He overhears her talking with the squirrel and thinks she is with another man. Paul throws his phone away and goes off to get drunk.

The next day, Veblen visits her mentally ill father to learn if he will be able to attend her wedding. Paul in the meantime, visits the VA to find his former office completely stripped of furnishings, and decides to write a whistleblowing letter about what Hutmacher has done with his device. As he exits the building, he sees Cloris driving off, headed directly at a squirrel, and irrationally throws himself between the car and the animal.

A humorous, frolicsome novel filled with well-drawn characters and a multitude of examples of sharply observed human behavior, *The Portable Veblen* has much to recommend it. Small photographs scattered throughout the pages serve to punctuate and emphasize particular scenes. Appendices—Melanie's letter to a clinical study center regarding her many physical symptoms, a clipped article about Paul and Veblen, a list of words for "squirrel" in sixty-five languages from Albanian to Zulu, an interview with Cloris Hutmacher, a questionnaire from Melanie to Veblen—add to the fun, furthering the story and underscoring characters' personality traits delineated throughout the novel.

Though ostensibly a comically dysfunctional love story, *The Portable Veblen* takes time to touch upon a number of serious issues in the process of unraveling the unpredictable plot. At the heart of the tale is the concept that the sins of the parents are visited upon their children; without the strong bond established between Veblen and Paul, it is doubtful that the psychological damage caused to them by bad parenting would ever be repaired. This thread is reinforced by reference to a book that sounds invented, but actually exists: Adolf Guggenbühl-Craig's *Marriage: Dead or Alive* (1977), which encourages committed partnerships so the participants can each become whole individuals. A related subtopic is the notion that medication is a poor substitute for caring human interaction.

Some of McKenzie's strongest condemnations are reserved for the pharmaceutical industry's penchant for taking shortcuts in its haste to bring profitable products to the marketplace. The military's glee in devising shiny and expensive hardware also takes a hit, as does the callous indifference towards wounded veterans who, having suffered grievously in their service, are manipulated into serving again as unpaid, voluntary test subjects, and are treated more like statistics than humans.

A strong thread running through the novel is the connection between Veblen and the man for whom she was named, economist-sociologist Thorstein Veblen (1857–1929). His best-known work, *The Theory of the Leisure Class* (1899), details the concepts of conspicuous consumption, and its companion conspicuous leisure, as indicators of social class—as exemplified in *The Portable Veblen* by such memorable characters as Cloris Hutmacher and Paul's best friend, Hans Borg.

Critical reception of *The Portable Veblen* was largely positive, with many reviewers particularly praising McKenzie's use of language. "[McKenzie] hears the musical potential in language that others do not," Jennifer Senior wrote for the *New York Times*. The character of Melanie is another stand-out; Scarlett Thomas, for the *Guardian*, calls her "a comic creation worthy of Dickens." Some critics found the book's quirkiness forced, but others found it endearing—what Sophie Elmhirst for the *Financial Times* complained of as "hyperactive eccentricity" and "self-conscious, chirpy voice," Senior praised as "festive originality" and "charm, bounce, and radiant eccentrics." Elizabeth Rosner, for the *San Francisco Chronicle*, went so far as to compare McKenzie with masters of dark, absurdist humor Joseph Heller and Kurt Vonnegut Jr.

A final layer in the multitextured work is the symbolism of the squirrel, which shows up almost everywhere, including in dreams. (A final hilarious chapter is presented from the point of view the squirrel itself). In literature, the furry, sociable animal by its constant movement represents boundless energy, and by its habit of collecting nuts demonstrates preparedness. In some cultures, especially Native American, the squirrel is considered a messenger; in other cultures, the animal represents unbounded passion. Mostly, however, the squirrel symbolizes the lasting impression that will be left with the reader of *The Portable Veblen*: a spirit of controlled playfulness.

Jack Ewing

Review Sources

Elmhirst, Sophie. Review of *The Portable Veblen*, by Elizabeth McKenzie. *Financial Times*, 22 Jan. 2016, www.ft.com/cms/s/2/5f0240ea-be05-11e5-9fdb-87b8d15baec2.html. Accessed 8 Nov. 2016.

Rosner, Elizabeth. Review of *The Portable Veblen*, by Elizabeth McKenzie. *San Francisco Chronicle*, 14 Jan. 2016, www.sfgate.com/books/article/The-Portable-Veblen-by-Elizabeth-McKenzie-6759548.php. Accessed 8 Nov. 2016.

Senior, Jennifer. "Facing Marriage and Befriending a Squirrel in 'The Portable Veblen.'" Review of The Portable Veblen, by Elizabeth McKenzie. *The New York Times*, 27 Jan. 2016, www.nytimes.com/2016/01/28/books/review-facing-marriage-and-befriending-a-squirrel-in-the-portable-veblen.html. Accessed 8 Nov. 2016.

Thomas, Scarlett. "'Raw, Weird and Hilarious." Review of *The Portable Veblen*, by Elizabeth McKenzie. *The Guardian*, 19 Feb. 2016, www.theguardian.com/ books/2016/feb/18/the-portable-veblen-elizabeth-mckenzie-review. Accessed 8 Nov. 2016.

Pumpkinflowers
A Soldier's Story

Author: Matti Friedman (b. 1978)
Publisher: Algonquin Books (Chapel Hill, NC). Illustrated. 256 pp.
Type of work: History, current affairs, memoir
Time: 1994–2002
Locales: Southern Lebanon, Israel

Pumpkinflowers *presents a brisk, tense account of an obscure and almost forgotten war that pitted Israeli forces against guerrillas in southern Lebanon—a conflict that mirrors the more widespread sectarian violence that has raged throughout the Middle East since the late twentieth century.*

(Courtesy of Algonquin Books)

Principal personages:

MATTI FRIEDMAN, the author of the book, who is now a journalist but who served for several years as a soldier in the Israeli army in the late 1990s

AVI "THE SKUNK" OFNER, a short, well-built, rebellious teenaged soldier and a voracious reader who served at Pumpkin, an army outpost in southern Lebanon

ERAN STERN, a soldier who loses an arm during a barrage aimed at the outpost

YOHAI BEN-YISHAL, Avi's commanding officer, who is severely wounded in a guerrilla attack

JONAH MANDEL, Friedman's childhood friend from Toronto

One of the basic tenets of journalism—along with such principles as accuracy, objectivity, and public accountability—is that journalists should not become embroiled in the stories on which they are reporting. To do so supposedly violates a significant ethical consideration: conflict of interest.

Sometimes, however, personal involvement in a particular story is unavoidable. A case in point is Matti Friedman's nonfiction work *Pumpkinflowers: A Soldier's Story*. The book is primarily a crisp retelling of an almost unknown series of skirmishes between the Israeli military and the Lebanon-based Islamist militant group Hezbollah. The book also incorporates the firsthand account of the author's own participation while he was performing compulsory army service, during part of an eighteen-year-long Israeli occupation of a volatile slice of Lebanese territory.

The Pumpkin of the book's title is the code name for a small, rectangular, concrete-reinforced army outpost on a hill in southern Lebanon, near an eight-hundred-year-old Crusader structure, Beaufort Castle. The Pumpkin, one of a similarly situated series of outposts (others nearby are named Red Pepper, Cyprus, and Citrus), was established in 1982 to provide a so-called "security zone" stretching fifty miles east and west to protect Israeli farmers just south of the Lebanese border from terrorist attacks. Visible from the fort's jury-rigged shipping-container observation post is a thick, concealing forest, and beyond lies the Shiite town of Nabatieh, a hotbed of Hezbollah guerrilla activity. Like French Foreign Legionnaires of yore, Israeli soldiers, equipped with armored tanks, night-vision goggles, and other technology, have been subjected to periodic violent enemy assaults, featuring rockets, improvised explosive devices (IEDs), grenades, artillery barrages, and machine-gun fire. Though the defenders inflict casualties on the attackers, they suffer losses of their own; wounded soldiers referred to in radio reports to Israeli headquarters are called "flowers" in military terms, and the dead are called "oleanders."

When *Pumpkinflowers* opens, it is early 1994, in the twelfth year of the Pumpkin's existence. The third-person narrative focuses on eighteen-year-old Avi Ofner, a typical soldier at the Israeli outpost and a member of an infantry brigade, the Fighting Pioneer Youth. Avi, symbolic of all the individuals who served at the isolated fortress, keeps a journal. Excerpts from Avi's writings reveal details about his varied relationships with his comrades-in-arms, about his future aspirations, his hobbies and interests, his hopes, dreams, and fears. The narrative enumerates daily chores and activities and captures the soldiers' cynicism and love-hate feelings toward their superior officers. This initial section of the book illustrates the modern equivalent of many of the common experiences of warriors from any place or time; those who fought in the Trojan War were probably just as annoyed at having to clean their weapons or perform menial KP kitchen patrol duties. Particularly evocative are passages dealing with the energy-sapping, morale-draining boredom of being stuck in the middle of nowhere with little to do in the long slack periods between the intense stimulation of attacks and counterattacks. Such life-or-death events, such as the Falcon Incident, in which twelve members of a thirteen-man Israeli patrol were killed in a brief but lethal firefight, are vividly recounted.

Avi's role, and Part One of *Pumpkinflowers*, ends suddenly on February 4, 1997. With just a month of his military service left, Avi is returning from leave in Tel Aviv, where he plans to attend university. Along with seventy-two other soldiers, he boards one of two helicopters for transportation back to the outpost. As they approach the Pumpkin, something goes horribly wrong: the two helicopters collide midair and crash, killing all on board both aircraft.

As Avi's story ends, Matti Friedman enters the story, and the narrative changes from third-person to first-person. A young man of Jewish heritage born in Canada, following high school graduation Friedman makes *aliyah*—the name given to the immigration to Israel of Jews from the diaspora. After working at a kibbutz dairy for eighteen months, Friedman receives his draft notice: he will need to serve in the army for three years. Along with his longtime friend Jonah Mandel, Friedman joins the same unit as the late Avi Ofner. In early 1998, Friedman and other replacement soldiers board trucks to travel north to the Pumpkin.

Meanwhile, in Israel, citizens outraged by the carnage of the helicopter crash begin to question the necessity of maintaining the security zone. A movement, led by kibbutzniks Bruria Sharon, whose son has been drafted, and Orna Shimoni, whose son Eyal, a tank commander, was killed at a Lebanese outpost, springs up.

By Part Three of the story, Friedman and the other new recruits have settled into the usual routine at the outpost, and readers are treated to the fresh perspective of a different narrator. Although conditions are still deadly—a guerrilla attack is launched just two weeks after the green soldiers arrive— elements of dark humor are introduced. Fireworks shot off to celebrate a wedding at a local village cause momentary panic when they are mistaken for incoming rounds. A potential gaggle of terrorists observed through thermal sights turns out to be nothing more sinister than a rooting herd of wild boars. To stave off ennui, outpost soldiers observing the landmarks of the nearby town of Nabatieh—monastery, hospital, gas station, mosques, villas damaged by shellfire—make up fanciful stories about the occupants, particularly a bottle blonde in a residence nicknamed the House of Babes.

(Courtesy of Sebastian Sheiner)

A reporter and former Associated Press *correspondent, Matti Friedman has written articles for the* New York Times, *the* Washington Post, *the* Wall Street Journal, *and many other periodicals. His first nonfiction book,* The Aleppo Codex: In Pursuit of One of the World's Most Coveted, Sacred, and Mysterious Books *(2012), won the Sami Rohr Prize for Jewish Literature, a Sophie Brody Medal from the American Library Association, and the Canadian Jewish Book Award for history.*

Particular aspects of Hebrew culture and history are also vividly described, appropriate to a nation and its military that are heavily steeped in and unified by traditional religious observations. Well sketched are the preparations for Passover, the annual celebration of the Jewish liberation from slavery in Egypt millennia ago. For the celebration, pots and utensils are scoured with blowtorches, matzah is brought in for the seder, and haroset (a paste of fruits and nuts) is served. The full, multistep ritual—from opening blessings (Kadeish) and ceremonial washing of hands (Ur'chatz) to final songs of praise (Hallel) and closing prayer (Nirtzah)—is performed in order according to the dictates of army-issued copies of the *haggadah*, a centuries-old Jewish text.

A wider view of the conflict is provided when Friedman is sent on a mission to the nearby Red Pepper outpost. The fortress is occupied by the South Lebanon Army, a ragtag and untrustworthy Christian militia left over from the bloody Lebanese civil war (1975–90) with whom Israel maintains an uneasy alliance.

As time wears on, the movement to end the security zone in Lebanon gains momentum in Israel. By the year 2000, when Friedman completes his military service, it has been decided the outposts will be abandoned and destroyed so guerrillas cannot use them later. The Pumpkin is duly stuffed full of fifty-pound mines one morning, and upon detonation the outpost explodes spectacularly.

In the final part of *Pumpkinflowers*, Friedman is a civilian working in a greenhouse, enrolled at the Hebrew University of Jerusalem. He is called up from reserve in 2001 and 2002 following an increase of incidents of terrorism, especially suicide bombings and guerrilla assaults launched upon soldiers and civilians from Lebanon. As the author notes, Israel was not the lone target in such acts: on September 11, 2001, the United States suffered devastating losses in the terrorist attacks on the World Trade Center and the Pentagon, which subsequently led to the invasions and costly, long-term occupations of Afghanistan and Iraq.

In the midst of the chaos and destruction, the author takes a risk at least as great as his military service: he will visit Lebanon and travel to the remains of the Pumpkin one last time. Traveling as a tourist on his Canadian passport, he sees the highlights of Beirut and then hires a taxi to Nabatieh and walks to the ruins of his former outpost.

Throughout *Pumpkinflowers*, the author—using short chapters, like a correspondent's dispatches from the battlefield where every word counts—compares aspects of the conflict he experienced with other historic wars. In occasionally lyrical, but more often stark and simple language, he draws parallels with the stagnation in the trenches of World War I, the emotions of the Spanish Civil War, the uncertainties of the Vietnam War, and the explosive violence of the Iraqi and Afghanistan wars. He notes that hilltops, such as that where the Pumpkin and other outposts were situated for strategic advantage, are particularly important in Israeli history and literature, reflecting Mount Sinai, Masada, Mount Carmel, and other such ancient landmarks.

Haunted, probably forever, by survivor's remorse like many surviving soldiers, with *Pumpkinflowers* Friedman has a produced a multilayered work with a uniquely existential flavor, encompassing the national need for Israeli citizens to prevent, with their lives if necessary, another Holocaust, another pogrom, another expulsion. For its structure, its insight into the causes and effects of war upon humans and its many often subtle literary qualities, *Pumpkinflowers* can stand proudly among the multitude of outstanding wartime histories and memoirs such as Barbara Tuchman's *The Guns of August* (1962), George Orwell's *Homage to Catalonia* (1938), or Tim O'Brien's *The Things They Carried* (1990).

Jack Ewing

Review Sources

Beckerman, Gal. Review of Pumpkinflowers: A Soldier's Story, by Matti Friedman. *The New York Times*, 3 May 2016, www.nytimes.com/2016/05/08/books/review/matti-friedmans-pumpkinflowers.html. Accessed 23 Aug. 2016.

Holahan, David. "*Pumpkinflowers*, a Memoir by an Israeli Soldier, Questions the Battle." Review of *Pumpkinflowers: A Soldier's Story*, by Matti Friedman. *The Christian Science Monitor*, 4 May 2016, www.csmonitor.com/Books/

Book-Reviews/2016/0504/Pumpkinflowers-a-memoir-by-an-Israeli-soldier-questions-the-battle. Accessed 23 Aug. 2016.

Lennox, Matt. "Review: Matti Friedman's *Pumpkinflowers* Is Not for the Faint of Heart." Review of *Pumpkinflowers: A Soldier's Story*, by Matti Friedman. *The Globe and Mail*, 20 May 2016, www.theglobeandmail.com/arts/books-and-media/book-reviews/review-matti-friedmans-pumpkinflowers-is-not-for-the-faint-of-heart/article30105713. Accessed 23 Aug. 2016.

Review of *Pumpkinflowers: A Soldier's Story*, by Matti Friedman. *Kirkus Reviews*, 1 Mar. 2016, www.kirkusreviews.com/book-reviews/matti-friedman/pumpkinflowers. Accessed 23 Aug. 2016.

The Queen of the Night

Author: Alexander Chee (b. 1968)
Publisher: Houghton Mifflin Harcourt (New York). 576 pp.
Type of work: Novel
Time: Mid-to-late nineteenth century
Locale: Paris, France, and other locales in Europe and the United States

(Courtesy of Houghton Mifflin Harcourt)

Alexander Chee's The Queen of the Night *is a rich, complex, and sometimes melodramatic historical novel that tells the rags-to-riches story of an orphaned American farm girl turned international opera diva, set amidst the turmoil of Second Empire France.*

Principal characters:

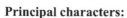

LILLIET BERNE, an opera singer with a remarkable voice and a tragic past
THE TENOR, a talented but controlling opera singer who buys her from a brothel
THE COMTESSE DE CASTIGLIONE, her mentor, a famous beauty and possible spy
ARISTAFEO CADIZ, a composer she falls in love with and lives with during the 1870–71 Siege of Paris
EMPRESS EUGÉNIE, wife of Napoleon III and Empress of France from 1853–1871
PAULINE VIARDOT GARCIA, a singer, musician, and composer known for her musical and literary salons
IVAN TURGENEV, Russian novelist and playwright, a lifelong admirer of Viardot Garcia
GIUSEPPE VERDI, Italian composer
GIUSEPPINA VERDI, Verdi's wife, an opera singer who retired from the stage early when her voice deteriorated

The Queen of the Night is Alexander Chee's long-awaited second novel, published more than ten years after his debut novel, *Edinburgh* (2001). The book was originally scheduled to be published in 2013, Chee said in an interview with *Slate* magazine, but he pulled it after finding a trove of research material about a historical figure, Pauline Viardot Garcia (1821–1910), who is an important character in the novel. *The Queen of the Night* mingles history and fiction in a style that may remind readers of E. L. Doctorow's 1976 novel *Ragtime*. Chee's operatic heroine, Lilliet Berne, is mentored by singer and composer Pauline Viardot Garcia, rubs shoulders with the likes of composer Giuseppe Verdi and writer Ivan Turgenev, serves as a wardrobe assistant for the Empress Eugénie, and spies on her for noted courtesan the Comtesse de Castiglione. Lilliet's story is like an opera in itself, larger than life and full of dramatic twists, acts of passion, and wild coincidences. Its "gorgeous prose style" and "ardent romanticism," critic Wendy Smith wrote in the *Washington Post*, are a perfect match for the diva whose tale Chee tells. In his notes following the novel, Chee says that his protagonist, Lilliet Berne, was very loosely based on nineteenth-century singer Jenny Lind as well as the character Pamina from the 1791 opera *The Magic Flute*.

Chee also told *Slate* magazine that he struggled with the form of the novel, rewriting it numerous times, but eventually came back to the structure he had originally conceived. Lilliet Berne, a celebrated opera singer known as "La Générale," is approached by Frédéric Simonet, a writer. He tells her he has written a novel about a circus performer, a singer known as "The Settler's Daughter," who was unable to speak but could sing one song she learned as a child. He proposes to turn his novel into an opera and asks Lilliet to star in it. As the writer describes his vision for the opera, Lilliet is taken aback, for the story he tells is that of her own secret past, and she wonders who in her life has revealed these secrets. Lilliet revisits her memories, revealing her tumultuous life and the many roles she has played, both onstage and off. Even her name, Lilliet Berne, is an adopted persona, taken from a stranger's gravestone. The reader never learns her real name. Her parents left Europe for America, and Lilliet grew up on a Midwestern farm. Her extraordinary voice reveals itself during church hymn singing, but her strict, religious mother regards the child's singing as vanity and tries to silence her, forcing her to wear a ribbon over her mouth. Lilliet later pretends she has become mute from a fever, and she will use muteness as a disguise or a form of self-protection at several points throughout the novel. Her "gift"—the beautiful voice that others cannot help but notice—is also at times a handicap, a danger, a source of jealousy, and a thing that isolates Lilliet from other people.

When illness wipes out her parents and brother, Lilliet plans to find her way back to Europe to look for relatives who may still live there, but her journey is not easy. Her money runs out in New York, and she is taken in as a housekeeper by an older, widowed man. She loses her virginity to him, and then, quite literally, runs away with a circus: Lilliet signs on as an "equestrienne rider" with a traveling show en route to Paris. Since she is able to ride and shoot, she fits the role of the "Settler's Daughter," a frontier girl who supposedly was captured by American Indians at a young age and forgot all her language except for one song her mother sang to her as an infant. Lilliet enjoys some success as a circus rider and performer—her voice even draws the attention of the emperor—but it is short-lived, and she falls into the life of a *fille en carte*, or prostitute, in a Paris brothel. When she catches the eye of the Tenor, a wealthy and celebrated opera singer, he buys her (like a pair of shoes, Lilliet muses) and supports her as his mistress, even arranging for her to take singing lessons, but Lilliet is not happy as a kept woman. In a series of plot twists worthy of Charles Dickens or Alexandre Dumas, she runs away, is jailed, switches identities with a dead girl, is sent to a convent, and ends up as a servant in the palace of Empress Eugénie de Montijo, wife of Napoleon III, emperor of France. Serving as a wardrobe assistant, Lilliet observes the opulence of life at court and reports on the empress's fashions to the Comtesse de Castiglione, a former mistress of the emperor. Still later, Lilliet develops her voice under the tutelage of Pauline Viardot-Garcia, an opera singer and composer, and is introduced to composer Giuseppe Verdi, writer Ivan Turgenev, and other legendary figures in the arts.

When the Franco-Prussian War topples France's Second Empire, Lilliet is trapped in Paris during the Siege of 1871. She nearly starves, as do many in the city, reduced to eating the bark off trees, but the time is also a romantic interlude for her, as she is finally able to live with her lover, Aristafeo, a composer she met in the palace. Eventually, in a scene as dramatic as it is outrageous, Lilliet escapes Paris in a hot-air balloon; unfortunately, it is the Tenor who orchestrates her getaway, and she returns to his control. She ascends in the world of opera, gains acclaim on the stage, but to finally gain control over her own life, she must take a risk even more desperate than all she has done before.

It is difficult to summarize the multilayered, complex, and ambitious novel that is *The Queen of the Night*. As readers follow the twists and turns of Lilliet's story, they may easily be distracted by the rich but sometimes overwhelming details Chee includes on various aspects of nineteenth-century life, from Empress Eugenie's extensive wardrobe to the scandalous 1875 debut of Georges Bizet's opera *Carmen*. Chee's heroine crosses paths with so many famous figures in music, literature, and politics that she might remind readers of a nineteenth-century Forrest Gump, of the book and film by the same name, or the eponymous hero of Woody Allen's 1983 film *Zelig*. While some critics thought the plot leaned too heavily on melodrama and fantastic coincidences, reviewers often noted that the stories of most operas are equally baroque, and that Chee's style matched his subject.

Alexander Chee achieved acclaim for his debut novel, Edinburgh *(2001), which won numerous prizes, including the Michener/Copernicus Prize in fiction, the Asian American Writers Workshop Literary Award, and the Lambda Editor's Choice Prize. He was the winner of a 2003 Whiting Award and received a fellowship from the National Endowment for the Arts in 2004.*

The Queen of the Night was seen as a surprising departure for Alexander Chee. While his contemporary debut novel drew almost universal acclaim, critics were divided over this second novel, which NPR called "sprawling, soaring, bawdy and plotted like a fine embroidery." *Kirkus Reviews* praised the strong voice Chee created for his heroine and the "richly researched" historical detail of the setting. The *Los Angeles Times* wrote that while the plot at times seemed overblown and the detail excessive, *The Queen of the Night* ultimately succeeded in telling a magical tale that is "historical, mythic and at the same time deeply personal." A starred review in *Library Journal* recommended the novel for all readers, especially those who enjoy historical fiction.

The cover image of *The Queen of the Night*, a historical photograph of the Comtesse de Castiglione, depicts a mysterious woman, elegantly dressed and coiffed, with most of her face hidden behind a black mask. This combination of display and withholding, of beauty and blankness, could be said to characterize Chee's novel. Every detail of setting, wardrobe, and historical background shows Chee's exhaustive research into the time period and milieu of his subject, yet the woman at the core of the story, Chee's protagonist, remains at a distance from the reader, as Joan Acocella pointed out in her

New Yorker review. The reader never learns Lilliet's real name or the name of the Tenor, the man who shapes so much of her life; the reader follows the rise and fall of her fortunes, but is seldom privy to her deepest feelings. Alexander Chee's elaborate plot, played out through flashbacks and flash-forwards, also makes it difficult for the reader to fully engage with the characters and story, Acocella wrote. Wendy Smith, writing for the *Washington Post*, also found the novel beautifully written but implausible and its major characters somewhat insubstantial, noting that Aristafeo, who is presented as Lilliet's great love, never develops beyond a "cloudy figure of romance." Similarly, Sarah Begley, for *Time* magazine, wrote that Lilliet was "more persona than personality," a glamorous but essentially shallow character. Like the great operas it pays homage to, *The Queen of the Night* is a dazzling and dramatic performance, designed for a grand stage: a novel larger than life and also removed from it.

Kathryn Kulpa

Review Sources

Acocella, Joan. "Night Music." Review of *The Queen of the Night*, by Alexander Chee. *The New Yorker*, 22 Feb. 2016, p. 74.

Akins, Ellen. "Alexander Chee's 'The Queen of the Night' Is an Operatic Novel of Opera." Review of *The Queen of the Night*, by Alexander Chee. *Los Angeles Times*, 11 Feb. 2016, www.latimes.com/books/la-ca-jc-alexander-chee-20160207-story.html. Accessed 10 Jan. 2017.

Cone, Edward B. Review of *The Queen of the Night*, by Alexander Chee. *Library Journal*, 1 Jan. 2016, reviews.libraryjournal.com/2016/02/books/fiction/the-queen-of-the-night-by-alexander-chee-lj-review. Accessed 10 Jan. 2017.

Flanagan, Margaret. Review of *The Queen of the Night*, by Alexander Chee. *Booklist*, 15 Dec. 2015, p. 35.

Review of *The Queen of the Night*, by Alexander Chee. *Kirkus Reviews*, 1 Oct. 2015, www.kirkusreviews.com/book-reviews/alexander-chee/the-queen-of-the-night. Accessed 10 Jan. 2017.

Review of *The Queen of the Night*, by Alexander Chee. *Publishers Weekly*, 26 Oct. 2015, www.publishersweekly.com/978-0-618-66302-6. Accessed 10 Jan. 2017.

Smith, Wendy. "The Girl Who Sang Her Way over the Sea." Review of *The Queen of the Night*, by Alexander Chee. *The Washington Post*, 2 Feb. 2016, www.washingtonpost.com/entertainment/books/the-queen-of-the-night-review-the-girl-who-sang-her-way-over-the-sea/2016/02/02/ab067cbe-c9d0-11e5-88ff-e2d1b4289c2f_story.html. Accessed 10 Jan. 2017.

Redemption Road

Author: John Hart (b. 1965)
Publisher: Thomas Dunne Books (New York). 432 pp.
Type of work: Novel
Time: Present day
Locale: North Carolina

Redemption Road, a crime thriller set in rural North Carolina, is American novelist John Hart's fifth book.

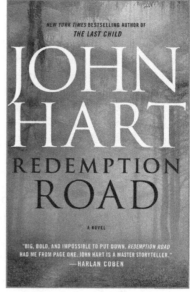

Principal characters:
ELIZABETH BLACK, a police officer who has been suspended for using excessive force
ADRIAN WALL, a former police officer who is being released from prison after thirteen years
GIDEON STRANGE, a fourteen-year-old boy seeking revenge for his mother's murder
CHARLIE BECKETT, a police officer who works with Elizabeth
CHANNING SHORE, the victim of a brutal crime

(Courtesy of St. Martin's Press)

There is a pivotal scene early in *Redemption Road* in which police officer Elizabeth Black takes Channing, a young woman she saved from abduction just six days earlier, to an abandoned quarry outside of their small North Carolina town. Consumed with anger, Channing is convinced that she will never be able to make peace with the horrible things that happened to her at the hands of her kidnappers. When she asks why Elizabeth has taken her to the quarry, Elizabeth reveals that it is the site where she was raped as a teenager. She urges Channing to do the one thing that enabled her to move on from her assault: take charge of her own life.

In addition to providing insight into Elizabeth's character, this scene introduces the novel's primary theme. As alluded to in the title, *Redemption Road* is an exploration of the human desire to be liberated from one's past. For most of the novel's characters, escaping the pain of their sins and traumas is a feat not easily accomplished. Although Elizabeth believes she has successfully claimed ownership of her life after the quarry incident, she remains haunted by the violent events that unfolded during Channing's rescue. Her former mentor, Adrian Wall, is being released from prison after serving thirteen years for the murder of a woman named Julia Strange. Wall, who was a police officer when Strange was murdered, has maintained his innocence. Elizabeth is the only person who still believes Wall despite the staggering DNA evidence against him. Meanwhile, fourteen-year-old Gideon is also seeking redemption for the horrible things that happened to his mother Julia Strange. However, unlike Elizabeth and

Adrian, Gideon believes that the only way he can achieve absolution for his family's past is by seeking revenge.

Darkness is an omnipresent force throughout *Redemption Road*. Hart's portrayal of evil and brutality is often unflinching. This becomes evident in the novel's first few pages, which comprise a flashback to Julia Strange's abduction from an unidentified character's point of view. The scene not only succeeds in establishing the event that becomes both the catalyst to the rest of the story and the link between the main characters but also effectively sets the narrative's chilling tone. Hart also uses a series of flashbacks to reveal what actually happened the day that Elizabeth rescued Channing. After discovering the basement where two men had raped and tortured Channing for over forty hours, Elizabeth engages in a violent struggle that ends with the captors being shot eighteen times. Hart initially provides some of the facts surrounding Channing's rescue in order to explain Elizabeth's tabloid nickname, "the angel of death," and why she has been suspended from the police force. However, he fills in the actual details of the event in a piecemeal fashion through flashbacks to infuse the narrative with a feeling of suspense. While this is a common literary technique in the mystery genre, Hart implements it in a highly effective way.

The cast of original, nuanced characters that populate the novel are arguably one of its strongest features. Hart uses characters strategically throughout *Redemption Road*. Sometimes they are the way in which he brings local, southern flavor to the story. This is especially evident in Crybaby Jones, an eighty-nine-year-old lawyer whose nickname stems from the fact that the beauty of the justice system once brought him to tears. More often than not, however, Hart uses characters as opportunities to examine the central narrative from a new angle or point of view. Written in third-person past tense, the chapters alternate between different characters' story lines. By doing this, Hart provides readers with new insight and then quickly makes them question the information. For example, one of the chapters that follow Gideon makes it seem as though Adrian is responsible for the murder of Julia Strange. When a later chapter depicts Adrian leaving prison, however, it becomes difficult to believe that he was ever capable of such brutality. Ultimately, the more characters Hart follows, the more effectively he obfuscates the truth.

In interviews, Hart has said that he sets all of his stories in North Carolina because it is where he grew up and consequently what he sees when he closes his eyes. The unnamed North Carolina town where *Redemption Road* is set reflects his familiarity with the state's culture well. Racial tensions are ubiquitous. The preacher is still viewed as an essential and untouchable leader. These details not only bring the novel's world to life but also contribute to the way in which the characters react to crimes within their community. The town has never recovered from the murder of Julia Strange, so when it appears that a serial killer is on the loose, tensions swell and people begin turning on one another. Ultimately, by portraying the town as being on the brink of chaos, Hart not only demonstrates the impact that violence and fear can have on a community but also raises the stakes for Elizabeth and Adrian. This makes the narrative more compelling.

Hart presents Elizabeth as the character that drives the plot forward. By solving the cold case of Julia Strange she will not only clear Adrian's name but also be able to identify the serial killer responsible, who has started murdering women again. While

John Hart is an American author of best-selling thriller novels, including The King of Lies *(2006),* Down River *(2007),* The Last Child *(2009), and* Iron Horse *(2011).*

spearheading this investigation, Elizabeth is also trying to prevent Gideon from enacting his revenge plan, protect Channing, and prove that her shooting of Channing's captors was not racially motivated. In many ways, Elizabeth is the novel's most familiar character; the police officer so devoted to her job that she does not have time for a personal life is a trope that originated from the narrative mediums of film and television. There is more to Elizabeth, however, than meets the eye. By gradually revealing her feelings and the events of her past, Hart effectively communicates to readers that the tough image Elizabeth maintains in public is far from her true self.

As a writer, Hart has been compared favorably to John Grisham, Lee Child, and Harlan Coben. *Redemption Road* furthers Hart's reputation as a masterful thriller writer by demonstrating his ability to cultivate suspense, narrative twists, and dark crimes. However, the novel also succeeds in highlighting the qualities that make Hart an unusual voice within the genre. While he depicts action and violence in an exciting and engaging way, Hart often spends an equal amount of time revealing how these events make the characters feel. Unlike the average crime novel, *Redemption Road* explores the nature of human emotion and relationships.

Positive reviews of *Redemption Road* have commended Hart for his adept storytelling. Writing for the *Huffington Post*, book critic Jackie Cooper calls the novel "the ride of a lifetime." Cooper's review is not alone in this sentiment; *Redemption Road*'s use of action and suspense has been a common point of praise across the critical community. This is arguably for good reason; many crime thrillers rely too heavily on the procedural elements of the story. Their detectives consequently spend most of the narrative piecing together evidence and analyzing suspects. While this classic "whodunit" style of storytelling can be enjoyable in its own right, Hart elevates the genre by ensuring the characters are constantly facing new sources of personal and professional conflict outside of the crimes they are trying to solve. This not only quickens the novel's pace and provides fertile ground for twists, but it also deepens the readers' feeling of empathy towards Elizabeth, Adrian, and Gideon.

Some critics have accused the plot of *Redemption Road* of being overstuffed. In his *Washington Post* review, Dennis Drabelle writes, "Stripped of two or three subplots, 'Redemption Road' might make a taut and believable novel. I wish it had been given that chance." Although Hart's decision to follow the dark, twisted stories of multiple characters simultaneously ensures the narrative is always moving forward and captivating the reader's attention, at times it can feel like a literary gimmick. In addition to several unsolved crimes, a serial killer, family conflicts, and past traumas, *Redemption Road* also includes a story about lost treasure. It can be argued that the number of conflicts that Hart decided to employ ultimately makes the novel feel disjointed and that it would be better served had it maintained a tighter focus. However, most readers are likely to feel that the numerous plotlines provide the novel with an action-packed quality. In line with this thinking, *Kirkus Reviews* says that *Redemption Road* has "enough characters, confrontations, secrets, and subplots to fill the stage of an opera house—and leave spectators from the orchestra to the balcony moved and misty-eyed."

Despite the fact that the critical response has been somewhat mixed, the public's reception of the novel has been overwhelmingly positive. In addition to receiving high ratings on online book forums, *Redemption Road* quickly became a *New York Times* best seller with more than two million copies in print. In part, the book's popularity can be attributed to Hart's well-established fan base, which has grown over time thanks to word-of-mouth recommendations. Hart's reputation as a writer is rooted largely in the success of his previous novels, including *The King of Lies* (2006), *Down River* (2007), *The Last Child* (2009), and *Iron Horse* (2011). While *Redemption Road* had the potential to disappoint fans who had been waiting five years for Hart's follow up to *Iron Horse*, it has instead solidified the author's status as one of the great American thriller writers. Rich in character, prose, and suspense, *Redemption Road* is an excellent addition to the murder-mystery genre.

Emily Turner

Review Sources

Cooper, Jackie K. "Redemption Road Gives Readers the Ride of a Lifetime." Review of *Redemption Road,* by John Hart. *The Huffington Post,* 19 May 2016, www. huffingtonpost.com/jackie-k-cooper/redemption-road-gives-rea_b_10054046. html. Accessed 26 Oct. 2016.

Cogdill, Oline H. "Book Review: 'Redemption Road' by John Hart." Review of *Redemption Road*, by John Hart. *Salon,* 4 May 2016, www.salon.com/2016/05/04/ book_review_redemption_road_by_john_hart. Accessed 26 Oct. 2016.

Drabelle, Dennis. "Redemption Road and the Problem of Thriller Killers." Review of *Redemption Road*, by John Hart. *The Washington Post,* 3 May 2016, www. washingtonpost.com/entertainment/books/redemption-road-and-the-problem-of-thriller-killers/2016/05/03/698bcdc8-e6d3-11e5-b0fd-073d5930a7b7_story.html. Accessed 26 Oct. 2016.

Review of *Redemption Road,* by John Hart. *Kirkus Reviews,* 3 May 2016, www. kirkusreviews.com/book-reviews/john-hart/redemption-road-hart. Accessed 26 Oct. 2016.

The Road to Little Dribbling
Adventures of an American in Britain

Author: Bill Bryson (b. 1951)
Publisher: Doubleday (New York). 400 pp.
Type of work: Travel, memoir
Time: 2014–15
Locale: Great Britain

The Road to Little Dribbling is a humorous travel memoir by American author Bill Bryson that explores the municipalities, landscape, and culture of Great Britain.

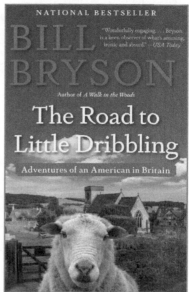

NATIONAL BESTSELLER

"Wonderfully engaging.... Bryson is a keen observer of what's amusing, ironic and absurd." —*USA Today*

BILL BRYSON

Author of *A Walk in the Woods*

The Road to Little Dribbling

Adventures of an American in Britain

(Courtesy of Doubleday)

Despite having lived and worked in England since 1973, American writer Bill Bryson was largely unknown among British readers until 1995, when his travelogue *Notes from a Small Island* was published. A record of the farewell tour that Bryson took around Great Britain before moving back to his native United States, the book was lauded for its ability to humorously capture the nation's history and cultural peculiarities. *Notes from a Small Island* went on to become one of the best-selling travel books of all time, solidifying Bryson's reputation as one of the United Kingdom's most beloved writers in the process. Published as a sequel twenty years later, *The Road to Little Dribbling* (subtitled *More Notes from a Small Island* for its British release) chronicles Bryson's most recent tour of the nation. Part travelogue, part autobiography, it explores the different ways in which both Bryson and Britain have changed over the past two decades.

The Road to Little Dribbling has a loose structure that successfully conveys the feeling of wandering. Early in the book, Bryson declares that on this particular nationwide tour he will only travel to places that he had never been; however, the guidelines of his itinerary quickly expand to include several destinations with personal meaning as well as a handful from his *Notes from a Small Island* tour. The resulting journey is undertaken in a series of small trips from his home in England, to which he returned in 2003 after living in New Hampshire for nearly eight years. Organized roughly in a south-to-north order, each of the twenty-six chapters in the book is devoted to a different city or region of Great Britain and Bryson's experiences there. The trip appears to have great sentimental value for Bryson, who often infuses the narrative with personal stories. When visiting the town of Virginia Water in Surrey, for example, he reveals how it was there that he happened upon a job at a local psychiatric hospital while hitchhiking around Europe in 1973. The event completely changed the trajectory of his life; not only would it lead to him spending the majority of the next forty years in

England, but it was at that hospital that Bryson met a student nurse named Cynthia who would become his wife. By using his journey as an opportunity to reflect on his life, Bryson gives the narrative an intimate tone.

It can be argued that Bryson's goal as a writer is not to incite others to travel to foreign places but instead to make readers feel as though they are already there. This is primarily evident in the prose of *The Road to Little Dribbling*. Instead of employing the salesman-pitch style that many other travel writers depend on, Bryson is often more cynical in his observations. In addition to making him seem more like a reliable narrator, this also informs readers as to what the truly spectacular sights are. Bryson uses detailed imagery to convey his enthusiasm for a place; for example, when recounting his walk along the Seven Sisters on the southern coast of England, he vividly describes them as "a hazy infinity of rolling hills, each ending at the seaward side in a sudden plunge of limestone cliffs." Another factor that distinguishes Bryson's travel writing from others is its accessibility, which can be attributed to both his writing style and the destinations on his itinerary. Throughout his nationwide tour, Bryson does not seek out luxurious or extreme locales. Instead, he spends his time meandering from small, fading seaside resorts, such as Bognor Regis on England's south coast, to the rugged peaks of Cape Wrath on the northwest tip of Scotland. By prioritizing places where "real" British people live and vacation, traveling exclusively by public transport, and eating at modest pubs rather than Michelin-starred restaurants, Bryson makes a case for travel being an act of exploration rather than escapism.

The perspective through which Bryson examines Great Britain is also highly unique. Typical travelogues encapsulate the experiences of authors who are exploring a new place for the first time. With no preconceived ideas or prejudices, it is easier for them to make raw, honest observations about a foreign place and its culture. Bryson, however, has spent most of his adult life in Great Britain married to an Englishwoman. It is where he raised his children and cultivated his voice as a writer. As a result, Bryson's journey across the land is described from an Anglo-American point of view. He strategically shifts between the two parts of his identity, leaning on one more heavily than the other depending on which best complements the material at hand. To emphasize the absurdity of the fact that parts of the British citizenship test are inaccurate, for example, Bryson assumes the perspective of a bemused outsider. When he writes from the perspective a longtime resident, however, it is often to lament how much Great Britain has changed over the years.

Central to *The Road to Little Dribbling* is the argument that although Britain is richer than it was twenty years ago, it has lost something along the way. Bryson comes to this conclusion after exploring a diverse swath of the country. He travels from bucolic villages that have been home to famous residents, such as Jane Austen's village of Chawton, to postindustrial cities such as Manchester and Liverpool and seaports such as Dover. He argues that because of outsourced manufacturing and cheap Mediterranean vacation packages, many of Britain's smaller towns and cities are being forgotten, and austerity measures are forcing many municipalities to become more utilitarian and less aesthetically nuanced. Ultimately, Bryson appears concerned that by participating in the new globalized economy, Britain has had to make cultural sacrifices.

Throughout the book, comedy is used as a tool to further reader engagement. By weaving humorous personal anecdotes into the narrative, Bryson ensures that his descriptions of British history, architecture, and wildlife do not become dull or tedious. Many of these anecdotes align to the book's theme of undesired change by targeting Bryson's age. In addition to portraying himself as increasingly frugal and cantankerous, Bryson also makes fun of the new health concerns he is confronted with now that he is in his sixties. At one point, he comically describes his dismay at learning that he is too old for early-onset dementia. While much of Bryson's humor is self-deprecating, he also mines material from conflicts he has with the people he meets on his cross-country tour. The comedy of these encounters is typically framed around his feelings of indignation at the stupidity of others. For example, after relating an argument he had with a woman who would not clean up after her dog on a hiking path outside Norfolk, Bryson fantasizes about beating her to death with his walking stick.

Despite Bryson's penchant for grumbling, *The Road to Little Dribbling* is ultimately a love letter to Great Britain. At one point in the narrative, Bryson argues that the British are an "ingenious" race of people, a recurring sentiment that he often supports with historical facts. While walking from the city of Oxford to the village of Iffley, for example, he describes how it was on a track near Iffley Road that, in 1954, a young doctor named Roger Bannister became the first man on record to run a mile in less than four minutes. In addition to devoting much of the book to the country's impressive history, Bryson also makes an effort to articulate his appreciation for the British people: their patience, their stoicism, and the way they take pleasure in small things like a cup of tea.

Bill Bryson is a best-selling writer. Originally from Des Moines, Iowa, he has resided in Britain on and off since 1973. He is best known for his books Notes from a Small Island *(1995),* A Walk in the Woods: Rediscovering America on the Appalachian Trail *(1998), and* A Short History of Nearly Everything *(2003).*

Yet although he admires the people, his deepest affection is reserved for the nation's countryside. After spending much of his nationwide tour on foot, Bryson concludes that there is no other landscape in the world as perfect or beautiful as Britain's. He marvels at how it feels like the world's most expansive park and how impressive sites such as the White Horse of Uffington, a three-thousand-year-old chalk carving, are so casually scattered around.

As a whole, *The Road to Little Dribbling* is an enjoyable addition to Bryson's extensive body of work. Over the years, Bryson has built a reputation as a writer who excels at seamlessly blending autobiography with history, science, and humor, and *The Road to Little Dribbling* continues this tradition. Like most of his previous works, it successfully delivers a significant amount of educational content in a highly entertaining way. To accomplish this, Bryson taps into his superior ability to contextualize obscure or complex information so that it becomes relevant to readers of all backgrounds. In his highly ambitious scientific book *A Short History of Nearly Everything* (2003), for example, Bryson illustrates just how powerful the big bang was by telling readers that its afterglow is still visible in the form of television static. In *The Road to*

Little Dribbling, he conveys the significance of Great Britain by comparing its small geographic area to the brilliance of its culture, the beauty of its land, and how much its people have accomplished. He argues that despite being an island only about 870 miles in length, Great Britain has produced an estimated 55 percent of the world's "significant inventions."

Reception of *The Road to Little Dribbling* has been mixed. A major New York Times Best Seller, the book has been a commercial success since its publication, but critics have been more tepid in their reactions. Among the book's positive reviews, there has been much praise regarding the quality of Bryson's prose as well as his effectiveness as a storyteller, and the book has been lauded as a satisfying sequel to *Notes from a Small Island*. The less favorable reviews have focused on Bryson's tendency to gripe. Annalisa Quinn wrote for National Public Radio that while *The Road to Little Dribbling* is often a pleasant and funny travel memoir, Bryson's complaints start to feel like a "long and grumpy Yelp review." It is true that Bryson's negative commentary is frequent throughout the narrative; whether or not readers find it to be tedious and repetitive depends exclusively on their sense of humor. For example, Michael Kerr wrote for the *Guardian* that Bryson is "better when he's harrumphing," and Griff Witte wrote in his *Washington Post* review that Bryson's complaints about British transit and service workers are nothing more than "good-natured grumbling." He claims that Bryson engaged in the same kind of mockery in *Notes from a Small Island* and that this was ultimately what made him beloved by British readers, whose humor typically demands that nothing be taken too seriously. Although it seems unlikely that it will live up to the acclaimed legacy of its predecessor, *The Road to Little Dribbling* is still a highly informative and entertaining travel book.

Emily Turner

Review Sources

Becker, Alida. Review of The Road to Little Dribbling: Adventures of an American in Britain, by Bill Bryson. *The New York Times*, 27 Jan. 2016, www.nytimes.com/2016/01/31/books/review/bill-bryson-the-road-to-little-dribbling-review.html. Accessed 25 Oct. 2016.

Kerr, Michael. "Splendid Harrumphs." Review of *The Road to Little Dribbling: Adventures of an American in Britain*, by Bill Bryson. *The Telegraph*, 13 Oct. 2015, www.telegraph.co.uk/books/what-to-read/the-road-to-little-dribbling-bill-bryson-review/. Accessed 25 Oct. 2016.

Quinn, Annalisa. "*The Road to Little Dribbling* Is a (Mostly) Pleasant Journey." Review of *The Road to Little Dribbling: Adventures of an American in Britain*, by Bill Bryson. *NPR*, 24 Jan. 2016, www.npr.org/2016/01/24/463226362/the-road-to-little-dribbling-is-a-mostly-pleasant-journey. Accessed 25 Oct. 2016.

Witte, Griff. "Wandering around Britain with a Good-Natured Grumbler." Review of *The Road to Little Dribbling: Adventures of an American in Britain*, by Bill Bryson. *The Washington Post*, 15 Jan. 2016, www.washingtonpost.com/opinions/wandering-around-britain-with-a-good-natured-grumbler/2016/01/14/403ecb60-b25c-11e5-9388-466021d971de_story.html. Accessed 25 Oct. 2016.

The Romanovs
1613–1918

Author: Simon Sebag Montefiore (b. 1965)
Publisher: Alfred A. Knopf (New York). 784 pp.
Type of work: History
Time: 1613–1918
Locale: Russia

(Courtesy of Knopf)

In The Romanovs, *award-winning historian Simon Sebag Montefiore traces the nearly three-hundred-year history of the Romanov family, rulers of Russia from the seventeenth century until the abolishment of the monarchy during the Communist Revolution in 1917.*

Principal personages:
MICHAEL I, first Romanov czar of Russia, r. 1613–45
ALEXIS I, czar of Russia, r. 1645–76
PETER I, czar of Russia, r. 1682–1721; emperor, r. 1721–25
CATHERINE II, empress of Russia, r. 1762–96
ALEXANDER I, emperor of Russia, r. 1801–25
NICHOLAS I, emperor of Russia, r. 1825–55
ALEXANDER II, emperor of Russia, r. 1855–81
ALEXANDER III, emperor of Russia, r. 1881–94
NICHOLAS II, emperor of Russia, r. 1894–1917
GRIGORY RASPUTIN, mystic and advisor to Nicholas II and his family

Writing dynastic histories is risky business. Unless one has the luxury of unlimited space—something not often accorded authors—the historian faces the daunting task of shaping a coherent narrative without overlooking important information, while still offering sufficient analysis to make sense of the disparate events that make up the historical chronicle. The desire to pay some attention to every ruler in a dynasty must be balanced by the need to emphasize the significant contributions or failures of those few whose actions shaped the future of their country. At the same time, the reading public generally enjoys these kinds of history books, and successful ones generate handsome sales for publishers. Witness, for example, the popularity of Dan Jones's *The Plantagenets* (2012), a chronicle of the family that ruled in England from 1154 to 1485.

Historian Simon Sebag Montefiore's *The Romanovs* covers a similar length of time, from 1613, when Michael I reluctantly accepted the Russian crown, until 1918, when the last of the Romanovs—Nicholas II and his entire family—were assassinated by revolutionaries near the end of World War I. Montefiore has spent a career writing about Russia and the Soviet Union, publishing award-winning books on Catherine the Great and Joseph Stalin. His interest is more than academic: his mother's family was from Lithuania and fled the Russian Empire in the early 1900s. Thus, his work combines the disciplined effort of the scholar to re-create and analyze the historical record with a passion for the history of one of his ancestral homelands.

Simon Sebag Montefiore is author of a number of popular historical studies, including Stalin: The Court of the Red Tsar *(2004),* Young Stalin *(2007), and* Jerusalem: The Biography *(2011). He is a member of the Royal Society of Literature.*

Nearly every one of the Romanov czars could be the subject of a full-length study (and many have been), and a good number of the stories about them, both true and apocryphal, could provide the spark for epic, romance, realist novel, or tragic drama. Condensing three hundred years of political strife and personal intrigue into a manageable narrative takes great skill. Montefiore proves up to the task. Arguing in his introduction that the Romanovs lived their lives in public, he organizes his book like a tragic drama in three acts. Carefully balancing stretches of narrative summary with detailed descriptions of key events in the personal and political history of the czars, he manages to hold readers' interest while still providing a sense of the historical framework in which these unusual personalities lived, loved, and ruled. The narrative is enhanced by maps and lists of principals in the saga. Additionally, at the beginning of each section, Montefiore provides helpful lists of important characters who appear in the narrative. For those desiring more detail, he includes copious notes. As the story progresses, the descriptions become more detailed (perhaps because the historical record is more complete), to the point where Montefiore re-creates scenes, complete with conversations, of the nineteenth-century czars' political and personal lives, going so far as to report on fashions for both the men and women. His exceptional command of language on occasion leads to florid descriptions that may distract some readers from the content of the narrative, but he often comes up with the perfect word to characterize a personality trait that distinguishes one Romanov ruler from their ancestors and descendants.

Montefiore never misses a chance to document the Romanovs' insatiable desire to expand their empire—a passion seldom controlled by Realpolitik. The czars believed that they ruled by divine right, and they maintained that belief long after other European countries had abandoned the notion in favor of some form of representative government. The czars' sense of duty was almost always matched by a sense of entitlement to rule by whatever means necessary to preserve security, peace, and their own place at the head of the nation and empire. From the beginning the Romanovs' rule was marked by exceptional cruelty; beheadings, impalings, butcherings, and dismemberments of dissidents, often done in public, were commonplace. Nearly every Romanov ruler relied on some version of a secret police to stay informed about intrigues, real or imagined, that might threaten the security of the monarch. Montefiore also chronicles the infighting of noble Russian families as they jockey for favor with the various sovereigns.

Equally common was the Romanovs' proclivity for taking lovers; both men and women slept around so frequently that the paternity of several members of the royal family was on occasion called into question. The sexual profligacy of the czars, and sometimes their wives, was so rampant that Montefiore finds it worth noting the rare phenomenon: a happy and faithful union between Alexander III and his wife.

One issue that becomes apparent in the early pages of *The Romanovs* is that Russia was not a kind place for women in the royal family. Early czars picked their brides out of a lineup—a "brideshow"—organized to make certain that no one noble family would be privileged. Later royal women were paired with members of European ruling families in marriages designed to create or maintain political alliances. Often the czarina and other females in the household were secluded in the palaces. Given the restrictions imposed on the royal women, it is remarkable that a number of women took command of the state as regents (such as Sophia) or ruled in their own right (such as Catherine I and Anna). Most notable, or perhaps most notorious, among these ruling women was Catherine II, also known as Catherine the Great, who assumed autocratic privileges normally reserved for the Romanov men and exhibited the same zest for power.

While Montefiore recounts in some detail the events of every Romanov ruler's time on the throne, some are afforded considerably more attention. Occasionally his judgments of their personality and accomplishments are at odds with conventional views. Of particular interest in this vein is his lengthy warts-and-all portrait of Peter the Great (Peter I), who created the Russian Empire with himself as its first emperor. Autocratic, mercurial, and given to extreme cruelty, Peter carried out his ambition to transform Russia into a European-style empire. Nowhere, however, is the integration of the political and personal more evident than in Montefiore's portrait of Alexander I. The long chapter on his rule offers a view of Russia's war with Napoleon from the czar's perspective; in it, Montefiore balances Alexander's management of the war with his constant pursuit of various mistresses. While acknowledging some of the czar's glaring blunders, Montefiore calls Alexander's overall leadership in thwarting Napoleon's ambition to rule all of Europe the greatest achievement of any Russian czar.

Montefiore rejects the conventional view that Nicholas I was an imperious, anti-Semitic martinet in favor of a nuanced portrait that recognizes his faults and foibles but finds significant merit in many of the actions he took to preserve the nation in times of crisis. Nicholas's son Alexander II stands in a much more favorable light; Montefiore presents him as the best of the Romanovs, emancipator of serfs and reformer of government. Ironically, Alexander's erratic efforts to introduce reforms while maintaining his position as autocrat cost him dearly: as he vacillated about reforms, revolutionaries became more active and eventually assassinated him. His son, Alexander III, showed no such indecision; he had little use for reform and kept the revolutionaries under control through his secret police. He also adopted the strong anti-Semitic policies of his grandfather. Like Alexander III, nearly all of the Romanov emperors were unwilling to consider significant reforms, convinced that the country would devolve into chaos if they relaxed their iron grip on their subordinates. When reformers pressed for change, the emperors generally responded by imposing more repressive measures.

The Romanovs offers an almost daily account of the march toward World War I in 1914 and the repeated defeats of Russian forces that led Nicholas II to assume personal command of the army, leaving his wife, the Empress Alexandra, to run the government. That decision proved disastrous, because she relied not on seasoned ministers but on a mystic who had wormed his way into the royal family to become an indispensable adviser: Grigory Rasputin. While the czars and their families tend to stand center stage in Montefiore's narrative, Rasputin becomes a major figure in the narrative of Nicholas II's reign. His influence is offered as a principal cause for the loss of confidence in the monarchy by those who might have propped it up against the growing tide of revolutionary activity that eventually forced Nicholas to abdicate. Montefiore's lengthy description of the Romanovs' arrest and assassination juxtaposes the dignity of the royal family with the ruthlessness of the Bolsheviks under Vladimir Lenin, who insisted that no revolution could be successful unless blood was spilled.

As Montefiore points out, it was dangerous for autocrats insistent on making every decision to surround themselves with advisers willing to take the risk of acting on their own. Doing so could, and often did, cost them their lives. The 1918 assassinations of Nicholas II, the Empress Alexandra, and their children, which ended the Romanov dynasty, may have been the most celebrated regicides in Russian history, but they were hardly unique.

If there is an insight that captures the essence of the Romanovs' rule, it is summed up in Montefiore's observation about the "Russian pattern of behaviour" that made the Romanovs' long-running dynasty possible: "servility to those above, tyranny to those below." Hence, Montefiore is able to use the story of the Romanovs to explain the behavior of subsequent leaders of Russia. One can see, for example, a precursor to Stalin's maniacal demands for security and his constant fear of conspiracy in Peter the Great's dismay at being unable to build a cadre of trusted subordinates. Montefiore sees the pattern continuing into post-Soviet times, explaining why elected leaders such as Vladimir Putin can act with impunity even in a so-called democratic state.

Attempting to capture the centuries of Russian history through the lens of the monarchy has its drawbacks. Montefiore seldom goes outside the story of the Romanovs to look at larger cultural and political forces impinging on the czars' efforts to carry out what they perceived to be their God-given mandate to rule the vast expanse of land and the millions of people who occupied it. As some reviewers have noted, Montefiore's narrative offers simplistic interpretations and stresses the sensational. Such is the fate of many books like *The Romanovs*, popular histories designed to satisfy the curiosity of the interested general reader rather than that of the specialist.

Laurence W. Mazzeno

Review Sources

Grushin, Olga. "Absolute Power." Review of The Romanovs: 1613–1918, by Simon Sebag Montefiore. *The New York Times* Book Review, 22 May 2016, p. 11.

Hughes-Hallett, Lucy. "The Romanovs' Only Loyalty Was to Absolute Power." Review of *The Romanovs: 1613–1918*, by Simon Sebag Montefiore. *New Statesman*, 5 Feb. 2016, www.newstatesman.com/culture/books/2016/02/romanovs-only-loyalty-was-absolute-power. Accessed 6 Oct. 2016.

King, Greg. "The Romanovs: Fascinating, Odd and Odious." Review of *The Romanovs: 1613–1918*, by Simon Sebag Montefiore. *Washington Post*, 13 May 2016, www.washingtonpost.com/opinions/the-romanovs-fascinating-odd-and-odious/2016/05/13/5979d084-fcc1-11e5-9140-e61d062438bb_story.html. Accessed 6 Oct. 2016.

Kotkin, Stephen. "Dwarf-Throwing and Other Delights." Review of *The Romanovs: 1613–1918*, by Simon Sebag Montefiore. *The Wall Street Journal*, 20 May 2016, www.wsj.com/articles/dwarf-throwing-and-other-delights-1463777504. Accessed 6 Oct. 2016.

Zamoyski, Adam. "The Ruthless Romanovs' Horrible History." Review of *The Romanovs: 1613–1918*, by Simon Sebag Montefiore. *The Spectator*, 30 Jan. 2016, www.spectator.co.uk/2016/01/the-ruthless-romanovs-horrible-history/. Accessed 6 Oct. 2016.

Secondhand Time
The Last of the Soviets

Author: Svetlana Alexievich (b. 1948)
First published: *Vremya sekond khend*, 2013, in Russia
Translated from the Russian by Bela Shayevich
Publisher: Random House (New York). 496 pp.
Type of work: History
Time: 1991–2012
Locales: Russia, Belarus, Chechnya

(Courtesy of Penguin Random House)

Secondhand Time: The Last of the Soviets *is a book of oral history that captures the last generation of those who lived under Soviet rule and the subsequent first generation to live under capitalism. Consisting of interviews with a wide range of individuals, the book is meant to create a symphony of voices that tell the story of how today's Russia came to be, politically, culturally, and emotionally.*

In her introduction to *Secondhand Time: The Last of the Soviets*, 2013 Nobel laureate Svetlana Alexievich writes, "The Soviet civilization . . . I'm rushing to make impressions of its traces, its familiar faces. I don't ask people about socialism, I want to know about love, jealousy, childhood, old age. Music, dances, hairdos. The myriad sundry details of a vanished way of life. It's the only way to chase the catastrophe into the contours of the ordinary and try to tell a story." And this is a large part of what makes Alexievich's latest "documentary novel" so important and profound; those small moments made up of tea, conversations between mothers and daughters, and the change of seasons serve to amplify the horror of what happened in the past. One man living a life of luxury becomes intoxicated and spills the details of his brutal past as an executioner for Joseph Stalin to his future son-in-law, while another woman tells the heartbreaking story of her second husband, who was a broken, solitary, but deeply caring, man. Each story is at once similar and distinct, and Alexievich reminds readers that only a Soviet can truly know a Soviet while she works to show the ways in which her cast of characters are connected through their pain.

Alexievich was born in the Ukrainian town of Stanislaviv, at the time part of the Soviet Union, and is the first Belarusian writer to win the Nobel Prize in Literature. Her father was Belarusian and her mother Ukrainian; she grew up in Belarus. An investigative journalist and nonfiction writer, Alexievich writes exclusively in Russian, and she has developed a unique oral history style for her storytelling, which is meant to act as witness to the emotional lives and upheavals of the Soviet people. She suffered political persecution in Belarus under the administration of Alexander Lukashenko and was in exile in Paris, Gothenburg, and Berlin for a decade before returning to Minsk in 2011, where she has become a prolific and important part of the international literary scene.

Alexievich's work is considered to be influenced by Belarusian writer Ales Adamovich, who used oral testimonies of witnesses to speak about atrocities of the twentieth century. Alexievich's other works include *Tsinkovye mal'chiki* (1990; *Zinky Boys: Soviet Voices from the Afghanistan War*, 1992), which tells the story of the Soviet occupation of Afghanistan (the coffins in which soldiers were sent back to Russia were made of zinc, hence the title), and *Tchernobylskaia moltiva* (1997; *Voices from Chernobyl*, 2005), an oral history of those who lived near the nuclear plant and who continue to suffer from the ramifications of radiation and environmental disaster. Her book *U voiny ne zhenskoe litso* (1985; *War's Unwomanly Face*, 1988), a collection of dialogues from women about war, has sold more than two million copies.

Though the stories in *Secondhand Time* take place after Stalin's era, his shadow is evident in much of the collection. An opening chronology subtitled "Russia after Stalin" offers a useful guide for following the historical moments and leaders referenced by many of Alexievich's interviewees, such as the Soviet invasion of Afghanistan in 1979; the quick succession of leaders in the 1980s, which included Leonid Brezhnev, Yuri Andropov, and Konstantin Chernenko; and the opening of the blockade between East and West Berlin and the subsequent declaration of the end of the Cold War in 1989. It also offers helpful explanations of the rise of inflation and some political movements that led up to the introduction of capitalism.

Told in two parts, *Secondhand Time* deftly balances the impact of the past, with the consequences suffered in the present. Part one, "The Consolation of Apocalypse," deals with stories about the Communist era in the Soviet Union; part two, "The Charms of Emptiness," focuses on the generation who became adults after the fall of Communism. By allowing for so many distinct voices, Alexievich creates a cacophony of ghostly memories and pressing desires, showing what was lost and mourned through the changing government and poignantly juxtaposing the older generation's fears and devastations against the younger's struggles and dreams. This is not a tome against Communism, nor is it a celebration of capitalism. Rather, *Secondhand Time* is a record of how the connections between neighbors, friends, families, and the government's investment and interest in its population become the stuff of history. No moment is too small to capture Alexievich's interest or ear.

Alexievich thoroughly explores all aspects of post-Communist Russian society. Frequently the younger interviewees are the most captivating subjects, because often they are the ones who have been most profoundly changed by the turn of events in the country. At one point, Alexievich speaks to a young man who talks about the beginnings of the free market in the country, and the pain that came with it. "You want to talk about the nineties . . . I wouldn't call it a beautiful time, I'd say it was revolting," the nameless man recounts. He continues by citing those who went insane after the fall and could not deal with the new society they found themselves in. However, he and many others embraced entrepreneurial enterprises with ambivalence. In the end he became very wealthy after selling wares he hauled in by the truckload, and at the time of the interview he owned a doctor's office. "What would I have been if not for perestroika? An engineer with a pathetic salary," he says. The combination of contempt for capitalism and his culture is captivating, as is the glimpse he offers as to what can become of a society when everyone is suddenly expected to look out for their own welfare after decades of communal living.

Many of the voices talk about the selection of new wares available to them in stores, specifically food items such as the salamis they had longed for as children, which are now available in dozens of varieties. The human tendency toward desire is openly and often discussed, but so is the dark side of that tendency, the economic hardships and inequalities experienced, and the lack of preparation for those who were ill-equipped to thrive in the new atmosphere. Many people recall being paid in goods under Communism and were subsequently left with pensions of fifty dollars a month as inflation climbed and climbed. Also of interest are the conversations of those who, in the words of one subject, "come from the kitchen generation," when friends would gather in each other's private homes at night to listen to music and discuss politics. Alexievich herself was a member of this generation and speaks warmly about the intellectual camaraderie experienced by so many, some of which is considered to have been lost with the coming of capitalism.

Svetlana Alexievich is the 2015 winner of the Nobel Prize in Literature. A Belarusian writer and investigative reporter, she is known for the oral history style of writing and gathering she applies to her work, which she has called documentary novels. Secondhand Time: The Last of the Soviets *is her fourth book to be translated into English.*

Themes of suicide and death run deep in these stories. In one chapter in the first half, called "On the Mercy of Memories and the Lust for Meeting," a mother tells the story of her fourteen-year-old son, Igor Poglazov, who committed suicide by hanging. She recalls her son being a sensitive, creative soul who was enraptured with death from a young age. "He just wanted to try it out, have a look," she says. The second half finds a chapter entitled "On Life the Bitch and One Hundred Grams of Fine Powder in a Little White Vase," as told by Tamara Sukhovei, a twenty-nine-year-old waitress. She has three times attempted suicide and speaks openly about having never seen any beauty or kindness in her life. Her mother is an oppressive, evil presence, and she has lived through the death of her father and stepfather and a divorce from her first husband. The story describes the long, painful decline of her mother and the abuse she suffers at the hand of her husband, who was stationed in Chechnya and suffers from trauma. A postscript reports that she attempted suicide a fourth time and succeeded.

The collection was reviewed widely and well, and is already considered a masterpiece in Europe. In his *New York Times* review, Dwight Garner commended Alexievich for allowing her subjects to speak with their own voices, unfiltered through an author's interpretive lens, and noted, "A freight of catharsis is on display. People gather around Ms. Alexievich to speak about their lives . . . because she's a conversational hearth." Andrew Riemer wrote in his review for the *Sydney Morning Herald*, "Apart from being a splendid instance of the craft of the oral historian, *Secondhand Time* is a magnificent work of literary art. This vast panorama can justly be regarded, I think, as the *War and Peace* of our age."

From Stalin to Putin, from dissident kitchen dwellers to full-blooded capitalists, S*econdhand Time* is indeed an important and necessary book that captures a fleeting generation and moment for those to come and offers an unprecedented look into the lives of those most are not likely to encounter. Not only an attempt at capturing voices, *Secondhand Time* also manages to capture the passing of history and time, while showing that much of what makes humans human is timeless and all in the details.

Melynda Fuller

Review Sources

Figes, Orlando. "Alexievich's New Kind of History." Review of *Secondhand Time: The Last of the Soviets*, by Svetlana Alexievich. *The New York Review of Books*, 13 Oct. 2016, pp. 18–19.

Garner, Dwight. "Review: In Secondhand Time, Voices from a Lost Russia." Review of Secondhand Time: The Last of the Soviets, by Svetlana Alexievich. *The New York Times*, 24 May 2016, www.nytimes.com/2016/05/25/books/review-in-secondhand-time-voices-from-a-lost-russia.html. Accessed 6 Oct. 2016.

Riemer, Andrew. "Review: Svetlana Alexievich's *Secondhand Time* Tells of Soviet Life from Stalin to Putin." Review of *Secondhand Time: The Last of the Soviets*, by Svetlana Alexievich. *The Sydney Morning Herald*, 3 June 2016, www.smh.com.au/entertainment/books/review-svetlana-alexievichs-secondhand-time-tells-of-soviet-life-from-stalin-to-putin-20160526-gp4jct.html. Accessed 6 Oct. 2016.

Review of *Secondhand Time: The Last of the Soviets*, by Svetlana Alexievich. *Kirkus Reviews*, 15 Apr. 2016, p. 43.

Review of *Secondhand Time: The Last of the Soviets*, by Svetlana Alexievich. *Publishers Weekly*, 25 Apr. 2016, p. 80.

Seinfeldia
How a Show about Nothing Changed Everything

Author: Jennifer Keishin Armstrong
Publisher: Simon and Schuster (New York).
Illustrated. 320 pp.
Type of work: Media
Time: 1988–the present
Locales: New York, Los Angeles

In Seinfeldia: How a Show about Nothing Changed Everything, *Jennifer Keishin Armstrong chronicles the making of the sitcom* Seinfeld *and its enduring influence on popular culture.*

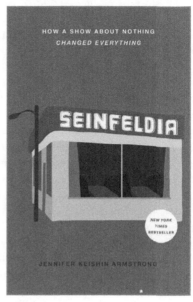

(Courtesy of Simon & Schuster)

Principal personages:
JERRY SEINFELD, a comedian and cocreator
    of Seinfeld; portrays a fictionalized version of himself in the show
LARRY DAVID, a comedian and cocreator of
    Seinfeld
JASON ALEXANDER, an actor; portrays George Costanza in Seinfeld
JULIA LOUIS-DREYFUS, an actor; portrays Elaine Benes in Seinfeld
MICHAEL RICHARDS, an actor; portrays Cosmo Kramer in Seinfeld

For many in the United States, it can be hard to escape the reach of *Seinfeld*. From the sitcom's near-constant reruns on US television channels to the various terms and catchphrases it popularized—the puffy shirt, "No soup for you," a close-talker—the show has spread far beyond its original timeslot in the two and a half decades since its pilot first aired. Indeed, *Seinfeld* has in many ways come to represent something far bigger than itself, and it is that phenomenon that fascinates pop culture writer Jennifer Keishin Armstrong, who terms the unusual half-real, half-fictional world that has sprung up around the show "Seinfeldia." In her book named after this idea, *Seinfeldia: How a Show about Nothing Changed Everything*, she chronicles the making of the show from its initial development as *The Seinfeld Chronicles* through its rocky years of low ratings to its eventual recognition as one of the greatest—perhaps even the greatest—sitcoms of all time. Although Seinfeld has often been described as a show about nothing, a term originating in a fourth-season episode in which the characters Jerry and George pitch a *Seinfeld*-like television show to the network NBC, Armstrong demonstrates clearly that the show meant much more than nothing to its creators, stars, and fans and in fact affected numerous lives in unusual ways. Building her narrative with the help of published interviews with Seinfeld's creators and stars as well as her own conversations with a variety of the show's writers, guest stars, and champions at its network, Armstrong reconstructs the chronicle of *Seinfeld* and provides compelling insight into what exactly made the show so special.

The story of *Seinfeld*—and of Seinfeldia—began in 1988, when comedians and friends Jerry Seinfeld and Larry David met up after performing at a New York City comedy club. Seinfeld, a popular comedian who had gained significant public recognition through a series of performances on *The Tonight Show*, had attracted the notice of NBC, and executives at the network wanted him to pitch them a show. As he did not have any ideas, he turned to David, who had previously worked on the television sketch show *Fridays* and completed a brief stint at *Saturday Night Live*. The two initially settled on creating a one-off special based in part on their banter during their time together. NBC liked the idea, but when the duo completed the script, they realized the material was better suited for a sitcom. With the network's approval, Seinfeld and David wrote the pilot for what was then titled *The Seinfeld Chronicles*. In addition to Seinfeld, who played a fictionalized version of himself, the pilot featured Jason Alexander as Jerry's friend George, based on David; Michael Richards as Jerry's neighbor Kessler, later renamed Cosmo Kramer; and Lee Garlington as Claire, a waitress at Jerry and George's usual restaurant. The pilot tested poorly with audiences and ultimately aired in the summer of 1989 as a stand-alone special. Unlike many poorly received pilots, though, *The Seinfeld Chronicles* received a second chance. Seinfeld and David revamped the show, replacing the character of Claire with Julia Louis-Dreyfus's Elaine Benes, Jerry's friend and ex-girlfriend, and the title of the show was shortened to simply *Seinfeld*. The first episode of the revamped series aired on NBC in May 1990, almost a year after the pilot's premiere.

Over the course of *Seinfeldia*, Armstrong chronicles the making of *Seinfeld* from its inauspicious beginnings to its finale in 1998, nine seasons later. Focusing on the full cast of characters who made the show a reality, she devotes individual chapters to specific groups of people, from the show's writers, discussed at length in "The Writers," to the various real-life individuals who inspired characters and events in the show, presented in "The Bizarros." In discussing such individuals at length, Armstrong provides an in-depth look behind the scenes of the show, revealing creative processes previously unrevealed to *Seinfeld*'s casual fans. Her discussion of the workings of *Seinfeld*'s writers' room is particularly fascinating. Although Seinfeld and David were ultimately in charge of the process, many of the most iconic episodes in the series were written by members of *Seinfeld*'s revolving stable of writers. The showrunners had the unusual policy of letting most of the writers go after a single season and replacing them with a fresh crop of new writers, thus ensuring a constant flow of new personal experiences on which to base storylines. Indeed, a significant number of *Seinfeld*'s memorable moments were based on incidents in the lives of the show's writers or those of their friends. Armstrong notes that a conflict in one episode caused by a typographical error in a Trivial Pursuit answer was based on an experience of writer Bill Masters, while a story from a friend of writer Peter Mehlman inspired an episode in which a valet's body odor permeates Jerry's car. Such anecdotes, taken to their most absurd extremes onscreen, formed the core of *Seinfeld*'s signature brand of comedy, based in the humorous nature of everyday life. As Armstrong explains, "if a pitch didn't sound real,

David didn't want it." In addition to providing key insights into the writing process, she delves at times into the conflicts that occurred among the show's writers, including the formation of alliances and even, according to one writer, deliberate sabotage.

In addition to chronicling the making of the show, Armstrong aptly demonstrates the profound effect *Seinfeld*'s popularity had on its cast and writers. As a tremendously popular sitcom, the show made Seinfeld himself a household name and propelled Alexander, Louis-Dreyfus, and Richards to a new level of stardom. Perhaps more striking, however, was the show's effect on those who were not part of the main cast. Among the examples Armstrong presents is that of actor Larry Thomas, who appeared as a brusque restaurateur known as the Soup Nazi in the 1995 episode of the same name as well as in the 1998 finale. Although the role was a relatively small one, Thomas's performance as the Soup Nazi both earned him an Emmy Award nomination and made him an iconic figure among *Seinfeld* fans. Armstrong recounts that in the decades since "The Soup Nazi" aired, Thomas's newfound fame helped him obtain many more guest roles in television and also made him a frequent guest on the convention circuit. A similar phenomenon occurred with Fred Stoller, a comedian who had a brief and largely unsuccessful tenure as a member of the *Seinfeld* writing staff but returned to the show a year later as an actor, playing one of Elaine's potential love interests. Following his appearance on the show, Stoller obtained numerous guest and recurring roles, becoming a recognizable character actor. However, Armstrong notes, he remained best known to many for his memorable appearance on *Seinfeld*.

Multiple times throughout the book, Armstrong returns to the idea of Seinfeldia, "a special dimension of existence, somewhere between the show itself and real life" that is characterized by a "strange intermingling of fiction and reality." In part, the concept encompasses the many ways in which *Seinfeld*'s characters, plots, and lexicon have become deeply ingrained in American popular culture. Perhaps the more intriguing form of Seinfeldia that Armstrong discusses, however, is the intermingling of fiction and reality that has come to surround various individuals who were themselves not officially part of the *Seinfeld* phenomenon but have become inextricably tied to it. One such individual is Kenny Kramer, a former neighbor of David and the real-life inspiration for Cosmo Kramer, who profited off of his connection to the show by offering a specialized tour of New York to *Seinfeld* fans. In a particularly Seinfeldian twist, the show in turn referenced the real-life Kramer's actions in an eighth-season episode in which the fictional Kramer operates a tour of his own. Armstrong argues that *Seinfeld* is unique in its ability to blur the line between fiction and reality to such an extent, and the stories she recounts provide ample evidence to support that point.

Jennifer Keishin Armstrong is the author of Mary and Lou and Rhoda and Ted *(2013), a history of* The Mary Tyler Moore Show. *She is a television columnist for* BBC Culture *and has contributed to publications such as* Entertainment Weekly *and the* New York Times Book Review.

In writing *Seinfeldia*, Armstrong drew extensively from conversations with individuals involved with the show as well as from previously published sources. Although she conducted interviews with various *Seinfeld* writers and actors as well as network employees and others deeply connected to the world of *Seinfeld*, all of whom are listed in the "Interview List" section that follows Armstrong's thorough source notes at the end of the book, she apparently did not interview cocreators Seinfeld and David or any of the members of the main cast. It is unclear from the work itself whether this was a conscious choice or whether she was simply unable to gain access to those particular individuals. Some readers, particularly those already familiar with the tale of the making of *Seinfeld*, will likely wish that *Seinfeldia* offered new anecdotes from David and the show's main cast. However, Armstrong's focus on the often-overlooked writers and studio employees who worked behind the scenes enables *Seinfeldia* to present new information on the making of the show from a variety of little-heard perspectives.

Upon its release in 2016, *Seinfeldia* met with largely positive critical reception. Reviewers praised Armstrong's attention to detail and lively style of writing, noting that she succeeded in transporting the reader into the 1990s writers' rooms she describes. In a review for the *Washington Post*, Carlos Lozada modified a memorable line from *Seinfeld* itself when describing the book, noting that Armstrong's "stories about 'Seinfeld' are real—and they're spectacular." *New York Times* reviewer Dwight Garner wrote that although he had "overdosed" on *Seinfeld* reruns years before, *Seinfeldia* renewed his interest in the show, a testament to Armstrong's engaging narrative. Critics did at times find fault with Armstrong's idea of Seinfeldia; Lozada, for instance, wrote that he was more interested in the "off-set drama and neurotic script doctors" prevalent in the story of the show's creation than in Armstrong's musings about the nature of Seinfeldia. Some critics also found that although the work presents a lively and coherent narrative of the development of *Seinfeld*, it "does little to broaden perspective on the show for its most ardent fans," as Matt Sedensky wrote for the Associated Press. Sedensky approved of Armstrong's tendency to highlight the many individuals who worked behind the scenes and are generally unknown to *Seinfeld*'s viewers. At the same time, he questioned Armstrong's decision not to interview more individuals involved with the show, including members of *Seinfeld*'s secondary cast, and present "morsels from more of the many hundreds involved with the show." Despite such critiques, however, reviewers generally found *Seinfeldia* to be an entertaining and enlightening work that provides an insider view into one of the United States' most popular and enduring sitcoms.

Joy Crelin

Review Sources

Balial, Nandini. "*Seinfeldia* Is a Deep Dive into TV's Greatest Non-Sitcom Sitcom." Review of *Seinfeldia: How a Show about Nothing Changed Everything*, by Jennifer Keishin Armstrong. *A.V. Club*, Onion, 11 June 2016, www.avclub.com/review/seinfeldia-deep-dive-tvs-greatest-non-sitcom-sitco-239170. Accessed 31 Oct. 2016.

Endrst, James. "*Seinfeldia* Celebrates a Comedy Classic." Review of *Seinfeldia: How a Show about Nothing Changed Everything*, by Jennifer Keishin Armstrong. *USA Today*, 2 July 2016, www.usatoday.com/story/life/books/2016/07/02/seinfeldia-how-a-show-about-nothing-changed-everything-book-review/86477876/. Accessed 31 Oct. 2016.

Garner, Dwight. "Review: Seinfeldia, on Why We Still Can't Escape 'Hello, Jerry.'" Review of Seinfeldia: How a Show about Nothing Changed Everything, by Jennifer Keishin Armstrong. *The New York Times*, 30 June 2016, www.nytimes.com/2016/07/01/books/review-seinfeldia-jennifer-keishin-armstrong.html. Web. 31 Oct. 2016.

Lozada, Carlos. "This New Book about *Seinfeld* Is Worth Double-Dipping." Review of *Seinfeldia: How a Show about Nothing Changed Everything*, by Jennifer Keishin Armstrong. *The Washington Post*, 4 Aug. 2016, www.washingtonpost.com/news/book-party/wp/2016/08/04/this-new-book-about-seinfeld-is-worth-double-dipping/. Accessed 31 Oct. 2016.

Sedensky, Matt. "Review: *Seinfeldia* Offers Little New on Landmark Comedy." Review of *Seinfeldia*: *How a Show about Nothing Changed Everything*, by Jennifer Keishin Armstrong. *Big Story*, Associated Press, 18 July 2016, bigstory.ap.org/article/ac85e6c4b2a04ab1b50f055f40620243/review-seinfeldia-offers-little-new-landmark-comedy. Accessed 31 Oct. 2016.

Review of *Seinfeldia*: *How a Show about Nothing Changed Everything*, by Jennifer Keishin Armstrong. *Kirkus*, 30 Apr. 2016, www.kirkusreviews.com/book-reviews/jennifer-keishin-armstrong/seinfeldia/. Accessed 31 Oct. 2016.

A Series of Catastrophes and Miracles
A True Story of Love, Science, and Cancer

Author: Mary Elizabeth Williams (b. 1965)
Publisher: National Geographic (Washington, DC). 304 pp.
Type of work: Memoir
Time: 2010s
Locale: New York, New York

A Series of Catastrophes and Miracles: A True Story of Love, Science, and Cancer *is Mary Elizabeth Williams's surprisingly witty account of her battle with a diagnosis of terminal cancer. Williams, now cancer free, benefited from cutting-edge immunotherapy treatment. Her book offers information about cancer and the history of its treatment.*

A Series of
Catastrophes
& Miracles

A True Story of Love,
Science, and Cancer

MARY ELIZABETH WILLIAMS

(Courtesy of National Geographic Society)

Principal personages:
MARY ELIZABETH WILLIAMS, the author,
    diagnosed with stage 4 melanoma
JEDD D. WOLCHOCK, her oncologist and an immunotherapy researcher
DEBBIE, her close friend, also struggling with cancer
JEFF, her husband
LUCY, her daughter
BEATRICE, her daughter

If it is possible to write a genuinely, consistently funny book about being diagnosed with terminal cancer, Mary Elizabeth Williams has done so. *A Series of Catastrophes and Miracles: A True Story of Love, Science, and Cancer* provokes a smile or laugh on practically every page, and some readers will find themselves at times literally laughing out loud. (The passage on enema purchases is in very bad taste but very good fun.) Williams's book, however, in no way trivializes the disease, nor is her humor either saccharine or cute. Wit is simply one more way for her to cope with the disease. It also seems a key part of her personality; she emerges from this volume as someone who would be fun to know. In any case, rarely does her wit seem strained. In addition to often being droll, her book is also often poignant, sharp-eyed, moving, and painful. Williams manages to write in ways that seem both brave and self-effacing, both inspiring and honest. In short, she manages to capture the full range of emotions that come with a diagnosis of a serious illness, including (although she does not acknowledge this herself) courage.

Williams begins by telling readers right away that her cancer was cured: that she, thanks to participation in a highly innovative medical trial, managed to beat the advanced disease that would otherwise have killed her. But her book never seems anti-climactic because of this; it is full of real suspense and consistently holds the reader's interest. Numerous memorable characters besides Williams herself appear in these pages, including a number of other cancer patients. The reader knows the odds are that many of these patients are unlikely to survive. One character in particular—a woman named Debbie, Williams's closest friend—eventually succumbs after a long, feisty battle. The book, then, has a bittersweet ending. Readers feel thankful that Williams herself emerged in good health, but they are constantly reminded that others were not so lucky.

Williams makes her living by writing, and her talent for effective phrasing appears on every page. The main narrative, for instance, begins by noting, "The thing that tried to take my life was as big as an eraser on a no. 2 pencil." A page later, she writes, "This is how the bottom drops out of your world, in ten seconds. It's the sound of your doctor telling you, 'I'm sorry.'" On the next page she comments, "My desk looks the same. My nearly finished story is still on the computer screen in front of me. And I have cancer." Later, she tells herself, "You are not a normal person anymore. You are a sick one. Your little bump on your head is not a little bump in your life. This thing is about to change all your goddamn plans." That last sentence captures the tone of frankness that frequently pervades this book. Williams is no shrinking violet; her prose often uses profanity, often in very funny ways, and the usage always seems appropriate.

A Series of Catastrophes and Miracles would be a satisfying read even if it did not deal with such a significant and widely relevant topic. Many readers, as they make their way through its pages, will wonder if they, too, may someday face the challenges Williams has had to confront, and how they might cope with similar situations. The book is partly a personal narrative and partly, if unintentionally, a training manual. In addition to telling her own story, Williams provides plenty of information about modern medicine, the latest treatments, available support systems, and especially the specifics of clinical trials of cutting-edge drugs.

Every so often, Williams shifts from her main autobiographical narrative to offer italicized sections that provide scientific facts as well as historical information. In these sections, she often functions as an insightful investigative reporter, not only explaining how she feels about her own situation but also revealing what she has learned about cancer in general. She comments, stunningly, that one-third of all women "will develop some form of cancer in their lives." She also notes,

Cancer has an exasperatingly bountiful array of manifestations. There are more than 100 different kinds of cancer that affect humans. . . . That's why there will likely never be a cure for cancer. And I say that as someone who has, for all intents and purposes, been cured. Cancer is not a single disease, and it almost certainly can't be addressed with a single magical potion. It has to be approached with a variety of protocols.

Williams shows just how long and complicated the process of developing new drugs can be, involving years of research, testing, and finally getting them approved for use in trials that can then take additional years to conclude. She shows how expensive the

(Courtesy of Chris Carroll)

Mary Elizabeth Williams is a staff writer with Salon.com *and has written for many other magazines, both in print and online. Her previous book,* Gimme Shelter *(2009), dealt with the rapid rise of real estate prices and the housing crisis that exists in certain highly populated urban areas.*

whole process can be and how many dead ends it typically involves. But she also shows the real progress that has been made in treating and in some cases even curing various kinds of cancer, her own included. Her outline of the history of immunotherapy is especially intriguing, showing how a method of treatment that was once widely ignored and even belittled now seems to hold enormous promise.

In one especially important passage, Williams takes to task conspiracy theorists who contend that cancer specialists and medical companies are merely out to make money and that they deliberately resist finding and developing cures. Williams cuttingly asserts, "My doctors have spent their whole adult lives allegedly investigating treatments and the researchers working on drug trials have done the same. It's pretty impressive to think they're really just sitting around letting everybody die. Totally had me fooled." Ultimately her book inspires real confidence in the medical profession and in most of its members, even if Williams is also willing to pen acid portraits of occasionally pompous physicians (whose names have been changed). Obviously she feels very grateful, not only for surviving but also for the many people who made her survival possible. Numerous heroes appear in this book, some of them professionally prominent and some of them mere parts of the vast medical bureaucracy. Quietly heroic patients also appear. Williams recognizes that she was lucky enough to have cancer in New York City, where she benefited from treatment at Memorial Sloan Kettering Cancer Center, one of the country's very best treatment facilities.

Friendship is an important theme in this book, as is family. Williams's two daughters were six and ten years old when she was diagnosed in her mid-forties. She and her husband had only recently reunited after a period of separation when the cancer struck. Williams was thus fortunate to have a supportive partner by her side as she dealt with the illness and its complicated treatment regimen. Her husband emerges as one of many good people in this volume. Readers also witness her children mature as the disease is slowly beaten back. In fact, the book often inspires good thoughts not only about doctors, nurses, and researchers but also about the kinds of people, especially family and friends, whom it is too easy to take for granted. Although it deals with a deadly disease, Williams's book is very much life-affirming in every way. It will remind most readers to feel grateful simply to have the chance to exist, to share life with people they care about and who care about them.

This is one reason the book's humor is ultimately so important and is, perhaps, the key feature that many readers will remember when they put this volume down or try to describe it to others. Williams quite literally laughs in the face of death. She makes it clear that death can only be postponed, not avoided entirely, and that in the meantime there can be plenty to enjoy, even in the grimmest of situations. She tells her husband, Jeff, "When it's my time, just give me a continuous loop of C-Span *Book TV*, so you can tell people I was literally bored to death." She recounts the last days of her cancer-stricken father-in-law, including this touching moment:

> He acknowledges my entrance with a faint nod and weakly extends his hand. I take it gently, my fingers caressing his papery flesh. "Can I go now?" he whispers. "I'm ready to go." He seems so serene.
>
> I pat his hand lovingly. "Soon," I say. "We're all right here with you."
>
> "I have to go," he says again. What beautiful acceptance, I think. With calm dignity. Then he adds, "I have to go pee." Oh.

Someday, of course, Williams herself will have to "go" in the way she mistakenly assumed here. But in the meantime, and forever, she has left behind this beautiful, powerful, and very funny memoir.

Robert C. Evans, PhD

Review Sources

Crum, Janet. Review of *A Series of Catastrophes and Miracles: A True Story of Love, Science, and Cancer*, by Mary Elizabeth Williams. *Library Journal*, 1 Feb. 2016, p. 98.

Dell'Antonia, K. J. "When 'Having It All' Includes Having Cancer." Review of *A Series of Catastrophes and Miracles: A True Story of Love, Science, and Cancer*, by Mary Elizabeth Williams. *Well*, New York Times, 22 Apr. 2016, well.blogs. nytimes.com/2016/04/22/when-having-it-all-includes-having-cancer/. Accessed 27 Jan. 2017.

Review of *A Series of Catastrophes and Miracles: A True Story of Love, Science, and Cancer*, by Mary Elizabeth Williams. *Kirkus Reviews*, 1 Feb. 2016, p. 10.

Springen, Karen. Review of *A Series of Catastrophes and Miracles: A True Story of Love, Science, and Cancer*, by Mary Elizabeth Williams. *Booklist*, 15 Feb. 2016, p. 14.

Shirley Jackson
A Rather Haunted Life

Author: Ruth Franklin
Publisher: Liveright (New York). 624 pp.
Type of work: Biography
Time: 1916–65
Locales: California, New York, Vermont

Shirley Jackson: A Rather Haunted Life re-counts the life of the often misunderstood and historically undervalued American fiction writer and essayist Shirley Jackson. In providing a thorough discussion of Jackson's life and work, literary critic Ruth Franklin aims to reemphasize the author's significance.

(Courtesy of Liveright Publishing Corporation)

Principal personages:
SHIRLEY JACKSON, the American writer most famous for her short story "The Lottery" (1948)
GERALDINE JACKSON, her emotionally abusive mother, a San Franciscan socialite
STANLEY EDGAR HYMAN, her unfaithful husband, a Bennington College professor and a literary critic for the New Yorker

Book critic and author Ruth Franklin has said in interviews that despite the fact that she loves ghost stories, she was never drawn to Shirley Jackson as a horror writer. Although Franklin appreciated the eerie, twisted fiction that Jackson was most famous for, including her short story "The Lottery" (1948) and National Book Award–nominated novel *The Haunting of Hill House* (1959), it was ultimately Jackson's memoirs on motherhood and domesticity that captured her attention. Fascinated by how sharply the memoirs contrasted the writer's public oddball persona, Franklin became determined to uncover who Jackson really was. She stays true to this objective throughout her second book, *Shirley Jackson: A Rather Haunted Life* (2016), a truly illuminating biography that posits that Jackson's experiences as a mother and a wife not only informed much of her dark writing but also deftly captured the frustrations of an entire generation of American women.

As the biographer of an individual who struggled with mental health issues, Franklin is deeply sympathetic. While relaying the details of Jackson's personal life, Franklin resists the temptation to leverage the many tragedies and scandals that the writer encountered for shock value. Instead, she chooses to examine these events in the context of Jackson's work. Throughout the biography, Franklin suggests that there were two people responsible for Jackson's emotional turmoil—her mother, Geraldine Jackson, and her husband, Stanley Edgar Hyman. A powerful antagonistic force in Jackson's life, Geraldine was a Californian socialite who treated her daughter as both an embarrassment and an inconvenience.

As a result of spending her childhood constantly harassed by Geraldine for her weight, bookishness, and general lack of feminine charm, Jackson's self-esteem never fully developed. Franklin illustrates the intensity of Geraldine's emotional abuse in one of the book's especially disturbing anecdotes, where Geraldine tells Jackson that she is the product of a failed abortion. Geraldine's cruelty never stopped; instead of congratulating Jackson on the glowing review her novel *We Have Always Lived in the Castle* (1962) received in *Time*, she wrote to tell her daughter how "awful" her photo was in the magazine. Franklin does not claim that Jackson's relationship with her mother had a silver lining; however, she does point out that Geraldine's qualities of malice and vapidity were often what Jackson depicted in her stories as the shortcomings of American society.

(Courtesy of Anthony Delmundo)

Ruth Franklin is an American book critic and writer whose work has appeared in the New Yorker, Harper's, *and the* New York Times Book Review. *Her first book,* A Thousand Darknesses: Lies and Truth in Holocaust Fiction *(2011) was a finalist for the Sami Rohr Prize for Jewish Literature.*

While Franklin's portrayal of Hyman is no more favorable, it is arguably more complex. Initially, Hyman is presented as the way in which Jackson chose to rebel against her mother's country-club values. In addition to being Jewish, Hyman was also a Communist and an ardent supporter of Jackson's work. Hyman declared that he would marry Jackson after reading one of her short stories in their college literary magazine—despite never having met her. Jackson was easily won over by Hyman; not only did he like her for who she was, but he also found her attractive. Their marital bliss quickly dissolved once they moved to Vermont where Hyman was offered a job as a professor at Bennington College. There, he insisted Jackson keep writing while also raising their children and playing the part of his dutiful faculty wife. Hyman, who claimed to not believe in monogamy, exacerbated Jackson's fragile self-esteem by not only being unfaithful but also regaling her with tales of his affairs. Franklin points out that ultimately the role that Hyman played in Jackson's life was a complicated and contradictory one. He was both her domestic captor as well as the biggest champion of her literary talent.

Franklin argues that a large part of what makes Jackson's work fascinating is how multifaceted it is. Many of Jackson's stories are important because they offer insight into the feeling of oppression that most American women experienced in the mid-twentieth century. This is primarily evident in Jackson's reoccurring motifs of lonely wives trying to escape oppressive households and romantic male figures whose initial promises of happiness ultimately prove to be illusory. Jackson's nonfiction pieces also address the harshly circumscribed societal roles of women at that time. In one particular essay, she reveals that only a few months after publishing her most famous short story, "The Lottery," in the *New Yorker*, she arrived at the hospital to give birth to her third child. The hospital clerk defiantly scribbled "housewife" in the paperwork, despite Jackson having declared "writer" as her occupation. To ensure that Jackson does not come across exclusively as a purveyor of darkness and lament, Franklin spends an equal part of her analysis on the writer's popular family stories. However restrictive she found the role of housewife to be, Jackson took great pleasure in motherhood and wrote several books while raising four children. Many of these titles, including the popular essay collection *Life among the Savages* (1953), are joyous, comedic accounts of her family. According to Franklin, Jackson could never have been a writer had it not been for her children; they forced her to be both creative and disciplined in her writing schedule.

If there is one central supposition to *Shirley Jackson: A Rather Haunted Life* it is that Jackson's gender has ultimately prevented her from being recognized as one of the most important American writers of the twentieth century. According to Franklin, the refusal by male literary critics to take Jackson seriously was in part due to the popularity of her essays on motherhood, which were published in women's magazines. Jackson furthered critics' dismissal of her talent with her unconventional sense of humor. On more than one occasion, the writer publically joked that she was an amateur witch who liked hexing publishers. Franklin illustrates the sexism and myopia of the literary community by comparing Jackson to writers such as Edgar Allan Poe and Nathaniel Hawthorne. Like these men, Franklin argues, Jackson was an American Gothic writer whose horror stories used irony to demonstrate the prejudice, evil, and hypocrisy that lurks within the human soul. This is especially evident in her short, twisted story about racism, entitled "Flower Garden" (1948), and "The Lottery," in which Jackson uses a quaint, bucolic town as the setting for a horrific act of community violence. By the end of *Shirley Jackson: A Rather Haunted Life*, it becomes clear that had Jackson been a male writer, her work would have earned the label of great literature long ago.

One of the most fascinating ways that *Shirley Jackson: A Rather Haunted Life* differs from other Jackson biographies is that it clearly defines her private voice. While conducting research for the book, Franklin was dismayed by the dearth of outgoing letters written by Jackson. Despite being an avid correspondent and having many high-profile friends to whom she wrote, few of Jackson's letters have been preserved. However, Franklin was able to right this wrong by tracking down the family of a Baltimore housewife named Jeanne Beatty. Beatty had started as a fan of Jackson's work and eventually became her pen pal. Beatty had kept Jackson's letters, which revealed the author's feelings of frustration about her personal life as well as her worries while writing her final novel, *We Have Always Lived in the Castle*. By incorporating and analyzing Jackson's letters to Beatty in the biography, Franklin provides readers with a more complete image of who Jackson was as both a woman and a writer.

Reviews of *Shirley Jackson: A Rather Haunted Life* have been overwhelmingly positive. Many critics have praised Franklin's decision to present Jackson as one of the most important American Gothic writers in literary history. In her *Washington Post* review, Elaine Showalter wrote that Franklin's book is a masterful biography that "both uncovers Jackson's secret and haunting life and repositions her as a major artist whose fiction so uncannily channeled women's nightmares." Similarly, *Kirkus Reviews* designated *Shirley Jackson: A Rather Haunted Life* as "consistently interesting" and claimed that it "deftly captures the many selves and multiple struggles of a true American original." Other reviewers have extolled Franklin for tapping into her own experience as a literary critic and writing the first Jackson biography that truly analyzes her work. For decades, the public narrative about Jackson focused exclusively on her tortured personal life. This image was furthered by Judy Oppenheimer's Jackson biography *Private Demons: The Life of Shirley Jackson* (1988), which sensationalized Jackson's tumultuous marriage, mental health issues, and the nervous breakdown that preceded her death in 1965. Ultimately, what makes *Shirley Jackson: A Rather Haunted Life* groundbreaking is that while it provides comprehensive biographical background, it examines Jackson primarily as an artist.

Some readers may find the book's tone to be too dry and academic—a result of Franklin's decision to incorporate a large amount of her research into the text. However, this is a subjective issue, as many Jackson fans will find Franklin's dedication to the details to be immensely rewarding. Another divisive aspect of the biography is the time it devotes to Hyman's career. Although Jackson's relationship with Hyman influenced her writing, Franklin's in-depth exploration of Hyman's separate professional life can often feel superfluous. Despite these shortcomings, *Shirley Jackson: A Rather Haunted Life* is an excellent book. In addition to Franklin's thorough, poignant writing, the biography proves immensely rewarding in its underlying mission to shine a light on the underappreciated genius of Shirley Jackson.

Emily Turner

Review Sources

Bradfield, Scott. "Shirley Jackson and Her Bewitching Biography, *A Rather Haunted Life*." Review of *Shirley Jackson: A Rather Haunted Life*, by Ruth Franklin. *Los Angeles Times*, 30 Sept. 2016, www.latimes.com/books/jacketcopy/la-ca-jc-shirley-jackson-bio-20160919-snap-story.html. Accessed 8 Jan. 2017.

Havrilesky, Heather. "Haunted Womanhood." Review of *Shirley Jackson: A Rather Haunted Life*, by Ruth Franklin. *The Atlantic*, Oct. 2016, www.theatlantic.com/magazine/archive/2016/10/the-possessed/497513/. Accessed 8 Jan. 2017.

McGrath, Charles. "The Case for Shirley Jackson." Review of Shirley Jackson: A Rather Haunted Life, by Ruth Franklin. *The New York Times*, 30 Sept. 2016, www.nytimes.com/2016/10/02/books/review/shirley-jackson-ruth-franklin.html. Accessed 8 Jan. 2017.

Miller, Laura. "Eerie and Cheery." Review of *Shirley Jackson: A Rather Haunt-ed Life*, by Ruth Franklin. *Slate*, 5 Oct. 2016, www.slate.com/articles/arts/books/2016/10/ruth_franklin_s_biography_of_shirley_jackson_reviewed.html. Accessed 8 Jan. 2017.

Review of *Shirley Jackson: A Rather Haunted Life*, by Ruth Franklin. *Kirkus*, 25 May 2016, www.kirkusreviews.com/book-reviews/ruth-franklin/shirley-jackson/. Accessed 8 Jan. 2017.

Showalter, Elaine. Review of *Shirley Jackson: A Rather Haunted Life*, by Ruth Franklin. *The Washington Post*, 22 Sept. 2016, www.washingtonpost.com/entertainment/books/shirley-jackson-a-rather-haunted-life/2016/09/15/4293b85e-5f2b-11e6-af8e-54aa2e849447_story.html. Accessed 8 Jan. 2017.

The Silence of the Sea

Author: Yrsa Sigurðardóttir (b. 1963)
First published: *Brakið*, 2011, in Iceland
Translated from the Icelandic by Victoria Cribb
Publisher: Minotaur Books (New York). 336 pp.
Type of work: Novel
Time: ca. 2009
Locales: Reykjavik, Iceland; Lisbon, Portugal; the North Atlantic Ocean

In The Silence of the Sea, *attorney Thóra Gudmundsdóttir investigates the disappearance of the passengers and crew missing from a yacht that arrives on autopilot in Reykjavik harbor, piecing together details about their fate from sparse forensic evidence in the absence of eyewitnesses to the tragedy that occurred at sea.*

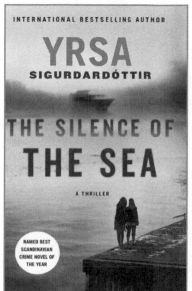

(Courtesy of St. Martin's Press)

Principal characters:
THÓRA GUDMUNDSDÓTTIR, an attorney
ÆGIR MARGEIRSSON, a representative of the resolution committee for a failed Icelandic bank
LÁRA, his wife
ARNA, their eight-year-old daughter, Bylgja's twin
BYLGJA, their eight-year-old daughter, Arna's twin
THRÁINN, a sea captain
LOFTUR, his mate
HALLDÓR "HALLI" THORSTEINSSON, a crew member
SNÆVAR THÓRDARSON, another crew member, Halli's friend
KARÍTAS, a socialite
MATTHEW REICH, a bank investigator, Thóra's beau
BELLA, Thóra's secretary

The Silence of the Sea, which received the Petrona Award for the best Scandinavian crime novel of 2015, is the sixth novel by Yrsa Sigurðardóttir featuring Thóra Gudmundsdóttir, an attorney living in Reykjavik, Iceland. A partner in a small law firm, Thóra often finds herself taking on cases that larger firms might not wish to deal with, which almost always involve her in significant investigations that usually result in murders being solved. This plot device has allowed Yrsa to create a mystery series that is at once suspenseful and somewhat quirky. That combination should not be surprising,

(Courtesy of Sigurjo´n Ragnar)

Yrsa Sigurðardóttir, a native of Reyk-
javík, Iceland, is the author of a crime
series featuring attorney Thóra Gud-
mundsdóttir as well as several stand-
alone mysteries. Several of her novels
have won or been nominated for presti-
gious awards. In 2015 she received the
Petrona Award, designating the best
Scandinavian crime novel of the year,
for The Silence of the Sea.

given Yrsa's own background. An engineer by training and a principal in one of Iceland's largest civil engineering firms, she began her career as an author in the 1990s by writing children's books, publishing her first adult mystery several years later. The social life of Iceland and its colorful, sometimes grim history form the backdrop for novels that give readers a sense of life near the Arctic Circle.

The series featuring Thóra Gudmundsdóttir is similar to conventional mysteries in that the novels contain a number of unusual occurrences that challenge the protagonist's (and readers') powers of deduction. Yrsa includes sufficient false leads and red herrings to keep both characters and readers off balance until the resolution, which can almost always be explained by a careful review of clues presented in the course of the narrative—although on occasion readers' credulity is strained, as in *Horfðu á mig* (2009; *Someone to Watch over Me*, 2013), when Thóra and others are stumped by a mysterious reference that would be apparent to any reader who has taken a course in high school chemistry.

As with most successful series, each book continues to develop Thóra's backstory. She struggles as a single parent and a grandparent when her teenage son gets his girlfriend pregnant. She tries to enjoy a personal life through her relationship with a German beau, Matthew Reich, whom readers meet in the first book of the series, *Þriðja táknið* (2005; *Last Rituals*, 2007), when he travels to Iceland to represent a woman whose son was murdered while in studying at university there. Matthew eventually moves in with Thóra in the fifth installment. The Thóra Gudmundsdóttir novels address a number of contemporary themes, including the presence of cults, the treatment of people with disabilities, and the impact of natural disasters. The collapse of Iceland's financial industry, which crumbled as a result of the worldwide recession in 2008, indirectly precipitates the action in *The Silence of the Sea*.

The plot is set in motion when a luxury yacht, the *Lady K*, departs Lisbon, Portugal, under command of an experienced sea captain, Thráinn, but arrives in Reykjavik harbor with no one aboard. What is known is that the yacht was being repossessed from an owner who defaulted on his payments to one of Iceland's failed banks. The yacht was to sail from Lisbon, where officials impounded it, back to Iceland, where the committee could sell it to settle some of the debt. Seven people sailed from Lisbon, among them Ægir Margeirsson, a member of the resolution committee set up to recover some of the bank's assets, who had been sent to Lisbon to repossess the yacht. When one of the two original crew members is injured just before departure, Ægir agrees to take his place on the voyage back to Reykjavik. His wife, Lára, and their twin eight-year-olds, Arna and Bylgja, who came to Portugal with him to vacation in the warm climate, decide to accompany him aboard the yacht on the voyage home. When none of the family arrives, Thóra is hired by Ægir's parents, who presume their son and most of his family have died. They need Thóra's help to claim Ægir's estate so they may raise the couple's two-year-old daughter, who was left in Iceland when the rest of the family traveled to Lisbon.

Although advertised as a mystery, *The Silence of the Sea* actually combines two popular genres, the mystery and the thriller. Chapters following Thóra's efforts to figure out what happened to Ægir's family alternate with ones providing a chilling first-hand account of what actually occurred aboard the yacht. Plot twists appear in almost every chapter, as it quickly becomes apparent that the yacht owner's wife, Karítas, has ostensibly disappeared as well. Sometimes aided (and occasionally thwarted) by the police, Thóra enlists Matthew and her secretary, Bella, to help understand what could have led to the crew and passengers either abandoning ship or suffering death at sea. In one of the many coincidences in the novel, Bella turns out to have been a classmate of Karítas; for once she sets aside the surly attitude that causes Thóra so much angst in earlier novels, as she is eager to unmask Karítas as a heartless social climber who managed to inveigle herself into the international jet set.

Because Thóra has no eyewitnesses to interview and virtually no communications records from the *Lady K* as it sailed northward, she seeks help from Snævar, the crew member whose inability to make the voyage forced Ægir to help sail the yacht back to Iceland. With his leg still in a cast from an injury suffered in Lisbon just before sailing, Snævar proves a willing and helpful source of information, although he seems mortified that his friend and fellow crew member Halli could be responsible for anything nefarious that may have happened on board.

Several days after the *Lady K* arrives in Reykjavik, the discovery of the bodies of the two crew members, one washed ashore on Iceland's coast and the other hanging in a makeshift sling beneath the boat, lends strong suspicion to the idea that Ægir and his family are not coming home. Making the most of small discoveries—blood on cushions, a garbled radio transmission sent to a passing ship about a body onboard, eyeglasses left behind by one of the twins, the absence of cell phones or cameras aboard the boat when it reaches Reykjavik—Thóra prepares documentation to convince a judge that Ægir's parents should receive the proceeds of his substantial insurance policy, thereby allowing them to care for the remaining child. The efforts of Ægir's parents to gain custody of their grandchild provide the author an opportunity to describe in some detail the unintended consequences of Iceland's social services policy that often denies older people the right to care for the very young, even if they are family members.

The alternate chapters read like a thriller, as readers learn what actually happened aboard the *Lady K*. Strange occurrences aboard the yacht—items moved, strange noises, the discovery of a body in a food storage locker—convince Ægir that he and his family are in serious danger. To complicate matters, he is unsure who among the crew he can trust, and as the boat sails farther north, the captain and crew come to suspect each other as well. Yrsa is not squeamish about describing the terror felt by the entire family—small children included—as they begin to suspect they will never reach Reykjavik harbor. The scene in which Ægir dons scuba gear and dives below the yacht to cut loose a large metal container that has become entangled with the *Lady K* rivals some of the best contemporary suspense fiction. Most readers will find themselves wishing the family could survive their ordeal, but at the same time, many will realize that both the plot and the novel's larger theme demand otherwise.

By employing this intriguing method of alternating chapters, Yrsa does more than simply create suspense. *The Silence of the Sea* is a kind of postmodern critique of the forensic process itself. The novel raises the epistemological question, how credible are the explanations offered for past events? Readers see that investigators (both Thóra and the police) are forced to draw inferences from the smallest details. Sometimes their deductions are remarkably accurate; at other times, they are far from the mark. One sees that it is possible to reach widely different conclusions from the same body of evidence, particularly when no one is able to corroborate a theory. The implications go beyond the reliability of criminal investigations, suggesting that any method for interrogating the historical past is open to question and that conclusions reached by investigators or researchers are often merely the most plausible—or most elegant—explanation for events that can never be fully known. Viewed from this perspective, *The Silence of the Sea* is much more than an exciting mystery; it is a deeply philosophical treatise on how people reconstruct and ultimately understand the past.

This is not the first novel by Yrsa Sigurðardóttir to weave together stories of past and present, but it is unquestionably her most successful in raising questions about the ability to know the truth about past events. Of course, in keeping with the conventions of the mystery genre, Yrsa creates an explanation that vindicates her protagonist. Some readers may find the conclusion to Thóra's investigation somewhat contrived, especially in light of the novel's larger thematic purpose. Yet even when Thóra has sufficient evidence to satisfy her clients' needs, some details about the fate of the crew and passengers of the *Lady K* remain unknown to the people who have an interest in the case. Additionally, although Thóra finally discovers two people still alive who played a role in the events on the yacht, these two offer decidedly differing views of what really happened and why. Readers, however, learn the full truth in a final chapter that provides a bittersweet ending to a novel that is likely to haunt them long after they finish the last poignant paragraph.

Laurence W. Mazzeno, PhD

Review Sources

Appell, Nelson. Review of *The Silence of the Sea*, by Yrsa Sigurðardóttir. *Emissouri-an.com*, 3 Aug. 2016, www.emissourian.com/blogs/mo_books/review-the-silence-of-the-sea/article_e05360d0-5931-11e6-af80-0bc8a0df5030.html. Accessed 16 Dec. 2016.

Lewis, Tony. "Yacht Mystery Creeps Out as It Sails Along." Review of *The Silence of the Sea*, by Yrsa Sigurðardóttir. *Providence Journal*, 24 Mar. 2016, www. providencejournal.com/entertainmentlife/20160324/book-review-yacht-mystery-creeps-out-as-it-sails-along. Accessed 16 Dec. 2016.

Review of *The Silence of the Sea*, by Yrsa Sigurðardóttir. *Kirkus Review*, 12 Dec. 2015, p. 334.

Steffens, Daneet. "*Silence of the Sea* a Compelling Mystery at Sea and on Land." Review of *The Silence of the Sea*, by Yrsa Sigurðardóttir. *Boston Globe*, 25 Feb. 2016, www.bostonglobe.com/arts/books/2016/02/24/silence-sea-compelling-mystery-sea-and-land/xp9oFxVciWRWmaTw4QHwlK/story.html. Accessed 16 Dec. 2016.

Williams, Wilda. Review of *The Silence of the Sea*, by Yrsa Sigurðardóttir. *Library Journal*, 11 Feb. 2016, reviews.libraryjournal.com/2016/02/books/fiction/fiction-from-ashe-box-and-sigurdardottir-plus-debuters-de-silva-and-kelly-xpress-re-views. Accessed 16 Dec. 2016.

The Silk Roads
A New History of the World

Author: Peter Frankopan (b. ca. 1971)
Publisher: Alfred A. Knopf (New York).
645 pp.
Type of work: History
Time: 550 BCE–present
Locale: Predominantly the former Persian
Empire

The Silk Roads: A New History of the World
tells the history of the world through the per-
spective of the rise of the Persian Empire
and the empire's subsequent effect on cul-
tural evolution in the rest of the world.

Principal personages:
CYRUS THE GREAT, founder of the Achaemenid Empire in Western Asia
GENGHIS KHAN, leader of the Mongol tribes
that conquered much of Asia
HAMMURABI, Babylonian king credited with creating one of the first known law codes
in existence

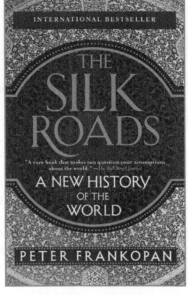

(Courtesy of Knopf)

While Oxford University historian Peter Frankopan's newest history, *The Silk Roads*,
bears the subtitle *A New History of the World*, it is, like any attempt to encapsulate
human history in a single volume, necessarily selective in perspective. Frankopan, an
expert in Near Eastern history, chooses the rise of the Persian Empire as the focal point
for a fascinating history anchored in the Middle East and shows how the rise and fall
of civilizations in this region affected the rest of the world. Frankopan opens the first
chapter of his book, "The Creation of the Silk Road," with the assertion that "from the
beginning of time, the centre of Asia was where empires were made." This statement,
however it might be debated by scholars in the field, guides Frankopan's examination
of history, which moves from the establishment of the first Persian Empire in 550 BCE
to a discussion of present-day Central Asia and the Middle East—a region in turmoil
that Frankopan believes is in the early stages of a renaissance that will eventually see
it dominant once again.

In the opening chapter, Frankopan makes a compelling argument that the kings
and emperors who vied for power in the Mediterranean considered the occupation of
Persia a necessary goal for true global advancement. Cyrus the Great, who founded
the Achaemenid Empire, more generally known as the Persian Empire, was killed in
his bid for expansion, but by that time, Persia had already become the cultural capital
of the world with material and cultural riches unequaled anywhere else. It is for this

reason, Frankopan asserts, that those who sought to build power learned from and imitated the Persian civilization. Alexander of Macedon, better known as Alexander the Great, for instance, did not seek to conquer the civilizations of Europe when he began his bid for global conquest in 336 BCE, but rather traveled to Persia, where there were far richer cultural and physical assets to be claimed. Alexander's death in 323 BCE left traces of Greek culture throughout Asia and led to one of the world's greatest transformations, Hellenization, through which aspects and elements of Greek philosophy and culture were deposited, absorbed, and adapted into the academic and popular philosophies and customs of civilizations from Egypt to what is now Afghanistan.

German geologist Ferdinand von Richthofen, who traveled extensively in Asia and published a highly influential series of historical and geographical volumes, is credited as the first to coin the term "silk road" for the trade arteries that ran through Asia and eventually connected the region to the Mediterranean and the rest of the world. Frankopan discusses the importance of silk textile as it connects to China's efforts to protect the nation's borders from the nomadic peoples that lived on the borders and had, for centuries, challenged the Han Chinese for control of parts of the territory that became China. The author is careful to refer to silk "roads" in the plural, because, as the book explains in detail, the silk trade used a complex network of passages, rather than a single road, to conduct trade from the Persian Gulf through Africa. While silk might have been one of the most prestigious and coveted materials to be shipped along these venerable trade routes, in the second chapter of Frankopan's history, he discusses how the silk roads were also an avenue for the transmission of religious philosophy. Further, Frankopan argues that Persia supported the world's great faiths centuries before there were major religious institutions in Europe and that Christianity might never have flourished in Europe and later North America had the faith been given room to grow and develop in the Middle East.

Frankopan also explores the rise of Islam in the Persian Empire and argues that the religion's success came because it appeared to offer a conciliatory message to the feuding Jews and Christians of the era. Early followers of Islam, Frankopan says, believed that Christians, Jews, and Muslims were all "people of the book," as all three faiths believed in the Hebrew Scriptures, in a single all-powerful God, and in the idea that God occasionally sends messengers. Islam therefore supported the belief that the three Abrahamic faiths should exist in peace. The rise of Islam accompanied a new renaissance in the Middle East that saw Baghdad become the most diverse, advanced, and richest city in the world.

Frankopan continues through major global transformations, providing an Eastern-centric view of the Crusades as the crusaders appeared to those in the East who opposed them, a depiction of the Mongol conquest through the eyes of the societies overtaken by Genghis Khan and his followers, and an Asian perspective on the West African slave trade. In each case, readers are invited to imagine some of the world's infamous military conquests through a different viewpoint. For instance, while most historians would likely agree that the Crusades were a dark point in European colonialism, of which there are many, to depict the Crusades from the view of the societies that stood opposed to the forceful encroachment of European armies is a departure from the typical Western discussion of the era.

The rise of the West begins in chapter 11 of Frankopan's book, "The Road of Gold," and Frankopan does not spare in his criticism of the Western world's obliteration of native cultures around the world as it grew in prominence. The remaining chapters of the book introduce various eras in the growth of modern Asia, the Middle East, Europe, and even the Americas, while, at each stage, filtering history through the transformations of

Historian Peter Frankopan is a senior research fellow at Worcester College, Oxford University, and director of the Oxford Centre for Byzantine Research. He has written numerous articles for the international press, including the Sunday Times, History Today, and the Sydney Morning Herald. The Silk Roads was a best seller in China, India, and the United States.

the former Persian Empire. Each era or major event is explored often through a brief look at a historical figure living then, and Frankopan's descriptions feature trivia that provide a vivid sense of the emotions behind the processions of major events and dates. For instance, in a chapter that deals heavily with the German invasion of Russia (again shifting the focus of World War II to its impact in Asia), Frankopan states that the German soldiers tasked with capturing the Russian wheat industry had been told to imagine that the Soviets were essentially eating food that had been "torn from the mouths of German children." Stimulating, visceral details like this power Frankopan's rapid advance through the centuries and help root his central thesis about the importance of the East.

Frankopan's exploration of the Cold War focuses on the Middle Eastern states and their unenviable position between the superpowers. While not writing an explicitly activist history, Frankopan provides a sufficiently damning case against both the former Soviet Union and the United States as they competed to control Middle Eastern oil. Out of this era came an image of the United States as "imperialists," "Zionists," or both, and this Middle Eastern perception endured into the 2010s, complicating relationships between the United States and the struggling nations in the oil-rich former Persian territories. As Iran, Iraq, Pakistan, and neighboring nations struggled to build new national identities within the midst of both pandering and threats from the superpowers, regimes grew, typically built on populist support but rapidly devolving into authoritarianism. The Cold War left the Middle East devastated. Regimes originally supported by the superpowers either developed into despotic governments or, in other cases, crumbled as the already oppressed and destitute populace overthrew governments, installing new governments, like the Taliban, to take their place.

Through the Cold War into the Arab-Israeli War of 1967, the Persian Gulf War, and the terrorist attacks of September 11, 2001, Frankopan remains dedicated to his thesis, linking many of the major transformative events of the twentieth and twenty-first centuries to the territories of the former Persian Empire. Frankopan concludes the central portion of his book with the observation that the West has seemed to lack historical perspective when determining policies, military, economic, and otherwise, regarding their approach to the Middle East. Frankopan calls the tumultuous popular movements in countries like Ukraine, China, Iran, and Afghanistan "birthing pains," as the region returns to the position of global importance it occupied for millennia. In Frankopan's opinion, hidden beneath the tumultuous politics of the region, an economic and cultural resurgence is also underway, with a host of new museums, cultural centers, and business districts rapidly emerging and countries like China and Russia investing in a "New Silk Road" connecting the Asian and Middle Eastern nations into a new economic partnership. China, for instance, which has maintained an isolationist economy for decades, has recently begun to expand, with investment in Africa, the Middle East, Asia, and parts of Europe.

Frankopan, who is also the author of a well-received 2012 book *The First Crusade: The Call from the East*, has dedicated much of his career to understanding the history of the Middle East. Reviewer Robert Irwin took issue with Frankopan's treatment of Western civilization in *The Silk Roads*, though, in most cases, Frankopan's take on Western politics can be seen as a natural outgrowth of his attempt to frame Western civilization through the perspective of the former Persian Empire. Several reviewers were skeptical about Frankopan's assertion that the East is rising again, citing the ongoing struggle against populists in the Middle East as an indication that the region seems far from a renaissance, for one. However, Frankopan's central argument on the "rise" of the East seems to be that the East will again become the most influential region in the world. The global focus on events there in the mid-2010s and the continued rapid growth of Middle Eastern and Asian economies are arguments in favor of Frankopan's thesis. Other reviewers, including Sadanand Dhume and Bettany Hughes, praised Frankopan's Eastern-centric approach and argued that his take on world history might encourage some readers to question many of their previously held historical assumptions. Western historians have a tendency to frame world history through the Western perspective, and for casual students, this may encourage the view that the Western historical view is the most accurate reading of global events. With *The Silk Roads*, Frankopan forces the reader to question this assumption, reviving the realization that historicity, or the accuracy of historical fact, is a relativistic record that depends largely on one's perspective.

Micah L. Issitt

Review Sources

Dhume, Sadanand. "The Thread That Bound the World." Review of *The Silk Roads: A New History of the World*, by Peter Frankopan. *The Wall Street Journal*, 11 Mar. 2016, www.wsj.com/articles/the-thread-that-bound-the-world-1457732631. Accessed 15 Nov. 2016.

Hughes, Bettany. "The Silk Roads by Peter Frankopan, Review: 'Charismatic.'" Review of *The Silk Roads: A New History of the World*, by Peter Frankopan. *The Telegraph*, 15 Aug. 2016, www.telegraph.co.uk/books/what-to-read/the-silk-roads-by-peter-frankopan-review/. Accessed 15 Nov. 2016.

Irwin, Robert. "The Silk Roads: A New History of the World by Peter Frankopan—
    All Loud on the Eastern Front." Review of *The Silk Roads: A New History of the
    World*, by Peter Frankopan. *The Telegraph*, 13 Aug. 2015, www.independent.
    co.uk/arts-entertainment/books/reviews/the-silk-roads-a-new-history-of-the-
    world-by-peter-frankopan-all-loud-on-the-eastern-front-10453668.html. Accessed
    15 Nov. 2016.
Sattin, Anthony. "The Silk Roads by Peter Frankopan Review—A Frustrating Trail."
    Review of *The Silk Roads: A New History of the World*, by Peter Frankopan. *The
    Guardian*, 29 Sept. 2015, www.theguardian.com/books/2015/sep/29/silk-roads-
    peter-frankopan-review. Accessed 15 Nov. 2016.
Thubron, Colin. "A Different Vision of History." Review of *The Silk Roads: A New
    History of the World*, by Peter Frankopan. *The New York Review of Books*, 21
    Apr. 2016, www.nybooks.com/articles/2016/04/21/silk-roads-different-vision-of-
    history. Accessed 15 Nov. 2016.

Small Great Things

Author: Jodi Picoult (b. 1966)
Publisher: Ballantine Books (New York). 480 pp.
Type of work: Novel
Time: Present day
Locale: Connecticut

Ruth has been a beloved labor and delivery nurse for twenty years; however, after a racist couple ask for her to be removed from the care of their newborn baby, she is blamed for his death, and her life spins out of control.

#1 NEW YORK TIMES BESTSELLER

Jodi Picoult

AUTHOR OF LEAVING TIME

small great things

a novel

(Courtesy of Penguin Random House)

Principal characters:
RUTH JEFFERSON, an African American labor and delivery nurse accused of murder
KENNEDY MCQUARRIE, her white lawyer
EDISON WESLEY JEFFERSON, her son
ADISA, her sister
TURK BAUER, a white supremacist and father of Davis
BRITTANY BAUER, a white supremacist and mother of Davis
DAVIS BAUER, baby who died

As a longtime labor and delivery nurse, Ruth Jefferson confronts life and death on a daily basis. She knows that "love has nothing to do with what you're looking at, and everything to do with who's looking." Though she understands this concept in connection to the new parents at work and with her own son, sometimes she is blind to it in the other relationships in her life. Throughout the course of this novel, she learns the deeper truth of this idea.

The book starts with an introduction to Ruth's story. She is a kind and compassionate nurse with whom patients build report while they toil through the labor process or settle into the reality of being parents of a newborn. The job is usually joyful, but there are moments when tragedy strikes and worlds are torn apart. Ruth usually gets to step back from those losses when the parents leave the hospital, but when Turk and Brittany Bauer arrive in the hospital, Ruth's life changes.

Turk and Brittany Bauer seem like normal new parents. They are excited about the birth of their first child, a son whom they name Davis. However, when Ruth steps into their room to do a routine examination after his birth, red flags are sent spiraling into the air. Turk protests her presence and demands that she be replaced by another nurse—all on the basis of her race. Ruth's supervisor caves to his demands and places a note in the baby's file: "NO AFRICAN AMERICAN PERSONNEL TO CARE FOR THIS PATIENT." Ruth, incensed with the parents' attitude but also with her boss for not standing up for her rights, is thrust into the reality that race does make a difference between love and hate, and fairness and unfairness, something she has long ignored.

Davis Bauer tragically dies a few days later, with Ruth in attendance and offering medical care despite the order in his file. For the first time in her career, she is torn between providing medical care and following orders. She begins to see in small ways that she is treated differently because of her skin color. Then, her life changes in ways she could have never suspected because despite her desire to protect the innocent life of Davis Bauer, her nursing license is suspended and she is escorted out of the hospital by security. Shortly after, she is arrested for murder in the baby's death.

Author Jodi Picoult skillfully weaves the stories of Ruth and Turk Bauer together alongside narratives from Kennedy, the public defense lawyer who is assigned to Ruth's case. The book itself is divided into four major sections based on labor and delivery stages: early labor, active labor, transition, pushing, and afterbirth. Within each section, readers are exposed to first-person narratives, mostly from the major players in the story: Ruth, Turk, and Kennedy. As Picoult exposes readers to the inner workings of each of these characters, they are taken on a rollercoaster ride through time with flashbacks interrupting the present scene, offering a glimpse into the motivations of these key players. The novel's structure keeps readers involved in the drama that unfolds. This technique allows Picoult to develop sympathy for all of the major characters as it delves into their deepest feelings and thoughts.

Jodi Picoult is a New York Times *bestselling author of adult and young-adult fiction. She has also written five issues of the DC Comics* Wonder Woman *comic book series. She has won numerous awards for her work, including the 2013–14 New Hampshire Literary Award for Outstanding Literary Merit.*

Ruth's sections tell the story of a life that has been lived as well as possible. An intelligent child of a domestic servant, Ruth is gifted with an education equal to the child of her mother's employees. She takes advantage of that gift, receiving strong grades and being accepted into a respectable medical school, where she works hard to get a nursing degree. Her dedication pays off and she lands a job in the hospital where, after twenty years of faithful service without a single complaint, she learns that one biased person can ruin another's life. Once her life changes, she is forced to really look at what it means to be African American in a society that claims to embrace equality. Her own experiences, combined with events that undermine her son's success and make her understand her sister's bitterness, open her eyes to a world she has been blindly ignoring for years.

In contrast to Ruth's stability in both childhood and adult life, Turk's sections tell the story of an emotionally and physically abused child who turns to violence to gain acceptance. The fact that the group of white supremacists who accepts him supports his own biased upbringing only reinforces his passionate hatred of people who are different than he is. Picoult creates in Turk a character that readers will want to hate but will also want to understand, one whose tragic loss of a child both supports and undermines everything that he has believed for most of his teen and adult life. Through this character, she provides glimpses of the white supremacy movement, its philosophies, activities, and members.

As Ruth's lawyer, Kennedy's sections waiver between telling her own present-day story and providing a semi-objective view of Ruth's present-day experiences. As a middle-class white woman, Kennedy has had an easy life, but her budding friendship with Ruth forces her to understand that not everyone is as privileged. By the end of Ruth's trial, Kennedy is forced to look at her own motivations, and she becomes a better person as a result.

One of the major themes in the novel is what people do with the lives they have been given. When Ruth was young, her Mama told her, "'You're destined to do small great things,' she told me. 'Just like Dr. King said.' She was referring to one of her favorite quotes: *If I cannot do great things, I can do small things in a great way*." This idea of being able to succeed one step at a time, making a positive effect on the lives of most of her patients as well as her son, carries Ruth throughout her life until the Bauers' accusation. She struggles with finding a way to hold onto this truth and carry on doing "small great things" even when she would like to give in to the negativity that surrounds her.

The other major thematic issue in the novel is race. Despite the murder case being directly focused on Ruth because she is African American, Kennedy's desire to leave race out of the trial proceedings raises questions about whether race should be a factor when the parties involved are so clearly immersed in a racially charged situation. Kennedy is torn between knowing

> there's no way you can look at a case that has, at its core, a nurse who is the only employee of color in the department, a white supremacist father, and a knee-jerk decision by a hospital administrator . . . and not assume that race played a factor.

> But.

> Any public defender who tells you justice is blind is telling you a big fat lie.

Ruth must learn to trust Kennedy's decision to leave race out of the arguments while Kennedy must learn to see what it is like to be African American in a racially charged world.

Since the issue of a white author writing about an African American character is sure to come up in a discussion of the novel, it will be helpful to note Picoult's authorial notes at the end of the book. In this section, Picoult reveals that this novel was inspired by real experiences. She discloses that she began a book about race years earlier after the shooting of an African American police officer, but she put it off because "I was having trouble creating a fictional character that rang true." Two decades later, she heard a story of an African American labor and delivery nurse and a white supremacist. That story became the basis for *Small Great Things*. Picoult's confession of concern over the creation of a character with whom she could not directly relate does soften the demand for authenticity while raising a question of authorial intention, which could become the basis for a solid book discussion. In addition to the author notes, there are three pages of acknowledgements and two pages of bibliography that offer readers further sources for information about the topics raised in the novel.

In addition to these major thematic concerns, the book also introduces a number of other thoughtful issues. Parent-child relationships, employer-employee connections, friendship, sibling relationships, and work ethic all show up in some form or another throughout the book, again raising ideas that could be developed into provocative discussions.

The reviews of the novel were primarily positive but confronted some issues that may concern readers. *Library Journal* lauded the work for its ability to appeal to fans expecting "plenty of courtroom drama and a surprise twist" as well as its background research. *Booklist* pointed out the "thought-provoking examination of racism in America today" while praising the story line as "gripping." Questions about the novel were, not surprisingly, focused on the ability of a white writer to delve into an African American character's experiences. *Kirkus Reviews* maintained that "Kennedy's journey of coming to terms with her own racist relatives and white privilege . . . is the real story here and the novel would have been stronger if it had been written from this perspective throughout." This review also challenged the somewhat "fairy-tale" ending of the book.

Theresa L. Stowell, PhD

Review Sources

Hoffert, Barbara. Review of *Small Great Things*, by Jodi Picoult. *Library Journal*, 15 May 2016, pp. 48–49.

Huntley, Kristine. Review of *Small Great Things*, by Jodi Picoult. *Booklist*, 1 July 2016, p. 31.

Review of *Small Great Things*, by Jodi Picoult. *Kirkus*, 19 July 2016, www.kirkusreviews.com/book-reviews/jodi-picoult/small-great-things/. Accessed 23 Feb. 2017.

Review of *Small Great Things*, by Jodi Picoult. *Publishers Weekly*, 29 Aug. 2016, www.publishersweekly.com/978-0-345-54495-7. Accessed 23 Feb. 2017.

Stenftenagel, Amy. Review of *Small Great Things*, by Jodi Picoult. *Library Journal*, 1 Aug. 2016, p. 85.

Smoke

Author: Dan Vyleta (b. 1974)
Publisher: Doubleday (New York). 448 pp.
Type of work: Novel
Time: Alternate nineteenth century
Locale: England

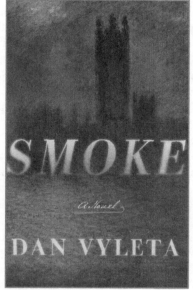

(Courtesy of Doubleday)

Dan Vyleta's novel Smoke *imagines an alternate nineteenth-century England in which sinful thoughts and bad deeds manifest themselves as Smoke excreted from one's body.*

Principal characters:
THOMAS, a newcomer and misfit student at an unnamed, prestigious boarding school who is prone to bursts of a fiery temper
CHARLIE, a fellow student and Thomas's only friend
JULIUS, the school's resident bully and prefect
DR. RENFREW, the school's forward-thinking but puritanical Master of Smoke and Ethics
LADY NAYLOR, an amateur scientist who studies Smoke
LIVIA, Lady Naylor's daughter, who is obsessed with purity

Dan Vyleta's *Smoke* is a historical fantasy novel set in an alternate, nineteenth-century England. In it, two schoolboys—a misfit, Thomas, and his only friend, Charlie—grapple with the meaning of purity. In Vyleta's England, humans must contend with an excretion called Smoke, a bilious, greasy cloud that can be emitted from a person's pores if they sin. In the book's gripping first scene, Thomas and Charlie are rudely awakened in the middle of the night. Prefect Julius has summoned all of the boys in the dormitory to gather in the cavernous bathroom. Pulling names out of a sack, Julius brings boys forward one at a time and forces them to submit to a strange interrogation. Under the guise of aiding self-improvement, Julius asks the humiliating or anger-inducing questions in an effort to get the boys to smoke. He succeeds in making one boy smoke in anger, which leaves a sweat stain, the color of ink, on his clean, white nightshirt. This is unfortunate for the boy, who will be punished for the stain when it appears in his laundry (Smoke is very hard to get out of clothes).

Smoke exits the body through the pores or mouth. It tastes bitter, and it can also be felt and smelled. Sometimes, Smoke leaves an ashy residue called Soot. The popular teaching is that Smoke comes from the soul; if a person is smoking, it is an indication that they have lied, committed a crime, had a lustful thought, or expressed anger. Smoke can only be controlled through arduous self-policing. The rich, already significantly divided from the poor by money and class, use Smoke as another way to separate themselves from the lower classes. The rich tend to smoke less, taught control in fancy schools like Thomas and Charlie's or able to afford secret aids to stop smoking, but it is all passed off as piety. In this way, it is a brilliant commentary on Victorian social mores and how they informed the era's deep class divide. Victorians believed that the poor were morally inferior. In *Smoke*, the rich, like Charlie and Thomas, attend elite schools to learn to control their Smoke. While powerful adults—all men—sample Smoke in the form of cigarettes made from Soot, and then suck on hard candies, a sort of anti-Smoke, to hide the evidence, the poor smoke constantly out of misery.

Vyleta explores class, but he also explores, at various points in the novel, sexuality, science, anti-intellectualism, political corruption, and colonialism. The world of *Smoke* is richly detailed but, as many reviewers pointed out, often collapses under its own intellectual weight. Charles Finch, who reviewed the book for the *New York Times*, wrote that Smoke, the book's unifying subject, is freighted by so much meaning "that it eventually becomes meaningless." Vyleta was inspired to write *Smoke* after reading a passage from the Charles Dickens novel *Dombey & Son* (1848), in which Dickens describes London's dank curtain of coal smoke. Dickens muses about the corruptible cloud: "But if the moral pestilence that rises with [it] . . . could be made discernible too, how terrible the revelation!" (The quote sheds light on another aspect of Smoke—wafting sin begets more sin.)

Vyleta was inspired by Dickens in subject but also appears to have been inspired in form as well. The mystery of where Smoke came from and a plot to uncover its source emerges, and Thomas, Charlie, and a young girl named Livia embark on an adventure through England to solve it. Unfortunately, critics uniformly agreed that the plot somewhat derails at this point, and is full enough of long lyrical asides that it becomes a bit difficult to follow. Frustrating as this may be for some readers, the confusion appears to be a part of Vyleta's larger, more cerebral intentions for the novel. In his afterword, he writes with conviction about the book's purpose—that it is "political" but also contains "no thesis." He describes *Smoke* as a "jazz solo," a riff on morality, rather than a straightforward thriller.

Regardless of Vyleta's intentions, *Smoke* has been compared to fantasy books such as J. K. Rowling's Harry Potter series and the His Dark Materials trilogy by Philip Pullman. (These novels are classified as young-adult literature; *Smoke* is not, though it features teenage protagonists.) In *The Golden Compass* (1996), the first book in Pullman's trilogy, a girl named Lyra becomes familiar with a particle known as Dust. Like Smoke, Dust is feared by the powerful as the manifestation of sin. (Finch suggests that Pullman falls prey to his own concept in the same way Vyleta does.) Lyra's uncle, Lord Asriel, is a rebellious figure who researches Dust. His intentions are ambiguous, but his discoveries fuel the subsequent novels in the series. Vyleta has a similar character in Lady Naylor. Continuing the work of her bedridden

Award-winning author Dan Vyleta was born to Czech parents and raised in Germany, though he attended school in the United States, Canada, and the United Kingdom. His other novels include Pavel & I *(2008),* The Quiet Twin *(2011), and* The Crooked Maid *(2013).*

husband, Lady Naylor seeks the origin of Smoke. Her research spawns a diabolical plan, the particulars of which become the novel's major plot line in the final stretch.

Vyleta is the author of three historical novels, his most recent being *The Crooked Maid* (2013), which is set in post–World War II Vienna. *The Crooked Maid* is a sequel to Vyleta's second book, *The Quiet Twin* (2011). Both novels are ostensibly murder mysteries, though reviewers noted Vyleta's loose allegiance to the genre and to realism in general. *The Quiet Twin* describes the surreality of life under the Nazis, while the tone of *The Crooked Maid*, as described by Esi Edugyan for the *Guardian*, is akin to works of German Expressionism in that its form is an inner darkness made manifest. Vyleta's debut, *Pavel & I* (2008), is a thriller set in the rubble and squalor of postwar Berlin. In *Smoke*, Vyleta stays true to form with a historical setting, a mysterious plot, and the cerebral nature of some of the writing, while diverging with a jump into fantasy.

Like Dickens, Vyleta has an eye for detail—particularly when he is describing the wretched or disgusting. In another well-executed early scene, Thomas and Charlie join their classmates on a trip to London. The trip was once a tradition at the school. The forward-thinking new Master of Smoke and Ethics, Dr. Renfrew, lobbied for the trip to be reinstated. It should be noted that the school is a cold and unwelcoming place. The food is bad and friends are hard to come by—thus the boys are eager to embark on a journey to an unknown place. None of them have ever been to London. Their excitement makes Vyleta's reveal all the more powerful. The train arrives in the station "literally encased in Soot," and when they arrive in the city, the Smoke of London blots out the sun. The Smoke stains their clothes and seeps into their skin, making them feel excited, irritable, aggressive, and afraid. As they make their way through the streets, Vyleta describes the queasy evil of Smoke:

> Drunks and beggars line the house fronts, slumped against the plaster; they display mangled limbs and open sores, or simply sleep away their stupor. Children dart through the press of the crowd, some in play, some loaded with goods for delivery or sale. The street is made of black muck five inches deep, soggy with meltwater. It takes Charlie a while to realize that it consists of Soot, deposited over decades and centuries.

Later, the boys watch a woman, a murderess swirling with Smoke, hanged for her crime. Underneath the platform of the gallows, Thomas witnesses an even more fearful sight—a hooded figure scraping Soot from the women's corpse and sealing it in a jar. Vyleta's London is horrifyingly specific; it sticks in the mind like Soot. Interestingly, it is also very close to the London of Dickens, who sought to make powerful people confront just how terrible the slums really were. Vyleta is at his best when his writing serves a similar purpose. The boys, wealthy and concerned only with their own Smoke, are shocked by what they see. Vyleta emphasizes this disconnect later when Thomas and Charlie visit Thomas's aunt, Lady Naylor, for Christmas. From the Naylors' wealthy estate, the boys find themselves, through an odd sequence of events, on the run and living with a family of coal miners. Livia, Lady Naylor's daughter who is with the boys, must grapple with her own privilege as it dawns on her that the miners' lives depend on the whims of people such as her parents.

Vyleta touches on a larger empathy divide in which the powerful focus on sin itself rather than the people committing the sins because they suffer. The English government has locked down its borders to keep the English people from learning about Smoke, or the lack thereof, in other countries—a modern, realistic corollary might be a church forbidding its congregants from learning about evolution. But the other end of the spectrum is just as dicey. Dr. Renfrew is a reformer and a scientist. He wants to understand Smoke, but like his mentor Lord Naylor, he falls prey to a kind of self-gratifying righteousness in pursuing that quest. (Another plot point, involving certain indigenous cultures that do not smoke, complicates the ethics of the book further.) He obsesses about Smoke—about his own sins and the sins of others, particularly his young niece—to such a degree as to obscure any value to the greater good. His goal becomes purity, a mastery of his own impulse to sin, rather than education or liberty. The resulting heady asides—about human imperfection, discipline, and empathy—can become convoluted, but at moments, provide serious food for thought in an ideologically divided age.

Molly Hagan

Review Sources

Finch, Charles. Review of Smoke, by Dan Vyleta. *The New York Times*, 10 June 2016, www.nytimes.com/2016/06/12/books/review/smoke-by-dan-vyleta.html. Accessed 17 Nov. 2016.

Mandelo, Brit. "Passions in Dust: *Smoke* by Dan Vyleta." Review of *Smoke*, by Dan Vyleta. *Tor*, 21 June 2016, www.tor.com/2016/06/21/book-reviews-smoke-by-dan-vyleta/. Accessed 17 Nov. 2016.

Quinn, Annalisa. "*Smoke* Author Dan Vyleta Keeps It Messy." Review of *Smoke*, by Dan Vyleta. *NPR*, 22 May 2016, www.npr.org/2016/05/22/478679677/smoke-author-dan-vyleta-keeps-it-messy. Accessed 17 Nov. 2016.

Roberts, Adam. "*Smoke* by Dan Vyleta Review—Visions of Sin." Review of *Smoke*, by Dan Vyleta. *The Guardian*, 13 July 2016, www.theguardian.com/books/2016/jul/13/smoke-by-dan-vyleta-review. Accessed 17 Nov. 2016.

Review of *Smoke*, by Dan Vyleta. *Kirkus*, 15 Mar. 2016, www.kirkusreviews.com/book-reviews/dan-vyleta/smoke-vyleta/. Accessed 17 Nov. 2016.

Soul at the White Heat
Inspiration, Obsession, and the Writing Life

Author: Joyce Carol Oates (b. 1938)
Publisher: Ecco (New York). 400 pp.
Type of work: Essays
Time: Twentieth and twenty-first century
Locales: Various

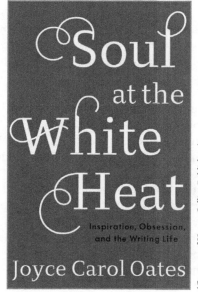

(Courtesy of HarperCollins Publishers)

Soul at the White Heat is a collection of essays from writer Joyce Carol Oates that spans her career as critic and literature lover. Derived from previously published work—many pieces coming from the New York Review of Books *and* Kenyon Review—*the pieces in the collection explore the writing life; offer lively discussion of literary figures, movements, and works; and afford brief glimpses into the author's own life. Beloved figures such as Virginia Woolf, Julian Barnes, and Margaret Atwood are all examined under Oates's careful eye, culminating in a respectful collection representative of contemporary literature.*

The opening essay of Joyce Carol Oates's collection *Soul at the White Heat* asks "Is the uninspired life worth living?" both in title and subject, and upon completion of the thirty-three pieces that follow, the reader is left with a collection of heavily examined inspired souls who have made their mark on letters and life through art, historical resonance, and prolific creation, attributes the author of the collection can claim as well. Divided into four sections—"The Writing Life," "Classics," "Contemporaries," and "Real Life"—*Soul at the White Heat* presents some of Oates's most vigorous and memorable criticism from her astonishing fifty-three-year-long career as a novelist, playwright, critic, poet, and essayist. Many of the pieces originally appeared in the *New York Review of Books*, *Kenyon Review*, the *New York Times Book Review*, the *Times Literary Supplement*, and the *New Yorker*. The collection's title comes from an 1862 poem by Emily Dickinson and opens the collection. Dickinson writes, "Dare you see a Soul at the White Heat? / Then crouch within the door."

Though these pieces deal mostly in critical work and essays, Oates's work as a writer of fiction and poetry is evident in the lyrical and insightful way she examines her subjects, and the range of literary subjects is what makes this collection exhilarating. Writings on Rebecca Mead's memoir *My Life in Middlemarch*, H. P. Lovecraft's strange and tragic life, and Georgia O'Keeffe and Alfred Stieglitz's doomed love affair pepper the "Classics," and in "Contemporaries," Oates examines more recent artists such as Julian Barnes, Derek Raymond, Lorrie Moore, Martin Amis, and Karen Joy Fowler. Curiously, this section finishes with a triptych of essays about boxing culture, including a review of Mike Tyson's memoir *Undisputed Truth* (2013) and his legacy as a boxing legend; a review of David O. Russell's film *The Fighter* (2010); and an examination of the career and near-mythic image of Muhammad Ali. One of the great surprises of the collection is that Oates seems to be an avid fan of the sport, displaying a thorough knowledge of boxing history and offering a careful, thoughtful portrait of her subjects.

Oates's other works include over forty novels, plays, and collections of short stories, four of which—*Black Water* (1992), *What I Lived For* (1994), *Blonde* (2000), and the short story collection *Lovely, Dark, Deep: Stories* (2014)—were Pulitzer Prize finalists, and her love and deep knowledge of writing is present as she skips between unlikely literary bedfellows and finds connections. In an essay about Anne Tyler's novels, including *Noah's Compass* (2009) and *Ladder of Years* (1995), she begins with a thorough examination of John Updike's and Philip Roth's treatment of the passage of time. Oates says, "'What to make of a diminished thing' is a proposition that becomes ever more crucial with the passage of time in our lives, and particularly in the lives of writers who began young, with early successes and early fame," noting that Updike and Roth, who are older contemporaries of Tyler, are similar to her subject in that way and in their focus on aging characters in their writing. By juxtaposing these three giants of literature, Oates is able to offer a fuller portrait of Tyler's later works, which she admits are less luminous than the writer's earlier ones, but nonetheless offer a singular voice about the aging process and how one develops socially and personally. It's worth noting that Oates finds a savagery to Roth's and Updike's treatment of their characters, often impotent men who have found a sympathetic and emotional tie to the past, while Tyler works to reassure her readers that "what we've always known, or should have known, about family life, romantic love, and loss is true after all."

Also of note is Oates's careful examination of the crime fiction of author Derek Raymond. It shows the range of Oates's knowledge and interest, and her elevation of the material shines new light on Raymond's gifts as a writer. She says in her essay that it's rare to see the combination of minimalism and "outbursts of passionate lyricism," particularly in detective novels. Through an examination of Raymond's characters and sparse language, Oates is able to perfectly capture his work and make it accessible even to those who are not familiar with the writer or genre. It is this skill that makes for quick, absorbing reading throughout.

Beyond Oates's engaging and informative criticism, the opening section dealing with the writing life is particularly interesting. Oates has a wealth of wisdom to offer aspiring writers and avid readers alike, and the four essays contained within do just that. The section follows an arch of sorts. The essay "This I Believe: Five Motives for Writing" follows "Is the Uninspired Life Worth Living?" and begins the personal portion of the section. Herein Oates lays out her processes for writing, offering observations of her own work, such as, "Much of my prose fiction is 'commemorative' in essence—it is a means of memorializing a region of the world in which I have lived, a past I've shared with others, a way of life that might seem to me vanishing, thus in danger of being forgotten," eventually parlaying this thought into the possible demise of the physical book. Perhaps most lyrical is the essay "The Writing Room." Oates says, "There is surely some subtle connection between the vistas we face, and the writing we accomplish, as a dream takes its mood and imagery from our waking life," as she describes the time she has spent gazing out the window of her writing space. Oates, who grew up in Lockport, New York, a town in the eastern part of the state, frequently writes of this area in her own work, and for avid readers of the author's fiction, the insights found in these essays become particularly valuable as they are offered an insider's view into her process and inspiration. The placement of these pieces in advance of her more critical pieces allows the reader to gain insight into Oates's work as a practitioner of the art she is about to analyze and to also appreciate the deep passion and drive she feels for the art form.

The weakest of the work found in *Soul* is the travelogue placed at the end in its own section titled "Real Life." The essay "A Visit to San Quentin" is an account of just that. Oates and a collection of laypeople and criminal justice students are led on a private tour of the maximum security prison, including a visit to the death chamber, a cell block, and the prison chapel. Oates mentions several times the irony of the prison being within view of the sparkling bay and nearly within view of San Francisco itself, while the inmates cannot see any of this. Her naïveté is exposed as she watches the others on her tour and talks of a tour she took in Trenton earlier in her life, while making off-handed jokes to herself and to the group. However, she is thorough in exploring the dark side of the tour as well, mentioning the days of depression to follow and experiencing a near fainting spell in the death chamber. The piece appeared in *Better Than Fiction: True Travel Tales from Great Fiction Writers* (2012), published by Lonely Planet, and while it offers an opportunity to see an alternative side to Oates's work, it feels like a superfluous add-on as a stand-alone piece unrelated to the rest of the collection.

Joyce Carol Oates is the author of over forty novels, in addition to plays, novellas, short story collections, poetry, and nonfiction. She is a four-time nominee for the Pulitzer Prize in fiction and has received the National Book Award, the O. Henry Award, and the National Humanities Award. With a career spanning over fifty years, she is currently the Roger S. Berlind Professor Emerita in the Humanities in the creative writing program at Princeton University, where she has taught since 1978.

Soul at the White Heat received a warm critical response. Nicholas Dames said in a *New York Times* review of several books about writing that Oates is often at her best in the collection when approaching more eccentric subjects such as Lovecraft. Joan Frank, for the website *SFGate*, said, "Oates has, it seems, read everything, and her deft, considered wisdom is pure treasure." Other outlets such as *Kirkus Reviews* and *Mother Jones* also gave *Soul at the White Heat* a positive reception.

Watching a master of the literary arts tackle the works of other iconic writers is a rare treat and with *Soul at the White Heat*, Oates gives her readers just this. The collection searches for inspiration in all corners of its subject matter, and with a thoughtful, precise mind in control, the result is one that is unique among collections of its kind. In "Is the Uninspired Life Worth Living?" Oates claims, "I have come to think that art is the formal commemoration of life in its variety," and she shows us that thought in action through her criticism.

Melynda Fuller

Review Sources

Dames, Nicholas. "Reading and Writing." Review of Soul at the White Heat: Inspiration, Obsession, and the Writing Life, by Joyce Carol Oates, et al. *The New York Times*, 2 Dec. 2016, www.nytimes.com/2016/12/02/books/review/reading-and-writing.html. Accessed 18 Jan. 2017.

Frank, Joan. Review of *Soul at the White Heat: Inspiration, Obsession, and the Writing Life*, by Joyce Carol Oates. *SFGate*, 15 Sept. 2016, www.sfgate.com/books/article/Soul-at-the-White-Heat-by-Joyce-Carol-Oates-9225495.php. Accessed 18 Jan. 2017.

Leach, Diane. "Joyce Carol Oates Is at Her Best with *Soul at White Heat*." Review of *Soul at the White Heat: Inspiration, Obsession, and the Writing Life*, by Joyce Carol Oates. *PopMatters*, 15 Dec. 2016, www.popmatters.com/review/soul-at-white-heat-joyce-carol-oates-at-her-best. Accessed 18 Jan. 2017.

Sammon, Alexander. "Writing Lessons from the Madly Prolific Joyce Carol Oates." Review of *Soul at the White Heat: Inspiration, Obsession, and the Writing Life*, by Joyce Carol Oates. *Mother Jones*, 10 Sept. 2016, www.motherjones.com/media/2016/09/joyce-carol-oates-soul-white-heat. Accessed 18 Jan. 2017.

Review of *Soul at the White Heat: Inspiration, Obsession, and the Writing Life*, by Joyce Carol Oates. *Kirkus Reviews*, 20 Sept. 2016, www.kirkusreviews.com/book-reviews/joyce-carol-oates/soul-at-the-white-heat. Accessed 18 Jan. 2017.

The Sound of Gravel

Author: Ruth Wariner
Publisher: Flatiron Books (New York). 352
pp.
Type of work: Memoir
Time: 1970s through the late 1980s
Locales: Mexico and Texas

(Courtesy of Flatiron Books)

The Sound of Gravel *is a memoir that recounts American writer Ruth Wariner's experience growing up in a polygamist Mormon cult. It is her first book.*

Principal personages:
RUTH, the author and narrator, who grew up
in a polygamist cult located in Colonia
LeBaron, Mexico
KATHY, her mother
LANE, her abusive stepfather
ALMA DAYER LEBARON, her paternal grand-
father and the founder of Colonia LeBaron
JOEL LEBARON, her father, the former leader of Colonia LeBaron who was murdered
by his brother when Ruth was an infant

Most people find religious cults to be fascinating. In addition to deviating from societal
norms, these groups are highly insular and removed from the public eye. This quality
enshrouds them in mystery, fostering widespread demand for any information on what
happens behind their members' closed doors. It can be argued, however, that too often
the books that recount the lives of people in cults tap into the human desire for voyeurism and schadenfreude. *The Sound of Gravel* breaks away from this trend. A memoir
written by Ruth Wariner, *The Sound of Gravel* is an in-depth account of the author's
life growing up in a polygamist Mormon cult. Straightforward and unsentimental, *The
Sound of Gravel* succeeds in its efforts to demonstrate the detrimental emotional and
psychological effects that polygamy has on women and children.

Despite being a memoir about a complex subject, *The Sound of Gravel* is surprisingly accessible—a testament to Wariner's storytelling skills; with a childhood that
comprises a number of disturbing elements, lesser writers might alienate their readers. Wariner, however, does not. In the first line of the first chapter, for example, she
states that she was her father's thirty-ninth child. It is a simple statement that quickly
establishes just how dramatically different her background is from most people's. To
prevent her story from becoming too extreme and foreign, she anchors the narrative in
universal human emotions. Instead of focusing on the bizarreness of her experiences,
she writes about how the experiences made her feel. Her depictions of fear, anger, and

love are unfiltered and honest, ultimately ensuring that the conflicts of her story are relatable to some extent.

By employing a matter-of-fact writing
style, Wariner demonstrates her refusal to
participate in sensationalism. Where many
depictions of religious cults utilize the tab-

*After leaving Colonia LeBaron at the
age of fifteen, Ruth Wariner raised her
younger siblings and put herself through
college and graduate school, eventually
becoming a high school Spanish teacher.
The Sound of Gravel is her first book.*

loid approach to storytelling by amplifying the most shocking aspects of former members' experiences, Wariner provides nothing more than the most necessary facts about
the history of her family's faith. Early in the memoir, she clarifies that Colonia LeB-
aron was founded by her grandfather, Alma Dayer LeBaron, a fundamentalist Mormon
who believed that he had been called upon by God to create a utopian, polygamist
society. She also describes how it was her father, Joel LeBaron, a self-proclaimed
prophet, who furthered the oppression of women in Colonia LeBaron by convincing
its members that men had to have at least two wives each in order to get into heaven.
Although Wariner does not initially provide any editorial comments on Colonia LeB-
aron, she indirectly reveals her opinion by describing the effects the community's way
of life had on her family. Her harrowing depictions of hunger and malnutrition, caused
by the unemployed husbands of Colonia LeBaron who were unable to provide for their
many wives and children, are especially convincing of the community's dangerous
shortcomings.

A large part of what makes *The Sound of Gravel* affecting is the perspective from
which the story is told. Wariner begins the book with her earliest memories from the
1970s, a decision that provides the narrative with a childlike quality. In the book's first
chapters, when Wariner is still very young, she is enchanted by the life she is born
into at Colonia LeBaron. She marvels at the beauty of the farmland and wonders in a
daydreaming fashion whether or not her father, who was murdered when she was an
infant by his brother in a religious power struggle, liked chocolate ice cream or vanilla,
like her. The love that she has for her mother is pure and unquestioning; by the age of
six, she is helping her cook, clean, and take care of her younger sisters. Her mother's
undivided attention proves to be the gift that she cherishes most. During the few occasions when she and her mother are alone, Wariner asks her what marriage is like. She
anticipates following in her mother's footsteps and marrying by the time she is a teenager. Despite the fact that her mother's life is an impoverished struggle of servitude,
she never tries to discourage the young Wariner from doing the same. She is a believer.

Wariner's journey into adulthood is portrayed as an awakening. As the chapters
advance and she grows older, her skepticism toward her family's faith deepens. Once
contented to believe that the people of Colonia LeBaron were obeying God's will, she
begins to question if she actually wants the life she was born into. In part, her doubts
are fueled by family trips to her grandparents' house in California. There, she and her
siblings enjoy full meals of store-bought food, hot showers, and electricity. Not only
is her grandparents' house paradise compared to their ramshackle house and endless
meals of rice and beans in Colonia LeBaron, but it also reminds her that another way
of living exists. Her stepfather, Lane, furthers this unraveling of her faith. Soon after

witnessing Lane mercilessly beat her mother with a belt over a trivial issue regarding a showerhead, Wariner becomes his next victim. Starting from the time she is eight years old until she is twelve, she is sexually abused by Lane. And when her mother does nothing to stop it, she independently realizes that she deserves a better life. When faced with another violent family tragedy, it is this long-brewing realization that provides her with the direction and determination necessary to escape Colonia LeBaron.

The Sound of Gravel successfully demonstrates the ways in which polygamy stunts women. Throughout the memoir, women are repeatedly portrayed as lacking agency over their lives. In addition to having to share their husbands, the wives of Colonia LeBaron are told that they must have as many children as possible in order to get into heaven. However, resources to support their children are scant. While their husbands occasionally perform odd jobs for money, it is the women's responsibility, in addition to cooking, cleaning, and raising the children, to travel regularly over the border between Mexico and the United States to collect their families' welfare checks. They are barely educated beyond learning how to bake bread and take care of their husbands. Wariner illustrates the irreparable damage this causes to women's minds, bodies, and souls through the character of her mother. Repeatedly throughout the novel, her mother's actions and decisions can be described as neglectful as she puts Lane and Colonia LeBaron's way of life above the welfare of her children. Still, Wariner continues to portray her in a loving light and even dedicates *The Sound of Gravel* to her. Ultimately, Wariner aims to elevate her mother's humanity so that she can better illustrate how polygamy made her into a lesser being. She succeeds in this effort.

Reviews of *The Sound of Gravel* have been largely favorable. *Publishers Weekly* called Wariner's memoir a well-written book that "is hard to put down and hard to forget." Similarly, *Kirkus Reviews* also praised the book's compelling narrative, calling it "engrossingly readable from start to finish." It is true that one of the strongest aspects of Wariner's memoir is her capacity for storytelling. Despite the fact that *The Sound of Gravel* focuses on more than fifteen years of her life, she provides a well-balanced blend of both significant events and everyday banalities to successfully illustrate her experience. The end result provides readers with a fully developed image of the world of Colonia LeBaron in a format of what is essentially a three-act story. While the foreignness surrounding Wariner's childhood creates intrigue, the narrative structure reinforces its engagingness.

While Wariner's storytelling is undeniably one of the strongest attributes of the memoir, it could be argued that at times her prose is somewhat unremarkable. There is a kind of simplicity to the writing that can occasionally feel distractingly incongruent to the complexity of the story being told. However, this is not necessarily a shortcoming; her plain words succeed in capturing the perspective of her younger self. Furthermore, her writing style allows the storytelling to be unsentimental. By sticking to the facts of the events and the effects they had on her and her family, she makes it more difficult for her critics, namely the people who still reside in Colonia LeBaron, to discredit her. In some ways, *The Sound of Gravel* is comparable to the investigative book *Under the Banner of Heaven: A Story of Violent Faith* (2003), which earned its author Jon Krakauer an enormous amount of criticism and personal attacks by the Church of

Jesus Christ of Latter Day Saints.

For many, the horrific events that comprise Wariner's formative years are unimaginable. By sharing her painful past in an honest and straightforward manner, she demonstrates how easily faith can be twisted to suppress and abuse others. More importantly, her depiction of how she was able to find and sustain the courage necessary to win her freedom is likely to provide many readers with inspiration. Isabella Biedenharn wrote in her review of the memoir for *Entertainment Weekly*, "Wariner is a survivor, but more important, she's a fantastic writer, letting the unbelievable events of her childhood speak for themselves while she wrestles with issues of blame and—miraculously—forgiveness." Ultimately, what makes *The Sound of Gravel* a worthwhile read is the fact that it does not aim to entertain through sensationalism. Instead, it is a well-written, compelling story of strength, hope, and resilience.

Emily Turner

Review Sources

Biedenharn, Isabella. Review of *The Sound of Gravel: A Memoir*, by Ruth Wariner. *Entertainment Weekly*, 23 Dec. 2015, www.ew.com/article/2015/12/23/the-sound-of-gravel-ruth-wariner-ew-review. Accessed 6 Dec. 2016.

Review of *The Sound of Gravel: A Memoir*, by Ruth Wariner. *Kirkus Reviews*, 5 Jan. 2016, www.kirkusreviews.com/book-reviews/ruth-wariner/the-sound-of-gravel/. Accessed 6 Dec. 2016.

Review of *The Sound of Gravel: A Memoir*, by Ruth Wariner. *Publishers Weekly*, 23 Nov. 2016, www.publishersweekly.com/978-1-250-07769-1. Accessed 6 Dec. 2016.

The Sport of Kings

Author: C. E. Morgan (b. 1976)
First Published: 2016
Publisher: Farrar, Straus and Giroux (New York). 560 pp.
Type of work: Novel
Time: Various periods from the 1700s through 2006
Locale: Paris, Kentucky

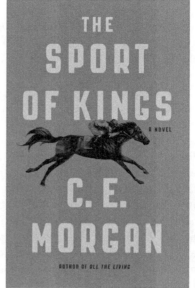

(Courtesy of Farrar, Straus and Giroux)

C. E. Morgan's sophomore novel, The Sport of Kings, *is a sprawling narrative about Kentucky, race, biology, and horse racing.*

Principal characters:

HENRY FORGE, the heir to a vast Kentucky fortune who grows up to raise Thoroughbred horses

HENRIETTA FORGE, Henry's daughter, who has an interest in, or perhaps obsession with, biology

ALLMON SHAUGHNESSY, a Cincinnati-born biracial man who takes a job on the Forge farm as a groom

Writer Kathryn Schultz, who reviewed *The Sport of Kings* for the *New Yorker* said it best when she described the book as "enormously flawed, ceaselessly interesting, and strangely tremendous." *The Sport of Kings* is a book of extremes and asks a lot of its readers, but gives a lot in return. Morgan's narrative spans over three hundred years and delves deeply into the lives of a handful of characters in service of a story about Kentucky, race, biology, and horse racing. It begins in the 1950s, when one of the main characters, Henry Forge, is a small child growing up on a Kentucky corn farm. The Forges are an old, moneyed Kentucky family; their forebear, Samuel Forge, along with an enslaved man named Benjohn, set out into the Appalachian wilderness from Virginia in the eighteenth century. He stakes his claim in what would later become Kentucky, a land of green, rolling hills and fertile soil. As one of the first Kentucky families, the Forge family built their name, though their enduring wealth come at the expense of countless slaves and ill-paid black staff who worked their land. One of Henry's earliest memories, illustrated with striking lyricism in the book's first pages, invokes that legacy of brutality in the image of a whipping post, built for beating slaves, in the backyard. In this scene though, it is Henry's father, John Henry, who ties his young son to the post and whips him with his belt as punishment for killing a bull.

This violence was the least among John Henry Forge's sins, and his many flaws and obsessions will eventually be taken up by his son. Breeding is first among them,

John Henry is consumed by his lineage and its purity and dignity. He also possesses a deeply entrenched racism. When faced with the prospect of his son attending school with black students as a result of 1960s integration, John Henry removes Henry from school. When the elder Forge learns from his own son of his wife's infidelity with a black farmhand named Filip, he promptly dispatches several men to lynch Filip in the woods.

Familial punishment is at the heart of Morgan's dark novel, but Schulz considered the heart of the novel to be "the way that African-Americans have been forced off track, literally and figuratively, to the psychological, political, and material advantage of whites." The novel as a whole has been described by various reviewers as a Southern gothic and, without derision, as a made-for-television melodrama; murder, arson, incest, as well as Filip's lynching can all be found within the novel's pages. Its trajectory is difficult to convey in summary, except to say that it tracks everywhere at once and across genres. Schultz detected the influence of

C. E. Morgan is an award-winning novelist who lives in Kentucky. Her debut novel, All The Living *(2009), landed her on the National Book Foundation's list of "5 Under 35." In 2013 she received the Whiting Award, and in 2016, she won the Windham-Campbell Literature Prize and the Kirkus Prize for fiction. Morgan has a master's degree in theological studies from Harvard Divinity School.*

William Faulkner and Herman Melville, while Dwight Garner of the *New York Times* saw shades of screenwriter Terence Malick for whom Morgan has expressed admiration. Biologists Richard Dawkins and Charles Darwin are quoted at length. *The Sport of Kings* is set up in six sections, with five interludes and an epilogue that spans hundreds of years and chronicles the lives of the Forges and generations of their slaves and workers, among others. The storyline leapfrogs through time and into the minds of its characters at will; interludes describe the geological history of the Ohio River and the evolution of human life on earth, the latter quoting, as Schultz points out, an author who is merely Morgan herself in disguise. Later in the book, an unnamed narrator, presumably also Morgan, steps out of the narrative, asking the reader, "Is all this too purple, too florid? Is more too much—the world and the words? Do you prefer your tales lean, muscular, and dry, leached of excess and honed to a single, digestible point? Have I exceeded the bounds of the form, committed a literary sin?" Critics responded, resoundingly, both yes and no.

No character emerges unscathed from *The Sport of Kings*, but as an author Morgan shows a remarkable sensitivity toward social justice. She manages to tap into a righteous rage that, crucially, never seems didactic—though other aspects of the novel do. Ostensibly, Morgan's novel is about horses, but horses, however beautifully depicted, are like so many other features in *The Sport of Kings*, merely a thematic device to describe the suffering of humans. The other two central characters in the book are Henrietta Forge, Henry's daughter, and Allmon Shaughnessy, a biracial groom at Forge Run Farm.

In the 1960s, Henry rebelled against his overbearing and violent father to transform the family property into a horse farm. Years later, Henry embodies some of his father's worst traits, in particular, his obsessive ambition and his racism. He pushes his daughter to take on the family legacy he remade in his own image. Henrietta's mother, Judith, walks out of the family when Henrietta is a child. The duration of her formative years are spent under the tutelage of her father who, skeptical of integration, refuses to send her to school and instead homeschools her. In this way, he is able to groom her to be both his successor and partner in his obsessive quest to breed a winning racehorse.

Throughout her life, Henrietta strains to extricate herself from her father. She loves horses, but is far more interested in science and biology. Later, as their relationship becomes intimate to the point of incest, she assuages her rage with anonymous sex. Her sexual desire, and her desire to rebel against her father, brings Allmon into the fold. Aware of Henry's racist views, she hires Allmon as a groom. Morgan goes back in time to describe Allmon's upbringing, which could not be more different from that of his wealthy employer and soon-to-be lover. He was raised across the Ohio River in Cincinnati. His father, a white Irishman, abandoned him and his mother when he was a small child. His underemployed mother did her best to make ends meet; she develops lupus but is unable to afford treatment. Desperate to help her, Allmon becomes a drug dealer, and after his mother's horrible death, he is arrested and sentenced to a long prison term. Allmon discovers his talent with horses while he is incarcerated, but the cruelty of prison warps and changes him. Allmon plasters over his grief and rage with a veneer of toughness to survive, but once he leaves prison, he has no way of accessing those parts of himself that will make him feel human again.

Allmon's arrival on the Forge farm is also a significant rejoinder of past and present. One of his ancestors, Scipio, was an escaped slave who swam the Ohio River to Cincinnati. A pregnant slave named Abby accompanies him, but does not survive the crossing. Scipio found the burden of this loss too much to bear and committed suicide a few years after his escape. Scipio was enslaved on the Forge plantation; Allmon's return of sorts to the Forge farm brings two of the key lineages in the book—the white lineage of the Forges and their black workers—together to attend to the third, Thoroughbred horses.

There is one other central figure in the book, a gifted filly, descended from the famed Secretariat, named Hellsmouth. Hellsmouth is as fierce as she is fragile. The fastest horses are often those that are inbred like she is, but as a result, her spindly legs—"dark and knotty rose stems"—make her prone to injury. Introduced late in the novel, Hellsmouth is the horse Henry has been waiting his life to breed. She makes it to the Kentucky Derby in 2006, but by then the plot has careened in another direction, setting its characters on a course for disaster with their various individual and historical pasts.

Morgan draws her characters in extraordinary detail. Alone with their own thoughts they are vivid, but within the context of the plot they feel just out of reach, seemingly created in service of the author, as Schultz put it, than built from their own desires. Young Henrietta's precocious knowledge of biology and geology is beautiful and brilliant as a stylistic choice, but as realism, it rings with the hollowness of a thematic device. Beguiling secondary characters like Allmon's grandfather, a preacher, and a verbose jockey named Reuben Bedford Walker III, come alive in bombastic sermons and monologues but falter in dialogue with other characters. The few flashes of truthful interaction are much quieter—among them, Allmon's mother's expressing her wounded pride or the undeserved care Henry's neighbor bestows upon him in an hour of need—but they are enough to sustain the book's five-hundred-plus pages.

Despite its flaws, *The Sport of Kings* dazzles the reader with its wealth of ideas, about legacy, history, and dreaming dreams at the expense of others. Morgan addresses the looming and ever-present specter of slavery head-on, and writes comfortably from the perspective of aristocrats, specifically those who benefit in the present-day from the past labor of enslaved people, and the poor who never amassed any wealth thanks to the same legacy. She finds "moral beauty" in a world suffering, but offers no guarantee that good prevails. In fact, in the true fashion of the Southern gothic, the book concludes in flame and tumult.

Molly Hagan

Review Sources

Cross, Stephanie. "*The Sport of Kings* Review—A Breathless Kentucky Tale." Review of *The Sport of Kings*, by C. E. Morgan. *The Guardian*, 22 May 2016, https://www.theguardian.com/books/2016/may/22/sport-of-kings-review-ce-morgan. Accessed 7 Feb. 2017.

Garner, Dwight. "Review: In C. E. Morgan's The Sport of Kings, Racing Against the Tide." Review of The Sport of Kings, by C. E. Morgan. *The New York Times*, 17 May. 2016, www.nytimes.com/2016/05/18/books/review-in-ce-morgans-the-sport-of-kings-racing-against-the-tide.html. Accessed 7 Feb. 2017.

Gordon, Jaimy. Review of The Sport of Kings, by C. E. Morgan. *The New York Times*, 10 June 2016, www.nytimes.com/2016/06/12/books/review/the-sport-of-kings-by-c-e-morgan.html. Accessed 7 Feb. 2017.

Review of *The Sport of Kings*, by C. E. Morgan. *Kirkus*, 29 Feb. 2016, www.kirkus-reviews.com/book-reviews/ce-morgan/the-sport-of-kings/. Accessed 7 Feb. 2017.

Schulz, Kathryn. "Track Changes." Review of *The Sport of Kings*, by C. E. Morgan. *The New Yorker*, 9 May 2016, www.newyorker.com/magazine/2016/05/09/a-sweeping-novel-about-race-in-america. Accessed 7 Feb. 2017.

Stamped from the Beginning
The Definitive History of Racist Ideas in America

Author: Ibram X. Kendi (b. 1982)
Publisher: Nation Books (New York). 592 pp.
Type of work: History
Time: Largely fifteenth century to the present day
Locales: United States; Europe

Ibram X. Kendi's sweeping history illustrates how racist ideas have been constructed and perpetuated in America, focusing on their essential beginnings in fifteenth-century Europe and ending in the present day.

Principal personages:
COTTON MATHER, a Puritan minister and writer
THOMAS JEFFERSON, a Founding Father and US president from 1801 to 1809
WILLIAM LLOYD GARRISON, a nineteenth-century abolitionist
W. E. B. DU BOIS, writer and civil rights leader in the nineteenth and twentieth centuries
ANGELA DAVIS, contemporary political activist and scholar

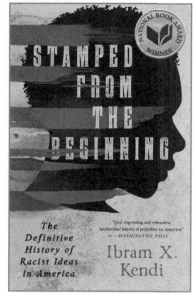

(Courtesy of Nation Books)

In his National Book Award–winning new book, *Stamped from the Beginning: The Definitive History of Racist Ideas in America*, Ibram X. Kendi erects an accessible framework through which his readers may view and comprehend American racist ideas. To structure his extensive narrative, which discusses hundreds of years of thought, Kendi has chosen to focus the discussion around five people, with each having served as one of the central intellectual figures of his or her historical era. These complex individuals are the New England Puritan minister and enthusiastic supporter of the Salem witch trials, Cotton Mather; Founding Father, third president of the United States, slave holder, and author of the phrase "all men are created equal," Thomas Jefferson; the prominent Civil War–era abolitionist and journalist, William Lloyd Garrison; the early twentieth-century African American writer and cofounder of the National Association for the Advancement of Colored People (NAACP), W. E. B. Du Bois; and Angela Davis, an academic and influential activist in the Black Power movement who remains an active participant in the prison abolition movement in the early twenty-first century.

In addition to declaring that his "definition of a racist idea is a simple one: it is any concept that regards one racial group as inferior or superior to another racial group in any way," Kendi presents a dual thesis in his introduction, asserting that, regarding issues of race, people can be roughly categorized into three groups: segregationists, assimilationists, and antiracists. Most figures in the book move fluidly among these categorizations. Du Bois for instance, was a champion of assimilationist thought as a young man, but became staunchly antiracist in his old age. But what do these terms mean? Kendi presents them in the context of racial disparities. For example, he cites a statistic in his introduction that claims that African Americans are five times more likely to be incarcerated than white people. Segregationists would argue that this disparity exists because of racial inferiority. Because antiracists reject this construct altogether, they would argue that this disparity exists because of racial discrimination. Assimilationists, meanwhile, try to find a middle ground between these two positions: they would argue that this disparity exists because of discrimination and also because of African Americans themselves.

The second part of Kendi's thesis is a reversal of a commonly held understanding of the relationship between racist policies (structural racism) and individual racist attitudes. It would seem logical to say that people are racist therefore they create racist policies, but as Kendi successfully argues, this is not the case. To begin supporting this theory, he begins discussing how in fifteenth-century Portugal, merchants bought and sold slaves from Africa and Eastern Europe. These merchants did not buy and sell slaves because they hated those particular people; they bought and sold slaves because it was an enormously profitable enterprise. As time went on—and Kendi describes this in more detail—more and more slaves came from African countries. What was the justification for why this was so? Scholars provided it in the form of racist ideas. Black people were biologically predisposed to bondage, these scholars claimed, and their lives in bondage were perceived as better than their seemingly barbaric lifestyles in Africa. The proliferation of these racist ideas and a host of others over time bred ignorance and hatred.

Kendi's argument—that racist policies lead to racist ideas that lead to hate and ignorance—is not only applicable to Portugal in the fifteenth century; the author illustrates this pattern perpetuating itself into the present day. That is perhaps the most disheartening aspect of Kendi's history; if ignorance were the root of the problem, education would be enough to overcome it, but self-interest is a much trickier foe.

Kendi is an assistant professor of African American history at the University of Florida. His first book, *The Black Campus Movement: Black Students and the Racial Reconstitution of Higher Education, 1965–1972* (2012), examines the student-led fight for diversity regarding faculty, curriculum, and campus culture in colleges and universities in the late 1960s and early 1970s. The fruit of that era, Kendi said in an interview with *Inside Higher Ed*, was an embrace of multiculturalism in higher education. This was a moment of true racial progress, but as Kendi explained in an op-ed for the *New York Times* in 2017, Americans tend to view racial progress as something like a stuttering car, inching slowly forward despite obstacles placed in its path. This is only partly true, Kendi wrote. What is missing is any acknowledgement of the car in the next lane inching forward at the same rate, which he identifies as the progression of racism.

This concept is exactly what Kendi illustrates in *Stamped from the Beginning*, his second book. The story of racism in America, Kendi asserts, is the story of resistance to African American political, financial, cultural, and sexual power. His book is intersectional; he acknowledges that all of these things are related, and makes a point of incorporating and centering the particular experiences of African American women; lesbian, gay, bisexual, and transgender (LGBT) people; and poor people in his narrative. Above all, Kendi challenges the reader to engage with ideas in a different way.

Take for instance, the concept of what Kendi calls "uplift suasion," the idea that the positive actions of one person might reflect back on a race as a whole. Kendi first identifies this concept in the 1790s, when white abolitionists pushed free African Americans to pursue perfection in every facet of their lives. If they succeeded, the thinking went, white people could be convinced to abandon their racist ideas and support abolition. Uplift suasion was rooted in a racist idea that

(Courtesy of Nation Books)

Ibram X. Kendi is an assistant professor of African American history at the University of Florida. He is also the author of The Black Campus Movement: Black Students and the Racial Reconstruction of Higher Education, 1965–1972 *(2012).* Stamped from the Beginning *won the 2016 National Book Award for nonfiction.*

black people occupied a lower station in society than white people not because white people had enslaved them and taken away their rights, but because black people were inherently inferior and uniquely vulnerable to vice. In this view, as Kendi writes, African Americans and their behaviors were responsible for racial discrimination, and thus the "burden of race relations was placed squarely on the shoulders of Black Americans. Positive Black behavior, abolitionist strategists held, undermined racist ideas, and negative Black behavior confirmed them."

Perhaps unsurprisingly, uplift suasion remains incredibly powerful. Unfortunately, as Kendi demonstrates, it has never worked. If a racist person sees a black person's face in a mugshot on the evening news, it will likely reinforce a negative stereotype that person holds about black people as a group. The same is not true of positive depictions of black people. African American achievement often falls prey to a counter stereotype Kendi identifies as the "extraordinary negro." When Du Bois became Harvard University's first African American doctoral student, his achievement did not force people to re-examine their racist ideas—the intended purpose of uplift suasion—it, perversely, also reinforced those same racist ideas. Du Bois succeeded because he was extraordinary, the thinking went; he was the exception, not the rule.

At the heart of uplift suasion, Kendi emphasizes, lies an important point about racist ideas in general. In ignoring the human flaws of African Americans, racist ideas are inherently illogical and, thus, cannot be fought with logic. "Uplift suasion," Kendi writes, "assumed, moreover, that racist ideas were sensible and could be undone by appealing to sensibilities." It goes back to his point about assimilationists. Can there really be a middle ground between reality and unreality? Is it really reasonable to suggest that the solution to racial discrimination lies in a standard of behavior set by the very people responsible for the discrimination in the first place? Kendi asks the reader to think critically about these things. One might shake their head in amazement at the absurdity of early racist arguments, but one will also recognize phrases such as "law and order" and "inner city" in later chapters. Might these phrases, and the concepts and prescriptions that accompany them, be just as ridiculous?

Stamped from the Beginning was only reviewed by a handful of publications, but those reviews were largely positive. Much has been made, however, about the prominent historical figures that Kendi accuses of having held, at one point or another, racist ideas, including Frederick Douglass and President Barack Obama. But to view Kendi's book through this lens does it a disservice. His aim is to interrogate how Americans talk about race and to what ends. Carlos Lozado, who reviewed *Stamped from the Beginning* for the *Washington Post*, lamented that so few people came out of the book "unscathed." This seems entirely beside the point. Kendi's book is a forceful yet thoughtful critique, not a witch trial, and in the end his point is plain. Engaging with racist ideas is necessarily complicated; antiracism is not. As Kendi writes in the book's epilogue, "There will come a time when Americans will realize that the only thing wrong with Black people is that they think something is wrong with Black people." In the second decade of the twenty-first century, as race has once again become an especially significant issue, particularly in the political arena, and as people take stock of American society in the time immediately following the country's first African American president's departure from office, *Stamped from the Beginning* adds crucial insight to the discussion.

Molly Hagan

Review Sources

Lozada, Carlos. "The Racism of Good Intentions." Review of S*tamped from the Beginning: The Definitive History of Racist Ideas in America,* by Ibram X. Kendi, and *Bind Us Apart: How Enlightened Americans Invented Racial Segregation,* by Nicholas Guyatt. *The Washington Post,* 15 Apr. 2016, www.washingtonpost.com/ news/book-party/wp/2016/04/15/the-racism-of-good-intentions/. Accessed 15 Feb. 2017.

Review of *Stamped from the Beginning: The Definitive History of Racist Ideas in America,* by Ibram X. Kendi. *Kirkus,* 2 Jan. 2016, www.kirkusreviews.com/book-reviews/ibram-x-kendi/stamped-from-the-beginning/. Accessed 15 Feb. 2017.

Vnuk, Rebecca. Review of *Stamped from the Beginning: The Definitive History of Racist Ideas in America,* by Ibram X. Kendi. *Booklist,* 1 Feb. 2016, pp. 16–17.

Sweetbitter

Author: Stephanie Danler
Publisher: Alfred A. Knopf (New York). 368 pp.
Type of work: Novel
Time: 2006–7
Locales: New York City; specifically Williamsburg, Brooklyn, Union Square, and the Lower East Side

(Courtesy of Knopf)

Sweetbitter *is the debut novel from writer Stephanie Danler. Loosely based on her real life experiences working in the Union Square Café in New York,* Sweetbitter *tells the story of a twenty-two-year-old woman newly arrived to the city and is as involved with food obsession as it is with the social aspects of a young person's life. She takes a job as a backwaiter (busser) at an unnamed restaurant where a colorful cast of characters* shows her the ins and outs of the restaurant business and life in the city. The story is told over the period of one year.

Principal characters:

TESS, a twenty-two-year-old who takes a job at "the best restaurant in New York City," where she has recently moved

HOWARD, the restaurant manager responsible for hiring Tess; he is lecherous, but an institution at the establishment

SIMONE, an older member of the waitstaff who takes Tess under her wing and introduces her to fine food, wine, and art

JAKE, Tess's love interest; a thirty-year-old dilettante who has worked at the restaurant for years and has a murky history with Simone

Sweetbitter, the first novel from writer Stephanie Danler, is a book perfectly placed in time and geography, told with a masterful knowledge of the landscape around it. Told from the point of view of twenty-two-year-old Tess, who recently fled her small town to follow her big city dreams, the novel mirrors much of its author's early twenties. Stephanie Danler also arrived in New York City at twenty-two and also worked at "the best restaurant in New York City," Danny Meyer's Union Square Café. Generally well-received by critics, *Sweetbitter* is an intimate story about a woman coming of age in the metropolis against the background of a bustling, prestigious restaurant. Not only does Tess dive into the New York restaurant world and learn about culinary appetites, but she also learns about her appetites for sex and drugs and begins to come into herself through the trials of experimentation.

When the reader first meets Tess, she has newly arrived in the rapidly gentrifying neighborhood of Williamsburg, Brooklyn. Tess has no real ambition or purpose in coming to the city—she is not a writer, artist, or musician. She has come to figure out what she wants, and her free-floating openness and eagerness to learn make her an intriguing protagonist. She has very little money and no prospects, but goes on a mission to find work, and ends up landing a spot as a trainee at the restaurant. In addition to her descriptions of Brooklyn in 2006, Danler successfully grounds her characters within the pop culture of that year, alluding to songs and books that allow the reader to engage with the experience, while also bringing to life what it was like to be alive during a particular time, experiencing a new place and lifestyle for the first time.

Danler's culinary knowledge is skillfully applied to Tess's progression into adulthood and her own gathering of culinary knowledge. For example, when Tess is interviewing with Howard, the restaurant's general manager, he asks her what kind of wine she likes. She replies, "White?", revealing her lack of knowledge and how much of an outsider she is. As Tess becomes a part of the restaurant's staff, she establishes her two most important relationships with Jake and Simone. Simone is a world-wearied woman in her late thirties who has a vast knowledge of culture, food, and travel. When Tess first sees her at the family dinner that begins each shift, Tess is intimidated and enthralled by Simone at once. Simone takes Tess under her wing and instructs her to study wine regions, teaches her how to taste them properly, and gives her books to read and maps to memorize. Jake is the dark, handsome, aloof bartender whom Tess is attracted to when they first meet. Tess can detect a connection between Simone and Jake, but doesn't know quite what it is.

Stephanie Danler is a New York–based writer and debut novelist of Sweetbitter. *She holds an MFA from the New School in creative writing.*

Tess's training goes beyond wine and books, as she tastes her first heirloom tomatoes, truffles, and chanterelle mushrooms. Danler's vivid descriptions of food—from oysters to chocolate to digestifs—create a convincing layer of intimacy with the world of the story and to Tess's coming of age. It is a pairing of oysters and beer that brings Tess and Jake together. One night while performing her closing duties, Tess is pulled aside by Jake, who takes her into the large walk-in refrigerator and pulls out two oysters and a beer to go with them. He teaches her how to consume the oysters, while Danler makes sure to capture the moment in taste as well. "I flipped the shell back. I was prepared for the brininess. For the softness of it. For the rigidity and strangeness of the ritual. Adrenalized, fiercely private. I panted slightly and opened my eyes. Jake was looking at me and said, 'They're perfect.'" From wine and oysters, she moves on to develop tastes for cocaine and sex, and Danler masterfully explores the intersections of these appetites.

Tess and Jake's steps towards a relationship are slow and halting—a kiss here, a brush there—and at times the process feels like it is in the way of the real story of the excitement of life inside a New York restaurant. The slowness of this relationship is something many critics complained about in their reviews. Though it may detract from the story by slowing the plot, the triangular relationship between Tess, Jake, and Simone is one of the pivotal points of the novel.

The arc of her relationship with Simone is the most captivating of the book, as is Simone as a character. Danler's descriptions of Simone—from her apartment in the East Village where she has a bathtub in the kitchen and books pulled out everywhere, to her hair and makeup, to her sartorial choices outside the restaurant, and her emotional neediness and past with Jake—create a woman who seems capable of capturing the attention and envy of a young woman like Tess. Collected, these details about Simone are somewhat superficial; Danler never affords the reader a look into Simone's inner workings or life.

The others who appear in Tess's life are never completely explored or developed. In fact, the development of the characters in the book was something critics pointed out as an overall flaw, particularly in the underdevelopment of Jake. As a flat and unrealized character, he speaks little for himself, has an unsatisfying backstory, and functions more as a sex object than anything else. Danler offers explanation for this: in an interview with the *Paris Review*, Danler stated that she does not think that rules for creating full characters necessarily exist anymore. Ultimately, however, the underdevelopment of both Jake and Simone makes it difficult for the reader to be as invested in their relationships and ultimate betrayal as Tess is.

Danler, a native of Los Angeles, worked in New York City restaurants like the Union Square Cafe, Buvette, and Tía Pol, and received her MFA from the New School. A story of her publishing deal circled claiming that she had met a prominent publisher during a shift and quickly received a seven-digit two-book publishing deal. Despite the many similarities between her own experience moving to the city and that of her protagonist Tess, Danler said in a *Vanity Fair* interview that although she had put many of her experiences into the novel, her overall story was more complex and less dramatic.

The story, in terms of the New York coming-of-age novel and New York restaurant confessional is nothing particularly new. *Guardian* critic Michelle Dean noted that the key difference between *Sweetbitter* and its peers is that Tess arrives in New York without specific goals or dreams. Gabrielle Hamilton, chef and owner of the New York restaurant Prune, reviewed the book for the *New York Times* and said, "The faults of the book are few . . . And although there are moments when you clutch the railing, tensed when Danler writes about flavor and food as metaphor, fearing she might cloyingly reduce the complexities of human pathos and desire to the common terms of palate and terroir, she catches herself. This excellent writer knows too well that a certain connoisseurship of taste, a mark of how you deal with the world, is the ability to relish the bitter, to crave it even, the way you do the sweet." She also noted that while Anthony Bourdain's *Kitchen Confidential* was the literary definition of New York restaurant's old guard, Danler's novel serves to define the restaurant industry of the newer generation. Where Bourdain and his (primarily immigrant) contemporaries were there because there was nowhere else to go, much of the newer workforce in New York restaurants are increasingly white, foodies, and college educated.

In the final pages of *Sweetbitter*, Tess is beginning to look outside the narrow world she has inhabited in the restaurant for the past year. Her growth can be measured in her friendships (or evolving relationships), the ways in which she relates to food and wine, and the confidence she seems to possess when three hundred pages earlier it was difficult to find. The coming-of-age novel may feel like an overplayed trope, but with *Sweetbitter*, Danler has created something fresh and potable that captures an intense time in every young person's life.

Melynda Fuller

Review Sources

Dean, Michelle. "*Sweetbitter* by Stephanie Danler Review—New York City's Bright Lights Dazzle." Review of *Sweetbitter*, by Stephanie Danler. *The Guardian*, 8 June 2016, www.theguardian.com/books/2016/jun/08/sweetbitter-stephanie-danler-review-new-york-city. Accessed 31 Oct. 2016.

Hamilton, Gabrielle. Review of Sweetbitter, by Stephanie Danler. *The New York Times*, 24 May 2016, www.nytimes.com/2016/05/29/books/review/sweetbitter-by-stephanie-danler.html. Accessed 31 Oct. 2016.

Heller, Karen. "'Sweetbitter': Stephanie Danler's Delicious Debut Novel." Review of *Sweetbitter*, by Stephanie Danler. *The Washington Post*, 15 June 2016, www.washingtonpost.com/entertainment/books/sweetbitter-stephanie-danlers-delicious-debut-novel/2016/06/15/4b1a6d08-319d-11e6-8758-d58e76e11b12_story.html. Accessed 28 Nov. 2016.

Quinn, Annalisa. "'Sweetbitter' Sings with Innocence and Experience." Review of *Sweetbitter*, by Stephanie Danler. *NPR*, 28 May 2016, www.npr.org/2016/05/28/478679741/sweetbitter-sings-with-innocence-and-experience. Accessed 28 Nov. 2016.

Swing Time

Author: Zadie Smith
Publisher: Penguin Press (New York). 153 pp.
Type of work: Novel
Time: 1980s–2000s
Locale: London, New York, West Africa

In Swing Time*, acclaimed novelist Zadie Smith traces the divergent lives of two dance-obsessed childhood friends who grew up together in council estates in Northwest London. In doing so, she weaves a multifaceted narrative about coming of age, the false promises of philanthropy, and the strange turns that life can take.*

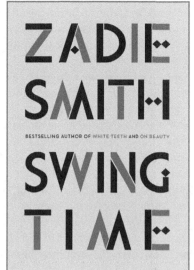

(Courtesy of Penguin Press)

Principal characters:

NARRATOR, the book's unnamed protagonist,
  a mixed-race girl from Northwest London who as an adult becomes a longtime assistant to the pop star Aimee

TRACEY, the narrator's best friend from childhood; as an adult, she enjoys a brief career in the theater before falling back into the trappings of poverty and estate life

NARRATOR'S MOTHER, a community activist and later member of Parliament. Originally from Jamaica, she is very focused on her Afro-Caribbean heritage.

NARRATOR'S FATHER, a postal service worker from a white, working-class family

AIMEE, a Madonna-like pop star and would-be philanthropist who employs the narrator

LAMIN, schoolteacher in an unnamed West African country who becomes the lover of both Aimee and the narrator

HAWA, schoolteacher in an unnamed West African country

A fraught friendship that is followed from childhood into adulthood is the basis of Zadie Smith's latest novel, *Swing Time*. Smith began her career by chronicling the lives of two wartime friends, a Bangladeshi and an Englishman, and their families as they grow in her 2000 book *White Teeth*. In *White Teeth*, as in her subsequent work, the courses of friendships are influenced not only by personalities, but by the complex class and social structures that have defined post-empire Britain, particularly from the 1970s onward.

Throughout her novels—and indeed in her nonfiction—Smith has exhibited a razor-sharp talent for observation, a wealth of wit, and has, in many different ways, picked apart the ways that people of different ethnicities and cultures interact and form relationships. Whether found in describing nuances of life in a mixed-race family or writing a treatise on the cultural importance of hip-hop, race and identity always make their mark in Smith's writing. Both her fiction and her essays have made her into one of the most important critical commentators on contemporary culture.

Throughout her next three novels, Smith continued her exploration of contemporary life and culture by exploring an autograph hunter's relationship with a reclusive actor in *The Autograph Man* (2002), a strained mixed-race marriage in *On Beauty* (2005), and the overlapping lives of four different Londoners in *NW* (2012). In all of these books, Smith employs a number of narrative viewpoints to illustrate the multiplicity of lives in contemporary Britain. In *Swing Time,* however, she confines her point of view to one character, employing a strict first-person voice. The unnamed narrator who, in the book's shifting timeline grows from a young girl to a thirty-something adult, is in many ways a vehicle for observing and commenting on the actions of the book's more dynamic characters. As she herself observes, "I had always tried to attach myself to the light of other people . . . I had never had any light of my own. I experienced myself as a kind of shadow."

(Courtesy of Dominique Nabokov)

Zadie Smith is a British novelist, essayist, and short story writer. She has published five novels, including White Teeth, *one of* Time *magazine's 100 Best English Language Novels 1923–2005 and* On Beauty, *winner of the Orange Prize for fiction. A native of London, she is a graduate of Cambridge University and has taught at Harvard and Columbia Universities. She is a fellow of the Royal Society of Literature and is currently a professor at New York University's creative writing program.*

The first person that the narrator meets that she attaches herself to in this way is Tracey. As biracial children in an otherwise white dance class, the narrator and Tracey form an unspoken alliance the first time they meet. The girls are drawn to each other because their "shade of brown was exactly the same." This develops into a proper friendship as the two spend more and more time with each other, watching classic musicals and writing lurid backstage dramas. Their love of dance becomes the cornerstone of their friendship, but only one of them shows any talent for it. Watching her friend, the narrator notes that, "every movement was as sharp and precise as any child could hope to make it, her body could align itself with any time signature, no matter how intricate. . . . I was—I am—in awe of Tracey's technique. She knew the right time to do everything."

By contrast, the narrator's own flat feet make her unfit for pursuing higher levels of dance. This is only one of several essential differences between the two girls. Although Tracey and the narrator each have one black parent and one white parent and both live in the council estates, the narrator lives in a nicer estate and is raised, for most of her childhood, in a two-parent household, while Tracey's father is in and out of jail. Similarly, while the narrator is a more passive participant in the events going on around her, Tracey is the more dominant figure, leading the activities of their playdates and goading the narrator into questionable behavior. She is also the more imaginative one, concocting fantastical, reality-defying scenarios, while the narrator remains more grounded in the circumstances of everyday life.

As the two girls grow older, they drift apart and lose touch. The narrator's autodidact mother, who pulls herself up from poverty to become a member of Parliament, creates a home environment that, no matter how much the narrator resists it, puts her on the path to a middle-class lifestyle. Tracey's rougher upbringing, as well as her self-destructive tendencies, relegate her to a life of single motherhood and impoverishment, despite her initial success in the theater world. She ends up in the same council estate she grew up in, mentally unstable, harassing the narrator's mother with a series of threatening e-mails. This behavior shows how Tracey's passionate personality has devolved into hatred and mental instability and draws a sharp contrast between her working-class status and the narrator's own life in the upper-middle class.

The second woman whom the narrator shadows is a Madonna-like pop star known only as Aimee. After taking a brief gig at an MTV-like station, the narrator meets Aimee, who hires her as a personal assistant. The narrator is employed by Aimee for nearly a decade. Aimee decides to fund a school in an unnamed West African country and the narrator makes frequent trips there to oversee the project. Although Smith often indulges in some rather easy barbs at white philanthropy, pointing at the self-serving, ignorant nature of Aimee's endeavors, she has far more in mind than simple point scoring. While she takes swipes at white philanthropy, Smith does not only look at the villagers (Lamin and Hawa in particular) from the perspective of the Western philanthropist. She instead delves into their culture and individual desires, as well as the complicated relationships with their own country and to the westerners who descend upon them.

Aimee herself is no mere caricature, but a woman who, for all her myopia, has a dynamism that has to be admired. Smith is on strong ground when she has her narrator consider this complex figure. The narrator smartly susses out that Aimee can only view human differences as "never structural or economic but always essentially differences of personality," a bit of willful naiveté. But then she works her way around to admiring what Aimee was able to build herself into by force of will. "Over ten years," she writes, "I saw how formidable [her] will could be, what it could make happen. And all the labor she put into it—all the physical exercise, the deliberate blindness, the innocence cultivated, the very many ways she fell in and out of love—all this came to seem to me a form of energy in itself."

This thoughtful observation on the narrator's part is one of the hallmarks of the book. She calmly considers the world in front of her, rarely taking any kind of definitive action, but reveals the complexities of the world around her. While this makes the narrator a conduit for insight into the other characters, she never becomes a fully realized character herself. When she finally does something drastic, however, her action leads to a dismissal from her position and creates a furor on the Internet. Smith is careful to make clear the difference between the narrator as she is writing the book and as she is living through the events she is narrating. The narrator frequently refers to her own act of writing, which provides a sense of retrospective to the story. Because the narrator has enough distance from the material, she can be a detached observer in much the same way that Smith, through creating and observing her fictional world, is able to operate.

As the novel continually expands outward, the relationship between the two childhood friends, the narrator and Tracey, is never far from the surface. This relationship, whether in the foreground or somewhere in the back of the narrator's mind, forms the sad heart of the book. The result is a nuanced, multifaceted work that, while confining its perspective to a single point of view, achieves a richness that rivals any of Smith's previous novels.

This was a view shared by many of the book's reviewers who praised the book's complexity and fluidity. Annalisa Quinn of *NPR* noted that "some writers name, organize, and contain; Smith lets contradictions bloom, in all their frightening, uneasy splendor," while Aminatta Forna of the *Guardian* found that "the novel's strength lies in its unflinching portrait of friendship." The book received plenty of mentions in year-end lists. It made the *Washington Post*'s "Ten Best Books of 2016" and was named a notable book by the *New York Times*.

Those critics who were less receptive to the novel often focused on the sketchy nature of the narrator. For example, John Boyne of the *Irish Times* finds that the book "lack[s] a consistent narrative drive, an interesting voice, or a compelling point of view," noting that "by the end, one feels no closer to understanding the central character." But this does not seem to be the majority viewpoint. Most reviewers recognize that the shadow-like nature of the protagonist is a deliberate, effective device on the part of Smith. By allowing her narrator to drift and observe, she is able to provide the reader with a unique perspective on our contemporary world which, since her precocious debut sixteen years earlier, is nothing less than what we have come to expect from Zadie Smith.

Andrew Schenker

Review Sources

Bass, Holly. "Zadie Smith's New Novel Takes on Dance, Fame and Friendship." Review of Swing Time by Zadie Smith. *The New York Times*, 10 Nov. 2016, www.nytimes.com/2016/11/13/books/review/zadie-smith-swing-time.html. Accessed 22 Dec. 2016.

Boyne, John. "*Swing Time* Review: Zadie Smith's New Novel Can't Overcome Faults." *The Irish Times*, 12 Nov. 2016, www.irishtimes.com/culture/books/swing-time-review-zadie-smith-s-new-novel-can-t-overcome-faults-1.2858001. Accessed 22 Dec. 2016.

Charles, Ron. "*Swing Time*: Zadie Smith's Sweeping Novel about Friendship, Race, and Class." *The Washington Post*, 9 Nov. 2016, www.washingtonpost.com/ entertainment/books/swing-time-zadie-smiths-sweeping-novel-about-friendship-race-and-class/2016/11/09/3975c488-a297-11e6-8832-23a007c77bb4_story.html. Accessed 22 Dec. 2016.

Forna, Aminatta. "*Swing Time* by Zadie Smith Review—An Unflinching Portrait of Friendship." *The Guardian*, 4 Nov. 2016, www.theguardian.com/books/2016/ nov/04/swing-time-by-zadie-smith-review. Accessed 22 Dec. 2016.

Quinn, Annalisa. "Know Thyself? *Swing Time* Says It's Complicated." Review of *Swing Time* by Zadie Smith. *NPR*, 16 Nov. 2016, www.npr. org/2016/11/16/501484095/know-thyself-swing-time-says-it-cant-be-done. Accessed 22 Dec. 2016.

Szalai, Jennifer. "In the Shade: Zadie Smith and the Limits of Being Oneself." Review of *Swing Time* by Zadie Smith. *Harper's*, Jan. 2017, http://harpers.org/ archive/2017/01/in-the-shade/. Accessed 25 Jan. 2017.

Tortorici, Dayna. "Zadie Smith's Dance of Ambivalence." Review of *Swing Time* by Zadie Smith. *The Atlantic*, Dec. 2016, www.theatlantic.com/magazine/ar-chive/2016/12/zadie-smiths-dance-of-ambivalence/505832/. Accessed 22 Dec. 2016.

Their Promised Land
My Grandparents in Love and War

Author: Ian Buruma (b. 1951)
Publisher: Penguin Press (New York). 320 pp.
Type of work: Biography, letters
Time: 1915–45
Locales: Great Britain, France, Germany, India

Based on a collection of family letters, Their Promised Land: My Grandparents in Love and War *recounts the story of the life and love of Bernard and Win Schlesinger. Spanning the eventful years between 1915 and 1945, this book uses the case study of this couple and their children to consider complex questions of identity and selfhood in a time of war and upheaval.*

(Courtesy of Penguin Random House)

Principal personages:
BERNARD "BUN" EDWARD SCHLESINGER, a medical professional whose career spanned both world wars
WINIFRED "WIN" HENRIETTA SCHLESINGER, his wife
JOHN RICHARD SCHLESINGER, their eldest son, a renowned filmmaker
IAN BURUMA, their grandson, the author

Their Promised Land: My Grandparents in Love and War is a project made possible by scholar Ian Buruma's rediscovery of a large collection of letters exchanged between his maternal grandparents, Bernard Edward and Winifred "Win" Henrietta Schlesinger, from their early romance in 1915 through the 1970s. Though Buruma was raised in the Netherlands, the Schlesingers were lifelong residents of Great Britain. Both were children of investment bankers and, thus, born into privileged circles in London. The book opens with Buruma's evocations of the lavishness and British nationalism that permeated the Schlesinger household, as epitomized by the family's multiday extravagant celebration of Christmas. Yet, although Buruma opens with the statement, "When I think of my maternal grandparents, I think of Christmas," the Schlesingers were Jewish. Win and Bernard had a complex relationship with their German heritage and their Jewish faith. Although they were largely secular and rejected their German ancestry, these identities played a significant role in their lives and also contribute some of the most significant material to this book. *Their Promised Land* offers a valuable study of the German Jewish diaspora specifically, as well as the complexities of immigrant identities in general. More intimately, this book is a thoughtful family reminiscence and a study of a devoted sixty-year marriage that survived several of the greatest hurdles of the twentieth century. Buruma describes his book as "a kind of novel in letters, with myself as a kind of Greek chorus," in which his characterizations of his grandparents and their children—most prominent among them the renowned filmmaker John Schlesinger, the author's uncle—"reflect my own preoccupations," thus integrating elements of memoir into the text.

Bernard and Win Schlesinger are not famous historical figures. As Buruma reflects, they are among the category of people who generally "slip away into oblivion when those who still remember them die in their turn." Yet the couple's legacy of several hundred letters, which span Bernard's service in France in World War I and in India in World War II, left an invaluable historical record, easily apparent to a scholar and descendant. The letters seem to have survived by accident, maybe because they were too precious for Win to discard, despite her belief that private correspondence should not be read by others. The couple's love letters certainly never were intended for descendants to read, let alone the general public. Perhaps for this reason, Buruma emphasizes that the couple's intimate relationship and their written expressions of this love are not the main subject of the book, though they are the principal theme of the letters. Instead, Buruma guides readers toward currents within the correspondence in which Bernard and Win "express how they saw themselves in relation to the world they lived in." Class,

Ian Buruma is the Henry R. Luce Professor of Human Rights, Democracy and New Media at Bard College. He is a prolific author, and several of his books concern the cultural and historical contexts of World War II.

family, nationalism, and music were all important identifiers to the Schlesingers, while ethnicity and religion were downplayed but were nevertheless significant factors at key junctures in their lives. Ultimately, Buruma presents *Their Promised Land* as an attempt to shed some light on the struggle of minority peoples to make sense of, and shape, the complexities of their relationship to the world around them.

Most readers will likely come to this book for its attention to the Jewish diaspora. *Their Promised Land* reveals a great deal about the attitudes the Schlesingers had toward their Jewish heritage and the complexities they negotiated in their identities as British Jews. The narrow focus of this book on the attitudes of two individuals allows Buruma to explore the contradictions and multiple faces of the Schlesingers' thoughts about the Jewish community, but it also of necessity limits the breadth of perspectives that the text offers. Between Bernard and Win the code word "45," for which Buruma can offer no origin point or additional information, was used to communicate that an individual was Jewish. Referring to moments when they themselves have faced prejudices, they easily attribute these issues to their "45" identity. Across the many cited instances throughout their correspondence in which this catchphrase is found, it is sometimes used to indicate a common identity, but it is just as often a descriptive category from which to launch into criticism of an acquaintance's personality or demeanor. Though Buruma's affectionate memory of his grandparents is clear, he does not hesitate to highlight their prejudices according to class and ethnic categories that color their assessments of other members of the Jewish community.

If their Jewish identity is complex, their German heritage is perhaps more troublesome. Both Bernard and Win were the children of immigrants from Germany, and both maintained family ties to the country. Despite the British identities that they projected, both were raised in German-speaking households. With bias against Germans heightened in the war years, it can be unclear whether challenges that they faced were due to their Jewish or German identities. During World War I, Bernard fretted that his last name was keeping him from being sent to the front, a goal that he dearly hoped to attain. During the same war, Win's brother changed his surname from Regensburg to Raeburn, superficially replacing German with Scottish ancestry. Bernard suggested she follow suit in order to attain a coveted post as a hospital nurse. In his correspondence from the military during World War I, Bernard conveys a clear, untroubled sense of Britishness, without ambivalence for the family that could be fighting for the German side. But, when the war ends and travel is again possible between the two countries, Win resumes visits with German relatives.

During World War II, Bernard would have been old enough to sit out the war, but instead he reenlisted. This decision produced much of the material of greatest interest in the book. Over the course of the war, Bernard was stationed away from home and eventually wound up in India. Though he would have preferred to serve closer to the military action, his letters provide interesting reflections on the final years of the British government in India. Meanwhile, Win's letters from home provide many details about the life of a Jewish family in Britain during the war. Though largely protected by their wealth, the Schlesingers nevertheless had to face the stark possibility that Nazi victory would mean almost-certain death for themselves and their children. In the darkest moments of the war, they seriously weighed the possibility of relocating their children to Canada. After the war, they would sadly learn of the deaths of many German friends and family members. Readers inclined to be put off by the privilege and biases of the Schlesingers will nevertheless recognize their vulnerability in this period.

The most memorable act of Bernard and Win Schlesinger's lives was their rescue of twelve Jewish children from Germany, a process that they presciently began before *Kristallnacht* in November 1938, which itself preceded Germany's invasion of Poland in 1939; their earliest documents related to this decision date to mid-October 1938. Although Buruma is unable to uncover the specifics of what triggered the Schlesingers to begin this process, their later correspondence connects the decision to Bernard having been subjected to a professional rejection a few months earlier for his Jewish heritage. The twelve children that the Schlesingers took in were from similar upper-class professional families and nearly all from the Berlin area. The children did not come to live in the couple's household; instead, they were cared for in the Schlesingers' London hostel until they, like the Schlesingers' own children, were sent to boarding schools. Although they did not live under the same roof, Bernard and Win did act as surrogate parents for these children, offering them not only safety, all of their necessities, financial resources, and education, but also advice, correspondence, and some degree of affection. In one account provided by the eldest of these children, Walter Bluh, Win is characterized as a reassuring presence who met the scared and forlorn child on the Liverpool Street Station platform, "welcoming him to England in fluent German."

Within these larger, more historically significant themes, *Their Promised Land* is also at heart the story of a family and of a relationship. From it, readers can learn about conventions of courtship and child-rearing quite distant from modern practices, despite being removed only by two generations. The mutual devotion of Win and Bernard is a touching tribute to the enduring potential of marriage. Their correspondence reveals the anxieties and trials inherent in maintaining a marriage, despite the obvious devotion and passion of the couple. Across the excerpts of correspondence, readers are also given a privileged glimpse into the concerns and confusions of parenting. Of particular historical interest are the struggles that the couple experienced with their son John. They fretted about facets of their son's character and demeanor, even as Win gave various forms of support to some of his more expansive early theatrical attempts. The earliest evidence of John's homosexuality and artistic persona manifested in an interest in cross-dressing and playacting, and the accompanying correspondence allows readers to trace attitudes toward his sexual orientation, alongside the other major concerns about self and society, within the text.

A theme that binds together all these threads of *Their Promised Land* is Britishness—or, rather, Bernard and Win's perceptions of their own Britishness. Proud and uncompromising nationalism is evident throughout their correspondence, despite the repeated reminders of their own difference from mainstream British norms. The children of immigrants, both Bernard and Win held dearly to as many symbols as they could claim of their own Britishness. Win, for example, was an avid gardener whose flower beds preoccupied her even during World War II. Buruma makes use of the contradictions between this aspiring Britishness and the Schlesingers' German Jewish heritage to further probe the complexity of identity. Though they evidently sought a tidier self-image, the aspiring Britishness that Buruma recovers for his grandparents is of a more dynamic nature.

Although the extant correspondence continues into the 1970s, Buruma concludes *Their Promised Land* with Bernard's return from India in the summer of 1945. In a brief passage he terms an "epitaph," Buruma closes the stories of their lives. Arriving at a description of the austere resting place that Bernard and Win share with their son John, Buruma recalls a passage from a December 1941 war letter. In it, Bernard reveals to Win his recent rejection of the existence of heaven and hell and recounts his opposing theory: "My idea is that our hereafter, good or bad, is the memory of ourselves we leave behind." In *Their Promised Land*, such an enduring memory is assured.

Julia Sienkewicz

Review Sources

Beckerman, Gal. "'How Marvelous It Is to Be British.'" Review of *Their Promised Land: My Grandparents in Love and War*, by Ian Buruma. *The Wall Street Journal*, 15 Jan. 2016, www.wsj.com/articles/how-marvelous-it-is-to-be-british-1452883476. Accessed 14 Jan. 2017.

Fraser, Nick. Review of Their Promised Land: My Grandparents in Love and War, by Ian Buruma. *The New York Times*, 12 Jan. 2016, www.nytimes.com/2016/01/17/ books/review/their-promised-land-my-grandparents-in-love-and-war-by-ian-buruma.html. Accessed 14 Jan. 2017.

Morrison, Blake. "*Their Promised Land: My Grandparents in Love and War* by Ian Buruma Review—A Fascinating Story of Assimilation." Review of *Their Promised Land: My Grandparents in Love and War*, by Ian Buruma. *The Guardian*, 26 Feb. 2016, www.theguardian.com/books/2016/feb/26/their-promised-land-my-grandparents-in-love-and-war-ian-buruma-review. Accessed 14 Jan. 2017.

Sheehan, Susan. "Ian Buruma's *Their Promised Land*: A Curious Tale of Jewish Assimilation." Review of *Their Promised Land: My Grandparents in Love and War*, by Ian Buruma. *The Washington Post*, 29 Jan. 2016, www.washingtonpost.com/opinions/ian-burumas-their-promised-land-a-curious-tale-of-jewish-assimilation/2016/01/28/9573a79c-a4fe-11e5-b53d-972e2751f433_story.html. Accessed 14 Jan. 2017.

Then Come Back
The Lost Neruda

Author: Pablo Neruda (1904–73)
First published: *Tus pies toco en la sombra y otros poemas inéditos*, 2014, in Spain
Translated from the Spanish by Forrest Gander
Publisher: Copper Canyon Press (Port Townsend, WA). Illustrated. 160 pp.
Type of work: Poetry

In these manuscript poems, written on playbills, napkins, and odd scraps of paper, the Nobel Prize–winning poet Pablo Neruda writes about love, friendship, and the complicated joys of life. The discovery of these poems has prompted fresh assessment of Neruda's late poems.

(Courtesy of Copper Canyon Press)

On June 18, 2014, the Barcelona-based publishing firm Seix Barral announced that it would publish twenty manuscript poems recently discovered in the archives of the Pablo Neruda Foundation in Santiago, Chile. The paperback volume *Tus pies toco en la sombra y otros poemas inéditos* (I touch your feet in the shade and other unedited poems) appeared soon after under Seix Barral's Planeta imprint with an introduction and notes by Darío Oses, director of the foundation's library. In his introduction, Oses explains that in 2011, twenty-five years after it took responsibility for preservation of Neruda's papers, the Fundacíon Pablo Neruda (Pablo Neruda Foundation) began a systematic review of its holdings. Oses and his assistants discovered numerous drafts and variants of the published poems, but also some "fugitive" works that resisted all attempts to connect them to one or another of the poems in Neruda's large canon. There were twenty-one of these poems in all, written over the last two decades of Neruda's life. Evidence for the dates was both external and internal, coming from printed information on the paper the poet used as well as from associations with events and writings over those years. (Notes on these associations and dates are included in an appendix to the volume.) Oses concludes the introduction by pronouncing the discovery of these previously lost poems both a literary event of great significance and a stimulus to fresh readings of Neruda's work.

In the English edition of this volume, published in 2016 under the title *Then Come Back: The Lost Neruda*, translator Forrest Gander writes about his own experience with Neruda. Gander, himself a celebrated poet with previous experience translating Neruda's work, admits that he originally felt he would rather direct his attention to any of several other contemporary Latin American poets, such as Coral Bracho or

Antonio Cisneros. But as he gained access to the digitized manuscripts, guarded as carefully as a Shakespeare first folio, he was drawn into the mysteries they presented. Some did not seem as puzzling to him as they had seemed to Oses and his associates. Rather than add notes of his own, he has made small departures from a strictly literal translation. In poem 10 ("Maravillosa oreja" / "Marvelous ear")—an ode to the ear of Matilde Urrutia, Neruda's third wife—Gander adds the word "abalone" to gloss the phrase "little ears of the sea" because, as he notes in the prologue, Chileans of an earlier generation used that circumlocution for those sea snails. Other small emendations are there for the bilingual reader to discover. In the last line of poem 1 ("Tus pies toco en la sombra, tus manos en la luz" / "I touch your feet in the shade, your hands in the light"), for example, Neruda writes that when he places his ear on Matilde's breast, he hears her "*sílaba araucana.*" Though the adjective "*auracana*" is more likely to refer to "Araucanians"—an old name for the indigenous Mapuche people of Chile and Argentina—than to Araucana, a prized breed of domestic chicken, Gander translates the phrase as "Araucan syllable," which allows for both possibilities.

Neruda is known as a great love poet, and the first half-dozen poems in this collection are unabashed love lyrics to the great love of his life, Matilde, who is named in poem 1 and who was his third wife when the others were written. But even in poem 4 ("Qué entrega a tu mano de oro la hoja de otoño que canta" / "What guides autumn's singing leaf into your golden hand"), where the poet aches for the return of his chosen lover, he addresses his words to "you with eyes yet to be born," which may refer to future generations as well as to the lover whose eyes he hopes to open so that she can see the world as her love helps him see it. Poem 5 ("Por el cielo me acerco" / "Crossing the sky I near") returns to her, specifically the glory of her red hair, and poem 6 ("Corazón mío, sol" / "My heart, sun") to their shared experience. Then in poem 7 ("Aun en estos altos" / "Even in these steep"), he recalls his callow youth, when he first came to Santiago, dreaming of poetry, and he gives some hard advice to others in the same position:

> toughen up
> take a walk
> over the sharp stones
> then come back.

Following poem 8, an ode to the lilac, poem 9 ("'No te envanezcas', alguien dejó escrito" / "'Don't be vain,' someone had scrawled") replies to those who consider Neruda vain. It states that his only cause for vanity is the poetry that has "coursed through [his] body" since childhood and notes that the words of that poetry have spoken for countless others, including the prisoners and forlorn lovers who have written to thank him for bringing back a sense of freedom and joy. As the speaker goes on to say that he takes more interest in the people of his country than in the suit of clothes he wears, the poem reminds us that Walt Whitman was among Neruda's favorite poets, a writer of free verse who wrote for the people of his country as though his story were theirs. This leads to poem 11 ("Al chileno" / "If they put"), which reflects on what Chileans of different classes and genders carry with them as they journey far from home. It goes there by way of Neruda's ode to the ear, which glories in "your ear"—the "you" being Matilde, according to Gander's prologue, although Oses notes that the poem bears similarities to the poet's other odes to various body parts, including the eye and the liver. Ear imagery recurs in poem 20 ("Del incomunicado" / "From isolation"), which talks mockingly about Neruda's adversarial relationship with the telephone; although he has "shake[n] hands with all the world" (*todo el mundo*, which can also be translated as "everyone"), he resents that maintaining his connections to the world requires him to

Pablo Neruda, born Ricardo Eliécer Neftalí Reyes Basoalto, grew up in the southern provinces of Chile, where he wrote his first poems. He went to Santiago to study for a career in teaching, but he devoted all his time to writing and soon began to publish books of poetry and fiction under his adopted nom de plume. He became a diplomat and was elected to the Chilean senate, where he served as a member of the Communist Party of Chile. During his lifetime he was awarded the 1953 Stalin Peace Prize (later renamed the Lenin Peace Prize) and the 1971 Nobel Prize in Literature.

"degrad[e] [him]self" by subjecting his "superior ear" to the "everyday prostitution" of telephone conversations—yet no more than he resents the silence when the phone does not ring.

In poem 21 ("Estos dos hombres solos" / "Those two solitary men"), included in the English-language edition although it has survived only in typescript, Neruda reflects on what Earth may have looked like to the first Soviet cosmonauts and how they "conquered an inanimate heaven" by bringing human life and emotions into what had been empty space. Politically, Neruda was a Communist, which forced him into exile in earlier periods of his life; although his politics later contributed to his celebrity, they may have ultimately cost him his life. Less than two weeks after the Chilean coup d'état of September 11, 1973, when the American-backed forces of military commander in chief Augusto Pinochet ousted the democratically elected socialist government of Neruda's friend Salvador Allende, Neruda, who had previously been diagnosed with prostate cancer, died at a clinic in Santiago. The cause of death was reported to be heart failure, but many long suspected Pinochet's involvement, and in 2011 the Chilean government opened an official investigation into Neruda's death.

The poems in *Then Come Back* are printed first in English and then in Spanish, accompanied by facsimile images of most manuscript pages, which were mainly written in the green ink that Neruda favored. They are untitled, listed in the table of contents by the first line of each poem; the title of the Spanish edition comes from the first line of poem 1. The English translation takes its title from the advice in poem 7, directed at Neruda's young self and others like him, but it echoes the first word of poem 18: *regresa*, from the line *"Regresa de su fuego el fogonero,"* which Gander translates as "Comes back from his blaze, the fireman." In the first thirty-six lines of this forty-one-line poem, representatives of different human professions come back from the poetic essence of their experience: "the hero comes back from oblivion, / the poor from another day gone, / the surgeon from staring down death . . ." Finally, "like the rest," the poet takes off his clothes, goes to bed with his partner, and enters the dream that keeps the world going.

Poem 19 ("Roa Lynn and Patrick Morgan") is the only one written about specific individuals other than Neruda and his muse. The pair are identified in the opening line, and the next lines locate them vaguely in space—"moored in these waters, / bewildered on this river," headed either "off to sea or to hell." Neruda's readers have learned much about the two since the poem was first published; their names are mentioned together in an Argentine newspaper notice from May 1968, which Gander reproduces in his prologue. According to the notice, Morgan was captivated by an interview with American poet Roa Lynn Lanou that was published in the *Buenos Aires Herald*, and he sought her out; the two met for the first time three days later, and they married three days after that. Lynn kept her own copy of the poem, which Neruda himself gave her, and she has since written about her story for the *New Yorker*. The poem ends with the pair heading up a "four-armed river"; Oses considers the line "quite cryptic" and notes its "apocalyptic" tone, although he was seemingly unaware of the identities of the named individuals at the time.

While he wrote everything from political manifestos to historical novels, Neruda is best known and loved for his love poems. Many of his poems have been translated into English, including the early volume *Veinte poemas de amor y una canción desesperada* (1924; *Twenty Love Poems and a Song of Despair*, 1969) and *Cien sonetos de amor* (1959; *100 Love Sonnets*, 1986). Translations by eight poets, including Gander, are included in *The Essential Neruda: Selected Poems* (2004).

Gander's new translations read very smoothly. One's reading may well break into two groups of ten, with "Those two solitary men" as a coda. The first group finds the poet in the heat of love and focused on the life of poetry, while the second finds him thinking about bidding farewell to his world—to the Andes and Chile and mornings on Earth. Although they are *disjecta membra*, the scattered remains of a distinguished poetic career, the twenty-one poems hold together nicely in the arrangement chosen by Oses and followed by Gander. They read well in either language and reverberate further when read in both languages with Oses's notes. The words of Oses are translated throughout by the American poet and translator Lizzie Davis.

Reviews of the collection have been relatively positive. *Washington Post* reviewer Elizabeth Lund noted that publication of the English edition was made possible by a Kickstarter campaign and that it serves as a reminder that Neruda's work "still matters." Sara Wilson for *World Literature Today* raved about the full-color reproductions of the original texts, which afford "a glimpse into the lived experience of this master." Lawrence Olszewski, in a review for *Library Journal*, called *Then Come Back* "a miniretrospective that captures the essence of his more famous works." In a well-argued minority report for the Indian website Scroll.in, former fan Sridala Swami criticized Neruda's tendency toward "the infantilising of the beloved" and noted that "if we must consider his politics and his diplomatic career as inseparable from his poetry," one must also take into consideration Neruda's alleged rape of a Tamil woman while serving as Chilean consul in Ceylon (now Sri Lanka) in the 1920s.

Thomas Willard

Review Sources

Lund, Elizabeth. "Newly Discovered Works by Pablo Neruda and Other Best Poetry This Month." Review of *Then Come Back: The Lost Neruda*, by Pablo Neruda, et al. *The Washington Post*, 26 Apr. 2016, www.washingtonpost.com/entertainment/books/newly-discovered-works-by-pablo-neruda-and-other-best-poetry-this-month/2016/04/26/78e5b784-07df-11e6-a12f-ea5aed7958dc_story.html. Accessed 17 Oct. 2016.
Olszewski, Lawrence. Review of *Then Come Back: The Lost Neruda*, by Pablo Neruda. *Library Journal*, 1 Feb. 2016, p. 80.
Swami, Sridala, "Pablo Neruda's Lost Poems Have Been Published, but Perhaps They Should Have Stayed Lost." Review of *Then Come Back: The Lost Neruda*, by Pablo Neruda. *Scroll.in*, Scroll Media, 29 June 2016, scroll.in/article/810732/pablo-nerudas-lost-poems-have-been-published-but-perhaps-they-should-have-stayed-lost. Accessed 17 Oct. 2016.
Wilson, Sara. Review of *Then Come Back: The Lost Neruda*, by Pablo Neruda. *World Literature Today*, May–Aug. 2016, p. 51.

This Must Be the Place

Author: Maggie O'Farrell (b. 1972)
Publisher: Alfred A. Knopf (New York).
  400 pp.
Type of work: Novel
Time: 1944–2014
Locales: Donegal, Ireland; San Francisco,
  California; London, England; Brooklyn,
  New York

In This Must Be the Place, *author Maggie
O'Farrell takes readers on a meandering
trip through time to understand the complications of protagonist Daniel Sullivan's life.
Conflicted relationships with the people he
loves lead to choices that may change his life
in ways he could never have imagined.*

(Courtesy of Knopf)

Principal characters:
DANIEL SULLIVAN, a linguistics professor
TERESA SULLIVAN, his mother
PHOEBE SULLIVAN, his oldest daughter
NIALL SULLIVAN, his oldest son
NICOLA JANKS, his first true love
CLAUDETTE WELLS, his second wife, a reclusive former film star
LUCAS WELLS, Claudette's brother
MAEVE, Lucas's wife
TIMOU LINDSTROM, Claudette's first love, a film director
ARI LEFEVRE LINDSTROM WELLS SULLIVAN, Claudette's son with Timou

Daniel Sullivan and Claudette Wells are a fairly unlikely couple. Daniel is a linguist
who teaches occasional college seminars; Claudette is a retired film star who avoids
the public. Daniel's first marriage ended in divorce after his wife had an affair, and he
lost custody of his children as a result of her machinations. Claudette's first relationship ended when she fled from her overbearing lover and the public spotlight, taking
her young son, Ari, away from his father, Timou Lindstrom. Daniel's past is peppered
with drug use, casual affairs, and problematic family relationships. Claudette's past
includes fame, fortune, and glamour. Despite these differences, Daniel and Claudette
share some similarities: they both love their children, they are both insecure in relationships, and they love each other regardless of the odds.

  Since their marriage seems strong, it is surprising when Daniel makes the choice to
pursue information about one of his past relationships without discussing the decision
with his wife. For Daniel, letting Claudette into that part of his life would change her

feelings about him. For Claudette, being left out of the details will test her security in the marriage and in her own sense of self.

O'Farrell challenges the motivations of these characters through one of the most noticeably unique aspects of the novel, which is its multiple narrative viewpoints. Though Daniel Sullivan and Claudette Wells are clearly the main characters in the novel, the book is broken into varied sections that share the viewpoints of not just these two but also many of the other characters who people their lives. The contributions of the other characters skillfully illustrate aspects of Daniel and Claudette that the two cannot perceive in themselves, a technique that enables O'Farrell to present protagonists who are more sympathetic and believable for being indelibly flawed, as real people often are.

The structure of the novel is built around the musings and remembrances of the narrating characters. As such, the book does not follow a strict chronological pattern, often jumping twenty or thirty years through time in one individual person's narrative. For instance, Teresa Sullivan, Daniel's mother, is the narrator of a chapter about two-thirds of the way through the book. In this chapter, Teresa is introduced lying on her deathbed and reliving a moment from her youth, one in which she met the man who would consume her thoughts and her heart for her whole life, although he was not the man she married. Teresa's story illustrates a mother's unconditional love for a child, but it does not contribute much beyond that to Daniel's story. It is more important for its revelation of yet another character who has struggled with fidelity and has made a difficult choice. Another chapter is narrated by Phoebe, Daniel's oldest daughter, a high school junior whose father has just reentered her life. As she relates this meeting, her mind wanders back to her childhood before her father left, and an omniscient narrator interrupts her musings to provide a flash-forward regarding the father-daughter relationship to come. This jump forward in time serves as a subtle foreshadowing of what will happen with Daniel's second marriage, but it will only be caught if the reader is paying close attention. There are elusive snippets of information such as this scattered throughout the novel.

Maggie O'Farrell is an award-winning Irish novelist. A former journalist, she was awarded the 2005 Somerset Maugham Award for her third novel, The Distance Between Us *(2004), and the 2010 Costa Novel Award for her fifth book,* The Hand That First Held Mine *(2010).* This Must Be the Place *is her seventh novel.*

The multiple narratives and nonchronological timeline challenge readers to pay close attention to the thematic ideas spread throughout the book. Fidelity is one of those major thematic issues. It is introduced early as Daniel recollects his first marriage and his wife's affair, which ended the relationship. Daniel unreservedly relates that he was involved in several sexual relationships during the divorce proceedings. At the point in his life when the book begins, years into his second marriage, however, he seems to recognize the trivial nature of those affairs. As readers follow Daniel's life, they are exposed to his almost casual turns to sex to cover up insecurities or hurts. The destruction wreaked in his life by those instances culminates in his realization that Claudette's insecurities regarding faithfulness and his own inability to communicate honestly may have undermined a marriage that truly means something to him. Claudette's connection with infidelity is more convoluted. As readers follow the meandering paths of her life, her former lover's faithfulness is questioned, and her own insecurity is brought to light when she doubts Daniel's motives for pursuing an old friend, suspecting immediately that he is pursuing another woman. The relationship between these two characters comes to a climax with this conflict. Daniel's mother's story also touches on the issue of fidelity, as readers are told about the man she has loved from afar all of her life, an emotional affair that never resulted in a sexual consummation.

Other themes that run through the novel include family relationships and loss. These two themes can be seen in many of O'Farrell's other books, but she introduces slight twists on the themes to make this novel stand out. For instance, though many of her works center on sisterly bonds, she steps out of that familiar territory in this book to showcase the loving link between Claudette and her brother, Lucas, instead. She also stresses brother-sister relationships with Daniel's children. His first two children are Phoebe and her brother, Niall, and his second family consists of his children with Claudette. The older two children's close relationship is revealed in chapters narrated by each of them; in her chapter, Phoebe repeatedly tells readers, "My brother is the coolest person in the world." Parent-child relationships are also central to the novel, explored through Daniel's glowing love for his children, Claudette's clear adoration of her children, and Teresa's "pure, animal avalanche of feeling" for her son. These familial ties are also associated with the losses. Daniel's losses include his separation from his older children, the death of his mother, and abandoned friendships and lovers. Claudette's loss of herself takes the story in a different direction.

Loneliness is another central experience for many of the characters. Phoebe reveals of Niall, "My brother smells of hard work. My brother smells of intelligence, of all-nighters, of education, of dedication and sometimes, I think, loneliness." Later in the novel, as Daniel recalls one of his first meetings with Claudette, he comments, "I caught wind suddenly, and for the first time, of her keen isolation, the bravery it must take for her to be there, alone with the boy." Other instances of loneliness that stand out in the novel are found in the side stories of Teresa Sullivan's unfulfilled love affair and of Lucas and Maeve's infertility problems, two narratives that add a layer of complexity to the development of Daniel and Claudette's characterizations as well.

Outside of the characterization and thematic intrigues, *This Must Be the Place* also reflects on the complexity of language and the ways people relate to each other through words. One way this is seen is through Daniel's very identity. As a linguist, Daniel's fascination with language comes across early in the novel when he travels to give a lecture on "pidgins and creoles, based around a single sentence," and he reveals that missing the lecture will leave "a group of undergraduates who will never be enlightened as to the fascinating, complex linguistic genealogy of the sentence: 'Him thief she mango.'" Later in the book, Ari's difficulties with stuttering bring to light the frustrations experienced by a child who cannot clearly express himself. It is Daniel's patience and understanding of her son's problem that draws Claudette to him.

One issue that might bother a certain audience is a casual reference to tobacco and drug use. One of Claudette's main vices, according to Daniel, is smoking. She carelessly smokes throughout the novel, even in the scenes set in 2010, when smoking would be known to be unhealthy. Daniel himself smokes as well, but his habit is, in 2010 at least, carefully controlled with a limitation of three cigarettes per day, smoked away from the children. More problematic is the almost constant reference to drug use by a younger Daniel and his friends Todd, Suki, and Nicola. While roommates in graduate school, Daniel, Todd, and Suki imbibe a variety of pharmaceuticals, seemingly without repercussion. A potential overdose by Nicola, Daniel's lover at the time, does not stop them from casually using drugs to overcome boredom or to compensate for a lack in their lives. This casual drug use by the of-age adults in the novel is tempered by an instance of peer pressure in which Phoebe decides to stand up for herself and walk away from a popular group of teens who are imbibing under the bleachers at their school.

Reviews of *This Must Be the Place* were mixed but generally positive. Poornima Apte's review for *Booklist* lauded the "flawless language" while cautioning that the "chorus of voices and constant time-frame switching occasionally threaten the clarity of the narrative." The reviewer for *Kirkus Review* noted that the characters "all have a magnetic star quality," adding, "The scenario is glamorous, the writing is stylish, the globe-trotting almost dizzying, but there's a satisfying core of untampered feeling as well." A complex and intriguing novel, *This Must Be the Place* will challenge readers to question their own motivations and relationships.

Theresa L. Stowell, PhD

Review Sources

Apte, Poornima. Review of *This Must Be the Place*, by Maggie O'Farrell. *Booklist*, 1 June 2016, pp. 45–46.

Graver, Elizabeth. "In Maggie O'Farrell's New Novel, a Film Star Flees the Fame Game." Review of This Must Be the Place, by Maggie O'Farrell. *The New York Times*, 5 Aug. 2016, www.nytimes.com/2016/08/07/books/review/maggie-ofarrell-this-must-be-the-place.html. Accessed 17 Feb. 2017.

Hoffert, Barbara. Review of *This Must Be the Place*, by Maggie O'Farrell. *Library Journal*, 15 Feb. 2016, p. 73.

Review of *This Must Be the Place*, by Maggie O'Farrell. *Kirkus Reviews*, 15 May 2016, pp. 30–31.

To the Bright Edge of the World

Author: Eowyn Ivey
Publisher: Little, Brown (Boston). 417 pp.
Type of work: Novel
Time: 1885 and present day
Locales: Vancouver, Washington; Alaska

Eowyn Ivey's second novel, To the Bright Edge of the World, *is an Alaskan adventure tale told through old letters, diary entries, photographs, and other ephemera.*

Principal characters:

COLONEL ALLEN FORRESTER, a newly married veteran of the Indian Wars, charged with leading an expedition up Alaska's Wolverine River in 1885

SOPHIE FORRESTER, his wife, an avid birdwatcher who takes up photography

LIEUTENANT ANDREW PRUITT, one of his men, a poetic soldier

(Courtesy of Little, Brown and Company)

SERGEANT BRADLEY TILLMAN, one of his men, a hot-tempered son of a miner

NAT'AAGGI, a young and resourceful Indian girl who accompanies Forrester and his men

THE OLD MAN, or "Man Who Flies on Black Wings," an old shaman who takes the shape of a raven with human eyes

Eowyn Ivey's second novel, *To the Bright Edge of the World*, is a magical realist tale of the Alaskan wilderness. Told through letters, diary entries, newspaper clippings, and photographs, Ivey's novel explores love, loss, loneliness, and survival through the story of Colonel Allen Forrester and his young wife, Sophie. The scraps of ephemera that describe their lives have been handed down through the Forrester family to the present day. Approaching old age—and fearful that the collection will be thrown away when he is gone—Walt Forrester, the Colonel's great-nephew, sends the box of papers to a man named Josh Sloan, the curator of a tiny museum in Alpine, Alaska. Walt and Josh, a young gay man and Alaska native grappling with the rapid changes confronting the town in which he grew up, correspond throughout the novel, contextualizing the stories in the collection with things they have heard or seen, and occasionally adding articles of their own. Still, the bulk of the novel belongs to 1885 and a dangerous and fantastical journey that changed Alaska forever.

Ivey's tale is fictional, but rooted in truth. In 1885, Lieutenant Henry T. Allen led an expedition into Alaska's interior, becoming the first white man to chart the Copper, Tanana, and Koyuku rivers. (The Wolverine River in the book is fictional.)

Allen's achievement, like the Colonel's, wrought complicated consequences for Alaskan tribes, helping to pave the way for the Klondike Gold Rush a decade later. As was true in the American West, the gold brought prospectors and homesteaders, but also death and disease for natives. In Ivey's telling, the Colonel's expedition represents a historical crossroads. If the gold rush marked the beginning of modernization—or perhaps more accurately, a forcible parting with old ways—the Colonel's Alaska was the last glimpse of an ancient world.

(Courtesy of Stephen Nowers)

Eowyn Ivey's first novel, The Snow Child *(2012), was a finalist for the Pulitzer Prize in 2013.* To the Bright Edge of the World *is her second novel.*

Ivey was born and raised in Alaska, and her first novel, *The Snow Child*, is also set in that state. In it, a barren, homesteading couple in the 1920s builds a child out of snow. Alan Cheuse for National Public Radio (NPR) wrote in 2012: "Ivey's delightful invention hovers somewhere between myth and naturalism." The same could be said of *To the Bright Edge of the World*, which combines American Indian origin stories with a true-to-life tale of survival in the Alaskan wilderness. Ivey imbues the land with peculiar, otherworldly powers. In her Alaska, a shaman can turn into a raven, a baby can be born of a tree root, and a man can be married to the winter mist. All of this might sound a bit whimsical for an adventure story, but like any good storyteller, Ivey is careful to withhold easy explanations from her readers. Did those women really turn into a flock of geese, or was it just a trick of the light? Ivey prefers to let strange events hover over her characters like ghosts of a forgotten past.

The story begins at an army outpost in Vancouver, Washington. Sophie Forrester excitedly prepares to accompany her husband on his adventure to the north until she discovers that she is pregnant. Disappointed, but equally excited about the child she carries, Sophie bids the Colonel good-bye only to be thrust into a demanding society of women who criticize her solitary and unladylike ways. They are appalled that she would rather walk in the woods than go to tea, for example, or that all of her dresses are a boring shade of grey. Her closest friends are a mischievous social butterfly named Evelyn and her eleven-year-old housemaid, Charlotte. At first glance, Sophie's story is mundane fare compared to that of her husband, who is, at the same time, nearly starving to death on a frozen river, but a devastating miscarriage and memories of her father's gruesome suicide plague Sophie. In the end, her mettle is tested just as the Colonel's is; only she must find the will to survive where he must find the way.

The Colonel, meanwhile, struggles with his crew. One of his men, the once-reliable Pruitt, is given to strange dark moods after his service in the Indian Wars. Later Pruitt reveals that he was at Elk Creek, a senseless massacre of Indian women and children likely modeled on the Sand Creek Massacre in 1864. The other man, Tillman, is a different kind of liability. He is gregarious and kind but a drinker who is always eager to fight. The men travel with a revolving band of hangers-on, including two trappers, Samuelson and Boyd, and a young Indian woman named Nat'aaggi. Nat'aaggi tells the men that she was once married to a man who turned into an otter, and further claims to have slit his throat one night when he was sleeping. She wears his pelt around her shoulders. Her story, though, is far less unsettling than the intermittent presence of the Old Man, an elderly and malevolent shaman with a lame leg who wears a black hat and goes by the name "Man Who Flies on Black Wings." He leaves the party only to show up again, further down the river, appearing as if out of thin air.

The first entry in the Colonel's diary begins with the Old Man. The Colonel is convinced that, waking in the middle of the night, he saw him sitting in the high branches of a tree. "I am left vaguely uneasy," the Colonel writes. "As if I witnessed a bird flying underwater or a fish swimming across the sky." It is an apt beginning for a novel in which the unsettling mysteries of nature are a running theme. The characters are forever running up against the bounds of what is possible. Like President Thomas Jefferson, who hoped that explorers Meriwether Lewis and William Clarke might encounter a woolly mammoth on their travels out west, the Colonel is not quite sure of what he will find in Alaska. Is this event real, he often asks himself, or is it just my imagination? If there really are, as he muses in the book, caves that breathe like animals—"blowing out air in the summer, sucking in air in the winter"—and "lantern-like creatures" at the bottom of the ocean, what really qualifies as strange at all?

Ivey is concerned with the magic of reality, or as Chris Bohjalian put it in his review for the *Washington Post*, "the inexplicable magic of the world—real or imagined—that hovers just beyond our conscious perceptions." Equally strange and mystifying for Sophie is photography, a relatively new technology at the time. Desperate for purpose after losing her child, Sophie—with the help of her delightful sidekick, Charlotte—sets out to become a nature photographer. She throws herself into the task with gusto, draining her savings account to buy equipment and even gutting her pantry to build a darkroom. She becomes particularly obsessed with capturing a hummingbird's nest. She waits—in a homemade deer blind—for hours on end for the perfect shot, like a traditional artist (her father, for instance) might wait for a bolt of divine inspiration. Ivey casts the making of art as a spiritual activity, like prayer. While the Colonel makes a map, Sophie looks for ways to communicate beauty that cannot be described.

Ivey intertwines Sophie and the Colonel's tales in near real time, but they only exchange a couple of letters that arrive months after they are written. The device has a satisfying symmetry; Sophie's miscarriage, for example, provides the inciting incident for her story line, and the crisis for his. Ivey's writing is lush but also restrained. Her characters are verbose Victorians, but Ivey admirably manages to convey their style without succumbing to its worst excesses. (This is universally true except for Pruitt, whose cryptic density is both amusing and sad.) *The Bright Edge of the World* is a thrilling read, though the end might be a bit too neat for some. Ivey is at her best when she holds a little something back, so when the time comes for answers, it is surprising that she overshoots the mark. Reviewers praised the book, though Bohjalian points out that both Sophie and the Colonel are "relentlessly good" people. Though they struggle with emotional and physical pain, their personalities remain uncomplicated by ambiguous deeds. Ivey suggests that the Colonel has had to make choices that he regrets, but these regrets are never explored. The same can be said of Pruitt, whose struggle with past mistakes—or rather, crimes—is largely internal. Relatedly, Ivey intermittently challenges the purpose of the men's mission. She is clearly interested in engaging with the relationship between the American Indians and the men that stole their land, but this theme ultimately plays a secondary role to her concern with the mysteries of nature and humankind's quest to interpret it.

Molly Hagan

Review Sources

Bohjalian, Chris. "'To the Bright Edge of the World': A Terrific Tale of Alaskan Adventure." Review of *To the Bright Edge of the World*, by Eowyn Ivey. *The Washington Post*, 5 Aug. 2016, www.washingtonpost.com/entertainment/books/to-the-bright-edge-of-the-world-a-terrific-tale-of-alaskan-adventure/2016/08/05/4e8d9a4a-5b29-11e6-9aee-8075993d73a2_story.html. Accessed 27 Oct. 2016.

Brooks, Geraldine. "A Journey into the Alaskan Wilds." Review of *To the Bright Edge of the World*, by Eowyn Ivey. *The Guardian*, 24 Aug. 2016, www.theguardian.com/books/2016/aug/24/to-the-bright-edge-of-the-world-by-eowyn-ivey-review. Accessed 27 Oct. 2016.

Greene, Amy. "A Novel's Team of Explorers Sets Out to Tame Alaska." Review of To the Bright Edge of the World, by Eowyn Ivey. *The New York Times*, 2 Sept. 2016, www.nytimes.com/2016/09/04/books/review/to-the-bright-edge-of-the-world-eowyn-ivey.html. Accessed 27 Oct. 2016.

Review of *To the Bright Edge of the World*, by Eowyn Ivey. *Kirkus*, 17 May 2016, www.kirkusreviews.com/book-reviews/eowyn-ivey/to-the-bright-edge-of-the-world. Accessed 27 Oct. 2016.

Review of *To the Bright Edge of the World*, by Eowyn Ivey. *Publishers Weekly*, 1 Aug. 2016, www.publishersweekly.com/978-0-316-24285-1. Accessed 27 Oct. 2016.

The Underground Railroad

Author: Colson Whitehead (b. 1969)
Publisher: Doubleday (New York). 306 pp.
Type of work: Novel
Time: Early to mid-nineteenth century
Locales: Georgia, South Carolina, North Carolina, Tennessee, Indiana

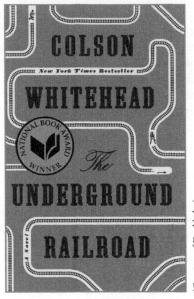

(Courtesy of Doubleday)

Cora, born into slavery on a Georgia cotton plantation, was left behind as a child when her mother escaped. After the plantation's ownership changes hands to a much crueler master, a newly arrived slave named Caesar convinces Cora to escape north on the Underground Railroad. Cora's journey, with its gritty realism and elements of fantasy, is harrowing, and Ridgeway, a slave catcher hired to bring her back, is determined to find her.

Principal characters:
CORA, a teenage slave on the Randall plantation who was left behind after her mother escaped when she was a child
CAESAR, a slave who has recently arrived at the Randall plantation and attempts to escape with Cora
MABEL, Cora's mother, a slave on the Randall plantation who escaped without Cora
AJARRY, Cora's grandmother and a slave on the Randall planation who was captured in Africa
ARNOLD RIDGEWAY, a slave catcher who is hired to capture Mabel, Cora, and Caesar

Colson Whitehead's novel *The Underground Railroad* is much more than a simple narrative describing the horrors of slavery. Instead, the novel uses slavery and the brutal treatment of African Americans during this period in history as a vehicle to illuminate contemporary racial and social problems. Whitehead blends history with elements of fantasy to follow his protagonist, Cora, on her bid for freedom, and he incorporates both the future and the past by alluding to other historic periods of exploitation and terror, such as the Salem witch trials and Tuskegee syphilis study. Through the creation of convincing and compelling characters and the inclusion of fantastical elements, Whitehead moves the story beyond a narrative of one character's horrific experiences to one that examines the profound and continuing legacy of slavery in the United States.

While the main focus of the novel is on Cora, who is a third-generation slave on the Randall cotton plantation in Georgia, Whitehead intersperses chapters detailing Cora's journey with chapters highlighting the lives and backgrounds of secondary characters. Whitehead begins by describing Cora's grandmother, Ajarry, who was captured in her native Ouidah, in modern-day Benin, and survived the inhuman suffering of the Middle Passage. After arriving, Ajarry never leaves the planation, as opposed to Cora's mother, Mabel, who escapes when Cora is ten years old and is never heard from again. Cora has an especially treacherous time navigating plantation slave life as an abandoned child, and although she resents her mother for leaving her behind, she also begrudgingly admires her successful escape. Cora dreams of freedom for herself, but it is not until the plantation is in the hands of an especially cruel master that Caesar, a recently purchased slave, convinces her to escape.

Much of the rest of the novel focuses on her quest for freedom, detailing the difficulty of the quest and Cora's dogged determination. Often, when Cora considers settling in a spot that seems ideal, circumstances emerge that force her to flee again. Other chapters focus on secondary characters Cora encounters on her journey, such as Ethel, the wife of an abolitionist who reluctantly shelters her, and Aloysius Stevens, a doctor who pressures African American women to be sterilized and has a shady past as a grave robber. A third chapter, and one of the most revealing, is dedicated to the slave catcher Arnold Ridgeway, who is determined to catch Cora and return her to the plantation. These three chapters on white secondary characters provide an insightful counterpoint on race relations and the horrors that often hid behind seemingly good intentions.

Although there are long sections of the novel where they do not interact, Cora and Ridgeway drive much of the suspense in the story—Cora in her determination to be free and Ridgeway in his obsession with finding and capturing her. Both are especially memorable and thought-provoking. Cora is courageous and keen, and her observations help her decide when to fight and when to stay silent. After her mother escapes, for example, she inherits her small vegetable plot and is determined to keep it, despite her young age. Older and physically stronger slaves try to take it from her, but she fights with the aid of a hatchet and wins.

Colson Whitehead is the author of five novels, including his acclaimed debut novel, The Intuitionist *(1999) and the* New York Times Best Seller Zone One *(2011). Whitehead's honors include the Whiting Award (2000), a MacArthur Fellowship (2002), and a Guggenheim Fellowship (2013).*

It is a small but significant triumph in a place where few victories are possible, and although she later pays a heavy price for winning that battle, it is evidence of the ingenuity and scrappiness she needs to survive. As the novel progresses and she attempts to build a new life as a free and independent woman, she continues to study the people and places around her. While the South Carolina town she first arrives in, with its soft cotton dresses and safe, campus-like atmosphere, appears to be the utopia she has been searching for, her keen observations about the mysterious situation of a woman in another dormitory and her conversation with a doctor pressuring her and others to take advantage of permanent birth control reveal that this is not the case. In Cora, Whitehead creates a protagonist to champion but also one who, despite her stubbornness and difficulty allowing herself to be emotionally vulnerable, is relentlessly strong. Through Cora, Whitehead implies that African Americans must be constant in their vigilance, that their guard cannot be lowered without the possibility of experiencing devastating consequences. Cora is continuously on the run, and often what seems on the surface to be paradise is not safe due to outside forces beyond her control, mirroring the plight of many African Americans in contemporary society.

Similarly, Ridgeway, the slave catcher, is also a strong and memorable character, but for entirely different reasons. He is Cora's equal in collecting details, such as when he questions the captured white abolitionists who helped Cora escape. He then investigates every lead, hoping to follow Cora's trail. He is also cruel and revels in his ruthlessness, further dehumanizing slaves by referring to them as "it" rather than he or she, and his delight in watching Cora's face when he recites the grim details of her loved ones' circumstances. Ridgeway had been hired to find Cora's mother, Mabel, years ago and failed, and that failure has affected him deeply. When he has the chance to redeem himself and find Cora, Mabel's daughter, he makes it his personal mission. Ridgeway is both cool, never losing his temper and remaining eerily calm, and he is even seemingly kind at moments, such as when he buys Cora a new dress, but ultimately he is relentless in his pursuit of fugitive slaves and his punishments are severe and chillingly cold-blooded. Critics such as Christian Lorentzen, in his review of the novel for *Vulture*, have equated Ridgeway's brand of racism and detailed scrutiny with some modern-day police officers.

It is the fantasy elements, however, that truly elevate the novel and encourage a depth of reading and comparisons, such as with Ridgeway, to contemporary society. The Underground Railroad is, in Whitehead's version, a literal underground train complete with tunnels, train tracks, stations, and boxcars rather than the legendary network of safe houses. In terms of the Underground Railroad being a literal train, for example, Cora is told that she will see the "true face of America" as she rides the train to freedom. Being the observant person she is, she is dismayed that there is nothing to see. She eventually realizes this was a joke, that "there was only darkness outside the windows on her journeys, and only ever would be darkness." Whitehead suggests that the true face of America is mired in a past it can neither face nor escape. He similarly uses Cora's job at the Museum of Natural Wonders, a living museum that enacts scenes from the past, including the lives of slaves, to show how often history is not written by the people who lived and experienced it but by others, in this case white Americans, who, although trying to be helpful, have little understanding and empathy, effectively whitewashing history. There are numerous other references to the Salem witch trials and the Tuskegee syphilis study, which occurred in the seventeenth century and the twentieth century, respectively, widening the scope of the novel's exploration of the terrors of history and how they recur at regular intervals. Whitehead implies that the past is not settled and over and that the legacy of slavery continues.

Although this novel is distinctly different from Whitehead's previous novels, those earlier novels did set the stage for *The Underground Railroad*, not in terms of providing a historical approach or his use of dark comic elements, but through raising questions about race in contemporary society and the incorporation of myth, fantasy, and even speculative fiction. In most of his novels, Whitehead has explored the impact of race and racism in a contemporary context. In *The Intuitionist* (1999), for example, Whitehead focused on protagonist Lila Mae Watson as the first female African American elevator inspector in a large city resembling New York. After the tragic crash of an elevator she has recently inspected, Whitehead, with ironic humor, explores a possible racially based conspiracy in which she is blamed for the accident. In a later novel, *Zone One* (2013), Whitehead presents a darkly comic zombie apocalypse in which the race of the protagonist, Mark Spitz, is not identified until very late in the novel, prompting readers to speculate about race and question their assumptions. In *The Underground Railroad*, Whitehead continues his discussion of race, and although it does have a small instance or two of dark humor, it focuses more on the role history plays in defining and perpetuating entrenched and often unconscious beliefs about race.

The *Underground Railroad* won the 2016 National Book Award for fiction, and critics have been nearly unanimous in their praise for Whitehead's deeply emotional, unflinching, and creative interpretation of the slave narrative. They praise protagonist Cora for her gritty determination in the face of the complex forces against her, ranging from her own mother's abandonment to Ridgeway's relentless pursuit. Critics were especially impressed with Whitehead's deft use of metaphor, making the Underground Railroad a literal train where the passengers travel in complete darkness and their destinations are unknown. Critics also appreciated Whitehead's ability to draw from other periods in history to show the fluidity of history and to explore how racial equality is in constant jeopardy by seen and unseen forces set to undermine and destroy it. Thus, when critic Michael Shaub called it "a novel against forgetting," in a review for NPR, he confirms that vigilance is necessary, and that questions about racial equality continue to be relevant.

The *Underground Railroad* is a timely and important novel, not just because of Whitehead's strong, moving characterizations and his characters' abilities to persevere despite horrific circumstances, but because he has found a way to make the past the present and to foster an awareness of the hard-won and ongoing efforts to advance racial equality.

Marybeth Rua-Larsen

Review Sources

Carroll, Rebecca. "Colson Whitehead's 'The Underground Railroad' Is Timely, Necessary and Shattering." Review of *The Underground Railroad*, by Colson Whitehead. *Los Angeles Times*, 26 Aug. 2016, www.latimes.com/books/jacketcopy/la-ca-jc-whitehead-underground-railroad-20160815-snap-story.html. Accessed 7 Nov. 2016.

Charles, Ron. "Oprah's Book Club Pick: 'The Underground Railroad,' by Colson Whitehead." Review of *The Underground Railroad*, by Colson Whitehead. *The Washington Post*, 2 Aug. 2016, www.washingtonpost.com/entertainment/books/the-underground-railroad-by-colson-whitehead-an-essential-american-novel/2016/08/01/4bcab684-55ad-11e6-b7de-dfe509430c39_story.html. Accessed 7 Nov. 2016.

Domestico, Anthony. "'Underground Railroad'—the New Oprah's Book Club Book—Is an Important American Novel." Review of *The Underground Railroad*, by Colson Whitehead. *The Boston Globe*, 4 Aug. 2016, www.bostonglobe.com/arts/books/2016/08/04/whitehead/I5baqZSXeDeLU6IcVEsRoL/story.html. Accessed 7 Nov. 2016.

Lorentzen, Christian. "How Pyrotechnic Comic Novelist Colson Whitehead Found His Way to the Grim, Measured Underground Railroad." Review of *The Underground Railroad*, by Colson Whitehead. *Vulture*, 13 Sept. 2016, www.vulture.com/2016/09/how-colson-whitehead-got-from-zombies-to-slavery.html. Accessed 7 Nov. 2016.

Schaub, Michael. "'Underground Railroad' Traces the Terrible Wounds of Slavery." Review of *The Underground Railroad*, by Colson Whitehead. *NPR*, 9 Aug. 2016, www.npr.org/2016/08/09/489208871/underground-railroad-traces-the-terrible-wounds-of-slavery. Accessed 7 Nov. 2016.

Vásquez, Juan Gabriel. "In Colson Whitehead's Latest, the Underground Railroad Is More Than a Metaphor." Review of The Underground Railroad, by Colson Whitehead. *The New York Times*, 5 Aug. 2016, www.nytimes.com/2016/08/14/books/review/colson-whitehead-underground-railroad.html. Accessed 7 Nov. 2016.

The Unseen World

Author: Liz Moore (b. 1983)
Publisher: W. W. Norton (New York). 464 pp.
Type of work: Novel
Time: Primarily 1980s and 2009
Locales: Boston, Massachusetts; San Francisco, California

Liz Moore's third novel, The Unseen World, *is a science-fiction mystery about virtual reality, artificial intelligence, and one woman's quest to decode her father's past.*

Principal characters:
ADA SIBELIUS, a lonely woman struggling to understand her father
DAVID SIBELIUS, her father, a brilliant computer scientist
DIANA LISTON, David's coworker and Ada's surrogate mother
ELIXIR, an artificial intelligence program created by David

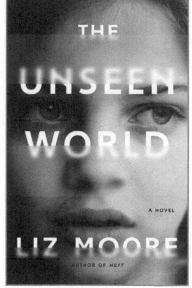

(Courtesy of Norton, W.W. & Company, Inc.)

Ada Sibelius has a life that other children her age might envy. She is twelve years old but has never set foot inside a classroom. Instead, her father, David, a brilliant computer scientist who runs a lab at the Boston Institute of Technology, simply brings her to work with him every day as he labors away at an artificial intelligence program called ELIXIR. Liz Moore's novel *The Unseen World* is, for the most part, set in the 1980s. In a world predating widely available cellular phones and the World Wide Web, Ada is surrounded by cutting-edge technology but still remains isolated. However, she minds this isolation only intermittently. Like her father, she is thrilled by working in the lab, where she is first adored as a mascot and then respected as a young colleague. Her formal education is supplemented by her doting, if not openly affectionate, father, who engages her in an ongoing dialogue about books, music, languages, proofs, and puzzles. David has instilled in his daughter a sense of intellectual independence, but socially, Ada is utterly dependent on him. Her only friends are the adults in the lab and the local librarian. When confronted with a child her own age, Ada is awed into silence, observing them like an alien species.

In the first scene of Moore's novel, set in the 1980s, David is quizzing Ada while preparing an elaborate feast for his students and colleagues. The gathering is an annual tradition, the meticulous details of which suggest David's patrician upbringing. There are place cards and table linens, and Ada mixes gin rickeys with the precision of a chemist, handing them out from a tray before formally inviting everyone to take a seat at the dining room table. At the end of the night, David offers a riddle, another long-running tradition. He sets forth the premise with gusto, but when his new students, the only two at the party to have never heard it before, are stumped, David goes blank. An awkward silence fills the room, and in that moment, just before David's close friend Diana Liston interrupts to come to his aid, young Ada realizes that there is something seriously wrong.

Moore unfurls the story of his illness slowly, but David has early onset Alzheimer's disease, and the diagnosis shatters Ada, slowly and irrevocably changing not only her daily life but also, and more painfully, the way she perceives her father. *The Unseen World* straddles several genres; it is a coming-of-age tale, a science-fiction story, and a mystery. But Moore's greatest achievement is her vivid depiction of Ada's slow-burning grief, her anguish made all the more visceral by her cloistered upbringing. She has a brilliant intellect but no emotional intelligence to guide her through the one problem she cannot solve.

Moore's previous novels include *The Words of Every Song* (2007), a series of vignettes about the music industry based on her own experiences as a musician, and *Heft* (2012), a dual narrative about an obese former professor and a teenager struggling with his mother's addictions. *Heft* was particularly well received, praised for its poignancy and its vibrantly drawn characters. *The Unseen World* may seem a bit of an outlier in Moore's oeuvre in its scope—later chapters skip from 1920s Kansas to Silicon Valley in 2009 and then beyond the present day—but at its heart, it inhabits a similar and carefully realized domestic world of parents and children, work and money, and the daily ennui of just getting by. The science-fiction aspects of the book, even the nonspeculative parts, effectively underscore Moore's rendering of everyday life, emphasizing human imperfection and mortality with the promise of something inhumanly perfect and, in the case of ELIXIR, possibly immortal.

ELIXIR is a self-teaching computer program that David developed as a challenge to computer scientist Alan Turing's famous test. Turing created the test, which he called the "Imitation Game" but has since come to be known more simply as the Turing test, as a means of detecting consciousness in machines. To pass the test, a person conversing with a machine must be convinced that they are really talking to a human. There are problems with and challenges to the test, but for the most part, Moore explores the philosophical implications of it as posited by Turing, one of David's heroes. Unlike its predecessor, the real-life ELIZA program from the 1960s, ELIXIR is a program capable of learning. When David and other lab members converse with it via a chat window, ELIXIR stores that information for future use. Over time, ELIXIR learns appropriate (i.e., human) responses to questions using the vocabulary it has been fed. David is adamant about constant engagement with ELIXIR. Each lab member—and Ada—has access to ELIXIR on their personal computer, and sometimes the program reproduces phrases of speech particular to one of them. In this way, Moore writes, "ELIXIR seemed to be a compilation of them all, a child spawned by many parents."

There are obvious parallels between Ada and ELIXIR. Ada also pulls from a growing stockpile of acquired knowledge, adding words such as "like" and "whatever" when she encounters a person her own age, to interpret her own life and the lives of

those around her. She also, thanks to essentially growing up in the lab, was "spawned
by many parents." The most important of
these surrogate parents is a woman named
Diana Liston, though everyone refers to her
by her last name. Liston, a relatively young,
single mother who grew up in Boston and
works in the lab, is David's closest friend.
She is maternal, friendly, a bit bawdy, and,
for Ada, blessedly normal. Liston is the first
person Ada calls when her father, in the early
throes of his illness, disappears for the first
time. A year later, David is living in a nursing home, and Ada moves in with Liston and
her brood.

*Liz Moore is a writer and a musician.
Her previous novels include* The Words
of Every Song *(2007) and* Heft *(2012).
She teaches writing at Holy Family University in Philadelphia, Pennsylvania.*

The new arrangement is complicated
by Ada's crush on William, Liston's handsome, popular oldest son. The other boys in
the house are Gregory, who is only a year
younger than Ada but is petulant and shy, and
Matty, who is nine. (Liston's oldest child,
Joanie, is an adult with a child of her own.) Ada longs to be one with the raucous clan
even as she seeks to avoid them, forever sneaking back into her old house down the
street to smell its familiar smells and talk to ELIXIR on her own computer. ELIXIR,
Moore writes, "triggered Ada's emotions in unexpected ways. . . . It brought out the
same warm feelings in Ada that a friend might have." ELIXIR becomes a diary and
confidant for Ada as she struggles to understand the social customs of teenagers—she
is enrolled in a real school at this point—and her father's past.

When Liston takes legal guardianship of Ada, she finds there are no records of a
man named David Sibelius. As she digs deeper—at first without telling Ada, which
causes a terrible rift—she discovers that almost everything she knew about her friend
and former boss was a lie.

Ada has some clues. Before her father became truly ill, he gave her a floppy disk
that contained a code and told her that she might later discover things about him that
she did not know. Ada enlists the members of the lab to help her crack the code, but to
no avail. Other resources, procured with the help of the local librarian, reveal information that cuts to the very core of Ada's identity. Ada's mother was a surrogate, and she
knew very little about her father's family—only that they were wealthy and dead. David always told her that he was estranged from his upper-crust New York City parents.
In the past, he had taken her to the city and pointed out their former stately home. He
even told her that his mother was descended from a voyager on the *Mayflower*. For
Ada, the depth and detail of the betrayal is stunning.

As Ada's quest intensifies, Moore's narrative begins to leap through time. Readers see an adult Ada living alone in San Francisco and working for a Silicon Valley

start-up, as well as a younger David following a surprising path. The decision to expand the story in this way is admirable, but the execution is ultimately disappointing. Other eras do not spring from the page in the same way that Moore's vision of Boston in the 1980s does, and the narrative pace slows. David's backstory in particular seems overly long and almost too revealing, suggesting that what Ada was really looking for from her father was not quite so literal. As Louisa Hall, who reviewed *The Unseen World* for the *New York Times*, wrote, "The novel is more enticing when it treats its characters as complicated and ultimately indecipherable puzzles, reminding us that Turing was right: When it comes to other intelligences, knowledge is a difficult game. Words sent out across distance are, at best, glistening and slippery clues, and the power of language isn't in the direct answers it gives us, but in the promise of endless approach." However, despite its flaws, *The Unseen World* is ultimately an engaging read that creatively deals with a number of significant themes, including identity, people's relationship with technology, and the meaning of family.

Molly Hagan

Review Sources

Campbell, Karen. "Across Decades, a Girl Unravels the Mystery of Her Computer Expert Father." Review of *The Unseen World*, by Liz Moore. *Boston Globe*, 28 July 2016, www.bostonglobe.com/arts/2016/07/27/across-decades-girl-unravels-mystery-her-computer-expert-father/BQAIenLlonXkKinQI7980M/story.html. Accessed 13 Jan. 2017.

Coll, Susan. "*The Unseen World*—a Cerebral Thriller about a Girl 'More Machine Than Human.'" Review of *The Unseen World*, by Liz Moore. *The Washington Post*, 19 July 2016, www.washingtonpost.com/entertainment/books/the-unseen-world--a-cerebral-thriller-about-a-girl-more-machine-than-human/2016/07/13/36a76e40-486b-11e6-acbc-4d4870a079da_story.html. Accessed 13 Jan. 2017.

Hall, Louisa. "Dementia Dims a Father's Brilliance in a Novel Plumbing Family Mysteries." Review of The Unseen World, by Liz Moore. *The New York Times*, 5 Aug. 2016, www.nytimes.com/2016/08/07/books/review/unseen-world-liz-moore.html. Accessed 13 Jan. 2017.

Review of *The Unseen World*, by Liz Moore. *Kirkus Reviews*, 1 June 2016, pp. 31–32.

Review of *The Unseen World*, by Liz Moore. *Publishers Weekly*, 16 May 2016, p. 28.

Until We Are Free
My Fight for Human Rights in Iran

Author: Shirin Ebadi (b. 1947)
Publisher: Random House (New York). 304 pp.
Type of work: Memoir

Writing in exile, Nobel laureate Shirin Ebadi chronicles her life and work in Iran under the brutal reign of former President Mahmoud Ahmadinejad.

Principal personages:
SHIRIN EBADI, a human rights activist and lawyer
JAVAD TAVASSOLIAN, her husband, a retired engineer
MAHMUDI, an intelligence officer bent on destroying her

(Courtesy of Penguin Random House)

Shirin Ebadi is an Iranian human rights lawyer and activist. She became the country's first female judge in 1975 but was stripped of her judgeship after the 1979 Iranian Revolution, which deposed Iran's shah and swept a conservative Islamist regime into power. As a woman, the new Islamic Republic argued, Ebadi was "unfit" to hold such a powerful position. In 1980, she became a clerk in her own courtroom. Undeterred, Ebadi began working pro bono as a human rights lawyer, representing women, intellectuals, dissidents, and religious minorities who had fallen prey to the regime. For her work she spent three weeks in jail in 2000 and, in 2003, became the first Muslim woman to receive the Nobel Peace Prize. In 2006 she published *Iran Awakening: A Memoir of Revolution and Hope*, in which she details her own participation in the 1979 revolution. Ebadi wrote about the revolution again in her 2011 book, *The Golden Cage: Three Brothers, Three Choices, One Destiny.*

Until We Are Free: My Fight for Human Rights in Iran is a chilling memoir that chronicles the author's life since winning the Nobel Peace Prize in 2003—the same year a little-known engineer named Mahmoud Ahmadinejad was elected mayor of Tehran, Iran's capital city, squeaking by thanks to a 12 percent voter turnout. Ebadi's fate had long been tied to the Islamic Republic, but Ahmadinejad's rise proved to be a dire threat not only to her precarious standing with the regime, which had been monitoring her since the 1990s, but also to her life and family. "The field of human rights is not about pretty words; it involves the abuse of the vulnerable by those who wield power," Ebadi writes in one of the book's later chapters. During the past decade, Ebadi, despite her international fame, became acutely vulnerable herself, engaging in psychological warfare with an intelligence officer named Mahmudi, a snakelike villain worthy of a spy novel who was bent on destroying her life. In an author's note at the end, Ebadi reveals that her intention in writing the book was to "bear witness" to the crimes inflicted against the Iranian people by their own government. "If a government can behave in this way with a Nobel Peace laureate who has access to the platform of world media, and who is herself a lawyer with intimate knowledge of the country's legal system, you can imagine what it does to ordinary Iranians, who have no such means or expertise at their disposal," she writes.

Ebadi's descriptions of living under the regime are studded with surprising and vivid details about everyday life in the once-cosmopolitan country, such as the ban on hotels and restaurants hosting "mixed" private events, such as weddings receptions, where both men and women are present, or her fears that if her daughter laughed too loudly in public, it would draw the unwanted attention of the morality police. She writes how most towns have at least one shop that sells artificial limbs, because Iran has an estimated sixteen million unexploded land mines—the second-highest number in the world—remaining in the ground after the devastating Iran-Iraq War of the 1980s. (Ebadi founded the Mine Clearing Collaboration Campaign in 2004 to address the problem.) These details strike a recurring theme, namely that Iranian citizens have little notion of the scope of their troubles. Until women must themselves tangle with the law, for instance, they have no idea how few rights they truly possess, and thanks to government censorship, most Iranians—despite the existence of those limb shops—do not realize just how dangerous it is to walk down the street. Despite this, people remain deeply unhappy but are afraid to rise up again, which Ebadi speculates is due to the ongoing civil war in neighboring Syria. The Iranian government is backing the brutal regime of Syrian president Bashar al-Assad and, in doing so, is sending a clear and violent message to its people: "If you rise up, we will crush you. . . . We will not be Hosni Mubarak of Egypt, who stepped down. We will be Assad, who would rather torch his country to the ground than relinquish power. The fate of Iran will be the fate of Syria."

As a lawyer, Ebadi became familiar with the quagmire of sharia and civil law, bribes, and political connections that warped Iran's legal system under the Islamic Republic. Her caseload included the brutal rape, torture, and murder of Canadian Iranian photojournalist Zahra Kazemi at the hands of prison guards in 2003, as well as the persecution of several Baha'i leaders by the hard-line Islamist government a few years later. (The Islamic Republic considers the Baha'i religion a heretical sect of Islam and frequently imprisons its followers.) Both cases received international attention but produced no satisfactory result in court.

Shirin Ebadi is an activist and human rights lawyer from Tehran. She founded the Defenders of Human Rights Center in 2001 and won the Nobel Peace Prize in 2003. Her other books include Iran Awakening: A Memoir of Revolution and Hope *(2006) and* The Golden Cage: Three Brothers, Three Choices, One Destiny *(2011).*

Ebadi recalls visiting the home of the family of Omidreza Mirsayafi, a young blogger who was tortured and killed by the government. Ebadi saw quickly that the family had no legal recourse to address their son's death, which was ruled a suicide; she told them she hoped his killers would be punished by God. In the book, she bitterly acknowledges that the only tangible thing she could offer many such parents was a cup of tea.

Ebadi recalls her stunningly ordinary family dinner the night before Ahmadinejad—whose campaign Ebadi described as a populist "gimmick"—was elected president in 2005. Unimpressed by the two more moderate frontrunners, Ebadi did not cast a vote. Her reasoning, though hard won through years of butting heads with a seemingly changeless regime, and the vivid descriptions of that family meal together illustrate how people, even politically well-informed people such as Ebadi, can focus their attention in such a way as to obscure the proverbial writing on the wall. (Elections at that time were competitive and clean, Ebadi writes, because each candidate was vetted by the regime.) In the final days of the campaign, Ahmadinejad visited rural towns and villages, drumming up support with funds that were later found to be drawn from Tehran's public coffers. Promising a comeuppance for the urban elite, he won in a runoff election. Ebadi, familiar with Ahmadinejad's religious extremism from his tenure in Tehran, realized immediately the grave implications of his election.

In 2006, Ebadi joined forces with other female Nobel Peace Prize laureates to found the Nobel Women's Initiative. Meanwhile, in Iran, government scrutiny of her work intensified. A strange man set up a shoeshine kiosk on her dead-end residential street, and Ebadi began carrying a bottle of pepper spray when she walked alone. "I wasn't afraid of thieves; I was afraid of spies," she writes. Ebadi had grown accustomed to regular meetings with a particular intelligence official, who stopped by her office to ask her questions about her work. In 2008, she was assigned a new officer named Mahmudi. Her life would never be the same. Months later, her office was forcibly closed.

Ebadi was not the only one feeling newly constricted by Ahmadinejad's regime. For the first time since the revolution, students and protesters rallied around reform candidates running in the 2009 presidential election. Ebadi was pleasantly surprised by their fervor, and in many ways she was carried away by it herself, confident that the election of a new president would restore her to her work. She conveys her sense of renewed hope so well that readers feel the blow of what happened next: traveling abroad in Spain for a lecture, Ebadi received news that Ahmadinejad had effectively stolen the election—an unthinkable move, even in corrupt Iran—and reelected himself in a landslide.

Outraged, Iranians flooded the streets in what would come to be known as the Green Movement. (Ebadi later writes of the Arab Spring, a chain of uprisings said to have begun in Tunisia in 2010, arguing that Iran's "awakening" came first.) But Ahmadinejad was ready to meet those protests with overwhelming force. The violence of his cronies has been personified in the filmed murder of Neda Agha-Soltan, a female protester who was gunned down by guardsmen in the street. Other protesters, both men and women, were systematically arrested and thrown in prison, where they were raped, tortured, and often killed. The protests stopped, but some Iranians, in a show of solidarity, began climbing to their rooftops in the middle of the night to shout "Allahu akbar!" (God is great!) into the dark. The benign, but in this case loaded, phrase became a sign of defiance. As for Ebadi, who had long been on the government's official "kill list," Ahmadinejad's reelection meant total exile. She is unable to return to Iran even today under Ahmadinejad's successor, Hassan Rouhani.

Ebadi continues her legal and humanitarian work. In 2013 she founded the Centre for Supporters of Human Rights in London, connecting human rights lawyers outside of Iran with those few who are left inside. But the second half of *Until We Are Free* is less about her work and more about the ways in which exile—and Mahmudi's relentless vendetta—has destroyed her personal life. She writes candidly about her own doubts; in one moving scene, even her husband tells her that her work is effectively fruitless. Still, Ebadi compulsively returns to the plight and deep-seated yearning of everyday Iranians in her mind. She writes, "Where did all that mistrust and resentment reside, I wondered. How could it just lie dormant inside so many people, as they went about their days, their multiple jobs, in this city choked with pollution, waiting and waiting for something to get better?"

Until We Are Free was widely praised by literary critics for Ebadi's painful, unflinching honesty, her attention to detail, and her measured, if ultimately pessimistic, assessment of Iran's political future. *Kirkus Reviews* called the book a "captivating and candid story of a woman who took on the Iranian government and survived, despite every attempt to make her fail"; the reviewer for *Publishers Weekly* wrote of Ebadi, "She is an inspiring figure, and her suspenseful, evocative story is unforgettable." In a review for the *Christian Science Monitor*, Denise Hassanzade Ajiri noted, "The book reminds us that tireless human rights activists are also human beings, with their own concerns, fears, attachments, and interests. . . . With her particular obsession in describing every detail, Ebadi does not just narrate a story but paints a scene." *New York Times* reviewer Jenny Nordberg described *Until We Are Free* as "powerful and deeply disturbing," adding, "[Ebadi's] excruciating personal story, glimpsed through her restrained and careful prose, tells of the almost unthinkable cost of one person's battle against a much stronger and very sophisticated enemy."

Molly Hagan

Review Sources

Ajiri, Denise Hassanzade. "*Until We Are Free* Tells of Shirin Ebadi's Fight for Human Rights in Iran." Review of *Until We Are Free: My Fight for Human Rights in Iran,* by Shirin Ebadi. *The Christian Science Monitor,* 23 Mar. 2016, www.csmonitor.com/Books/Book-Reviews/2016/0323/Until-We-Are-Free-tells-of-Shirin-Ebadi-s-fight-for-human-rights-in-Iran. Accessed 6 Oct. 2016.

Nordberg, Jenny. "One for the Oppressed." Review of Until We Are Free: My Fight for Human Rights in Iran, by Shirin Ebadi. *The New York Times* Book Review, 20 Mar. 2016, p. 23.

Review of *Until We Are Free: My Fight for Human Rights in Iran,* by Shirin Ebadi. *Kirkus Reviews,* 12 Dec. 2015, p. 101.

Review of *Until We Are Free: My Fight for Human Rights in Iran*, by Shirin Ebadi. *Publishers Weekly*, 4 Jan. 2016, p. 43.

Waterbury, John. Review of *Until We Are Free: My Fight for Human Rights in Iran*, by Shirin Ebadi. *Foreign Affairs*, May–June 2016, p. 184.

Valiant Ambition
George Washington, Benedict Arnold, and the Fate of the American Revolution

Author: Nathaniel Philbrick (b. 1956)
Publisher: Viking (New York). Illustrated.
448 pp.
Type of work: History
Time: 1775–80
Locale: Colonial America

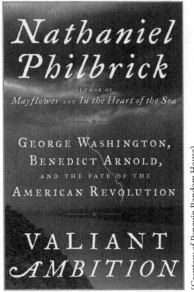

(Courtesy of Penguin Random House)

Nathaniel Philbrick provides an incisive study of the relationship between George Washington and Benedict Arnold, who began as comrades in arms during the Revolutionary War but ended up bitter enemies. Both were daring and fearless soldiers, but what eventually separated them was character. Washington learned to tame his furies and place the common good before his own; Arnold did not, and his name became a synonym for treason.

Principal personages:
GEORGE WASHINGTON, commander in chief of the Continental Army
BENEDICT ARNOLD, a major general in the Continental Army
PEGGY SHIPPEN ARNOLD, his Loyalist wife
HORATIO GATES, a major general in the Continental Army, victor at the Battle of Saratoga and rival of George Washington
JOSEPH REED, a former Continental Army officer turned Pennsylvania politician
JOHN ANDRE, a major in the British Army, Arnold's main contact

Nathaniel Philbrick is fast becoming one of the United States' best-known popular historians. He first gained widespread notice with *In the Heart of the Sea: The Tragedy of the Whaleship* Essex (2000), which won the National Book Award for nonfiction and was made into a 2015 film directed by Ron Howard. Philbrick produced another tale of nautical adventure with *Sea of Glory: America's Voyage of Discovery; The US Exploring Expedition, 1838–1842* (2003), then dove into more mainstream American history in *Mayflower: A Story of Courage, Community, and War* (2006), *The Last Stand: Custer, Sitting Bull, and the Battle of the Little Bighorn* (2010), and *Bunker Hill: A City, a Siege, a Revolution* (2013). Along the way, he has picked up a shelf of prizes to put alongside his National Book Award. With these works Philbrick is continuing a tradition of historical writing that in the United States can be traced back to nineteenth-century masters such as William Hickling Prescott and Francis Parkman.

He produces well-written, serious history for a broad, nonacademic audience. David McCullough is one of the few modern masters of this genre with a comparably eclectic range of subject matter.

Valiant Ambition is the second book of what is shaping up to be a trilogy on the American Revolution. Where *Bunker Hill* looked at the beginning of the war of independence, *Valiant Ambition* takes the story through the middle years of the war, and a projected volume on the Battle of Yorktown would focus attention on the conclusion of the conflict. *Bunker Hill* is a portrait of Boston and its environs as the fulcrum of revolution in 1775; it brought to life a rich lode of dramatis personae, including such well-known figures as Samuel Adams and John Hancock. That work also highlights the largely forgotten role played by Dr. Joseph Warren, who was a mainspring of Patriot resistance until his untimely death at the battle that gives the book its name. *Valiant Ambition* has a geographically wider range, shifting back and forth from the wilds of upstate New York to the well-settled region around New York City and Philadelphia. Chronologically it moves from the end of 1775 to 1780. While inevitably the cast of characters is large, Philbrick primarily focuses on two men, George Washington and Benedict Arnold. In doing so, he has written a modern variant on Plutarch's *Parallel Lives*, which compared and contrasted eminent Greeks and Romans with roughly similar careers. Like Plutarch's biographies, Philbrick's book is a study in character.

On the surface, Washington and Arnold seem to have had much in common. They were both brave to the point of rashness. Both were refugees from the battlefield law of averages, surviving numerous close encounters with death, though here Washington proved the more fortunate, escaping the debilitating wounds that periodically sidelined Arnold. Both men possessed a fierce temper that could explode to stunning effect on those around them. Above all, Washington and Arnold both yearned for the glory won by the sword, which drove them on as they risked their lives and honor in a rebellion against the most powerful empire in the world. What decisively set them apart was that Washington came to realize that he needed to master his passions. He learned to discipline his combative impulses and cultivate strategic patience. Washington always recognized that he served a cause greater than himself, and he submitted to feckless political masters and endured endless frustrations because he understood that he was defending an infant republic, a delicate experiment in popular government.

Such was not the case with Arnold, a swashbuckler who never learned to tolerate slights from military or political superiors. He could only pay lip service to the common good, which he came increasingly to identify with his own reputation and financial security. Arnold never escaped a heroic solipsism; too self-centered to be a republican hero, he was an atavist who more properly belonged to an earlier and more piratical age. Ironically, Philbrick notes, on at least two occasions Arnold attempted to transfer to naval service and lead raids on British shipping. How different Arnold's fate might have been if he had been allowed to engage in a profitably independent war on the high seas. Instead, Arnold's egotism and avarice would tempt him into a treasonous plot that might have changed the course of the Revolutionary War. Until the final betrayal, Washington always loyally supported his tempestuous subordinate. It is the final measure of Arnold's perfidy that he hoped to betray to the British his commander in chief along with the garrison and fortress of West Point.

In the beginning, though, Arnold was one of the darlings of the Revolution. In 1775, he became known as the "American Hannibal" after leading a small army through the trackless wastes of Maine to link up with another American contingent invading Canada. The ultimate American assault on Quebec miscarried, in part because Arnold was wounded at the head of his men. In 1776 Arnold commanded the American force charged with parrying a British thrust south from Canada. The British would descend Lake Champlain, the waterway that formed the traditional invasion route to and from Canada. Arnold constructed a small fleet of gunboats and, in October, fought a naval battle against a superior British squadron near Valcour Island. Though Arnold lost the battle, he won the campaign. His resistance so delayed the British that their invasion was put off until the following year.

Washington displayed an aggressive willingness to fight comparable to that of Arnold as he prepared to defend New York City against a massive British invasion force that arrived by sea. It nearly cost him his army. British naval supremacy in New York Harbor and along the Hudson River rendered Washington's position untenable, and he was

> *Nathaniel Philbrick won the 2000 National Book Award for nonfiction for* In the Heart of the Sea: The Tragedy of the Whaleship Essex *(2000). His work* Mayflower: A Story of Courage, Community, and War *(2006) was a finalist for the 2007 Pulitzer Prize for history.*

briskly chivvied out of New York by General William Howe, who used his command of the water to repeatedly land troops in unexpected places and roll up the American flank. By the end of 1776, Washington had been driven across New Jersey and the Delaware River into Pennsylvania. These were what Thomas Paine, at the time one of Washington's volunteers, described in *The American Crisis* (1776–83) as "the times that try men's souls." Washington's army was melting away and the American cause seemed lost. The commander in chief saved the situation with a brilliant winter campaign that surprised and captured a Hessian garrison at Trenton and overwhelmed a British detachment at Princeton. Washington had retrieved his honor and revived American morale. He realized, though, that it had been a near-run thing. He resolved to pursue a more cautious strategy. He recognized that it was the existence of his army, not the fortunes of a battle, that would win the war. Risking the army risked the revolution. Washington began the hard process of transforming himself from a fighter into a general.

The year 1777 saw Arnold win more battlefield laurels. Despite quarreling with his commander, General Horatio Gates, he played a key role in winning the great victory of Saratoga, which eliminated the British army that had invaded from Canada. General Howe left that invasion force in the lurch and instead advanced on Philadelphia, where he once again bested Washington in battle and captured the city. The American army settled into winter quarters at Valley Forge. Here Washington had to resist the intrigues of the Conway Cabal, an effort by some politicians and military officers to get him replaced as commander in chief by General Gates. Washington survived this political test with his reputation enhanced. Increasingly he was coming to be seen as the sturdy bulwark of the new republic.

Arnold suffered a severe wound to his leg at Saratoga, forcing him into a prolonged period of recuperation for which he was ill-suited and giving him time to mull over his grievances. Arnold's promotion to the rank of major general was held up for political reasons: Congress had imposed a quota of two major generals per state, and Connecticut's slots were filled. Arnold raged at the thought that political appointees stood between him and the rank that he had shed blood earning. He also grew increasingly restive at the financial losses that he, like most Continental Army officers, had suffered while in service. As he convalesced, Arnold was made military governor of newly liberated Philadelphia. He proceeded to use his position to launch a series of questionable business endeavors, seeing no reason not to use his insider knowledge and authority to line his pocket. He also began consorting with wealthy Loyalists who had collaborated with the British during their occupation of the city. He fell in love with Peggy Shippen, who had played a conspicuous part in a fete organized by the British officer John Andre. Arnold's behavior was loudly condemned by Joseph Reed, the leader of the "democratic" faction in Pennsylvania politics, who initiated a congressional investigation of Arnold's behavior in Philadelphia.

Washington tried to help Arnold by getting him back into action. He offered Arnold a field command with his army. Unfortunately, by this point Arnold had other plans. He had reconsidered his loyalties. He had no respect for the politicians who refused to accord him the deference he believed that he deserved, and he convinced himself that a bold stroke that won the war for the British would lead to national reconciliation. He also expected that the British would pay very handsomely for the execution of such a stroke. Arnold's decision to commit treason was enthusiastically seconded by Shippen, who had by then become his wife, and she helped him arrive at an arrangement with Major Andre in New York. Arnold convinced Washington to give him command of the strategically important American outpost of West Point on the Hudson River. His plan was to surrender the place along with its garrison to the British. If the timing was right, he might be able to trap Washington there as well. Only the fortuitous American capture of Andre with compromising papers foiled Arnold's scheme. Arnold escaped to a British warship.

Washington and Arnold began as comrades in arms and ended at opposite extremes of the American revolutionary experience: Washington became the father of his country, while Arnold became the archetypal American traitor. Philbrick's assertion that the discovery of Arnold's treason helped rally American opinion behind the war effort is probably overstated, but he is certainly correct that Arnold's infamy heightened Americans' appreciation of the steadfast virtues embodied by Washington. Philbrick brilliantly demonstrates how Arnold helped shape the way that the new nation saw itself and its founders, albeit in a way that he never could have anticipated.

Daniel P. Murphy

Review Sources

Davidson, John Daniel. "The Seduction of Benedict Arnold." Review of *Valiant Ambition: George Washington, Benedict Arnold, and the Fate of the American Revolution*, by Nathaniel Philbrick. *National Review*, 15 Aug. 2016, pp. 37–39.

Hooper, Brad. Review of *Valiant Ambition: George Washington, Benedict Arnold, and the Fate of the American Revolution*, by Nathaniel Philbrick. *Booklist*, 15 Mar. 2016, p. 18.

Kappanadze, Margaret. Review of *Valiant Ambition: George Washington, Benedict Arnold, and the Fate of the American Revolution*, by Nathaniel Philbrick. *Library Journal*, 1 Mar. 2016, p. 110.

Maslin, Janet. "Benedict Arnold's Road to Betrayal, Map by Map." Review of Valiant Ambition: George Washington, Benedict Arnold, and the Fate of the American Revolution, by Nathaniel Philbrick. *The New York Times*, 13 May 2016, pp. C19+.

Review of *Valiant Ambition: George Washington, Benedict Arnold, and the Fate of the American Revolution*, by Nathaniel Philbrick. *Kirkus Reviews*, 15 Feb. 2016, p. 74.

Review of *Valiant Ambition: George Washington, Benedict Arnold, and the Fate of the American Revolution*, by Nathaniel Philbrick. *The New Yorker*, 6 June 2016, p. 96.

Review of *Valiant Ambition: George Washington, Benedict Arnold, and the Fate of the American Revolution*, by Nathaniel Philbrick. *Publishers Weekly*, 15 Feb. 2016, p. 55.

Waldstreicher, David. "Sympathy for the Devil." Review of Valiant Ambition: George Washington, Benedict Arnold, and the Fate of the American Revolution, by Nathaniel Philbrick. *The New York Times* Book Review, 22 May 2016, p. 27.

The Vegetarian

Author: Han Kang (b. 1970)
Translated from the Korean by Deborah Smith
First published: *Ch'aesikjuuija*, 2007, in South Korea
Publisher: Hogarth (London). 188 pp.
Type of work: Novel
Time: Present day
Locale: Seoul, South Korea

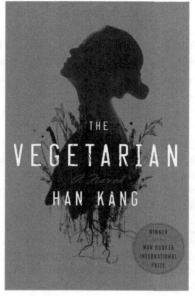

(Courtesy of Penguin Random House)

When Yeong-hye, an unremarkable Korean homemaker, declares herself a vegetarian after having a deeply disturbing dream, her life and the lives of her husband, her sister, and her brother-in-law change in drastic ways. This novel provides an internationally relevant and thought-provoking study of family and mental illness.

Principal characters:
YEONG-HYE, a young woman who becomes a vegetarian
IN-HYE, Yeong-hye's motivated and successful older sister
MR. CHEONG, Yeong-hye's husband
IN-HYE'S HUSBAND, Yeong-hye's brother-in-law, an unnamed artist
JI-WOO, In-hye's young son
YEONG-HO, the brother of Yeong-hye and In-hye

In *The Vegetarian*, readers are given a rare glimpse into the dysfunctions of a Korean family. The story is broken into three parts. In the first part, "The Vegetarian," readers meet Yeong-hye, a young married woman. This first part of the story is narrated by Yeong-hye's status-conscious husband, Mr. Cheong. The second part, "Mongolian Mark," continues with a focus on Yeong-hye, but the story is narrated by Yeong-hye's obsessive brother-in-law. In the final segment of the story, "Flaming Trees," In-hye, Yeong-hye's sister, tells the tale.

One major thematic issue discussed in the novel is family relationships. Although sisters In-hye and Yeong-hye are not particularly close, their family does still celebrate together and rely on each other during difficult times. In-hye and Yeong-hye grow increasingly intertwined as the story progresses, and it is to Yeong-hye's parents and In-hye whom Mr. Cheong turns when he cannot convince his wife to give up her vegetarian diet. Familial violence is revealed when their father physically attacks Yeong-hye for refusing to eat meat, and In-hye later remembers that her sister, after their mother, had taken the brunt of their father's abuse when they were children. The stigma of having a daughter, sister, or wife who does not fit into the expected norms of their society leaves In-hye as the only family member who cares enough to support Yeong-hye after things fall apart.

The meaning of marriage in Korean culture is a secondary focus of the novel. Though four marriages are mentioned, the marriages of the two sisters are the driving force of the story. Their parents' marriage, however, provides a backdrop to understanding the girls' poor choices in husbands. As the novel progresses, the patriarchal nature of South Korean society is made apparent. Mr. Cheong's narration in the first portion of the novel clearly showcases his desires in the marriage as more important than anything his wife may be thinking, feeling, or needing. In-hye's marriage is slightly different, as she is the sole breadwinner, but her husband's selfish ambitions and lack of personal responsibility further display the woman's lack of control. The final marital relationship is Yeong-ho's, and although his marriage is only briefly mentioned in two places, both times it appears to be a fairly stable imitation of the parents' traditional relationship, with Yeong-ho possessed of his father's quick temper.

Faithfulness is another central idea that works alongside family and marriage. A fairly flat character, Mr. Cheong is sexually faithful, but he is never emotionally committed to his marriage. When his wife stops being the mild-mannered doll who can be manipulated to fulfill his desires and needs, he takes the easy route and divorces her. In-hye's marriage struggles more with faithlessness, as her husband leaves all of the economic and emotional responsibility in her hands. His satisfaction with just drifting through life doing what he wants leads to his most egregious sin, his obsession with and abuse of her younger sister. In-hye's husband is more developed than Yeong-hye's husband, but the fact that Kang never gives him a name suggests that this character is less socially important. In-hye sees this as not only a marital failure but a lapse in moral judgment, as her husband has taken advantage of a mentally unstable person.

The infidelity of In-hye's husband results partially from his self-centered belief that his artistic obsessions justify almost any behavior. In his obsession, the sensitive issue of art versus erotica becomes a thematic consideration for the second episode of the novel. In-hye's husband is a video artist, and he has envisioned a film in which two people whose bodies are covered with paintings of flowers emulate pollination of sorts. In his vision, his models make love and the floral patterns merge in a beautiful imitation of nature. When he talks Yeong-hye into being the female model, his male model shrinks at the thought of having intercourse with her, so the film is put on hold until he can talk another artist into turning him into the model who will fulfill the role of sexual partner. After he does this, he initiates a sexual situation with the vulnerable girl, filming each moment of the encounter. Although the video turns out beautifully, his wife's discovery of his infidelity with her sister undermines his ability to ever produce it

A poet, novelist, and professor, Han Kang has won numerous awards for her writing, including the Yi Sang Literary Award, one of South Korea's most prestigious prizes for literature. Originally from Gwangju, South Korea, Kang teaches at the Seoul Institute of the Arts. She has also participated in the University of Iowa International Writing Program.

in a public forum. The episode also raises questions about sexual identity, rape, voyeurism, and the graphic description Kang provides, making a circular connection to what she is protesting in the story itself.

The film is the artist's dream, but more literal dreams are also integral to the novel. The importance of dreams particularly follows the two women, providing them with a psychological depth. Dreams are the instigators of change and a revelation for the characters. Yeong-hye's declaration of vegetarianism is the direct result of a disturbing dream, and when asked why she has chosen to give up meat, she simply answers, "I had a dream," no matter who is asking. The mild-mannered young woman's disturbing dreams show her consuming animal flesh in an almost fiendish way. Ironically, her fear of becoming that almost demonic projection of herself leads her to a rejection of nutrition that ultimately devours her whole being. As the story draws to a close and Yeong-hye lies on her deathbed, In-hye, who has also struggled, tells her, "I have dreams too, you know. Dreams . . . and I could let myself dissolve into them, let them take me over . . . but surely the dream isn't all there is? We have to wake up at some point, don't we?" This revelation of a common thread may have helped her sister earlier in Yeong-hye's illness; however, at this point in Yeong-hye's mental and physical deterioration, it seems to serve more as an outlet of In-hye's fear of her own instability, and it leaves readers wondering whether she will be able to go back to her successful life or if she will succumb to the darkness that has consumed Yeong-hye.

Mental stability is, perhaps, one of the strongest themes brought to light in the novel. Yeong-hye's dreams set her on a journey of self-annihilation, which culminates in a suicide attempt and hospitalization. For her sister, this raises the question of whether she should have done more to protect Yeong-hye when they were young, a dilemma that many readers will understand. Yeong-hye is not the only character to deal with mental issues, as In-hye fights depression after the destruction of her marriage. This aspect adds depth to her character, making her a bit less perfect and more relatable.

Kang's organization of the novel into three sections describing Yeong-hye's experience provides a complicated and detailed glimpse into the thought processes of multiple characters, showing the author's strong grasp of both story and character development. The first portion is narrated by Mr. Cheong, a comparatively uptight businessman who has chosen his wife simply because she was "unremarkable." During the first five years of their marriage, she continues to be quiet and undemanding, but when she has a grotesque dream, she changes. The "completely ordinary wife who went about things without any distasteful frivolousness" becomes someone he cannot accept, upsetting his life in a way that reveals an inner cruelty in this self-centered man. Interspersed through her husband's first-person narration are a few short passages of internal dialogue from Yeong-hye herself, the only instances when readers are exposed to the young woman's own thought processes and the content of her dreams. The second portion of the novel is also narrated by a man, Yeong-hye's brother-in-law. In-hye's husband is a self-proclaimed artist who has never produced anything particularly fantastic and who relies on his wife to financially support his ambitions. When he becomes obsessed with an idea for a video piece, he centers his mania on Yeong-hye, using her vulnerability to fulfill his own erotic desires. The final section of the novel is narrated by In-hye and is split in focus between the sisters as she takes on the burden of caring for her mentally ill sibling.

Reviews of the novel have been positive. Terry Hong, in a review for *Library Journal*, called Deborah Smith's translation "seamless." The organizational structure of the novel's three sections that could be read as separate stories is another area lauded by reviewers. Colleen Lutz Clemens, writing for *World Literature Today*, for instance, pointed out that the narrative structure enhances the "gulf between its characters." Hong also noted that "while Yeong-hye remains the crux of the disturbing narrative, her voice is rarely heard. Instead, she's ignored, interpreted, spoken over, and silenced to devastating effect" throughout the triple narrative. Joanna Walsh, in a review for the *New Statesman*, drew a comparison between Kang and such classical authors as Herman Melville and Franz Kafka and suggested that Hang is a Korean Margaret Atwood. The novel has only limited questions regarding its quality, with the main concern being a Korean reviewer's concern that the characterization is too extreme.

Although this is not Han Kang's debut novel, it is her first piece that has been translated into English. Her fresh voice and Yeong-hye's plight will add to any library collection that strives to challenge the cultural status quo, especially when the voices of the marginalized are sought. In recognition of Kang's remarkable achievement and Smith's excellent translation, *The Vegetarian* received the prestigious Man Booker International Prize in 2016.

Theresa L. Stowell, PhD

Review Sources

Clemens, Colleen Lutz. Review of *The Vegetarian*, by Han Kang. *World Literature Today*, vol. 90, no. 3/4, 2016, pp. 91–92. *Humanities International Complete*, search.ebscohost.com/login.aspx?direct=true&db=hlh&AN=115195778&site=ehost-live&scope=site. Accessed 12 Jan. 2017.

Hong, Terry. Review of *The Vegetarian*, by Han Kang. *Library Journal*, vol. 140, no. 20, 2015, p. 94. *Education Research Complete*, search.ebscohost.com/login.aspx?direct=true&db=ehh&AN=112171802&site=ehost-live&scope=site. Accessed 12 Jan. 2017.

Walsh, Joanna. "First Refusal." Review of *The Vegetarian*, by Han Kang. *New Statesman*, 20 Feb. 2015, p. 51. *Social Sciences Full Text*, search.ebscohost.com/login.aspx?direct=true&db=ssf&AN=101078582&site=ehost-live&scope=site. Accessed 12 Jan. 2017.

Version Control

Author: Dexter Palmer
Publisher: Pantheon Books. 512 pp.
Type of work: Novel
Time: Near future
Locale: New Jersey

Dexter Palmer's second novel, Version Control*, is a time-travel epic and a domestic drama that explores modern life through the lens of technology and science in a near or alternate future.*

Principal characters:
REBECCA WRIGHT, a recovering alcoholic who works for a dating website called Lovability
PHILIP STEINER, her husband and a brilliant physicist working on a major project
ALICIA MERRILL, his former graduate student and current laboratory coworker
WOODY WRIGHT, her father, a Unitarian minister
KATHRYN, her lifelong best friend and a serial dater
CARSON, his laboratory coworker, a physicist, Kathryn's sometimes boyfriend
SEAN, their young son

(Courtesy of Pantheon)

In a near future or perhaps an alternate universe, a woman named Rebecca Wright feels ill at ease. She believes that the world is plagued by "a certain subtle wrongness," as if that at first glance, everything appears as it should, but in looking deeper, everything also appears intangibly and slightly not quite right. Rebecca is a recovering alcoholic and has been sober for two years. She works for a dating website called Lovability, which is also the same site through which she met her husband, Philip, who is a brilliant physicist. Recently, Rebecca feels that Philip has been emotionally distant. Since the death of their young son, Sean, he has become increasingly involved with and distracted by a long-running special project in which he and several others are developing a machine he calls a causality violation device. The device is complicated, and Philip, in an interview for a popular science television show tries valiantly to explain it without uttering its crudest description—time machine.

The causality violation device, to Philip's enduring horror, appears to be a failure. Funds for the project are drying up, and each experiment with over three-hundred test runs on the device turn up the same disappointing result. But as a scientist, Philip is used to failure and he believes that failure drives him and the entire scientific field. In an effort to remind himself of this, he hops out of bed each morning and performs

(Courtesy of Bill Wadman)

Dexter Palmer is the author of the 2010 novel The Dream of Perpetual Motion.

push-ups "to the point of failure." He reasons "If I didn't do them to the point of failure," he reasons, "I'd probably be stronger. But getting stronger isn't the point. The failure is the point." He applies this logic to his work, knowing that if some experiments did not fail, others would not succeed. Still, it is hard for Philip to not feet frustration and loss of hope as he continues to work on the losing end of the spectrum while his colleagues pass him by.

The realistic grind of Philip and Rebecca's unhappy marriage—and the time machine's prominent place within it—makes Dexter Palmer's sprawling second novel, *Version Control*, as much a domestic drama as it is a science fiction epic. A reviewer for *Kirkus* compared the novel to one of Jonathan Franzen's "state-of-the-union" novels, calling to mind his 2010 novel *Freedom* or his 2015 work *Purity*, which explore larger political issues like computer hacking or climate change alongside the subtleties and realities of human relationships. Palmer, who coincidentally shares a literary agent with Franzen, frames *Version Control* in much the same way with the exception that he explores contemporary life through the lens of the future. Big data and privacy figure prominently into his story, and interactions with technology and corporate entities shape the way his characters move about in their lives, despite taking such interactions for granted.

Dating website Lovability, for instance, sells its user information to corporations, and when Rebecca video chats with her father, a Unitarian preacher named Woody, she has to endure the ads that pop-up around his face. These irritating invasions would not seem out of place in our own world, but for Palmer, they foreshadow more sinister intrusions of privacy. When Rebecca goes to the mall to shop for a dress, mannequins with life-like eyes follow her around the store while her body is measured and her online shopping profile is identified. There are no racks of clothes in these stores. Instead, a saleswoman with a tablet approaches Rebecca. There are three dresses displayed on the tablet's screen, and they each fit to Rebecca's size and their styles are based on her online purchasing history.

Stranger still are the regular communications from the president of the United States, who is shown sitting at his desk and speaking to the camera as he introduces every television program on every channel. When Rebecca and her friend Kathryn go out to eat, he appears on their electronic menu in order to lament about the sad state of affairs in the Dakota territories, which is a minor subplot in the novel and involves secession and violence in those states. The president refers to the women by name and, using an identifying algorithm it seems, is able to ascertain facts about them. Based on what they have ordered, the president guesses that Kathryn and Rebecca are mother and daughter because only Kathryn has ordered alcohol. In exchange for this interruption, the president offers to pay for their dessert.

Palmer's rendering of this almost-present is striking in its balance between technological innovations a reader can easily imagine and those that are at first unimaginable yet could take place if the world and technology allow it. Rebecca often contemplates technology and whether it has shaped her own desires and interests. Is her trust misplaced, she wonders, and is its basis so influenced and molded by technology that her trust is not truly hers? Along those lines she wonders if she chose the blue dress because she truly liked it or because the data and technology told her she did.

Palmer's academic background can be seen as an influence in *Version Control* as well as in his first novel, *The Dream of Perpetual Motion* (2010). Palmer earned his PhD in English literature from Princeton University, where he specialized in the cerebral works of writers like James Joyce, William Gaddis, and the challenging postmodernist Thomas Pynchon. One can also recognize in Palmer's novels what some critics have characterized as a variation of steampunk, the science-fiction subgenre that combines futurism with the aesthetics of nineteenth-century steam-powered technology. In *The Dream of Perpetual Motion*, for example, a man narrates his life story while trapped on an airship powered by a perpetual motion machine. He is with a cryogenically frozen body of an inventor named Prospero and the disembodied voice of his daughter Miranda. Prospero and Miranda are characters in Shakespeare's *The Tempest*, which is a story that also figures heavily in the plot. Joyce's masterpiece *Ulysses* appears briefly in *Version Control* when Philip, who is reading the book, describes it as "not a story" but "a system of the world." The reader may then apply this simple description of one author's work to *Version Control* in particular, which does not so much move forward as a traditional story might, but instead blossoms outward with all of its branches leading back to one event: the death of Philip and Rebecca's young son.

Philip began his work on the causality violation device long before his son was killed, but the tragic car accident gives Philip's work an unspoken weight and urgency. It is not as if Philip pines to finish the device in order to see his son again. Rather, Palmer appears to go out of his way to not cast the device as anything a reader might recognize as a traditional time machine found through literature and films where the travel aspect of time travel is emphasized. In *Version Control*, Palmer is more interested in the implications of such a device: If a life is constructed by chance, with each choice a person makes solidifying one narrative instead of another, how does a person live in such a way as to ensure the best possible outcome?

This of course is a question that cannot be answered, but it is one that Palmer exhaustively explores. Some passages, particularly ones involving complicated philosophical arguments between Woody and Philip, are a bit dense, but as the novel's complex structure reveals itself, so do its dizzying implications. Software developers use the term "version control" to organize and keep track of different versions of programs. For instance, in the novel, Philip and his lab coworkers collaborate to write the code that runs the causality violation device. On a suggestion, they begin working separately, each writing code on a separate copy of the master. Over time the problems become obvious: How far afield has each coder strayed? How will they reconcile all of the versions of code to create one definitive master? The anecdote is illustrative of the implications of the device on chance and choice and the multiverse, the theory on which Palmer's novel hangs.

The multiverse theory says that there is an infinite number of universes. Contained in that infinite number are universes in which, hypothetically speaking, Dexter Palmer writes *Version Control*, Dexter Palmer writes a slightly different version of *Version Control*, and Dexter Palmer never writes *Version Control*—and on and on. If the number of universes is truly infinite and without end, there is then a universe for every choice an individual has ever made. Alicia Merrill, a straightforward character who works in Philip's lab, explains, "One of the hard things to deal with in life is the fact that you destroy potential information whenever you make a decision. You could even say that's essentially what regret is," Alicia continues: "a profound problem of incomplete information."

No wonder Rebecca feels so disoriented. In a multiverse, how would she ever know which timeline is the "right" one for her and her happiness? Such sleight-of-hand in which dense theory is loaded with emotional weight is Palmer's forte. *Version Control* is quite long and at times a bit slow, but viewed as a system rather than a story, the novel continues to unfold itself long after it is over. The novel is not as much a narrative as it is a way in which to view the universe, the modern world, and the choices that make us who we are.

Molly Hagan

Review Sources

Heller, Jason. "'Version Control' Is a Dizzying Elevation of the Time-Travel Tale."
    Review of *Version Control*, by Dexter Palmer. *NPR*, 26 Feb. 2016, www.npr.
    org/2016/02/26/467133235/version-control-is-a-dizzying-elevation-of-the-time-
    travel-tale. Accessed 15 Oct. 2016.
Hightower, Nancy. "Best Science Fiction and Fantasy for February." Review of
    Version Control, by Dexter Palmer. *The Washington Post*, 16 Feb. 2016, www.
    washingtonpost.com/entertainment/books/best-science-fiction-and-fantasy-for-
    february/2016/02/16/0187f10a-d02d-11e5-abc9-ea152f0b9561_story.html. Ac-
    cessed 15 Oct. 2016.
Review of *Version Control*, by Dexter Palmer. *Kirkus*, 8 Dec. 2015, www.kirkusre-
    views.com/book-reviews/dexter-palmer/version-control/. Accessed 15 Oct. 2016.
Review of *Version Control*, by Dexter Palmer. *Publishers Weekly*, 1 Feb. 2016, www.
    publishersweekly.com/978-0-307-90759-2. Accessed 15 Oct. 2016.
"Time Travel from H.G. Wells to 'Version Control.'" Review of *Version Control*, by
    Dexter Palmer. *The Economist*, 6 June 2016, www.economist.com/blogs/pros-
    pero/2016/06/science-fiction. Accessed 15 Oct. 2016.

The View from the Cheap Seats

Author: Neil Gaiman (b. 1960)
Publisher: William Morrow (New York). 522 pp.
Type of work: Essays

(Courtesy of HarperCollins Publishers)

In award-winning novelist and comic book writer Neil Gaiman's first long work of non-fiction, he has collected some of his favorite pieces, delving into his ideas about reading, fiction, writers, and other sundry topics.

Neil Gaiman has built a writing career on shifting genre and medium. He made his name in the late 1980s in comic books and since then has written novels for children and adults, as well as screenplays and teleplays. Gaiman started his career as a journalist, and all through publishing his other works, he continued to write essays, speeches, and book introductions. The best of what he estimated to be a total of three hundred pieces was collected in the hefty volume that is *The View from the Cheap Seats*. The book opens with a dedication to his son: "For Ash, who is new, for when he is grown. These were some of the things your father loved and said and cared about and believed, a long time ago." Though Gaiman has yet to produce anything like a memoir or autobiography, his varied musings on writers, writing, his influences, and experiences in this collection provide a picture of Gaiman the writer as clearly as any book written expressly for that purpose. As the reviewer for Kirkus notes, "if the idea of going on a long, rambling walk with Gaiman and asking him about his influences is appealing, this is the book for you."

The essays are grouped by subject into ten sections of varying length; section nine, for example, only contains a single piece, the "Make Good Art" speech Gaiman gave as the 2012 commencement speech at the University of the Arts. Though the book is over five hundred pages long and features individual pieces, the longest essay is only fifteen pages and most of the others range from three to seven pages. Each piece provides a look into Gaiman's personality and views; his desires for himself and the world; his interests in writers, music, and film; and his own reading and writing processes. As a result, the reading experience is fast and filled with tidbits and profundities, although (as many reviewers noted) the book does get occasionally repetitive as certain subjects and anecdotes appear multiple times across pieces and chapters.

Reviewers have been primarily positive in their commentary about *The View from the Cheap Seats*. *NPR Books* points out the strength of tone with "his musings shine with wit, understatement, and a warm lack of pretention" and concludes that the book "is not only invaluable, but engrossing." A review from the *Guardian* adds that the book is "hugely enjoyable, thoughtful, and wise" and "like a series of thoughts for the day via the enthusiastic worldview of one of our most inquisitive writers, it's a perfect antidote to cynicism and a paean to the power of reading."

Gaiman devotes the most space in the book to discussions of and with other influential writers. Each of these pieces shares either an anecdote, if Gaiman knew the writer, or a story that establishes that writer's significance in Gaiman's life. Gaiman reveals that as a child he was a voracious reader, and accordingly, his pool of influences is wide and varied. In his first chapter, "Some Things I Believe," for instance, he provides a speech he gave to MythCon in 2004 in which he talks about C. S. Lewis, J. R. R. Tolkien, and G. K. Chesterton. He extolls Lewis as "the first person who made me want to be a writer," while his relationship with Tolkien was a bit more complicated. He explains that he decided to be a writer, but also that he wanted to have been the writer of the Lord of the Rings series. With the books already written and barring travel to alternate universes where the books had not yet been written, he concluded that he could not write them, but that he would write. He also discusses his admiration of Chesterton's masterful use of words. He concludes his tribute with strong words: "And without those three writers, I would not be here today." In chapter six, "Introductions and Contradictions," he expands on his tribute to Chesterton with a short essay titled "The Mystery of G. K. Chesterton's Father Brown" while he only briefly comments on Lewis and Tolkien in other essays. Additional writers noted throughout the book include (but are not limited to) Harlan Ellison, Geoff Notkin, Fritz Leiber, Ray Bradbury, Edgar Allan Poe, Rudyard Kipling, H. G. Wells, H. P. Lovecraft, Stephen King, and James Thurber.

Throughout the book, Gaiman also provides memorial essays for writers and other artists who are friends. In these pieces, his relationships are noted through anecdotes and honest commentary on their personalities and writing. For instance, in chapter two, he provides the forward he wrote for the book *Hitchhiker: A Biography of Douglas Adams*. As he relates the moment when he heard about Adams's death, readers get a sense of his profound grief over the loss of his friend. His admiration for Adams is established in his note that "he had never been a novelist, not really, despite having been an internationally bestselling novelist who had written several books which are, a quarter of

Neil Gaiman is a writer known for his work in comics, fiction, and film. He has won numerous awards, including the Hugo Award for Best Novel, the Nebula Award for Best Novel, and the Carnegie Medal.

a century later, becoming seen as classics . . . I think that perhaps what Douglas was probably something we don't even have a word for yet. . . someone whose dreams and ideas, practical or impractical, are always the size of a planet, and who is going to keep going forward, and taking the rest of us with him." He also pays tribute to Terry Pratchett, with whom he collaborated on the novel *Good Omens*. Though there are two pieces on Pratchett in the book, the closing essay, "A Slip of the Keyboard: Terry Pratchett," is a heartfelt tribute to a fellow writer who was not only influential to a young journalist and a partner, but a friend. Written as the introduction to Pratchett's nonfiction collection *A Slip of the Keyboard*, the essay reveals Pratchett's almost constant and feverish passion that goaded him into writing. Gaiman discusses throughout what writing means to him and what drives him to do it, but in this essay on Pratchett, he is in the unique position of being able to identify and explain these things in another writer. Collected in this fashion, Gaimain's body of nonfiction work appears to have been, at least in part, a project of celebrating and defining creativity and the artistic process. Essays such as those about Adams and Pratchett give the book larger scope than a memoir would do.

The single chapter that has only one piece is "Make Good Art," a commencement speech given in 2012. In this chapter, Gaiman offers advice to a group of college graduates. His advice is simple, including remarks such as, "The things I did because I was excited, and wanted to see them exist in reality, have never let me down, and I've never regretted the time I spent on any of them." The most inspirational message of the chapter is "Life is sometimes hard. Things go wrong, in life and in love and in business and in friendship and in health and in all the other ways that life can go wrong. And when things get tough, this is what you should do. Make good art." Gaiman has noted in interviews that this piece was a last-minute addition to the text, and that he sees it as a thesis of sorts for the book up to that point.

In addition to the praise of those who influenced him, the tributes to people he knows, and the encouragement to pursue art, Gaiman provides quite a bit of information about his own prolific career and touches on miscellaneous issues that will reach readers from a myriad of interest levels. From television and film writing to journalism to novels, Gaiman's writing has been influenced by multiple genres and has been influential, in turn, as a result of his unique style. Chapters on science fiction, comics, and fairy tales provide a platform for his fans to learn about his own works as well as his relationships with his contemporaries in these fields and those writers he admires. In "Films and Movies and Me" he talks about *The Bride of Frankenstein*, *MirrorMask*, and *Doctor Who*. In "Music and the People Who Make It," he gives tribute to his friend Tori Amos and memorializes Lou Rccd. In his final chapter, "The View from the Cheap Seats: Real Things," he once again touches the hearts of his readers when he reveals that he did not want to attend the Oscars when the film version of *Coraline* was nominated because it was on the anniversary of his father's death. Ironically, while walking past the cameras, this man notices, "'I'm invisible'" and concludes, "I feel as if I've sleepwalked invisibly through one of the most melancholy days of my life. There are glamorous parties that evening, but I don't go to any of them, preferring to sit in a hotel lobby with good friends." In stark contrast to his experience at the Oscars, Gaiman next relates his experiences visiting Syrian refugees living in refugee camps in "So Many Ways to Die in Syria Now," appealing for help for the helpless living in often deplorable conditions. After nearly a whole volume of discussing art and making things up, it is a sharp dose of realism.

Theresa L. Stowell

Review Sources

East, Ben. "The View from the Cheap Seats Review—Wisest of Worldviews." Rev. of *The View from the Cheap Seats* by Neil Gaiman. *The Guardian*, 3 July 2016, https://www.theguardian.com/books/2016/jul/03/view-from-cheap-seats-neil-gaiman-review. Accessed on 26 Sept. 2016.

Heller, Jason. "Neil Gaiman's Nonfiction, Seen from the 'Cheap Seats.'" *NPR Books*, 31 May 2016, http://www.npr.org/2016/05/31/479728667 /neil-gaimans-nonfiction-seen-from-the-cheap-seats. Accessed on 26 Sept. 2016.

Malone, Tyler. "Neil Gaiman on Making Art, Mistakes and His *View from the Cheap Seats*." *Los Angeles Times*, 24 June 2016, http://www.latimes.com/books /jacket-copy/la-ca-jc-neil-gaiman-20160616-snap-story.html. Accessed on 31 Oct. 2016.

Rev. of *The View from the Cheap Seats* by Neil Gaiman. *Kirkus Reviews*, 13 Apr. 2016 https://www.kirkusreviews.com/book-reviews/neil-gaiman/the-view-from-the-cheap-seats/. Accessed on 31 Oct. 2016.

Rev. of *The View from the Cheap Seats* by Neil Gaiman. *Publishers Weekly*, 29 Aug. 2016, http://www.publishersweekly.com/978-0-0622-6226-4. Accessed on 31 Oct. 2016.

Vinegar Girl

Author: Anne Tyler (b. 1941)
Publisher: Hogarth (New York). 224 pp.
Type of work: Novel
Time: Present day
Locale: Baltimore, Maryland

In Vinegar Girl, *protagonist Kate Battista, who has always taken care of her father and her little sister, must take control of her own destiny after her father asks her to marry his lab assistant.*

Principal characters:
KATE BATTISTA, preschool teacher
DR. LOUIS BATTISTA, her father, a brilliant scientist
PYOTR SHCHERBAKOV (ALSO KNOWN AS PYODER CHERBAKOV), Louis Battista's lab assistant and her potential beau
BUNNY BATTISTA, her fifteen-year-old sister
THEA BATTISTA, her dead mother
MRS. DARLING, head teacher at the daycare where she works

(Courtesy of Penguin Random House)

Vinegar Girl is a part of the Hogarth Shakespeare series. This series provides contemporary reinterpretations of some of William Shakespeare's most popular plays. The authors involved in the project are all popular writers familiar to British and American audiences, such as Jeanette Winterson, Howard Jacobson, and Margaret Atwood.

Vinegar Girl is Anne Tyler's reimagined *Taming of the Shrew*. In *Taming of the Shrew*, Baptista has two daughters: Katherina (the shrew) and Bianca, her prettier and more desirable sister. Baptista will not hear the petitions of Bianca's many suitors until his eldest daughter is married. Petruchio comes to town for a rich wife, agrees to marry Katherina, and then woos and tricks her into marriage. Petruchio then takes her home and denies her food, sleep, and new clothes until she becomes submissive and obedient. The play endures in popularity, though many modern readers have taken issue with the plot, often inexplicable behavior of the characters, the abusive behavior of Petruchio, and what many have interpreted as the sexism of the play. Anne Tyler has stated that she hates all of Shakespeare's plays, but *Taming of the Shrew* in particular, which led to her decision to rewrite it.

In Anne Tyler's hands, Katherina becomes Kate Battista, a grouchy twenty-nine-year-old preschool teacher who takes care of her widower father and younger sister. Kate is not the shrew that inspired her, but is witty, sharp-tongued, and lacks tact and understanding of social conventions. She was kicked out of college in her sophomore year and never tried to complete a degree. She has taught preschool for six years, a job she does not enjoy and that both she and the children know she is not suited for, and satisfies her interest in botany through gardening. Her father, Louis Battista, is a scientist sure that he is on the brink of a research breakthrough. He asks Kate to marry his brilliant lab assistant, Pyotr, whose visa is about to expire.

Reviews of the book are mixed. Positive reviews focus on Tyler's writing more than the story itself. Most reviewers have noted the book's fun and readability. Most hailed the substitution of the green card marriage for an arranged marriage as a brilliant interpretation. Many also appreciated Tyler's elements of screwball comedy and her signature fluidity of her characters and depth of family dynamics. Tyler removed the play's subplots, such as Bianca and her suitors, and softened most of the characters, Kate and Pyotr in particular, to make them both more believable and palatable. Whether Tyler's resulting novel is a sweet love story about a woman taming herself, or a somewhat unsuccessful experiment in retelling is where critics differ most significantly. Heller McAlpin, reviewing for *NPR*, called the book "a fizzy cocktail of a romantic comedy, far more sweet than acidic, about finding a mate who appreciates you for your idiosyncratic, principled self—no taming necessary." The reviewer for *Kirkus Reviews*, however, says Tyler's "special qualities as a writer don't make a very good fit with the original" and the book is "neither a faithful retelling nor a trenchant counter tale, though agreeable enough as an afternoon's entertainment."

Anne Tyler is an award-winning author who earned the Pulitzer Prize in 1988 for the novel Breathing Lessons. *In addition to writing novels, Tyler has produced a number of short stories and children's books.*

At the beginning of the book, Kate is in a bit of a rut. She takes care of her father and his house; though he is dependent on her, he does not value her as he should. Despite possessing a considerable intelligence and a love of botany, Kate has kept her job teaching preschool partially because she does not know what else to do. She is allowed to retain the job even when the school's headmistress reprimands her for being "flippant" with a parent and pointing out that Kate needs to "develop some social skills. Some tact, some restraint, some diplomacy." Kate's snarky comments, which are often spoken aloud, are a source of humor throughout the book. Although Kate is snide and combative with most everyone else, Kate is uncharacteristically obedient to her father.

While Shakespeare's heroine fights marriage proposals at all turns, Kate has not had a real romantic relationship. In fact, she is rather confused by them. She clumsily flirts with Adam Barnes, a coworker at the preschool, but quickly finds herself out of her depth. She wishes that she had had a better example in her parents' marriage, or in her mother when she was alive. Later in the novel, the narrator tells readers that Kate "had always been such a handful—a thorny child, a sullen teenager, a failure as college student," and this is how Kate sees herself.

When her father first proposes to Kate that she marry Pyotr to save him from deportation, pointing out her lack of romantic prospects, she is furious. Bunny, her younger sister modeled loosely on Shakespeare's Bianca, also protests the proposed marriage. She tells Kate bluntly that their father is treating her poorly: "'What are you?' she asked Kate. 'Chattel? . . . We are supposed to be the center of his life,' Bunny said. 'What is it with him? The man forgets for months at a stretch that we even exist, but at the same time he thinks he has the right to tell us who we can ride in cars with and who we should marry.'" Bunny's desire to stand up for her sister makes her so unpleasant to Pyotr that he later unjustly accuses her of criminal activity, the only thing that truly upsets his burgeoning relationship with Kate. After her initial anger and Louis and Pyotr's desperate efforts to persuade her, however, Kate agrees to the marriage. Some reviewers found this enjoyable and believable, but some did not: James Walton for the *Telegraph* suggested that "the real explanation for whatever Tyler's Kate does is that someone did something similar in a play in the 1590s."

One positive aspect of this modern retelling is that Pyotr is a much kinder and gentler version of Petruchio. Where Petruchio and Kathryn insult each other in the beginning of their courtship, Pyotr is always pleasant. This does not mean that Pyotr is saved from Kate's verbal barbs, and Kate's interplay with Pyotr's bluntness and sometimes curiously constructed English is another significant source of comedy in the novel. While their relationship did begin as a sham marriage, the convenience does eventually turn into romance. The reviewer for *Kirkus* noted that, despite their short and uncomfortable courtship, the two genuinely do care for and respect each other. While in Shakespeare's *Shrew*, Petruchio employs abusive behavior to tame the headstrong Katherina into submission, Kate becomes more agreeable as she and Pyotr get to know and genuinely fall for each other, and, as Jane Smiley for the *New York Times* noted, once Kate understands that the marriage could "lead to independence and even pleasure."

As Kate finds her way to some happiness, she and Bunny switch characters in an example of the kind of character depth and fluidity that Tyler is known for. Bunny is an attractive, boy-crazy fifteen-year-old who is popular at school and has an active social life. Though Kate finds her sister shallow, Bunny has always been the more pleasant and socially adept of the two. Bunny, who has been unpleasant to Pyotr throughout the novel, finally berates Kate for changing so much and becoming sweet, while Bunny herself turns into something of a shrew.

One surprising characterization is in Louis Battista. Tyler has turned Shakespeare's rather despicable father into an absent-minded but ultimately well-meaning professor. His desire to keep Pyotr in the country is primarily selfish, as Pyotr is the first assistant to truly find Battista's work worthy of praise, but he is not as insensitive to his older daughter's feelings as it first appears. Nonetheless, he does not realize that Kate does not understand his love for her, and it is not until one evening of drinking wine that he admits that he has been selfish in keeping her home because he likes being around her. Prior to this discussion, Kate had always felt that she had lost her father's approval after she was expelled from college.

Vinegar Girl is a quick, and overall enjoyable, reading experience. The novel ultimately reflects the plot and intent of the source material, even as Tyler has attempted to justify some of the action with explanations that might satisfy a twenty-first century audience. While Tyler does not turn the play, controversial for its treatment of women, into a feminist manifesto of any sort, she does warmly portray the inner working of an offbeat family, and gives Kate the room to discover herself.

Theresa L. Stowell, PhD

Review Sources:

Charles, Ron. "Anne Tyler Loathes Shakespeare. So She Decided to Rewrite One of His Plays." Review of Vinegar Girl, by Anne Tyler. *Washington Post*, 21 June 2016. www.washingtonpost.com/entertainment/books/in-a-rare-interview-anne-tyler-talks-about-her-unusual-new-novel/2016/06/21/640b99c0-3311-11e6-8ff7-7b6c1998b7a0_story.html. Accessed on 13 Oct. 2016.

McAlpin, Heller. "Fizzy *Vinegar Girl* Tames Shrewishness to Sparkle." Review of *Vinegar Girl*, by Anne Tyler. *NPR*, 21 June 2016. www.npr.org/2016/06/21/482023595/fizzy-vinegar-girl-tames-shrewishness-to-sparkle. Accessed on 13 Oct. 2016.

Smiley, Jane. "Touch Up Your Shakespeare: Anne Tyler Recasts The Taming of the Shrew for Our Time." Review of Vinegar Girl, by Anne Tyler. *The New York Times*, 6 July 2016. http://www.nytimes.com/2016/07/10/books/review/touch-up-your-shakespeare-anne-tyler-recasts-the-taming-of-the-shrew-for-our-time.html. Accessed on 13 Oct. 2016.

Review of *Vinegar Girl* by Anne Tyler. *Kirkus Reviews*, 15 Mar. 2016. https://www.kirkusreviews.com/book-reviews/anne-tyler/vinegar-girl/. Accessed on 13 Oct. 2016.

Walton, James. "*Vinegar Girl* by Anne Tyler, Review: 'Hardly a Shrew, Not Really a Taming.'" Review of *Vinegar Girl*, by Anne Tyler. *Telegraph*, 18 June 2016. http://www.telegraph.co.uk/books/what-to-read/vinegar-girl-by-anne-tyler-review-hardly-a-shrew-not-really-a-ta/. Accessed on 13 Oct. 2016.

The Wangs vs. the World

Author: Jade Chang (b. 1976)
Publisher: Houghton Mifflin Harcourt (Boston). 368 pp.
Type of work: Novel
Time: 2008
Locales: Bel-Air, Santa Barbara, Vernon, and Twentynine Palms, California; Phoenix, Arizona; El Paso and Austin, Texas; New Orleans; Opelika, Alabama; Atlanta, Georgia; High Point, North Carolina; Helios, New York; Taipei, Taiwan; Beijing and Gaofu, China

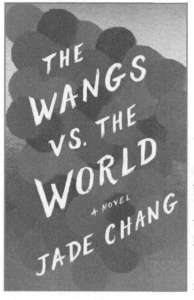

(Courtesy of Houghton Mifflin Harcourt)

A bittersweet debut novel, The Wangs vs. the World *humorously and poignantly portrays the effects of the 2008 recession on a fragmented Chinese American family. The Wangs, a family of individuals each with distinctive personalities and ranging in age from mid-teens to mid-fifties, overcome their differences to reunite in a common cause during an epic cross-country road trip.*

Principal characters:

CHARLES "BABA" WANG, a.k.a. Wang Da Qian, a Chinese American entrepreneur
SAINA WANG, a.k.a. Jiejie, his eldest daughter, an artist living in upstate New York
ANDREW WANG, his son, a college student and aspiring stand-up comedian
GRACE WANG, a.k.a. Meimei, his teenage daughter
BARBRA WANG, a.k.a. Hu Yue Ling, his second wife
AMA, his former wet nurse
MAY LEE, Charles's deceased first wife and the mother of his children

As *The Wangs vs. the World* opens, disaster has struck the titular family. Protagonist and family patriarch Charles Wang is the middle-aged father of three children, who range in age from sixteen to twenty-eight. He is a Chinese immigrant from Taiwan, his family having fled mainland China during the latter stages of the Chinese Civil War, leaving their ancestral lands behind following the Communist takeover. Charles first came to the United States as a single man in the 1970s, sent by his father, a manufacturer of synthetic urea for use in fertilizer, to approach similar American firms. However, on the flight over, he had a brainstorm when he read the label of a bar of soap in the airplane's bathroom and saw that one of the ingredients was urea. Based on that inspiration, Charles carved out an empire founded on urea-based cosmetics that were pumped out in vast quantities from an expanding network of factories. He married a beautiful but brainless Chinese American woman who gave birth to three intelligent, attractive children—Saina, Andrew, and Grace—before dying in a tragic accident. Charles then acquired a former movie star's mansion in Bel-Air, a fleet of pricey vehicles, a second wife, and a crowd of wealthy acquaintances—all the trappings of the good life.

Then he loses everything. All of his possessions—home, furniture, factories, cars—are seized in foreclosure following an aggressive and ill-advised financial overextension of his business just before the 2008 investment banking collapse and resultant recession. With nowhere else to turn, Charles decides to seek refuge with his adult daughter, Saina, who owns a roomy, century-old farmhouse in upstate New York.

Unbeknownst to Charles, Saina has suffered her own recent disasters. A commercially and critically successful performance artist until her last exhibit created a storm of protest, she has retreated from the glitz of New York City to lick her wounds in a village in the Catskill Mountains and is recovering from the collapse of her volatile love affair with a handsome but fickle artist. Despite her own problems, Saina answers the call of family and agrees to let her father, stepmother, and siblings stay at her home.

In a borrowed 1980 Mercedes station wagon and with a secret cache of hoarded hundred-dollar bills, Charles sets out on a road trip with his taciturn Taiwan-born wife, Barbra (who married him for his money after the death of his first wife), and his elderly nanny, Ama. Along the way they collect Charles's other two children: his rebellious, fashionable, sexually precocious, suicide-obsessed teenaged daughter, Grace, whose exclusive private boarding school Charles can no longer afford; and his handsome, witty son, Andrew, attending college in Arizona.

The Wang family's meandering trip northeast is a series of lessons in humility, during which everyone draws closer thanks to their shared misery. Along the way, Charles and his passengers keep in touch with family members, friends, and business contacts (including Charles's high-priced lawyer, still on retainer, who is working on a clandestine project for his client) via cell phones, knowing that their cell phone accounts could be shut down at any time for nonpayment. They stay overnight with Ama's daughter, Kathy, in her tacky home near a Marine Corps base and dine on hot dogs. They stay in inexpensive motels, sleeping on rough-textured sheets. They take advantage of the hospitality of scattered friends and relatives, and they endure the slow deterioration of their vehicle, which ultimately loses worn-out parts, spins out of control, and is demolished in a spectacular crash in which the passengers miraculously receive only minor injuries. Piling into a purple PT Cruiser, the only car available at the rural rental agency where the accident occurred, the family drives on, finally pulling up to Saina's farmhouse after a journey of more than three thousand miles. While the distance traveled is significant, it is not as noteworthy as the transformation in attitudes of the travelers. Even after their safe arrival, the journey is not over, because Charles has developed a new plan: to travel to China in order to reclaim his family's lost estate.

The Wangs vs. the World is an incongruously entertaining account of the effects that financial catastrophe can have on a family that is uniquely American, as viewed through the prism of Asian heritage and sensibilities, but understandable to anyone of any culture and background who has experienced success and failure. Author Jade

Chang portrays complex, well-rounded characters who possess all-too-human foibles. The relationships between Charles and his children, and among the siblings themselves, are warm, loving, and believable.

The story is told in third-person past tense, with the viewpoint shifting among the various characters. Two brief chapters in the book are told from the point of view of the aged car. Each chapter is headed by a Chinese character, and many untranslated Chinese phrases are scattered in dialogue throughout the novel, which will undoubtedly provide those who understand the written or spoken language with extra layers of meaning.

The novel contains many memorable, character-illuminating scenes. Charles, for example, breaks into his former factory to retrieve boxes of magnolia-scented cosmetic products to deliver, via rented U-Haul trailer, as promised to young, trusting clients in Alabama; when he arrives, however, the products have been damaged by the heat, and Charles has to write out a refund check that he knows cannot be cashed on his defunct account. Andrew gives a series of laughably awful stand-up routines during amateur night at nightclubs along the way before surrendering his virginity and briefly running off with a predatory older woman. There is also an ironic flashback to the death of Charles's first wife, May Lee, during a "Lover's Special" helicopter tour of the Grand Canyon. The two were on the tour because they were attempting to reconnect after ten years of marriage. When the helicopter went into a spin, Charles, who had not buckled his seat belt, was thrown out and landed safely on a ridge; May Lee, safely strapped in, plunged a mile into the canyon and perished in a fiery crash.

The narrative of *The Wangs vs. the World* touches on myriad subjects and themes that are introduced organically at appropriate intervals, critically examined, sometimes satirized, and then discarded in favor of freshly intriguing ideas. One such thread within the story deals with the contradictory nature of manufacturing, in which attractive finished products are created from ugly, unappealing ingredients—such as beauty products that are made from urea, a by-product of urine, or hot dogs that are homogenized into uniformity by processing the less desirable parts of animals. The very cosmetics that

Jade Chang has written and edited for numerous periodicals, including the Los Angeles Times *magazine. She has received a Sundance fellowship for arts journalism, a Winterhouse Award for Design Writing and Criticism, and a scholarship from the Squaw Valley Community of Writers Workshop. The Wangs vs. the World is her first novel.*

were responsible for Charles's immense fortune are savaged as a false concept: the industry is based on the notion that masking imperfections will allow "true beauty" to be revealed. Similarly, the financial business, which was responsible for both Charles's steady rise and his sudden downfall, is subjected to harsh criticism through the unflattering portrayal of insular banking executives who control the fates of real people by arbitrarily passing judgment according to impersonal and arcane economic formulas.

The art world also takes a major hit in Chang's book. Saina considers the pros and cons of falling in love with an artist and wonders at what point she will change from being an object of affection to merely being subject matter for a painting. She fumes that "art" is only designated as such by the approval of critics whose opinions help set prices for collectors, who then gather together expensive pieces to bask in reflected glory as supporters of artistic movements and collaborators in art history.

History in general is a recurring theme, particularly as it applies to the myths of young America and old China. According to Charles Wang, Christopher Columbus, a poor and unintelligent sailor, was unable to navigate beyond a whole continent and was too incompetent to have been the discoverer of America. Charles believes that the Vikings, under the leadership of Leif Eriksson, are much better candidates than Columbus for the discoverers of the New World. He also maintains that the ancient Chinese really deserve the credit, and that his forebears traveled across the Bering Land Bridge during the Ice Age to eventually become indigenous Americans.

Two key themes that run through the novel are luck and family. It was serendipity that Charles found a way to parlay a waste product into a fortune; it was just bad luck and bad timing that led to his ruin. Saina had success through her first three shows, but her fourth exhibit—fittingly, as the number four is considered bad luck in Chinese culture—led to her tarnished reputation. Finally, as demonstrated throughout the novel, family harmony and familial love, though fraught with difficulties, can conquer all, even the worst of luck.

Jack Ewing

Review Sources

Brownrigg, Sylvia. "A Richly Entertaining Debut." Review of *The Wangs vs. the World*, by Jade Chang. *The Guardian*, 22 Nov. 2016, www.theguardian.com/books/2016/nov/18/the-wangs-vs-the-world-by-jade-chang-review. Accessed 20 Jan. 2017.

Nguyen, Kevin. "Caught between the New Country and the Old." Review of The Wangs vs. the World, by Jade Chang. *The New York Times*, 14 Oct. 2016, www.nytimes.com/2016/10/16/books/review/wangs-vs-the-world-jade-chang.html. Accessed 20 Jan. 2017.

Shea, Lisa. "Read the Riches-to-Rags Novel That Has the Literati Buzzing." Review of *The Wangs vs. the World*, by Jade Chang. *Elle*, 3 Oct. 2016, www.elle.com/culture/books/news/a39744/wangs-vs-world-jade-chang/. Accessed 20 Jan. 2017.

Stapley, Marissa. "Review: Jade Chang's *The Wangs vs. the World* Is a Damn Good Debut." *The Globe and Mail*, 29 Nov. 2016, www.theglobeandmail.com/arts/books-and-media/book-reviews/review-jade-changs-the-wangs-vs-the-world-is-a-damn-good-debut/article33088275/. Accessed 20 Jan. 2017.

Review of *The Wangs vs. the World*, by Jade Chang. *Kirkus Reviews*, 1 Aug. 2016, p. 216.

When Breath Becomes Air

Author: Paul Kalanithi (1977–2015)
Publisher: Random House (New York). 256 pp.
Type of work: Memoir
Time: 2013–15
Locale: California

When Breath Becomes Air *is a memoir that examines the meaning of life from the perspective of author Paul Kalanithi, a dying neurosurgeon.*

Principal personages:
PAUL KALANITHI, the author, a neurosurgeon who was diagnosed with stage IV lung cancer at the age of thirty-six
LUCY KALANITHI, his wife, also a doctor
ELIZABETH ACADIA KALANITHI, his infant daughter
EMMA, his oncologist

#1 NEW YORK TIMES BESTSELLER

WHEN BREATH BECOMES

air

PAUL KALANITHI
FOREWORD BY ABRAHAM VERGHESE

(Courtesy of Penguin Random House)

When the subject of human mortality is explored in literature, more often than not it is from the perspective of someone who is learning to cope with the loss of a loved one. For example, in her award-winning memoir *The Year of Magical Thinking* (2005), American author Joan Didion writes about how mourning the death of her husband affected her emotionally and physically. Similarly, C. S. Lewis's *A Grief Observed* (1961), written after the death of his wife, American poet Joy Davidman, functions primarily as a collection of personal and spiritual reflections on his experience with bereavement. What makes *When Breath Becomes Air* (2016) more unique is the fact that the author, Dr. Paul Kalanithi, writes about death while he is dying.

After being diagnosed with terminal lung cancer at the age of thirty-six, Kalanithi was asked by his oncologist, Emma, what he would like to do with the rest of his life. He replied that he was unsure; only a few months earlier he was on a self-designed forty-year career track, of which he planned to spend the first half as a neurosurgeon and the second half writing books. However, with an estimated two years left to live, he decided that his dream of becoming a writer would have to be expedited. His first piece was an essay titled "How Long Have I Got Left?," about the first eight months of his life as a terminal patient, which was published on January 24, 2014, in the *New York Times*. Readers responded quickly and emphatically to his writing, ultimately moved by his beautiful prose, honesty, and optimism. Kalanithi decided soon afterward to turn "How Long Have I Got Left?" into a memoir.

Kalanithi chose the title *When Breath Becomes Air* for his memoir because it both captured the existential journey he was on and paid tribute to his love of literature. It is paraphrased from the first lines of Fulke Greville's seventeenth-century sonnet "Caelica 83," which read, "You that seek what life is in death / Now find it air that once was breath." The underlying message of "Caelica 83" aligns neatly with Kalanithi's purpose in writing *When Breath Becomes Air*: just as Greville concluded the poem by writing, "Reader! then make time, while you be / But steps to your eternity," Kalanithi's decision to write a memoir was his attempt to make the most out of the limited time he had left while immortalizing his life.

In the first half of his memoir, Kalanithi describes his life before cancer. Relatively spare in the details of his childhood, the anecdotes that he does provide about growing up in New York and Arizona are intended to illuminate how he came to love literature and why he always felt conflicted about medicine as a profession. He reveals that as a young child, he blamed medicine for keeping his father, a cardiologist, away from their family. As he got older, however, he felt he could no longer deny his own personal calling to become a doctor. After earning two bachelor's degrees and a master's degree in literature from Stanford University as well as a master's degree in the history and philosophy of science and medicine from the University of Cambridge, Kalanithi went on to graduate in the top of his class from the Yale School of Medicine. He was finishing his residency in neurosurgery at Stanford when he learned that he had terminal lung cancer.

Paul Kalanithi was a neurosurgeon and writer who graduated from Yale School of Medicine. He died on March 9, 2015. He is survived by his wife, Lucy, and their daughter, Elizabeth Acadia.

By contextualizing who he was before his diagnosis, Kalanithi amplifies the tragedy of it. For most of his life, he was training for a career that he would never have. He reveals that this is one of the most difficult truths he ever had to face: in the years prior to his diagnosis, his education and training prevented him from learning how to truly live; then, suddenly, he had no choice but to learn how to die. While the process of dying would be difficult for most people to articulate, Kalanithi brings unprecedented, eloquent insight to the experience. In part this is due to his background in philosophy and literature, which drives him to look for meaning in his mortality. However, what really makes Kalanithi an interesting and effective writer on the subject of death is his medical perspective. As a doctor, he knows exactly what is happening inside of his body and what his odds of survival are. Subsequently, *When Breath Becomes Air* is both a physical and a metaphysical examination of the nature of death.

Arguably one of the most affecting elements of *When Breath Becomes Air* is Kalanithi's unwavering honesty. Throughout the memoir, he is consistently willing to share his most personal experiences, emotions, and fears, even when they make him look flawed. For example, in the prologue, he reveals that he instinctively knew that he had cancer for months before he received the test results. In addition to losing a significant amount of weight, he was in tremendous pain all of the time. However, he did not tell his wife, Lucy, also a doctor, about his suspicions. When she discovered that he was looking for the statistical likelihood of cancer in people in their thirties on a medical search engine on his smartphone, Lucy questioned whether or not they should separate. Ultimately, she was devastated that he could not share his thoughts and fears with her. Kalanithi reveals later the bittersweet irony that his cancer helped save their marriage in the end by forcing them to address their issues and make the most of the time they had left together.

Much of *When Breath Becomes Air* is about anticipating and mourning the loss of one's own life and saying good-bye to loved ones. Beneath Kalanithi's honest portrayal of fear and grief, however, is a message of hope. Halfway through the book, he learns that the tumors in his lungs have shrunk and that he is getting stronger, which means there is a chance that he could live for longer than he originally anticipated. With this news, he struggles to decide whether or not he wants to return to practicing medicine. He reflects on the fact that Friedrich Nietzsche and Charles Darwin agreed on only one thing: that the defining characteristic of an organism is "striving." He decides that he cannot stop trying to live and briefly returns to medicine. It is this same logic that fuels his decision to have a baby with Lucy before he dies. When she asks him if he is certain that he can handle the fact that having a baby might make dying even more emotionally painful, he replies that he hopes it does. The wisdom that he aims to impart with these anecdotes is that people must never stop trying to infuse their lives with ambition and meaning.

In the epilogue, Lucy Kalanithi reveals that her husband died on March 9, 2015. The epilogue is written in a style that emulates Dr. Kalanithi's previous pages; it is an account of his final days, including his last breath, that blends raw, human emotion with scientific fact. Ultimately, this is what makes *When Breath Becomes Air* a truly engaging book: the Kalanithis are deft writers with a powerful story. Since its publication, the book has received overwhelmingly positive reviews, with many critics praising the memoir for its courage. What makes *When Breath Becomes Air* feel remarkable at times is the fact that Kalanithi is willing to look deeply upon an event that most people are too scared to think about when they are healthy, and he never falters in his quest to understand the nature and meaning of death. Book critic Nora Krug praised this effort in her review for the *Washington Post*, writing that Kalanithi's "words are bracing for their honesty." It is the honest insight that Kalanithi provides regarding his experience that makes the memoir feel simultaneously personal and universal.

The universality and humanness of Kalanithi's message is likely to resonate long after readers have finished his book. Alice O'Keeffe commented on this impact in her review for the *Guardian*, noting, "The power of this book lies in its eloquent insistence that we are all confronting our mortality every day, whether we know it or not." In addition to the universality of his message, Kalanithi has also been praised for his ability to craft beautiful prose about a scientific, medical phenomenon. Where a lesser writer might have produced a drier, less accessible narrative, Kalanithi's love for the written word enabled him to express complex ideas in a lyrical way. In her *New York Times* review, Janet Maslin wrote that much of the memoir's poignancy stems from the way Kalanithi "conveys what happened to him—passionately working and striving, deferring gratification, waiting to live, learning to die—so well. None of it is maudlin. Nothing is exaggerated." Indeed, Kalanithi's intelligence and eloquence are a large part of what make his memoir arguably one of the best books ever published on the subject of death. One of the few negative attributes of *When Breath Becomes Air* is that, at times, Kalanithi's medical perspective, and the ideas and jargon that accompany it, makes parts of the narrative feel as though they are only for fellow doctors. Besides these rare moments, however, *When Breath Becomes Air* is an immensely compelling and worthwhile read.

Emily Turner

Review Sources

Krug, Nora. "*When Breath Becomes Air*: Young Doctor's Last Words of Wisdom, Hope." Review of *When Breath Becomes Air*, by Paul Kalanithi. *The Washington Post*, 8 Jan. 2016, www.washingtonpost.com/entertainment/books/when-breath-becomes-air-in-a-young-doctors-final-words-wisdom-and-hope/2016/01/08/aa5a8402-b60e-11e5-9388-466021d971de_story.html. Accessed 16 Nov. 2016.

Maslin, Janet. "In When Breath Becomes Air, Dr. Paul Kalanithi Confronts an Early Death." Review of When Breath Becomes Air, by Paul Kalanithi. *The New York Times*, 6 Jan. 2016, www.nytimes.com/2016/01/07/books/review-in-when-breath-becomes-air-dr-paul-kalanithi-confronts-an-early-death.html. Accessed 16 Nov. 2016.

O'Keeffe, Alice. "How to Live, by a Doctor Who Died Aged 37." Review of *When Breath Becomes Air*, by Paul Kalanithi. *The Guardian*, 3 Feb. 2016, www.theguardian.com/books/2016/feb/03/when-breath-becomes-air-paul-kalanithi-review. Accessed 16 Nov. 2016.

Where It Hurts

Author: Reed Farrel Coleman (b. 1956)
Publisher: G. P. Putnam's Sons (New York).
   368 pp.
Type of work: Novel
Time: Present day
Locale: Long Island, New York

Award-winning and best-selling author Reed Farrel Coleman introduces a new series character, Gus Murphy, in Where It Hurts. *A psychically damaged ex-policeman, Murphy embarks on an informal investigation into the murder of the son of a felon, encountering violent crime and deep-seated corruption in the process of crisscrossing his socially diverse home territory of Long Island, New York.*

(Courtesy of Penguin Random House)

Principal characters:

JOHN AUGUSTUS "GUS" MURPHY, retired Suffolk County, New York, policeman; works as a courtesy van driver and provides security for the hotel he lives in

THOMAS DELCAMINO, a.k.a. Tommy D, former petty criminal

ANNIE, Murphy's ex-wife

KRISTEN, a.k.a. Krissy, Murphy and Annie's twenty-year-old daughter, a college dropout and drug user

PETER FRANCIS XAVIER "PETE" McCANN, a detective at the Fourth Precinct, once had an affair with Annie

BILL KILKENNY, a.k.a. Father Bill, a former police union chaplain

AL ROUSSIS, a homicide detective at the Suffolk County Police Department

KAREEM SHIVERS, a.k.a. K-Shivs, a former boxer, current heroin dealer

RICHIE ZITO, a.k.a. Zee, former motorcycle club member, current bar owner

SLAVA PODALAK, from Warsaw, Poland; the night bellman and doorman at Murphy's hotel

LOU CAREY, a policeman, former coworker of Murphy's

MILT PAXSON, a policeman, Lou's partner

SMUDGE, Tommy D's friend

John Augustus "Gus" Murphy is at a low ebb in his life when *Where It Hurts* first opens. A twenty-year veteran of the Suffolk County Police Department on New York's Long Island, Murphy left the force in despair following the sudden death two years earlier of his adult son (and namesake) from an undiagnosed heart condition. The tragic event also resulted in the breakup of his marriage and eventual divorce from his wife, his teenaged daughter's descent into drug use and addiction, the loss of most of his friendships, and his resulting emotional instability. Working to make some sense of what his life has become, Murphy attends regular therapy sessions to help him deal with and process his grief. To make ends meet, he works for the substandard hotel where he now lives, driving their courtesy van and occasionally serving as the hotel's security and bouncer.

One day, Murphy is approached by Thomas "Tommy D" Delcamino, a petty criminal whom Murphy had arrested many times in the past and who now works as a laborer for a masonry and paving company. Delcamino explains that he wants to hire Murphy, who he feels always treated him fairly, to investigate the murder of his son TJ. Four months earlier, the young man was tortured and brutally beaten to death, his body burned and then dumped in an empty lot, but Tommy D believes the police are barely working the case. Thinking Tommy is exploiting his own anguish over his dead son, Murphy angrily dismisses the ex-con, who leaves behind a newspaper clipping of the crime. Later, Murphy reconsiders, believing Tommy's request was genuine, and he also feels guilty for not being more sympathetic to a fellow father who had lost a son.

Before he can do anything, however, Murphy must rescue his daughter, Kristen, who is called Krissy, from the police station where she is being held after being arrested for smoking marijuana and having an open bottle of vodka in her car. While he is at the precinct, Murphy decides to ask his former department colleague, Detective Peter Francis Xavier "Pete" McCann about TJ Delcamino. Pete points him towards the men who are assigned the case, detectives Lou Carey and Milt Paxson, and at the same time warns Murphy off the investigation, which instead only encourages Murphy to pursue it.

Murphy explores the site where TJ's battered body was found. Afterward, he visits an old friend and retired chaplain, Father Bill Kilkenny, to talk about the case. Murphy

Since publishing his first novel, Life Goes Sleeping *(1991), Reed Farrel Coleman has written several critically acclaimed and commercially successful books. He is best-known for his Moe Prager series and continuing the late Robert B. Parker's Jesse Stone series. Coleman has won three Shamus Awards as well as Anthony, Barry, and Macavity awards.*

then heads to Tommy D's workplace where someone shoots at him, grazing his leg with the bullet, before fleeing in a dark SUV. When the assailants have left, Murphy finds Tommy D's body in the mobile home where he lived—which has been thoroughly searched—and calls the police. An old friend from the force, Al Roussis, responds to the call, and in the course of their conversation, he also warns Murphy off the case.

Returning home to the Paragon Hotel, Murphy finds a man called Smudge waiting for him. Smudge is a friend of the late Tommy D's, and at Tommy's request, Smudge has brought Murphy a backpack containing a book of names, addresses, and phone numbers of possible leads in his son's murder. Smudge relays the message from Tommy that if Murphy needs anything, to talk to Richie "Zee" Zito. Murphy travels to Zee's business, Harrigan's Pub, where Zee informs him that TJ was a thief and an addict and suggests Murphy abandon the case.

Back at the hotel, Murphy is accosted by Kareem Shivers and two other men, who by their vehicle were apparently the ones who shot at him at the scene of Tommy D's death. Kareem says that Murphy has something that belongs to him. Before Murphy can deny it, Kareem and his companions are subdued by Slava Podalak, the hotel's doorman and night bellman who is also concerned for Murphy's welfare. As a precaution, Murphy switches rooms at the hotel, a procedure he will repeat several times.

Despite the numerous warnings he has received to stay away from the investigation into TJ's murder, Murphy doggedly pursues information and leads while also investigating the murder of Tommy D. He questions a series of cops, follows up leads provided by Tommy's notebooks, performs one-man stakeouts, witnesses additional crimes, and risks his life entering dubious neighborhoods and risky situations, all for the sake of keeping an unmade promise to a dead man and fellow grieving father. Murphy follows a tortuous path littered with dead bodies in the often frustrating process of following clues that appear to lead nowhere. Slowly he realizes who killed the men, why they were killed, and why nobody in authority seems to be interested in solving the murders. Eventually, he arrives at a startling and potentially deadly conclusion.

Where It Hurts is the first installment in a planned series and presents a modern take on the conventional hard-boiled detective subgenre. In many ways, the Murphy stories will be an update of Coleman's acclaimed 1980s-era Moe Prager series, which also features a divorced former cop.

First-person narrator and lead character Gus Murphy—upon whom the success or failure of the new series will ultimately rest—is a former policeman who has the requisite skill-set to carry out a coherent investigation. His abilities include training and experience in law enforcement techniques, familiarity with firearms, and established relationships with networks of various police and criminal figures. What he does not possess (an oversight that will presumably be addressed in future books) is a private investigator's license, which is a requirement in the State of New York. Additionally, many of Murphy's activities are actually illegal, especially anything done in connection with the investigation of murder, which is beyond the normal purview of even licensed investigators, who are generally confined to gathering information about suspect individuals, searching for lost persons, conducting surveillance, and providing security. Murphy has survived the highs and lows of both professional and personal life. He exhibits a certain level of cynicism and world-weariness that is tempered by empathy, humanity, and vulnerability. He regularly searches his soul in order to examine his own behavior and character in an attempt to understand and improve his downbeat outlook. Murphy is physically imposing and can hold his own against the violent people he sometimes encounters. He is attractive enough and sufficiently unattached to stimulate the romantic interests of women, and he is intelligent enough to develop a plan of attack, to piece together bits of information in order to form a conclusion, and to take appropriate measures to achieve desired objectives. Whatever results Murphy obtains will be due more to his persistence than to his deductive capabilities, and in perilous moments, he is more likely to respond with brute force than with brainpower.

In keeping with traditional detective fiction, *Where It Hurts* presents a realistic, somewhat jaundiced ambiance that is complete with unexpected bloody violence, dark humor, philosophical musings, R-rated sexual situations, and dialogue that alternately sinks into the gutter or rises toward poetry. As in real life, people are neither all good nor all bad, and situations typically resolve inconclusively and in shades of gray rather than in sharply defined black-and-white outcomes. A particular strength of the novel is the depiction and incorporation of the colorful setting: the socially, geographically, and ethnically diverse Long Island, New York, where the author makes his home. One of the world's largest and most densely populated islands, Long Island provides a wide range of character types, from venal policemen to drug dealers and from aging bikers to low-intelligence accomplices. This cast of characters allows Murphy to demonstrate his flexibility in dealing with a ranges of personality types.

Because of Reed Farrel Coleman's outstanding critical and commercial reputation as a writer in the crime and mystery field, it is likely that his new Gus Murphy series will quickly find an enthusiastic audience among fans of his work.

Jack Ewing

Review Sources

Cooper, Jackie K. "Reed Farrel Coleman Impresses with 'Where It Hurts." Review of *Where It Hurts*, by Reed Farrel Coleman. *The Huffington Post*, 6 Feb. 2016, www.huffingtonpost.com/jackie-k-cooper/reed-farrel-coleman-impre_b_9178716. html. Accessed 6 Dec. 2016.

Corrigan, Maureen. "'Where It Hurts': Reed Farrel Coleman Captures Long Island's Seedy Side." Review of *Where It Hurts*, by Reed Farrel Coleman. *The Washington Post*, 24 Jan. 2016, www.washingtonpost.com/entertainment/books/where-it-hurts-reed-farrel-coleman-captures-long-islands-seedy-side/2016/01/24/18788798-ae41-11e5-9ab0-884d1cc4b33e_story.html. Accessed 5 Nov. 2016.

DeSilva, Bruce. "Reed Farrel Coleman's New Series Leads with Superb Detective Novel." Review of *Where It Hurts*, by Reed Farrel Coleman. *St. Louis Post-Dispatch*, 30 Jan. 2016, www.stltoday.com/entertainment/books-and-literature/reviews/reed-farrel-coleman-s-new-series-leads-with-superb-detective/article_dd9fbda8-1c44-5995-89f0-d2e55b9f6068.html. Accessed 5 Nov. 2016.

Review of *Where It Hurts*, by Reed Farrel Coleman. *Kirkus*, 23 Sept. 2015, www.kirkusreviews.com/book-reviews/reed-farrel-coleman/where-it-hurts/. Accessed 5 Nov. 2016.

Wilde Lake

Author: Laura Lippman (b. 1959)
Publisher: William Morrow (New York).
  368 pp.
Type of work: Novel
Time: 1980–2015
Locale: Columbia, Maryland, and environs

*A suspenseful examination of how past
crimes, lies, and secrets can adversely affect
present lives, Laura Lippman's* Wilde Lake
*continues the author's outstanding record of
producing literary crime fiction featuring an
intelligent, sympathetic, and strong-willed
woman as the central protagonist.*

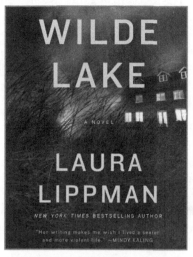

(Courtesy of HarperCollins Publishers)

Principal characters:

LUISA FRIDA "LU" BRANT, newly elected state's attorney of Howard County, Maryland

AJAX HOMER "AJ" BRANT, her brother, a former stockbroker turned travel writer and lecturer

DAVEY ROBINSON, his friend from high school

ARNOLD "BASH" BASTROP, another of AJ's high school friends

TOM FLOOD, a high school dropout

 BEN FLOOD, his brother, also a high school dropout

JUANITA CORDELIA "NITA" FLOOD, a.k.a. Jonnie Forke, their sister

FREDERICK C. "FRED" HOLLISTER III, her former boss

MIKE HUNT, a police detective

Wilde Lake opens with a dramatic account of an incident from the past that will later figure prominently in the plot. As first-person narrator Luisa "Lu" Brant tells it, on an evening in mid-June 1980, when she was just ten years old, her brother, AJ Brant, and his friends were partying at Wilde Lake, celebrating their high school graduation. In the midst of the festivities, Tom and Ben Flood, two high school dropouts, arrived and approached Davey Robinson, one of AJ's friends. Ben stabbed Davey in the back, declaring that he was doing it for Nita, his sister. AJ wrestled with Ben, who broke away and ran into the nearby woods with AJ in pursuit. The rest of the graduates subdued Tom, cared for a severely injured Davey, and called for emergency services. AJ soon reappeared, covered in blood, his elbow broken. He reported that he was hurt when he tackled Ben, who fell on his own knife and was killed. In the aftermath of the event, Juanita "Nita" Flood accused the now-paralyzed Davey of rape, a charge that was dismissed when it was revealed that the two teenagers were secret lovers. Tom Flood was charged as an accomplice to the assault on Davey and sent to prison. AJ, having acted in self-defense, was allowed to remain free and go on to attend Yale University.

The scene then shifts to early 2015, establishing a pattern that will be repeated throughout the novel. Scenes set in the present, narrated in third-person present tense and indicated by text set in serif type and chapter headings consisting solely of the date, alternate with accounts of past incidents, which are narrated in first-person past tense, set in sans-serif type (although this first section is not), and presented under more descriptive chapter headings. Contemporary segments advance the plot, while their historic counterparts retreat into the past, providing details of key characters and occurrences and dropping hints that the deeds described will have consequences down the road

In January 2015, Lu Brant is now forty-five years old. She is moving into the office of her former boss, Fred Hollister, having just been elected to a four-year term as the first female state's attorney for Howard County, Maryland. As Lu unpacks, she reminisces, and readers gain insights into her personal history and glimpses of her personality. Lu, whose mother died in childbirth, is a widow with young twin children, living beside Wilde Lake with her aged father in a home that was once a Revolutionary War–era tavern. In subsequent alternating chapters, further information is revealed about Lu's family members, friends, and acquaintances. Lu herself confesses to her torrid affair with one of AJ's high school friends, Arnold "Bash" Bastrop, now a high-powered lobbyist and sexual athlete who is serially unfaithful to his beautiful young wife

Within days of Lu moving into her new office, a murder is reported, and Lu visits the scene of the crime. There, Detective Mike Hunt walks her through the crime scene: a middle-aged waiter, Mary McNally, has been brutally beaten and strangled in her low-rent apartment during what appears to be a break-and-enter. Fingerprints and DNA found at the apartment lead to the quick apprehension of Rudy Drysdale, a middle-aged, medically disabled vagrant with only petty crimes and no acts of violence on his record. In the course of investigating the suspect, it is revealed that he went to Wilde Lake High School, where Lu and her brother also attended. Shortly after Rudy's arrest, his incompetent public defender is replaced with high-priced Fred Hollister, now working as a criminal defense attorney for one of the largest law firms in Baltimore.

As the murder case unfolds, Lu visits Rudy's aged mother and father. She uncovers an incident that indicates Rudy once stabbed his father with a pair of scissors while sleeping over at his parents' house, suggesting he might be capable of murder after all.

In the course of checking out leads in preparation for the prosecution of her murder case, Lu asks her brother, who lives nearby with his second wife, if he knew Rudy. AJ, however, only wants to talk about having children via surrogacy, the process by which Lu's twins were born, since she underwent a hysterectomy in her late twenties. Lu later questions the murder victim's next-door neighbor, Jonnie Forke, and learns that she is the former Nita Flood. She begins to wonder if Nita was perhaps the intended murder victim. This theory of the crime leads her to again question AJ about the incident in which Nita was supposedly raped by Davey.

After Lu obtains a formal indictment against Rudy, the criminal trial begins. Soon after the jury is seated, Rudy attacks Lu, knocking her down in the courtroom, and runs out, attempting to escape, but is tackled and handcuffed. Slightly bruised, Lu contemplates the reason for Rudy's assault—perhaps he desired suicide by cop, since he is somewhat claustrophobic—when she receives a phone call. Rudy is dead, having committed suicide in prison by smashing his skull against the wall of his cell.

Wilde Lake is logically divided into three parts. Part 1 introduces all the major players while highlighting some of their strengths and flaws, provides background to the often-complex relationships among the various characters, and details the history and description of the setting. Columbia, Maryland, an actual place with a colorful past—it was initially established as a utopian community between Baltimore and Washington, DC, in the 1960s, as Lu explains in the book—has special significance to Lippman, since she lived there and graduated from Wilde Lake High School in 1977. The first part also sets the plot into motion with a seemingly routine crime that, as time passes, takes on deeper and more sinister implications.

In Part 2, characters and motivations are more closely examined. Troubling contradictions arise as different characters give different versions of key events, secrets hidden in the recent and distant past are exposed, and assumptions and conclusions previously drawn begin to unravel. The sudden suicide of Rudy Drysdale at the end of part 2 seems to bring an end to Lu's case, but in reality, thanks to her dogged insistence in excavating the truth, the case is only just beginning in earnest. Part 3 presents the tying up of numerous loose threads in unforeseen ways. Lippman always plays fair, planting clues along the way that alert readers can connect along with, or even ahead of, the ever-vigilant Lu Brant.

Characterization is a particular strength for Lippman, who has carved a successful fiction-writing career out of developing three-dimensional, flawed yet determined, intelligent, often witty female protagonists with a unique sense of justice. Male characters are more broadly and less intimately drawn but nonetheless still come across as believable. Dialogue among characters is natural and realistically conversational. Plots are convoluted enough to keep most crime-story fans guessing. Underlying themes, such as loss of childhood innocence, adult cynicism, the difficulty of prosecuting the crime of rape because of widely differing public perceptions of victim and perpetrator, and a hidden past coming back to haunt the present and future, are handled with subtlety and grace.

A former reporter for the Baltimore Sun, Laura Lippman turned to writing crime fiction in the 1990s. Her popular series featuring private investigator Tess Monaghan began with the publication of Baltimore Blues (1997) and, as of 2017, includes a dozen entries. She has also published a number of stand-alone novels. Her fiction has won Agatha, Anthony, and Edgar Awards, among many others.

Beneath Lippman's work is a solid literary foundation that raises her novels above the popularly perceived limitations of genre. This is particularly true in the case of *Wilde Lake* which, as some reviewers have noted and Lippman has acknowledged, contains elements that echo Harper Lee's *To Kill a Mockingbird* (1960). The name of Lippman's protagonist, Luisa, even echoes that of Lee's narrator, Scout, who is formally named Jean Louise Finch. The family units are similar: a widower father, a young girl and her older brother, and a housekeeper as a substitute for an absent mother. In each instance, a black man with the surname Robinson (Tom in *Mockingbird*, Davey in *Wilde Lake*) is accused of raping a woman, and each suspect is violently assaulted by outraged citizens. In both novels, revenge-seeking assailants die, supposedly by falling upon their own knives. Such parallels do not detract from Lippman's work but rather enhance it. The similarities underscore the sad fact (reinforced with her passing reference to riots in Baltimore in the wake of the unexplained, and ultimately unpunished, death of Freddie Gray while in police custody in April 2015) that even with the passage of time, prejudice seems to be a permanent and insoluble feature of the national landscape.

Jack Ewing

Review Sources

Anderson, Patrick. "*Wilde Lake*, One of Laura Lippman's Finest Novels, Feels Personal." Review of *Wilde Lake*, by Laura Lippman. *The Washington Post*, 28 Apr. 2016, www.washingtonpost.com/entertainment/books/wilde-lake-one-of-laura-lippmans-finest-novels-feels-personal/2016/04/27/b034e9e0-fcd5-11e5-80e4-c381214de1a3_story.html. Accessed 17 Jan. 2017.
Hughes, Declan. "*Wilde Lake* Review: A Great Crime Writer at the Top of Her Game." Review of *Wilde Lake*, by Laura Lippman. *The Irish Times*, 30 July 2016, www.irishtimes.com/culture/books/wilde-lake-review-a-great-crime-writer-at-the-top-of-her-game-1.2735079. Accessed 17 Jan. 2017.
Turow, Scott. Review of Wilde Lake, by Laura Lippman. *The New York Times*, 31 May 2016, www.nytimes.com/2016/06/05/books/review/laura-lippmans-wilde-lake.html. Accessed 17 Jan. 2017.

The Wonder

Author: Emma Donoghue (b. 1969)
Publisher: Little, Brown (New York). 291 pp.
Type of work: Novel
Time: 1850s
Locale: Irish Midlands, Ireland

Elizabeth Wright is sent to Ireland for a nursing position. When she arrives, she discovers that her patient, eleven-year-old Anna O'Donnell, is an "extraordinary wonder" who has not eaten in four months. As she observes the child to determine whether this is a hoax, the nurse uncovers a dark twist behind the so-called miracle.

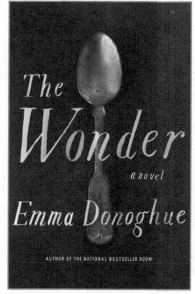

(Courtesy of Little, Brown and Company)

Principal characters:
ELIZABETH "LIB" WRIGHT, nurse trained by Florence Nightingale
ANNA O'DONNELL, the Wonder, a child who has reportedly not eaten for four months
WILLIAM BYRNE, a newspaper reporter
SISTER MICHAEL, fellow nurse and observer
ROSALEEN O'DONNELL, Anna's mother
MALACHY O'DONNELL, Anna's father
KITTY, Anna's cousin, a servant in Anna's home
PAT O'DONNELL, Anna's deceased brother
DR. MCBREARTY, Anna's family physician

The Wonder is a tale of determination fueled by fear and love. Deeply religious, eleven-year-old Anna O'Donnell claims not to have eaten for four months, and yet seems to thrive. She catches the attention of the local doctor, Dr. McBrearty, and clergy, as well as townspeople who believe Anna's survival to be a miracle and trek to her home to visit her and leave donations. This part of Donoghue's story is based in the historical phenomenon of the Fasting Girls; girls primarily in Ireland who, from the sixteenth to the twentieth centuries, claimed, by the grace of God, to be able to survive without food.

A local committee, of which the local doctor and pastor were a part, decided that the veracity of Anna O'Donnell's miracle needed to be proven, or disproven. They hire two nurses, Sister Michael and Elizabeth "Lib" Wright, to watch over Anna for two weeks to see if she is eating or how she is surviving.

The book's chapters are organized around the dual themes of nursing and religion. Each chapter is named according to a shared duty and includes a dictionary-like listing of each title's meaning. In the first chapter, titled "Nurse," Lib arrives in Ireland from England and meets the O'Donnells, of whom she is very skeptical. In the subsequent chapters, readers follow Lib and her patient through "Watch," "Fast," "Vigil," and "Shift." As "Watch" unfolds, Lib's main duty is to watch Anna eight hours a day to find out if she is being fed and to see if any of the family or visitors are interacting with Anna in a way that would provide nutrients. When Lib arrives, Anna is surviving and, lack of food aside, is doing well. Within a week of Lib and Sister Michael's arrival, however, she takes a turn for the worse.

The novel also provides a scintillating glimpse into the early days of the nursing profession. Early on, Lib explains her pedigree in her profession, that her father was a gentleman and she received a formal nursing education. As readers come to know the somewhat prickly Elizabeth Wright, they are exposed to a lesson on Florence Nightingale's mission in the Crimean War (1853–56), specifically in Scutari, where Lib served as a nurse under the famous Miss N. Under the horrific conditions for soldiers on the battle field, and the scarcity that Nightingale's nurses had to endure while caring for them, Lib received a different sort of formal, pedigreed training. What is most important regarding Lib's experience there is what she was taught; little nursing lessons from Nightingale are scattered throughout the chapters, and Lib's reliance on her teacher is revealed in phrases starting with "Miss N. always."

The central conflict in this book is between the religious and medical ideologies of the time and how they assist or hinder efforts to keep Anna alive. In contrast to the positive picture that most readers will have about Nightingale, this novel reveals some of the problematic aspects of her nursing ideas in addition to the misguided thoughts of the doctors of the day. For instance, Lib carries with her a notebook where she keeps detailed records of Anna's condition from the very first day. Though Lib finds this to be comforting, she remembers that "Miss N. thought some nurses relied on note-taking too much, laming their powers of recall." Despite her training and experience, as a nurse and a woman, Lib has difficulty making her convictions heard. When Lib challenges Dr. McBrearty regarding Anna's treatment, she is admonished: "Are we beginning to stray beyond our remit? . . . Leave such mysteries to those who've been trained for them." Later in the novel, Lib notes that Miss N. frowned on developing relationships with patients, but fortunately the nurse cannot help herself from coming to care for the starving child.

Although Lib, who is an atheist and harbors a dislike and distrust for Irish Catholicism, puts her store in science and medicine, the science of the day is lacking and, by modern standards, woefully ignorant. Dr. McBrearty lessens Anna's already limited fluid intake and bleeds her to release swelling. A visiting physician who, after diagnosing Anna with hysteria (the era's catch-all term for women suffering from premenstrual syndrome, who were particularly nervous or outspoken, or depression, and anything in between), and tells Lib that his nurses are under strict orders to force-feed patients refusing meals with a rubber tube. Satisfied with his superior understanding of the situation, the great man sweeps out, leaving Lib feeling more protective of Anna than she had before. Dr. McBrearty's fantastical hypothesis that Anna is turning reptilian, however, is, perhaps, the most outrageous instance of medical absurdity. Dr. McBrearty also suggests, after some research, that Anna could be "reabsorbing, subsisting on [her] own menses."

Anna's Catholicism plays a very large role in her survival. Lib struggles with the existence of God, telling newspaper reporter William Byrne, "At Scutari . . . I found myself thinking, If the Creator can't prevent such abominations, what good is he?" Despite Lib's atheistic leanings, the O'Donnell family and the town in which they live are very staunchly Catholic. And regardless of her youth, Anna is the most devout of them all. Her fast, she believes, is divinely inspired, and her daily activities center on prayer and singing. This confounds Lib, who is so far away from understanding the Catholic rituals that she calls one of Anna's recitations the "Dorothy prayer" because she cannot understand what the child's low voice is muttering. Her frustration over this is shared with Byrne, when she tells the reporter that

(Courtesy of Nina Subin)

Emma Donoghue is an award-winning author of nine novels, five short story collections, a children's book, and three literary history books. She has also written for screen and the stage. She holds a PhD from the University of Cambridge.

Anna wants to die, "Perhaps because your religion's filled her head with morbid nonsense." This "morbid nonsense" includes the idea that a living person can pray a dead one into heaven, and Lib realizes that Anna's prayers are centered around the death of her older brother, Pat, whom the child believes has angered God, thus being banished from heaven unless his sister can gain favor through the fasting and constant prayer.

Throughout the novel, Donoghue's characters are deftly crafted, providing surprising depths that add to the suspense of the story. Lib is introduced as a rather stark, narrow-minded widow who begrudges the time she will have to spend in the Irish Midlands with, as she sees it, uneducated and overly religious peasants who live there. Readers discover a softer side to Lib as she interacts with Anna and as pieces of her own difficult past are revealed. By the end of the novel, she becomes an unlikely champion for Anna. Anna is another well-developed character whose motivations will shock readers as the story draws to a close.

As Anna continues to deteriorate, Lib and William are the only ones who see Anna's condition for what it is and understand that she is dying. No one in the family or on Anna's committee is willing to listen to Lib over the word of Dr. McBrearty, or to consider, as they see it, the lack of faith acknowledging the truth would require. Lib finds herself caught between respecting everyone's wishes and being complicit and Anna's suicide, or force-feeding the dying child. The relationship between mother and child is also explored in this story. Rosaleen O'Donnell clearly loves her child, but Lib establishes an early hostility toward Anna's mother because she believes Rosaleen is purposely fooling the world for financial gain. The women never truly form any positive relationship as the mother fears for her daughter's life, but not enough to save the child in Lib's eyes. Lib, on the other hand, finds the mother inside as she grieves for Anna's declining physical and mental condition. The conflict between the two women raises an ethical question of belief and protection.

In addition to the historical perspectives on science and religion, the novel show-cases an innate prejudice on the part of the English as Lib unwittingly discloses an ignorance of the English population regarding the conditions in Ireland. When Lib arrives, she sees dirty and hungry people, shabby cottages, and poor road conditions. She does not understand, thinking, "But this was high summer. How could food be scarce now, of all times?" Her lack of true knowledge over the plight of the Irish people is further revealed throughout the novel.

Reviews on the novel were positive, though some reviewers had problems with the book that ranged from mild to major. Donoghue is undoubtedly most famous for her psychological thriller novel *Room* (2015), and many praised the move back to a deeply psychological novel contained in small spaces. Most praised Donoghue's pacing and her innate ability to create suspense and complex drama. Other reviewers, such as Michael Schaub for *NPR*, levelled heavier criticisms against *The Wonder* than others, but most reviewers did agree that Donoghue's tendency to over-explain was a consistent defect in the novel.

Criticisms aside, *The Wonder* is a thought-provoking novel that will make readers stop and think about their own preconceived notions and professional resolutions in a fresh way.

Theresa L. Stowell, PhD

Review Sources

Donaldson, Emily. "Emma Donoghue Follows Up *Room* with Tale of a Miracle Girl." Review of *The Wonder*, by Emma Donoghue. *Maclean's*, 25 Sept. 2016, www.macleans.ca/culture/emma-donoghue-follows-up-room-with-tale-of-a-miracle-girl/. Accessed 22 Feb. 2017.

Johnson, Sarah. Review of *The Wonder*, by Emma Donoghue. *Booklist*, 1 July 2016, www.booklistonline.com/The-Wonder-Emma-Donoghue/pid=8227040. Accessed 22 Feb. 2017.

Justine, Jordan. "*The Wonder* by Emma Donoghue Review—A Thrilling Domestic Psychodrama." Review of *The Wonder*, by Emma Donoghue. *The Guardian*, 23 Sept. 2016, www.theguardian.com/books/2016/sep/23/the-wonder-by-emma-donoghue-review. Accessed 22 Feb. 2017.

King, Stephen. "Stephen King Reviews Emma Donoghue's Latest Novel." Review of The Wonder, by Emma Donoghue. *The New York Times*, 27 Sept. 2016, www.nytimes.com/2016/10/02/books/review/stephen-king-emma-donoghue-the-wonder.html. Accessed 22 Feb. 2017.

Schaub, Michael. "*The Wonder* Is a Hard-to-Believe Tale of Belief." Review of *The Wonder*, by Emma Donoghue. *NPR*, 22 Sept. 2016, www.npr.org/2016/09/22/494916738/the-wonder-is-a-hard-to-believe-tale-of-belief. Accessed 22 Sept. 2017.

Words Are My Matter
Writings about Life and Books, 2000–2016, with a Journal of a Writer's Week

Author: Ursula K. Le Guin (b. 1929)
Publisher: Small Beer Press (Easthampton, MA). 352 pp.
Type of work: Essays

This generous collection of nonfiction by celebrated speculative fiction author Ursula K. Le Guin includes essays, addresses, reviews, and introductions to the works of others.

(Courtesy of Small Beer Press)

Words Are My Matter: Writings about Life and Books, 2000–2016, with a Journal of a Writer's Week collects sixteen years of nonfiction writing by celebrated speculative fiction author Ursula K. Le Guin. The works contained within are divided into three main sections—"Talks, Essays, and Occasional Pieces," "Book Introductions and Notes on Writers," and "Book Reviews"—followed by a journal Le Guin kept during her stay at the Hedgebrook women-only writer's retreat in 1994.

The essays in the first section are addressed to various audiences, both professional and public. They are arranged chronologically and have been revised from the original versions only minimally. Two recurring themes in these essays are Le Guin's exploration of the speculative fiction genre and her defense and celebration of women's writing. In an essay for the *Washington Post* in which he briefly reviewed four recent releases by Le Guin—*Words Are My Matter*, plus three new collections of her short stories and novellas—book critic Michael Dirda wrote that the collection "spills over with insight, outrage and humor."

One of the longest pieces in the book is the essay entitled "Living in a Work of Art," which Le Guin notes in the foreword is "probably" her favorite. Part of this is because the essay was not written for a particular audience or commissioned for a publication, unlike most of the other pieces in this section. Rather, Le Guin says, "It was something I wanted to write, purely on the principle of E. M. Forster's lady who said, 'How do I know what I think till I see what I say?'" Although the essay primarily focuses on the house in San Francisco in which she grew up, it begins with a description of that city's Palace of Fine Arts, as both buildings were designed by architect Bernard Maybeck. This essay may also rank among Le Guin's favorites because it is a personal, descriptive narrative rather than an expository or argumentative essay about literature like the other pieces in this section, although it does move at the end to a consideration of the nature of beauty and how such novels as Jane Austen's *Pride and Prejudice* (1813), Virginia Woolf's *To the Lighthouse* (1927), and J. R. R. Tolkien's *The Lord of the Rings* (1954–55) might indeed be called beautiful. In trying to understand why the house she lived in has always been important to her, Le Guin concludes that perhaps all her life she has been trying to rebuild it around herself out of words—an ultimate and personal example of how, as she asserts in the collection's title, words are her matter.

One of the shortest pieces, and one that caused Le Guin the most anxiety, is the speech that she delivered upon receiving the National Book Foundation's Medal for Distinguished Contribution to American Letters in 2014. In this six-minute talk, Le Guin scolds publishers for eschewing their responsibility to support their writers by giving over editorial control to their sales departments, which, she says, "sell us like deodorant, and tell us what to publish, what to write." Books are more than simply commodities, Le Guin argues, and now that she

(Courtesy of Jack Liu)

Ursula K. Le Guin has won numerous awards for her writing, including the 1973 National Book Award for children's books, the 2002 PEN/Malamud Award, and the 2014 National Book Foundation's Medal for Distinguished Contribution to American Letters. In 2000, she was recognized as a Library of Congress Living Legend.

is nearing the end of her career, she does not "want to watch American literature get sold down the river." She proudly insists that while writers should insist on their "fair share" of profits, ultimately "the name of our beautiful reward isn't profit. Its name is freedom."

"The Operating Instructions," a speech that Le Guin gave at a meeting of Oregon's Literary Arts organization in 2002, is an argument for the power of the imagination—which she calls "the single most useful tool mankind possesses"—and the importance of literacy as a means to listen to others. She describes reading as an active, rather than passive, process of listening, and listening itself as "an act of community, which takes space, time, and silence." For Le Guin, imagination is most powerfully expressed through language, for, as she says, "we are a wordy species," and "nothing quite equals poem and story."

In "Genre: A Word Only a Frenchman Could Love," a speech given at a Public Library Association preconference in Seattle in 2004, Le Guin makes a distinction between genre as a tool that allows for the delineation of different types of narrative fiction and genre as a negative value judgment that critics often use to characterize popular forms of narrative outside the realm of literary fiction. She quite rightly reminds her audience that genre as a descriptive tool still serves an important purpose: "If you don't know what kind of book you're reading and it's not a kind you're used to, you probably need to learn how to read it. You need to learn the genre"—that is, its common characteristics, tropes, and conventions. However, she insists, this does not give critics justification for using genre as a tool of valuation. Her favorite illustration of this issue, which she uses several times in her talks and essays, is science fiction, the genre into which much of her own fiction falls. She argues throughout these essays that the way people think about genre needs to be reformed; primarily, she says, there needs to be a distinction between genre and formula, because fiction of any genre—even the realism of so-called literary fiction—can be fitted into easy formulas that prioritize broad commercial appeal over skillful and imaginative storytelling. "There are many bad books," Le Guin pronounces. "There are no bad genres."

Tailoring her talks to the audience to which they are presented, Le Guin often focuses on more specific literary subjects. For example, her piece "The Beast in the Book," given to a conference on literature and ecology, focuses on literature, primarily children's stories, about animals. Such stories are important, she says, because they are usually about wilderness, which "scares us because it is unknown, indifferent, dangerous, yet it is an absolute need to us; it is that animal otherness . . . that we must join, or rejoin, if we want to stay sane and stay alive"—and children are far closer to that otherness than adults.

After the issue of genre in general and speculative fiction genres in particular, the next most important subject for Le Guin is evident in her two talks at the Winter Fishtrap writers' gathering in Oregon in 2010, both collected under the title "What Women Know." She introduces the first talk with the question, "What do we learn from women?" The most basic answer to this question, which Le Guin admits is a "huge generalisation," is "we learn how to be human"—more specifically, "how to walk, talk, eat, sing, pray, play with other children, and which adults we should respect, and what to fear, what to love—the basic skills, the basic rules." These are "largely genderless" skills, says Le Guin, whereas the lessons that children learn from men are more often to be gendered, often involving enforcement of societally approved gender roles. She goes on to say that much of what human beings learn is taught in the form of stories, and that historically it has been the women who preserve and pass on the stories of the family and the tribe. Le Guin is very much committed to challenging the overwhelming focus on male authors and male-oriented stories in both media and the classroom, and to supporting and encouraging the growing interest in literature written by women. In the piece immediately following, a previously unpublished essay entitled "Disappearing Grandmothers," she discusses four common methods by which women are often excluded from the literary canon—"*denigration, omission, exception*, and *disappearance*"—the cumulative effect of which is the continuing marginalization of women's writing.

The second section of this book consists primarily of introductions, usually for books released as new editions. All of the books Le Guin writes about here are ones she admires, for, as she says, she would not agree to write an introduction for a book she did not like. Moreover, since Le Guin is world renowned as the author of speculative fiction, most (though not all) of these introductions are for classics of the science-fiction and fantasy genres. One such book is Philip K. Dick's *The Man in the High*

Castle, originally published in 1962 and republished in 2015 as a Folio Society edition. It is a "what if" story about American life after an alternate World War II in which the Axis powers won, giving control of the East Coast to the Germans and the West Coast to the Japanese. Praising Dick's imagination and his prose style, Le Guin draws on her vast knowledge of speculative fiction to properly situate *The Man in the High Castle* as a model of its genre.

The longest piece in this section is a composite essay based on several pieces on the work of Portuguese writer José Saramago, winner of the 1998 Nobel Prize in Literature, who died in 2010. The essay, a conventional biographical and analytical piece, discusses several of Saramago's novels, including *Ensaio sobre a cegueira* (1995; *Blindness*, 1997), *A caverna* (2000; *The Cave*, 2002), *Ensaio sobre a lucidez* (2004; *Seeing*, 2006), and his second-to-last novel, *A viagem do elefante* (2008; *The Elephant's Journey*, 2010), which Le Guin says "may be his most perfect work of art." She concludes that "Saramago writes with wit, heartbreaking dignity, and the simplicity of a great artist in full control of his art" and calls him "a true elder of our people, a man of tears, a man of wisdom."

The last section of the book consists of book reviews, most of which were originally published in the national British newspaper the *Guardian*. This is perhaps the least rewarding section, at least for readers more interested in Le Guin's own words than her recounting of the words of others; although reviews often allow writers to talk about profound issues, primarily the job of the reviewer is to describe the book, which often just leads to plot summary. The reviews are organized by author's last name; among the books reviewed are three by Margaret Atwood, two by Kent Haruf, two by Salman Rushdie, and two by Saramago, as well as books by J. G. Ballard, T. C. Boyle, and Jeanette Winterson, among others. As might be expected, many of the books reviewed have been classified as science fiction or fantasy, and, as she does in her more developed essays, Le Guin makes clear that she is very much aware of the importance of recognizing and characterizing genre. Most of the pieces are positive assessments, although she is not reluctant to challenge or chide writers who she thinks are not taking their work as seriously as she does her own.

The book ends with a piece entitled "The Hope of Rabbits: A Journal of a Writer's Week." In typical diary fashion, it records a week Le Guin spent in 1994 at Hedgebrook, a writer's retreat north of Seattle that accepts only women, thus offering what Le Guin calls a "once-in-a-lifetime gift" for many women who still find it frightening to call themselves scholars, scientists, or artists. In it, Le Guin recounts her daily activities at the retreat, primarily her work on a novella, which, like the journal itself, she wrote in bound notebooks by hand. It is the most personal piece of writing in the collection, giving readers the voice of Ursula K. Le Guin living and feeling, rather than analyzing and asserting.

Charles E. May, PhD

Review Sources

Brewer, Jenny. Review of *Words Are My Matter: Writings about Life and Books, 2000–2016*, by Ursula K. Le Guin. *Library Journal*, 15 Sept. 2016, p. 84.

Cart, Michael. Review of *Words Are My Matter: Writings about Life and Books, 2000–2016*, by Ursula K. Le Guin. *Booklist*, 1 Sept. 2016, p. 32.

Dirda, Michael. "At 86, Ursula K. Le Guin Is Finally Getting the Recognition She Deserves—Almost." Review of *Words Are My Matter: Writings about Life and Books, 2000–2016*, et al., by Ursula K. Le Guin. *The Washington Post*, 6 Oct. 2016, www.washingtonpost.com/entertainment/books/at-86-ursula-k-le-guin-is-finally-getting-the-recognition-she-deserves--almost/2016/10/03/8753524c-8654-11e6-92c2-14b64f3d453f_story.html. Accessed 1 Dec. 2016.

Review of *Words Are My Matter: Writings about Life and Books, 2000–2016*, by Ursula K. Le Guin. *Kirkus Reviews*, 1 Aug. 2016, p. 181.

Review of *Words Are My Matter: Writings about Life and Books, 2000–2016*, by Ursula K. Le Guin. *Publishers Weekly*, 4 July 2016, p. 51.

The Year of the Runaways

Author: Sunjeev Sahota (b. 1981)
First published: 2015, in Great Britain
Publisher: Alfred A. Knopf (New York). 496 pp.
Type of work: Novel
Time: 2003; ca. 2014
Locales: Sheffield, England; India

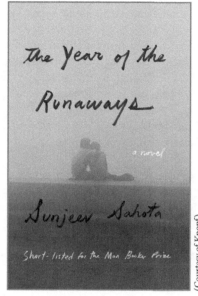

(Courtesy of Knopf)

Sunjeev Sahota's critically acclaimed novel The Year of the Runaways *focuses on the vulnerabilities and hardships of Indian immigrants as they negotiate visas, jobs, and living conditions in England in their quest for a better life. Sahota narrates the story through four key characters, three men and one woman, whose struggles are compounded by issues of class, caste, spirituality, and moral obligation.*

Principal characters:
RANDEEP SANGHERA, college student in India
NARINDER KAUR, his visa-wife
AVTAR NIJJAR, his sister Lakhpreet's secret lover
TARLOCHAN (TOCHI) KUMAR, his roommate

Sunjeev Sahota's *The Year of the Runaways* is a compelling and deeply moving novel addressing the obstacles and hardships faced by three young men in their quest to better their own lives and those of their families by illegally emigrating from India to England. Their journeys are difficult, complicated, and often dangerous, and Sahota, a highly skilled writer, humanizes this polarizing political topic through his use of a flowing narrative structure; the inclusion of vivid, detailed descriptions; and the creation of fully drawn, complex characters. Set in 2003, the novel traces the lives of Randeep, Avtar, and Tochi through a full year, exploring the reasons they leave India, their often frightening passages, and their adjustment to life in England, where work is scarce and they are treated, at best, like second-class citizens. Narinder, the lone female protagonist and the only main character native to England, is a devout Sikh and the moral compass of the novel, offering kindness and compassion as she attempts to meet her family's rigid expectations while dedicating herself to humanitarian causes. Ultimately, Sahota illuminates the treacherous and exploitative world of illegal immigration and chronicles the ways in which his characters are irrevocably shaped by it, shedding light on both Indian and English societies.

While Sahota applies a conventional and roughly chronological structure to the novel, that of the seasons, he also provides extensive backstories, which can sometimes be a challenge. The novel begins in the winter of 2003, a month or so after the three young men arrive in England and find work. Then, Sahota shifts the story back in time to recount each main character's individual and family story. Once those individual stories are established, the novel continues forward chronologically through the rest of 2003. Though Sahota keeps the story moving by writing in an episodic style, jumping back and forth between characters and scenes, he undercuts that approach with chapters 2, 4, and 6, which provide novella-length histories for the major characters. Separate chapters are dedicated to Tochi (chapter 2) and Narinder (chapter 6), with Randeep and Avtar sharing chapter 4, since their family lives interconnect through Randeep's sister, Lakhpreet, who is secretly Avtar's lover. The extensive backstories flesh out each character in voluminous detail, much of which will inform their future choices and behavior. The details are rich and beautifully rendered, and the individual stories are powerful, and yet the level of detail slows down the story considerably.

In chapter 2, "Tochi: Autorider," for example, Sahota describes Tochi's life as a "chamaar," or untouchable, in great detail. There are numerous examples of the rampant discrimination Tochi and his family face because of their caste, and it is only when Tochi stumbles into buying a rickshaw through an installment plan and gets his taxi business underway that he finally begins to believe he can improve his life and help his family. Before he realizes success, however, tragedy strikes, and it is this horrific tragedy that shapes who Tochi becomes and explains his anger, apathy, and loss of spirituality through the rest of the novel.

One of Sahota's greatest strengths as a writer is his character development and the way he builds complexity within each character. While the story is bleak and the main characters experience significant aguish, Sahota manages to infuse them with some hope by having them focus on their immediate goals as well as look toward their futures. The three male protagonists, Randeep, Avtar

Sunjeev Sahota is a British novelist. His first book, Ours Are the Streets *(2011), earned him inclusion on Granta's list of the twenty best young writers in 2013. His second novel,* The Year of the Runaways *(2015), was short-listed for both the 2015 Man Booker Prize and the 2016 International Dylan Thomas Prize.*

and Tochi, for example, are relentless in their pursuit of work, and once they have one job, they often begin hunting for a second. They are motivated to help themselves and their families, and they pursue every work lead and rumor. No job is beneath them, not even cleaning out sewers. Rather than surrender, they search for another way to achieve their goals, and Sahota's inclusion of telling details, such as the welcome note Randeep leaves for Narinder to find in a kitchen cabinet, hoping it will endear her to him, counter an earlier, more violent encounter Randeep has with another young woman, suggesting Randeep is more complex than he might first appear.

Similarly, Sahota portrays Narinder, the female protagonist, as steadfast in her commitment to helping others through charitable work, yet questioning a God who would allow people to suffer. When she agrees to be Randeep's visa-wife, she does so not for monetary reasons but out of guilt, having earlier refused someone in similar circumstances who later died trying to immigrate illegally. Narinder also helps others at her own personal cost. Her brother, in particular, worries that Narinder will bring shame upon the family, and she is punished because of it, yet she continues to help others knowing there will be consequences. She sacrifices herself willingly for the greater good. At the beginning of the novel, Narinder is a devout Sikh, but by the end, after witnessing Tochi's caste discrimination and many other instances of racism and classism, she questions her beliefs. Again, Sahota builds many contrasting details into Narinder's story, creating a character that is steadfast in her religious devotion until the numerous events she witnesses make it impossible for her not to question that devotion.

While Sahota shines an intense light on the underbelly of illegal immigration, he also explores the degree to which illegal immigration exacerbates other of society's many existing problems, such as the sale of human organs, sexual assault, and domestic violence, infusing the novel with even more depth and poignancy. Sahota takes great care to include these tangential issues not merely for the sake of creating sensationalized, hot-button plot points, but to show the lengths to which his characters will go in search of a better life and the heavy price they pay for the constant stress they experience, resulting in deeply flawed yet sympathetic characters. Randeep, for example, as a young college student in India, is initially a pampered, entitled eldest son, but he is also naïve, having little understanding of women or how to truly help his family after his father's debilitating illness prevents him from working. Randeep is kind but simpleminded, offering to take on as much work as is needed to keep his family financially afloat. He attends school during the day and takes a night job at an Amritsar call center to send money home. His exhaustion mounts, his school work suffers, and though he is gratified to begin a relationship with a young woman, Jaytha, he becomes overwhelmed.

As the pressure on Randeep intensifies, his relationship with Jaytha turns unexpectedly and uncharacteristically violent, yet Sahota's descriptions of Randeep, which underscore his insecurities, set the stage for this behavior. Later, at the construction house, Randeep's housemates often tell him, "You'll be OK," when he is hesitant to be on his own or take initiative. Even Avtar tries to distance himself from Randeep at certain points, believing Randeep is preventing his success and ability to move forward. In the end, the violent outburst is a consequence of his constant insecurity, and Sahota depicts that well and fully. Randeep, the character from the most well-off family, who has the luxury of applying for a visa-wife when his friends must take a harder and more dangerous path, is the least sympathetic initially. As the novel progresses, however, and the degree to which he is vulnerable to the deceptions of others and his own lack of ingenuity is revealed, he becomes much more sympathetic.

While the critical response to the book has been overwhelmingly positive, a few critics noted their difficulty in getting through the backstories at the beginning of the book or their dissatisfaction with the cursory epilogue. The long character histories include small but illuminating details on the characters' family dynamics and motivations, such as the fact that Randeep and Avtar are connected through family, though Randeep is not privy to the fact that Avtar is his sister Lakhpreet's lover and they intend to marry. Details such as these create drama and intrigue, but the sheer volume of information sometimes dazes more than it enlightens. The novel does, however, take full flight in chapter 7 and moves much more quickly after that point. Additionally, the epilogue, at eleven pages, feels rushed and incomplete after experiencing the previous level of detail throughout the novel. The epilogue updates the characters' lives ten-plus years later, and while Sahota is clear about how they are generally living, he does not delve into their psyches about how much or little they have changed as a result of their immigration experience. The fact that the novel does not tie up loose ends is understandable, but providing no insight into how at least some of the characters have been able to overcome obstacles in their way and make a new life is not.

The Year of the Runaways continues to garner critical acclaim for its humanizing depiction of illegal immigration. Sahota avoids sentimentality, and while the writing is not graphic in its depiction of violence, neither does it look away from the hardship and despair his characters endure. They may be exploited, imprisoned even, and still they fight. Giving up is not an option for them, and Sahota, through the creation of these unforgettable characters, paints a necessary, moving portrait of the grittiest, most self-preserving kind of resilience.

Marybeth Rua-Larsen

Review Sources

Bose, Mihir. "*The Year of the Runaways* by Sunjeev Sahota, Book Review: A Picture of Modern Immigration." Review of *The Year of the Runaways*, by Sunjeev Sahota. *The Independent*, 18 June 2015, www.independent.co.uk/arts-entertainment/books/reviews/the-year-of-the-runaways-by-sunjeev-sahota-book-review-a-picture-of-modern-immigration-10328722.html. Accessed 16 Aug. 2016.

Calagiovanni, Julia. "Man Booker Shortlist 2015: *The Year of the Runaways*." *The Atlantic*, 12 Oct. 2015, www.theatlantic.com/entertainment/archive/2015/10/man-booker-shortlist-2015-the-year-of-the-runaways-sunjeev-sahota/409888/. Accessed 16 Aug. 2016.

Charles, Ron. "*The Year of the Runaways* Review: *The Grapes of Wrath* for the 21st Century." Review of *The Year of the Runaways*, by Sunjeev Sahota. *The Washington Post*, 21 Mar. 2016, www.washingtonpost.com/entertainment/books/the-year-of-the-runaways-review-the-grapes-of-wrath-for-the-21st-century/2016/03/21/e6e09a8c-e97c-11e5-b0fd-073d5930a7b7_story.html. Accessed 16 Aug. 2016.

Dahiya, Nishant. "Weeping for All That Is Lost: A Harsh Migration out of India." Review of *The Year of the Runaways*, by Sunjeev Sahota. *NPR*, 30 Apr. 2016, www.npr.org/2016/04/30/476070048/weeping-for-all-that-is-lost-a-harsh-migration-out-of-india. Accessed 16 Aug. 2016.

Kakutani, Michiko. "Review: The Year of the Runaways, about Fighting for Scraps in a New Country." Review of The Year of the Runaways, by Sunjeev Sahota. *The New York Times*, 21 Mar. 2016, www.nytimes.com/2016/03/22/books/review-the-year-of-the-runaways-about-fighting-for-scraps-in-a-new-country.html. Accessed 16 Aug. 2016.

Sipahimalani, Sanjay. "*The Year of the Runaways* Book Review: The Wanderers." Review of *The Year of the Runaways*, by Sunjeev Sahota. *The Indian Express*, 15 Aug. 2015, indianexpress.com/article/lifestyle/books/the-year-of-the-runaways-book-review-the-wanderers/. Accessed 16 Aug. 2016.

You Will Know Me

Author: Megan Abbott (b. 1971)
Publisher: Little, Brown and Company
(Boston). 340 pp.
Type of work: Novel
Time: Present day
Locale: United States

Megan Abbott's novel You Will Know Me *is a psychological thriller and murder mystery that centers on the budding career of a teenage gymnast.*

Principal characters:
KATIE KNOX, the novel's protagonist and Devon's mother
DEVON KNOX, a fifteen-year-old elite gymnast and Olympic hopeful
ERIC KNOX, Devon's father
DREW KNOX, Devon's perceptive kid brother
COACH T, Devon's kindly older coach
HAILEY, Coach T's niece and an assistant coach at his gym

(Courtesy of Little, Brown and Company)

Katie Knox is an ordinary suburban mother with an extraordinary child. Her fifteen-year-old daughter, Devon, is an elite gymnast and aspiring Olympian. Devon's all-consuming training schedule dictates the lives of everyone in her family—including her father, Eric, and her younger brother, Drew—but, Katie believes, it also serves as the family's lifeblood. With an obsessive devotion to what Devon's coach calls the Track, Devon's high-stakes path to Olympic stardom, Katie comes to see just how much she is willing to sacrifice for her daughter's dream. Author Megan Abbott writes with the skill of a genre specialist, carefully building a sense of unease in a series of escalating events. Scenes that would be mundane in any other story—a parent booster party, a trip to the gym—become nightmarish and strange in Abbott's hands. At the heart of *You Will Know Me* is the fear of the known: how well do you know those people closest to you? Or, perhaps a more frightening question for Katie, how well do you know yourself?

Abbott, the author of eight novels, is best known for plumbing the darker depths of teenage girlhood. Jia Tolentino, who reviewed *You Will Know Me* for the *New Yorker*, referred to her oeuvre as "furtive, sticky, iconographic teen-girl noir." In her 2012 novel *Dare Me*, Abbott writes about competitive cheerleading from the perspective of two teenage girls. The plot is similar to that of *You Will Know Me*—youthful ambition, bodily punishment, a suspicious death—but its focus is the brutal ennui of adolescence. The characters describe being a teenage girl the way young men in old novels describe being at war: excruciating boredom punctuated by moments of raw adrenaline and fear. In Abbott's *The Fever* (2014), inspired by a real mystery illness in Le Roy, New York, in 2012, a handful of teenage girls succumb to seizures and strange physical tics. Abbott recasts the epidemic as a kind of dark magic and uses its implications as a lens through which to view young female desire.

Abbott is also the author of a nonfiction book called *The Street Was Mine: White Masculinity in Hardboiled Fiction and Film Noir* (2002). The book critiques the function of the solitary white man in classic crime and noir stories. This archetypal "tough guy," Abbott writes, is the centerpiece of films like *Double Indemnity*, *The Big Sleep*, and *Chinatown*. Abbot's interest in the subject matter has clear influences on her own fiction. Abbott, a recipient of the Edgar Award for mystery writing, centers women in her work. Her early novels—*Die a Little*, *The Song Is You*, *Bury Me Deep*, and *Queenpin*—are classic noir tales, set in midcentury America. They feature gangsters, femme fatales, and Hollywood hustlers—but unlike classic noirs of the past, they all feature female protagonists.

In *You Will Know Me*, Abbott combines expertly noir tropes and contemporary female angst. Katie, the novel's protagonist, is no hard-boiled detective, but like the heroes of noirs past, she alone is left to interpret a world gone mad. Describing a bacchanalian booster club party in the book's first pages, Abbott writes, "Later, Katie would come to think of that night as the key to everything that came after, the secret code." Through the clusters of neon tiki drinks (and "momtinis"), the swirling smoke of "purloined cigarettes," and the thumping bass of the music from her youth, Katie encounters Devon, oddly stoic in the bathroom, after she cozies up to Ryan, the young and handsome boyfriend of the coach's niece, Hailey. The central plot of the novel hinges on Ryan's sudden death a few months later. For the parents whispering anxiously in the stands of the gym, the tragedy could not have come at a worse time. Elite Qualifiers, a necessary obstacle to be overcome on Devon's Track, are coming up, and now big-hearted Coach T is skipping out on practice to comfort Hailey. Things only get worse when the police get involved, and word spreads that Ryan's death—he was hit by a car while walking home alone at night—might not have been an accident.

The girls at BelStars, the elite gym where Devon reigns like a silent queen, are distraught but resigned. Even the youngest ones, those for whom Ryan is the first person in their lives to ever have died, know better than to take their eyes off the prize. Among them, Devon is the living embodiment of focus. She is distant to her teammates—she is after all, the gym's superstar—and even Katie, her own mother, cannot quite seem to figure her out. Abbott, writing through the eyes of the other characters, purposely casts the young gymnast as unknowable, inhuman. Her parents see her as a workhorse, and her little brother is convinced that she can fly. Physically, Devon is tiny, a fifteen-year-old with the body of a child, but mentally, she is more akin to Sun Tzu. "That was what gymnastics did, though," Abbott writes in Katie's inner voice. "It aged girls and kept them young forever at the same time." This tension between gaining experience and staying young sustains the novel with crackling force. Preteens watch their breasts and hips expand in dread, and a period feels like a death sentence. One thing about Devon is clear: she is at war with her own body, or as Katie puts it, "She was the most

(Courtesy of Drew Reilly)

Megan Abbott is an award-winning writer whose previous novels include The Fever *(2014),* Dare Me *(2012),* The End of Everything *(2011),* Bury Me Deep *(2009), and* Die a Little *(2005), among others. She lives in New York City.*

dangerous thing in her own life. Her body, the only dangerous thing."

Katie, meanwhile, struggles with the nagging feeling that she might not be a good mother. She and Eric married young, their union precipitated by Katie's pregnancy, and as a toddler Devon had an accident that still haunts Katie. When she was three years old, Devon tripped on a running lawn mower and the blade sliced off two of her toes. A pediatrician suggested that tumbling class might help Devon achieve a better sense of balance; the recommendation changed the family's life forever. The doctor also suggested soccer or ice skating, and Katie wonders what might have been different had Devon taken up one of those instead. Deeply in debt to finance Devon's career, Katie and Eric are perpetually exhausted. "All their duties hung like heavy raiment over them all the time," Abbott writes, "only the sight of Devon spearing into the air lifting them up."

Though Katie is involved in the nitty-gritty of Devon's routine—the leotards, the groin pulls, the driving back and forth—she claims to be the least obsessive of the BelStar parents. "She just does it on her own," Katie likes to say, when mothers ask how their daughters can be like Devon. But underneath, Abbott teasingly suggests over the course of the novel, Katie is in far deeper than she realizes.

You Will Know Me is as much about the existential inertia of adulthood as it is about the brutality of being a teenage girl. Early on in the novel, at the booster club party, a zealous mother named Molly Chu—"who rarely talked about anything but gymnastics and carpooling"—corners Katie and drunkenly tells her a story about her own youth. When she was a little girl, Molly says, she wanted to be a majorette. She stole a piece of pipe from her father and painted it silver, poking a cork in one end. "I'd twirl it in the front yard for hours," she tells Katie, with tears in her eyes. "It looked like a pinwheel in the sun." She continues: "Remember that kind of wanting? That kind that's just for yourself? And you don't even have to feel guilty about it? You wouldn't know you should."

Katie's desire to see Devon succeed is wrapped up in memories of her own turbulent youth. Those memories, incidentally, mirror those of another prominent female character. Hailey, the coach's niece, is the subject of gossip among the mothers. She had a troubled childhood, after which her aunt and uncle took her in as their own. The depths of Hailey's character—her grief, her mental illness—showcase Abbott's range but also make a larger point about the inevitability of experiencing pain specifically tied to one's womanhood. *You Will Know Me* is a story about mothers and daughters and protection from harm; it is also about putting a pretty face on violence. Tiny girls crunch, batter, and bloody their bodies for the sake of beauty, wearing sleek, expensive leotards and glittering high ponytails. Gymnastics is one of the most grueling and gruesome of sports, but female participants are required, to paraphrase Tolentino, to display a kind of hyper-femininity while doing it. Devon, the ascendant, certainly feels the pressure to perform and destroy, but also be beautiful in equal measure. She feels these things, one could argue as the book progresses, to the exclusion of all other feelings. In the gym, girls are hushed in her presence, but at school, as Katie discovers in one heartbreaking scene, boys harass her for her "freakishly" underdeveloped body. Devon's condition, Tolentino observes, "is an exaggerated version of the condition of every teenage girl. Her body is a source of glory and terror, beauty and castigation; it belongs to her deeply, and to everyone else, too."

Molly Hagan

Review Sources

Hannah, Sophie. "In Megan Abbott's New Murder Mystery, a Teenage Gymnast Sharp as a Knife." Review of You Will Know Me, by Megan Abbott. *The New York Times*, 27 July 2016, www.nytimes.com/2016/07/31/books/review/megan-abbott-you-will-know-me.html. Accessed 22 Oct. 2016.

Quinn, Annalisa. "'You Will Know Me' Says No, You Won't." Review of *You Will Know Me*, by Megan Abbott. *National Public Radio*, 28 July 2016, www.npr.org/2016/07/28/485865091/you-will-know-me-says-no-you-wont. Accessed 22 Oct. 2016.

Review of *You Will Know Me*, by Megan Abbott. *Kirkus*, 5 May 2016, www.kirkus-reviews.com/book-reviews/megan-abbott/you-will-know-me. Accessed 22 Oct. 2016.

Senior, Jennifer. "Review: In Megan Abbott's 'You Will Know Me,' Gymnast Girl and Cute Dead Guy." Review of You Will Know Me, by Megan Abbott. *The New York Times*, 18 July 2016, www.nytimes.com/2016/07/19/books/review-in-megan-abbotts-you-will-know-me-gymnast-girl-and-cute-dead-guy.html. Accessed 22 Oct. 2016.

Tolentino, Jia. "The Bodily Terror of Women's Gymnastics." Review of *You Will Know Me*, by Megan Abbott. *The New Yorker*, 11 Aug. 2016, www.newyorker.com/culture/jia-tolentino/the-bodily-terror-of-womens-gymnastics. Accessed 22 Oct. 2016.

Zero K

Author: Don DeLillo (b. 1936)
Publisher: Scribner (New York). 288 pp.
Type of work: Novel
Time: Present
Locales: New York City and a desert near
Kazakhstan

Don DeLillo's new novel Zero K *imagines a
world in which people opt to be cryogenically
preserved in hopes of living again in a distant
future.*

Principal characters:
JEFFREY LOCKHART, a thirty-four-year-old
American man who is adrift in his own
life
ROSS LOCKHART, his extraordinarily wealthy
father, a Convergence evangelist and
donor
ARTIS MARTINEAU, his dying stepmother, an archaeologist

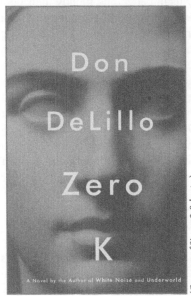

(Courtesy of Simon & Schuster)

The pleasure of Don DeLillo's latest novel is experiential. The plot of *Zero K* centers on a strange compound, part tech start-up, part hospice, part installation artwork, called the Convergence. Jeffrey Lockhart, the novel's thirty-four-year-old protagonist, arrives at the Convergence, located in an isolated stretch of desert near Kazakhstan, after days of sleepless travel. The place has the surreality of a mirage; there are life-like mannequins and twisting hallways with rows and rows of doors painted different shades of gray. There are no phones, no clocks, no Internet, and only a handful of windows. There is a garden but it is filled with fake plants. The compound alone makes Jeffrey feel unmoored, but his reason for being there is just as strange. His once-estranged father, billionaire Ross Lockhart, is an investor in the Convergence and also, it seems, a client. But what is the Convergence? DeLillo is deliberately elusive on this point. People come to the Convergence to die, and after they are dead, their bodies are cryogenically preserved in pods, the thought being that they will be "reborn," with the help of nanobots powered by as-yet-undiscovered technology, sometime in the distant future. Ross's young wife and Jeffrey's stepmother, Artis, an archaeologist, is terminally ill. She and Ross have come to the Convergence—Ross compares them and fellow believers to pilgrims—to end her life and intern her in her pod.

There is something seriously suspicious about the whole enterprise, though Jeffrey seems to be the only one who sees it. The technology behind the process is too vague; its founders too charismatic; its donors too rich. When Jeffrey stumbles across what appears to be a meeting of investors, it sounds like a recruitment pitch for a religious cult. They even call the Convergence "faith-based technology," but just what or who exactly the people of the Convergence are placing their faith in is unclear. As Jeffrey grapples with Artis's coming death (or non-death), Ross makes a stunning announcement: he has decided to join her. The Convergence has a special unit for people like Ross, people who are healthy but wish to end their life in this world in the hopes of more quickly entering another, called Zero K.

DeLillo is one of the best-known American writers of the late twentieth century. With his first novel, *Americana* (1971), he established himself as a postmodernist in the purest sense of the word, a writer devoted to interrogating people's flawed perception of reality. If the post–World War II world—nuclear proliferation, the Cold War, the rise of the Central Intelligence Agency (CIA), the assassination of John F. Kennedy, the evolution of computer technology and the Internet—seemed like sensory overload to the people that lived it, DeLillo saw it that way too, only more so. People often use the word "hallucinatory" to describe his kaleidoscopic vision of American life; others call it dystopian, paranoid or, as the *New York Times* dismissed the prose of *Americana*, "word-salad." DeLillo's books are not always popular or critically acclaimed, though a few of them are considered masterpieces of American literary fiction. His nearly one thousand-page opus *Underworld* (1997) was a finalist for both the Pulitzer Prize in fiction and the National Book Award. In it, he weaves an intricate web encompassing seemingly every major social movement of the second half of the previous century. Federal Bureau of Investigation (FBI) director J. Edgar Hoover has a role in the story along with comedian Lenny Bruce. In his novel *Libra* (1988), DeLillo imagines the Kennedy assassination as a CIA conspiracy gone awry and delves into the minds of the men, chief among them Lee Harvey Oswald, who made it happen.

DeLillo's style—from the way he constructs sentences to his bleak worldview—is so singular that it has been a subject of parody. He has been criticized for his clunky, aphoristic dialogue and his sketchily drawn characters, many of whom are apathetic men with scant emotional depth. Indeed, many reviewers noted that like his previous work, *Zero K* will not necessarily be lauded for multidimensional, well-rounded characters. In his review for *Slate*, Mark O'Connell wrote, "DeLillo's characters often feel less like fully realized human beings than conduits for the various preoccupations and ideas at work in the narrative." At the same time, however, he can just as easily be counted on for flashes of brilliant insight couched in passages about ordinary things. For example, DeLillo wrings a divine message about life and death from the final image of *Zero K*, in which a little boy watches a strange and beautiful event known as Manhattanhenge—a twice annual alignment of Manhattan's grid and the setting sun—on a grimy crosstown bus. Few writers can describe scenes and images like DeLillo can, but for all of his breathtaking imagery, he has very little interest in plot. The trajectories of his books do not move forward so much as they proliferate around a philosophical point. Critic James Wood described *Underworld*, in an article for *New Republic*, as a "flawless carpet of fine prose on page after page, a soothing sense that it might never have to end, that another thousand or two thousand pages might easily be added." Even at less than three hundred pages, the same description could be applied to *Zero K*.

Zero K is about people coming to grips with their own mortality—but as the author is DeLillo, that struggle is shaded by commentary about the double-edged sword of technology (how it can be both beneficial and burdensome), the twin threats of global climate change and terrorism, and the selfish whims of a wealthy elite. Nathaniel Rich, who reviewed the book for the *New York Review of Books*, compared Jeffrey's father, Ross, to Virgin Mobile founder and roguish human lifestyle brand Richard Branson, though Peter Thiel, the radical Libertarian tech magnate, would also be apt. Thiel is a transhumanist who believes that he will live forever. He has invested millions of dollars in exploring life-extending technology, some of it—the work of the Alcor Life Extension Foundation, for example—very similar in nature to DeLillo's fictional Convergence. The relationship between dreams of immortality and wealth is central to DeLillo's story. Ross is important in this world, and therefore cannot imagine a world in which he does not exist. In theme (though not in style), *Zero K* could be compared to *The Waterworks* (1994), a novel by DeLillo's contemporary, the late E. L. Doctorow. In the book, a commentary on contemporary society though it takes place in 1870s New York City, poor children are sacrificed to supply experimental treatments for the city's wealthiest men.

Not all of *Zero K* takes place within the confines of the Convergence. A good deal of the narrative follows Jeffrey after his return to New York City. He dates a school councilor named Emma Breslow, who has an adopted son, a teenage savant named Stak. The introduction of these characters is central to a recurring image in *Zero K*. This image is DeLillo's interpretation of mortality, and it involves a character separating a thing—an object or an event—from the world and paring it down to its essence in an effort to understand it. Twice this image involves art installations—one of DeLillo's favorite devices, because conceptual art asks viewers to alter their perception of reality. In one scene, late in the book, Jeffrey takes Emma and the troubled Stak to an art installation in New York City where the exhibit is a single rock. Throughout the book, Jeffrey struggles with a childhood tic, a habit of falling down the rabbit hole of his own mind in pursuit of the definition of words like rock. What is a rock? The exercise can be singularly maddening.

This is also what the Convergence asks of its clients; through aggressive disorientation, it asks people to look inward and define their own existence. Every aspect of the Convergence demands this of its guests except for one. As Jeffrey wanders the hallways of the compound, he occasionally comes across a floating screen. The screen plays footage of atrocities: the aftermath of terrorist attacks, environmental disasters, epidemics, and war. The effect is overwhelming but also distancing. The film is meant to represent what the clients of the Convergence have opted out of; all of that horror, for them, is just a memory of the world in which they used to live. However, it is oddly ineffective—not as a literary device, but for its intended purposes on Jeffrey—because it attempts to do his own work for him, and poorly. The footage reduces humanity without capturing its essence. In one of his last interactions with Artis, Jeffrey asks her if she ever thinks about the world in which she will be "reborn." She thinks about a particular memory, she says, about a time when she stood in the shower and watched a water droplet form and ooze down the wall. As DeLillo renders it, readers are meant to understand that this is her distillation of humanity. If being reborn means going back to the beginning, this, for Artis, is the beginning.

To question the root of humanity in this way is a way of thinking about death, and for DeLillo, all roads lead to death. In her review of *Zero K* for the *New York Times*, Michiko Kakutani quoted the narrator of DeLillo's National Book Award–winning novel *White Noise* (1985), who says, "All plots tend to move deathward." In *Underworld*, characters Klara and Miles attend an art exhibit in the 1970s. The exhibit involves a bootleg copy of the then-unknown Zapruder film, a twenty-second video recording of the Kennedy assassination. Today, the Zapruder film is a deeply familiar cultural artifact, but DeLillo imagines people watching it for the first time on a wall of television screens, each screen looping the film at a different speed. After a while, the images themselves lose their meaning. Klara begins to focus on the movements of the film itself, and DeLillo writes of her, "She thought to wonder if this home movie was some crude living likeness of the mind's own technology, the sort of death plot that runs in the mind . . . a model of the nights when we are intimate with our own dying." DeLillo has taken this theme a step further with *Zero K*, using the concept of cryogenics and the potential for expanding human life as a literal means to explore mortality.

Molly Hagan

Review Sources

Daum, Meghan. "Death and Don DeLillo." Review of *Zero K*, by Don DeLillo. *Atlantic*, May 2016, www.theatlantic.com/magazine/archive/2016/05/death-and-don-delillo/476367/. Accessed 14 Feb. 2017.

Jordison, Sam. "*Zero K* and Making Sense of 'Late Period' Don DeLillo." Review of *Zero K*, by Don DeLillo. *The Guardian*, 24 May 2016, www.theguardian.com/books/2016/may/24/zero-k-and-making-sense-of-late-period-don-delillo-white-noise. Accessed 14 Feb. 2017.

Kakutani, Michiko. "Review: In Don DeLillo's Zero K, Daring to Outwit Death." Review of Zero K, by Don DeLillo. *The New York Times*, 25 Apr. 2016, www.nytimes.com/2016/04/26/books/review-in-don-delillos-zero-k-daring-to-outwit-death.html. Accessed 14 Feb. 2017.

O'Connell, Mark. "The Disembodied." Review of *Zero K*, by Don DeLillo. *Slate*, 2 May 2016, www.slate.com/articles/arts/books/2016/05/don_delillo_s_novel_zero_k_reviewed.html. Accessed 14 Feb. 2017.

Rich, Nathaniel. "When High Technology Meets Immortality." Review of *Zero K*, by Don DeLillo. *The New York Review of Books*, 9 June 2016, www.nybooks.com/articles/2016/06/09/don-delillo-when-high-technology-meets-immortality/. Accessed 14 Feb. 2017.

Category Index

TITLE INDEX

Author Index